Shots in the Dark

• • •

SHOTS

• • •

IN THE DARK

*The Policy, Politics, and Symbolism
of Gun Control*

WILLIAM J. VIZZARD

ROWMAN & LITTLEFIELD PUBLISHERS, INC.
Lanham • Boulder • New York • Oxford

ROWMAN & LITTLEFIELD PUBLISHERS, INC.

Published in the United States of America
by Rowman & Littlefield Publishers, Inc.
4720 Boston Way, Lanham, Maryland 20706
http://www.rowmanlittlefield.com

12 Hid's Copse Road
Cumnor Hill, Oxford OX2 9JJ, England

Copyright © 2000 by Rowman & Littlefield Publishers, Inc.

Parts of *In the Crossfire: A Political History of the Bureau of Alcohol, Tobacco, and Firearms* (copyright © 1997 by Lynne Rienner Pub.) reprinted by permission.

British Library Cataloguing in Publication Information Available

Library of Congress Cataloging-in-Publication Data

Vizzard, William J., 1944–
    Shots in the dark : the policy, politics, and symbolism of gun control /
William J. Vizzard.
        p. cm.
    Includes bibliographical references and index.
    ISBN 0-8476-9559-X (alk. paper) — ISBN 0-8476-9560-3 (pbk. : alk. paper)
        1. Gun control—Government policy—United States. 2. Gun control—Political
    aspects—United States. 3. Gun control—Law and legislation—United States.
    4. United States—Social policy. 5. United States—Politics and government. I. Title.
    HV7436 .V59 2000
    363.3'3'0973—dc21

                                                                        00-038739

Printed in the United States of America

∞™ The paper used in this publication meets the minimum requirements of American
National Standard for Information Sciences—Permanence of Paper for Printed Library
Materials, ANSI/NISO Z39.48–1992.

FOR JAMES AND JENNIFER

who have made me proud

CONTENTS

PREFACE

Gun control shares one characteristic with a multitude of other policy issues: the less one knows about it, the simpler it seems. Invariably, when others become aware that I have written on the topic, their response begins with, "what is your position on gun control?" It quickly becomes clear that they are not asking for a two-hour colloquium. What they assume is that their inquiry will result in an expression of support or condemnation. Yet virtually all Americans support some forms of gun control and oppose others. For instance, few would support legalizing the sale of guns to felons, the mentally ill, or children; nor would they advocate free commerce in implements of modern warfare, such as Stinger missiles or howitzers. At the same time, the majority of Americans have consistently opposed a general prohibition of private gun ownership by the general public. Asking how one stands on gun control is much like asking how one stands on traffic laws; it is meaningless without more specificity.

I spent 27 years as an agent, supervisor, and manager in the Bureau of Alcohol, Tobacco, and Firearms, dealing with the administration and enforcement of federal firearm laws. I have written a doctoral dissertation and a number of papers on the topic of gun control policy. I also have read virtually every serious work published on the subject and have at least a nodding acquaintance with most of the serious scholars in the field. But I must admit that there are a number of questions about the topic that I, and I suspect others, cannot answer.

I wrote this book to answer the questions that I believe can be answered, to put gun control in its political and historical context, and to demonstrate what gun control tells us about our political and policy process. Others have covered some, but not all, of this ground. I believe that my description of the events leading to the passage of the Gun Control Act in 1968 constitutes the most complete history available. Likewise, I have presented the only comprehensive history and analysis of the implementation of that law. I sought to link, both in theory and narrative, these earlier events with more contemporary issues, such as the Brady Law, assault-weapons laws, concealed-carry laws, and class-action lawsuits.

I also attempted to bring a unique combination of knowledge and perspective to these topics. My knowledge results from years of working in law enforcement and with those who possess, use, collect, and deal in firearms. In addition, almost 50 years of personal experience with firearms provides me with a technical understanding that many academics lack. This background gives me hope that I can present a balanced examination of the subject, unattractive though that may be to extremists on both sides of the gun issue.

ACKNOWLEDGMENTS

I would like to thank all those people who consented to interviews for this book. Advocates on both sides of the issue, legislators, legislative staff members, and current and retired government officials all contributed to this book. In particular, my friend of many years, Steve Helsley, provided information and support, in spite of our opposing positions. Thank you to Michael Beard, Phil Cook, and C. B. Kates for their reviews and comments and Jennifer Knerr for her guidance and support. In addition, editorial assistance from my wife, Diana, my friend Cynthia Ragland, and my son, James, made this book possible.

I would also like to acknowledge the support of Lynne Rienner Publishing for their permission to reprint portions of *In the Crossfire: A Political History of the Bureau of Alcohol, Tobacco, and Firearms,* copyright © 1997 by Lynne Rienner Publishers, Inc.

INTRODUCTION

Congress first addressed comprehensive national gun-control legislation in 1933 at the beginning of Franklin Roosevelt's presidency. Although the issue disappeared from the political agenda between 1938 and 1964, it has been a topic of continuous national discussion for the past 35 years. Yet it remains as contentious and unresolved a public-policy issue as ever.

This book examines the history of that policy debate. Although it is my intent to make a useful contribution to the social science literature on the topics of gun control and public policy, this book is neither a vehicle for new quantitative research nor a comprehensive review of such research by others.[1] Instead, it is an effort to place the issue in a context that provides the reader a greater insight and understanding of both gun control as a policy issue and the policy process itself. Although I offer proposals for policy options, I do so with no illusions that these options could either eliminate all the problems associated with firearms or end the controversy surrounding gun control. These conflicts, rooted in the very fiber of American culture and values, will not soon abate, even in the unlikely eventuality that more orderly and rational policies are adopted.

In fact, it is the intractable nature of the gun issue, combined with the role of symbols, myth, cultural paradigms, and language, that makes it such an important and interesting case study. Gun control's lack of clear boundaries in jurisdiction, time, and place challenges the researcher. It has been on the agendas of municipalities, states, and the federal government, weaving among intergovernmental complexities and multiplying them. Although this presents methodological problems, it offers the opportunity to advance the understanding of policy processes. Gun control confirms the contention of political-scientists Roger Cobb and Marc Ross that politics is not just about economic interest, but also about identity and worldview.[2]

The examination of decisions to site a public facility, fund a project, or even go to war provides a particular type of perspective on the policy process. These are often issues forced onto the agenda of a single level of government by external events, which impose certain time constraints. An alternative is to examine issues that lack these clear edges. Abortion, health care, sex education, immigration, and welfare all fit this latter category. Policy advocates have expanded these policies beyond the purview of policy elites—or what political scientists Frank Baumgartner and Bryan Jones call "policy monopolies"[3]—by expanding the issues and enlisting broader advocacy coalitions. However, because these policy coalitions lack the ability to generate strong public consensus, the issues endure—existing in intellectual paradigms, infused with values, perceptions, and linguistic meanings. If governmental processes are to be understood, it is essential to deal with these issues as well as those that are more convenient to research.

Policy researchers face a number of difficult methodological concerns when they choose such amorphous issues. Where does one draw the lines for the limits of study? Where does the process begin and end? How does one apply quantitative analysis? There may be, however, an even more fundamental frustration. As has often been observed, Americans are a mostly optimistic people. They also favor pragmatic resolution to problems and want to believe that democratic government can eventually provide such resolution, albeit imperfectly. The examination of unresolved issues, influenced more by symbolism than reason, challenges our faith in the efficacy of the governmental system and our rationality as a people. Political-scientist Aaron Wildavsky approached this perspective when he said that problems are never resolved, they are just replaced by new problems.[4] Even Wildavsky, however, assumed that the political process would produce decisions to alter the nature of particular problems. The more one deals with an issue such as gun control, the less sanguine one becomes about reaching any sort of resolution of contentious policy issues.

Failure to resolve the gun-control issue springs from the nature of the issue itself and from our political culture and structure. Political-scientist Robert Spitzer has pointed out that gun control is a textbook example of what Theodore Lowi described as "regulatory policy."[5] Lowi theorized that regulatory policy constituted the most problematic form of policy to enact, because it directly affects personal behavior in an immediate way.[6] In addition, gun control involves numerous stakeholders, cultural symbolism, and well-organized interest groups. Regulatory policy that involves only a few stakeholders, even powerful ones, allows for private negotiation. Since the regulated parties are usually motivated by financial goals and a desire to minimize costs, they find private negotiation and bargaining highly desirable. They often prefer a clearly defined regulatory environment to uncertainty. This has not proven to be the case for gun control. Although some have tried to characterize the gun lobby as being a front for gun manufacturers, it is a classic example of dispersed power and grass-roots activity motivated by worldview. A large body of stakeholders view gun control as an attack on their core cultural values, and organizational leaders ignore constituents at their peril. Thus the structure of firearm interest groups does not lend itself to negotiation or accommodation. Finally, the devil is in the details. Policy options that appear to be simple become far more complex in implementation for the very reasons cited by Lowi.

THE POLICY AGENDA

Significant and comprehensive national gun regulation has seldom, if ever, fully gained access onto the public agenda.[7] Although Congress has considered various initiatives, only one comprehensive regulatory bill has ever become law.[8] While agenda-setting remains one of the least-examined aspects of the policy process, some political scientists have addressed the issue. Roger Cobb and Charles Elder's classic work on agenda-setting recognizes the political nature of policy-making[9] and postulates that conflicting interests will attempt to expand the conflict by engaging others, primarily by controlling the language and symbolism of the debate,[10] a pattern confirmed by the case of gun control. Cobb and Elder divided agendas into two categories: *systemic* and *interest*. *Interest* agendas consist of narrow, specialized, and low-in-visibility issues of little general interest, while the *systemic* agendas address issues with high visibility and wide impact. Cobb and Elder argued that four conditions must be met for an issue to reach the systemic political agenda: widespread public awareness of the issue, consensus that the issue is an appropriate public concern, consensus that the issue necessitates a remedy, and consensus that a remedy is available.[11] Subsequently, Cobb, along with Ross, divided the policy agenda into *formal* and *public* agendas. The *formal* agenda constituted those issues under active consideration by government entities. Issues that make the formal agenda are characterized by their being evidence of a real problem, their presence on the wider public agenda, and their presence on the agendas of other nations with similar social systems.[12] Comprehensive gun control would seem to provide a case establishing that these three criteria, while perhaps prerequisites, are not adequate to ensure agenda access.

John Kingdon advanced a modified garbage-can model in which agenda access depends on policy entrepreneurs seizing upon opportunity when various policy streams merge in a favorable environment. Kingdon referred to these opportunities for matching favored solutions with perceived problems as the "opening of the policy window."[13] As he predicted, gun-control advocates have responded to a variety of perceived problems with gun-control solutions. Often the perception of a problem has resulted from a highly visible assassination or mass shooting. In his work on focusing events, Thomas A. Birkland has built on Kingdon's model to examine the role of such events in the opening of policy windows.[14] Although Birkland specifically addressed disasters, mass shootings, and assassinations of prominent persons appear to fit well into his thesis and have allowed policy entrepreneurs and interest groups to mobilize support and move gun-control proposals temporarily onto the formal policy agenda.

Although political scientists have examined the issue of agenda access, this examination has largely failed to consider the influence on the nature of policy options of tactics employed to attain agenda access. In an effort to gain agenda access, policy advocates and entrepreneurs redefine problems and reshape policy solutions as strategies to overcome opposition or apathy. In gun-control policy, the "Saturday-night-special" issue provides an excellent example. However, by subdividing policy into smaller and more symbolically appealing issues, policy advocates risk reducing the rationality and utility of their own proposals. Given the serial nature of the policy agenda, such strategy has the potential for undercutting long-term policy goals by encouraging legislators to enact fragments of symbolic policy and then move on to new issues. Although policy advocates may view these episodes as successful steps in an incremental process, these episodes of agenda access may serve to strengthen opponents in several ways: by raising legitimacy issues regarding the policy area, by generating incoherent and fragmented policy with significant implementation problems, and by providing politicians with future excuses for not revisiting a controversial or risky policy issue.

Even accessing the policy agenda with coherent, well-crafted proposals provides no guarantee of policy enactment. Once on the agenda, a policy issue becomes subject to the forces within the political system. The unique American system, with its divisions of powers between levels and branches of government, allows far more opportunity to thwart the formulation of policy than to craft it. Beyond these major divisions, the very nature of the legislative branch adds confusion to the policy process. On several occasions the bicameral nature of Congress has thwarted the passage of firearm legislation.[15] The disproportionate power of rural states in the Senate, combined with Senate rules, allows the representatives of a small portion of the population to block any legislation. In addition to the difficulties of policy formulation, Congress has skewed and even thwarted the implementation of legislation it passed in its legislative role by exerting pressure on the bureaucracy in its oversight role.[16] Finally, the division of authority under the Constitution has constrained rational policy-making. As items of commerce, firearms are subject to regulation at the federal level. Yet regulation of their possession and use constitutes an exercise of the police power and thus is a state responsibility. Not only does the political system influence the likelihood of policy implementation, it also limits potential policy options, shapes the crafting of law and regulations, and dictates the implementation of policy. In short, the political process molds every aspect of policy.

THE AUTHOR'S PERSPECTIVE

I do not come to the issue of gun control as an impartial policy analyst. This book owes much to my personal experience and perspective developed over years of working with the issue as an interested observer, practitioner, teacher, and researcher. I have had a strong interest in firearms from childhood. I obtained my first hunting license at age 10, shot competitively in high school, belonged to the National Rifle Association for a decade, taught hunter-safety classes, and carried guns routinely for over 30 years as a soldier, a police officer, and a federal agent. I also spent the better part of a 27-year career with the Bureau of Alcohol, Tobacco, and Firearms (ATF), enforcing and administering gun laws. I have experienced a long history of friendly relations with a variety of people interested in this topic, including the founders of two gun-control organizations, several NRA officials, a multitude of gun dealers and enthusiasts, and numerous authors and researchers on every side of the gun issue. I am *both* a gun owner and an unabashed advocate of gun control.

In fact, it is difficult to find a person who is not an advocate of some form of gun control, as the alternative implies the unrestricted access of any type of arms by any person at any time. *"Do you support gun control?"* constitutes a question so imprecise as to be almost meaningless. The question presumes a world composed of two discreet classes of people: those who favor guns and oppose all gun control, and those who detest guns and seek their prohibition. I, like most Americans, reside in neither camp.

Just as I bring to this book more than one perspective on guns and gun control, I also bring multiple and conflicting perspectives on social science, public policy, and government. I am an avid consumer of quantitative and qualitative social-science research and policy analysis. Still, I remain skeptical regarding our capacity to understand complex social processes and predict outcomes given the limits on our ability to gather accurate information and the difficulty of constructing effective models of real-world activity. Combined with our inability to identify all relevant variables and our less-than-perfect tools for analysis, these limitations provide good reason for caution about our conclusions. Not many years ago, activist social scientists advanced interventionist government agendas and brushed aside skeptics. Today, public-choice and economic theorists dismiss intervention with equal disdain. I am skeptical of both extremes.

Although with most Americans I share skepticism regarding the efficacy of government intervention and reservations regarding excessive government power, I am no libertarian. I assume that laissez-faire policies impose their own costs, and I fear anarchy with the same intensity as I fear government tyranny. Humans are social animals and as such have never had an absolute right to be left alone. Thus my focus on accommodation of gun owners, which many gun-control advocates may find excessive, will not satisfy libertarian readers.

The issue of gun-control policy has been examined by lawyers, sociologists, historians, political scientists, public-health theorists, and economists, each with their own unique perspective. My examination of the topic differs from others primarily in my focus on the details of implementation. My years of

experience in dealing with gun laws and my knowledge of firearms have provided me with a perspective shared by few researchers and writers. To this
experience I have added study in the areas of crime and public policy. Thus
this book brings together both my background and my academic interests in a
unique way.

FOCUS AND STRUCTURE OF THE BOOK

I advance three interrelated theoretical arguments in this book. The first is that
comprehensive gun control has seldom, if ever, fully accessed the public agenda.
The second is that the inability to resolve agenda conflict has produced policy
proposals that lack rationality and consistency, and that political expediency has
shaped policy that lacks impact and presents significant implementation problems.[17] Finally, I argue that both advocates and critics of gun control, locked in
a battle over symbolism and worldviews, have contributed to policy deadlock
and irrational policy outcomes. They have also misconstrued the potential benefits of well-crafted and -implemented gun control. Almost universally, firearm
laws have been characterized as ante facto mechanisms for denying dangerous
persons access to guns or discouraging the carrying of firearms in certain situations.[18] I offer an alternative conceptualization of gun regulations as a mechanism for enhancing the efficiency in 1) identifying and controlling persons
responsible for violent offenses, 2) incarcerating career offenders, and 3) dis-
rupting the illegal firearm markets.

While I bring certain experience, knowledge, and perspective to this topic,
I also bring limitations. I am not a quantitative methodologist; my critique of
the quantitative methodology in the field relates to its assumptions, structure,
and symbolic uses. When I offer a technical critique—beyond structural critique—of any specific method used by a researcher, I depend on the analysis of
others. I am also not a constitutional lawyer. Although I have devoted considerable amount of scholarship to the Second and Fourteenth Amendments of
the Constitution, I do not purport to be a constitutional authority. I am far less
interested in "*original intent*" than in the political and symbolic impact of the
constitutional argument.

This book is organized into three sections: The first one addresses the current status of the issue and endeavors to provide the reader with the background information necessary to understand the subsequent sections. The
second section provides a narrative of the evolution of gun policy. The final
section addresses options and trends for the future, then closes with an examination of what gun control conveys about the policy process. I have included a
bibliographical essay at the end of this book that many readers may find useful
reading *before* they read the text. It provides substantial background on the current state of the literature, and those who have contributed to that literature.

Part One

WHERE WE ARE

• • •

CHAPTER ONE

FRAMING THE ISSUE

O N THE MORNING OF April 20, 1999, Americans watched on live television as terrified students fled Columbine High School in Littleton, Colorado. While police SWAT teams rushed students from the building and medical personnel worked frantically to save injured victims, it became apparent that two heavily armed students had systematically murdered over a dozen of their fellow students and faculty members and severely injured many more before committing suicide. Americans groped for some understanding of this horrific and apparently irrational event by applying a variety of explanations ranging from a decline in the role of religion in American life to inadequate security precautions in schools. Many focused on the necessary implements of the carnage—guns—and their ready availability. A new wave of gun-control activity began in Congress, and suddenly the press featured a plethora of articles on guns and gun laws. Yet, almost two years later, no new legislation has passed Congress and media interest appears in decline. For many, these events demonstrated the capacity of a narrow special interest to thwart common sense and the will of the people; for others, they symbolized the victory of reason over emotional scapegoating.

Would different gun-control policy make such events less likely? If so, what policy? For those hostile to guns, the need for new and far more restrictive policy seems obvious. How can one explain two teenagers acquiring the firepower necessary to commit such a deadly massacre? For those raised in rural areas, where young people have always had easily available guns without perpetrating mass killing, access seems no more unusual than access to automobiles, alcohol, or cigarettes, all of which kill people.

The dilemma is captured by a recent event in Northern California. Two young gang members, armed with pistols and wearing masks, forced their way into the home of a couple, both prominent physicians, in Alamo, California. The intruders held the wife and her brother at gunpoint but apparently were unaware of the husband, who responded by firing his own gun. In the ensuing battle the husband and one of the intruders were fatally shot, and the wife and the second intruder were seriously wounded.[1] Does this event demonstrate the futility or utility of guns for home defense? Did the presence of a firearm in the home result in the unnecessary death of the husband and injury of his wife? Did the husband's action benefit the larger society by preventing future crimes by these two offenders or by deterring other potential offenders from similar crimes? Did the failure of existing gun laws to prevent the convicted felon-intruders from acquiring guns confirm the futility of all gun control, or did it highlight the inadequacy of current laws and the need for stricter controls? Finally, would any gun law likely to be adopted nationally have changed any aspect of this event?

As policy theorist Deborah Stone has so aptly conveyed, policy-making is a political process in which competitive interests vie to control policy process by controlling the language and definition of events.[2] Each of the events just described offers rich potential for building a narrative that gives it meaning and potential influence on policy. No policy arena provides a clearer example of the role of politics, language, and symbolism in the policy process than does gun control. No realm for quiet accommodation among political elites, gun control generates the rough and tumble of the American democratic process, warts and all. It is political trench warfare in which each side distrusts and dislikes the other and views neutrality or compromise as moral failure.

CONCEPTUALIZATIONS OF THE ISSUE

Previously, I have argued that both advocates and opponents have conceptualized gun control in the context of four basic paradigms.[3] The most persistent of these paradigms characterizes gun control as a mechanism for crime control. A second paradigm places gun control in the context of social order or sovereignty. In the third, sociologists have conceptualized the issue as a symbolic conflict over values and worldview, and recently the issue has been couched in a fourth: the language of public health. To these four I have added a fifth—political symbolism. Although politicians formulate their positions in the language of ethics, rationality, and public interest, they are keenly aware of the importance of symbolism. I progressively am convinced that many politicians view gun control more as a potent political symbol for defining themselves and their opponents than as a critical policy question.

Each of these paradigms has components of reality and myth, and each emphasizes different language, values, and assumptions. Clearly, these paradigms overlap. Both the crime control and social-order paradigms emphasize restriction of access to instruments of force and violence. The crime-control paradigm, however, focuses on individual acts of violence, while social control focuses more on the right of the state to maintain a monopoly on legitimate force. The greater the willingness to rely on government for social order, the greater the acceptance of gun control as a legitimate mechanism of social control.

The struggles between opponents and proponents have been directed as much to controlling the language and presumptions of these paradigms as at the direct control of the political process. As such, the issue of gun control offers a look at the policy process in the United States from a unique perspective. This has not been a conflict over who gets what, when, and how, as Harold Lasswell characterized politics. This has been a conflict over ideas, values, perceptions, and, most of all, the role of government. The history of gun control confirms that sometimes ideas matter more than assets. This has been a struggle over what Robert Reich has called "public ideas" more than over process, power, or resources.[4] Underlying this entire issue are powerful American myths that make compromise difficult, if not impossible.

The importance of the gun as a mythical symbol in the United States can be demonstrated by any review of popular culture. The frontiersman, cowboy, soldier, private detective, and policeman have provided this country with most of its mythical heroes, and each has been conspicuously armed. No other object is so common in the popular culture. At times, dogs, horses, airplanes, and automobiles have rivaled firearms, but the latter seem always to prevail. As such, the firearm has taken on a cultural importance in the United States unrivaled in any other industrialized nation.

Paradigms

Intellectual and cultural paradigms provide the primary conceptual structures for the examination, discussion, and understanding of public policies. Each policy area has dominant paradigms at any given time in history. Crafted in language, these paradigms provide a structure for use in examining any problem. The field of international affairs has, for instance, been replete with such intellectual structure. The Cold War was the most basic of paradigms for over 30 years. As a result of the Vietnam War, Watergate, U.S. action in Chile, and other events, an alternative paradigm gained widespread legitimacy. Each of these paradigms served as an intellectual prism for its user, as it was used to organize and interpret data. Understanding the structure, emphasis, and language of paradigms provides insight into how an issue is perceived.

In the case of gun control (and probably many other policy issues), some paradigms have alternative constructions in which conflicting groups concur on focus but disagree as to interpretation. An example would be a power paradigm, in which both radicals and conservatives perceive the issue as control of power, while moderates perceive it otherwise. In this case, both radicals and conservatives agree on the integral role of power in politics but disagree on *who* should exercise that power and to *what* purpose. Gun control highlights a critical fault line in American political thought between a *collective* and *individual* focus. This difference in intellectual orientation has proven critical in the analysis of gun-control proposals. In addition, the issue of gun control itself is conceptualized in several paradigms that must be understood to facilitate examination of the issue.

Crime Control

Built on the assumption that easy access to firearms either encourages crime or exacerbates the level of violence associated with it, the crime-control paradigm has been at the center of most arguments by control advocates and is the one most frequently attacked by opponents. Advocates find the widespread criminal use of firearms in the United States evidence of a need for more restrictive firearms policies. Although it has occasionally been argued that the availability of guns exacerbates the attitudes that motivate crime,[5] most argument centers on the escalation of violence facilitated by the presence of firearms.[6] When proponents utilize this paradigm, they focus primarily on handguns, "Saturday night specials," assault weapons, or other categories of firearms believed to be particularly suitable for criminal purposes.[7] The language is often cost/benefit in orientation, and the narrowing of application serves to minimize their apparent cost and impact of controls.

Opponents respond with direct attacks on the assumption of benefit. Their arguments historically have centered on the inability to obtain compliance with the law by criminals. They stress the impracticality of controlling over 220 million firearms, point to the 20,000 existing firearm laws that "do not work," and generally attack the cause-and-effect argument.[8] Opponents generally concentrate less on the specifics of cost when dealing with the general public than when addressing core constituencies.[9] Costs usually consist of inconveniences for some gun owners that would not be fully appreciated by the general public. Most recently, opponents have attempted to control the public conceptualization of this paradigm. The research of Gary Kleck and John Lott has provided considerable legitimacy to the arguments that the presence of guns reduces crime through deterrence.[10]

Cultural

In 1972, the *Wall Street Journal* portrayed the battle over gun control in the United States as a symbolic conflict between two identifiable social groups. The advocates were characterized as the "cosmopolitans" and the opponents as the "traditionalists." The former were urban, educated, and internationalist in their orientation; they looked to Western Europe as a model for governance and tended toward liberal, democratic values on most social issues. The traditionalists were viewed as rural or small town in orientation, their frame of reference for governance was domestic, and they were less tolerant in their social values.

Invoked more by scholars than by policy advocates or politicians, this paradigm lies just below the surface of many advocacy arguments. Barry Bruce-Briggs picked up the theme in his 1976 essay, as did Lee Kennett and James

Anderson, who characterized the widespread gun ownership in the United States as embarrassing to internationally oriented, cosmopolitan America.[11] Osha Davidson's history of the NRA focused more on politics than culture, but found the cultural paradigms and stereotypes to be a critical component of the political history.[12]

Other writers have gone beyond simply characterizing the advocates and opponents of gun control. William Tonso concurred with the characterization of the groups but criticized the advocates for the practice of "sagecraft" based on their personal biases rather than any utilitarian purpose.[13] John Kaplan argued that the movement for gun control parallels the Prohibition movement and is primarily symbolic, with a goal of declaring some people less worthy than others.[14] Don Kates has characterized opponents of gun control as being motivated by a normative opposition to self-defense,[15] a perspective that is surprisingly close to that of gun-control advocate Robert Spitzer.[16] Franklin Zimring and Gordon Hawkins have couched their perspective of this concept in crime-control language, with advocates seeing crime as an outgrowth of social forces, and opponents perceiving sharp definitions of good and evil between ordinary citizens and criminals.[17]

Many people probably arrive at their positions on gun control based primarily on their perceptions of its utility. Many more most likely come to their positions based on self-interests or innate acceptance of or distaste for guns. No doubt both of these elements influence those who have strong ideological leanings. But repeated interviews with persons having strong views on the subject of gun control reveal certain defined and consistent ideological patterns. Advocates are more collectively oriented and more disposed toward governmental solutions, while opponents are far more suspicious of collective decisions and solutions and are more likely to look to the individual for solutions. This difference becomes particularly fractious over the issue of self-defense. Opponents of gun control view the use of violence in defense of oneself or one's property as a fundamental right, while gun-control advocates more often view individual self-defense as counter-productive or illegitimate. Ultimately, gun control may be more a test of libertarianism than of liberalism versus conservatism.

Three primary influences have contributed to a highly individualistic and libertarian strain in American cultural tradition. The first of these was a tradition of suspicion of authority born of revolution and independence. The second was a vast frontier, offering space and free land to all who would claim it. The third was Protestantism of the most decentralized type, which placed the maximum emphasis on the individual's relationship with God. Historian Richard Hofstadter traces the roots of the American obsession with firearms to both the frontier and the Lockeian tradition that looked to an armed populace.[18] Although he did not consider the gun issue, political-theorist Robert Dahl attributed the lack of European-style class conflict in the United States as being largely due to this independence spawned by philosophy and opportunity for land.[19] Evidence of this persistent national trait appears in the resistance to national health care, the absence of a national identity system, resistance to mass transit and land-use planning, and the recurrent American preference for suburban and rural living.

Political theorist Benjamin Barber characterized American political thought as being heavily anarchist. He also saw strong elements of minimalism and pragmatism that combine with suspicion for authority to produce two distinct approaches to government.[20] In Barber's view, minimalism combined with anarchy results in support for Madisonian restraints on government. Pragmatism combined with anarchy results in commitment to preservation of rights through government action. In either case, Barber argues, the result is concentration on individual rights and the restraint of government in preference to collective rights and government action.[21]

This historic American focus on the individual provides an explanation as to why gun-control advocates have been less than successful in advancing their worldview, and even why they have often focused on particular "evil guns." In American political values, the individual is supreme and the state must justify every intervention. Clearly, narcotics were demonized to justify the type of strict control and intervention that has been imposed.[22] With over 220 million firearms in the United States, most of which are not being unlawfully used at any given time, similar demonization is not likely. In addition, the historic reverence Americans extend to individual rights and the Constitution constitutes an additional burden for control advocates, even though the courts have not invalidated any gun-control law as a violation of the Second Amendment.[23]

As with all issues in the United States, ideology and worldview alone are not the only components of the cultural paradigm. Guns themselves evoke strong symbolic reaction among much of the population either as positive symbols of recreation and healthy activity or negative symbols of danger and violence. Both gun ownership and positive attitudes toward guns correlate positively with early exposure to recreational use of firearms.[24]

Sovereignty and Social Order

Historically, control advocates have been reticent to address the topic in the context of order and state sovereignty. No such hesitancy is found on the part of the most ardent foes of gun control.[25] Even more, scholarly opponents such as Kates and law professor Robert Cottrol trace the origins of most gun-control efforts to the desire of a dominant population to control political or social unrest.[26] It is not surprising that advocates tread lightly on the issue of sovereignty and social order. The underlying question is one of legitimate control of power. Legal scholar Sanford Levinson opines that the view of state resides at the very heart of the conflict over the Second Amendment and gun control, with advocates accepting a Weberian definition of the state as an institution with a monopoly over the use of force, and opponents being tied to a populace view.[27]

Americans have long been ill at ease with the issue of sovereignty. This concern can be found in the discourse on control of the militia during the debate over ratification of the Constitution.[28] Although the issue was largely resolved by the Civil War, the subsequent decline of the state militias, and the creation of a standing army, it does not appear to be an issue with which Americans are fully comfortable. This may ultimately be because, as political theorist John Rohr argues, the concept of state, in the European sense, does not exist in the United States.[29] If the ultimate legitimate authority is the Constitution, who then has a legitimate monopoly on the use of force?

It is in this area of order—control over legitimate use of force and sovereignty—that Barber's paradigms of American political thought become most significant. The minimalist seeks to disperse power and its means through limiting government—thus opposing controls on weapons by the state. The pragmatist seeks controls that protect one citizen against another, and therefore looks for "reasonable controls." The issue of state sovereignty is essentially avoided because of the character of the political value system. Even the pragmatist can be expected to be less than enthusiastic in actually implementing sanctions to enforce controls, particularly against those who cannot be seen as immediately and directly threatening others. This pattern, in fact, is common.[30]

Although many Americans are ill at ease with the sovereignty and social-order paradigm, it is likely the heart of the gun-control issue. Unlike the issue of crime control, for which the practical utility can be debated forever, sovereignty and control of force are value issues. As such, positions can be pursued on principle as opposed to research and evidence. Scholarly debate relating to this paradigm has centered around the meaning of the Second Amendment. In general, a commentator's view of the controlling constitutional law can be assumed to closely coincide with his or her position on sovereignty and attitude toward firearms; however, there are exceptions.[31] At a more pragmatic policy level, debate centers around the legitimacy of individual self-defense and the authority of the state to control when, where, and how persons may possess guns.

Public Health

In many ways, the public health paradigm is the diametric opposite of the sovereignty paradigm. Instead of the language of law and rights, it is cast in the language of utility, risk, and social costs. Although it considers crime, it is focused on accidents and suicides. References to these topics were uncommon prior to the 1980s, when the public health community began to study the health implications of guns. By the end of the decade, a variety of articles began to appear, primarily in medical journals, that focused on the public health implications of the presence of firearms in society.[32]

In the 1990s the public health paradigm largely solidified around issues of firearm access, storage, and safety devices. It differs from the crime-control paradigm by expanding from a focus on the impact of guns on crime to the impact on accidents and suicides as well. This presents a challenge for opponents of gun control that is very different than those presented by other paradigms. Here the analysis is primarily cost benefit, and the ability to demonstrate benefit is limited by the structure of the paradigm. In addition to introducing new language and perspective into the gun debate, this new paradigm has facilitated the expansion of interest in gun control among the medical community. Physicians such as Garen Wintemute have become some of the most prominent advocates of gun control.

Although gun-control opponents have begun to respond to this paradigm, they have not presented an alternative construction as yet.[33] Many control advocates viewed this new paradigm as a means for shifting the debate away from deadlocked positions and accessing concerns over public costs and safety.[34] Although control opponents have been less than successful in accessing the public health literature, they have responded in other media.[35] For many opponents of gun control, the public health community has become the focal point of their fears and hostility.

Political Symbolism

It is difficult to sort political ideology from political expediency in any issue. When a politician holds a position that places him at political risk or in opposition to his natural allies and supporters, ideological commitment can be inferred. Thus there is little doubt that liberal Democratic Representative John Dingell's (Mich.) opposition to gun control is heartfelt. On the other hand, adequate historical record exists to demonstrate rather conclusively that some positions are rooted almost exclusively in opportunism. Such was likely the case in the late Senator Thomas Dodd's (D-Conn.) pursuit of firearms legislation in the 1960s (see chapter 7). In most cases, however, ideology and opportunity most likely overlap, making differentiation difficult.

Although a majority of individual legislators can calculate the political risks and benefits of specific gun-control positions, determining the impact on a national political party constitutes a more elusive task. The Democratic Party controlled Congress and the White House at the passage of the National Firearms Act (NFA), the Gun Control Act (GCA), and the Brady Law. In spite of this, numerous Republicans supported the NFA and GCA, and the Republican Party did not incorporate a position in opposition to gun-control legislation in its national platform until 1976.[36] Even then, the platform reflected more the emerging Reagan faction than the position of President Gerald Ford.[37] Likewise, Democrats have been divided, with most Southern and Western democrats opposing gun control.[38]

By 1980, however, the Republican Southern strategy, which began in 1964, had reached full fruition. Gun control took its place among social issues such as abortion and school prayer as a critical part of the symbolic campaign to break Southern and Western voters permanently away from the Democrats.

Opposition to gun control has remained a core social issue for Republicans since that time and has proven useful at least at the congressional level.[39]

So long as the Democrats enjoyed Western and Southern support, the issue of gun control was highly problematic at the national level.[40] Support for gun control was expected by their Northern liberal base but was symbolically damaging to both congressional and presidential candidates in the West and South. After modest efforts by the Carter administration generated substantial reaction, Democrats largely avoided the issue until the campaign of 1992. In that campaign and in the presidential campaign of 1996, Bill Clinton openly espoused support for the limited, and largely symbolic, firearm legislation. Gun control became a key component of Clinton's strategy to nullify the "soft on crime" label that the Republicans had managed to hang on Democrats in every election since 1968. It would appear that gun control has moved onto the permanent political agenda as a *symbolic* issue, although, as I will explain later, not on the *real* issue agenda of either party. Gun control, as a symbolic mechanism for attracting and holding voter loyalty, has not received the same scholarly attention as the other four paradigms. It should not be surprising, however, that those who have used symbolic stands on gay marriage, domestic abuse, capital punishment, flag burning, and a host of other issues that either lack substance generally or in the form presented might view gun control as a political mechanism. Substantial evidence to support the rising importance of gun control as a symbolic issue can be seen in California's 1998 election campaigns.[41]

THE SYMBOLIC CONTEXT OF HISTORY

Symbols, myth, culture, and paradigms do not provide the entire context for understanding the evolution of gun-control policy, but they do provide a critical element. In the following chapters I address the specifics of gun control, with a primary emphasis on national rather than state and local policy. Although the ensuing chapters move from the conceptual and theoretical to the specific and concrete, they seek to explain the development of events in light of the theory presented in this chapter, while recognizing the limits of that theory. Some events owe as much to unique, idiosyncratic circumstances as to larger forces.

• • •

CHAPTER TWO

CRIME, CULTURE, AND MARKETS

M OST AMERICANS CONCEPTUALIZE gun control within a crime-control paradigm. Thus any examination of gun control necessitates some understanding of the current state of knowledge regarding crime. My intention is not to provide the reader with a comprehensive understanding of crime and its causes. I am constrained not only by limited space, but also by the current state of knowledge. No absolute consensus exists, even among scholars, regarding the causes, nature, or appropriate responses to crime. The debate becomes even more acrimonious when expanded to public officials, politicians, and the public, all of whom seem to feel qualified as being experts on the subject. Therefore I offer only a few fundamentals that are rather widely accepted.

CRIME, VIOLENCE, AND GUNS

Although most laymen perceive the crime rate as a well-documented statistic, scholars are far less sanguine.[1] Since 1933, the Federal Bureau of Investigation (FBI) has gathered and published national crime statistics, commonly referred to as the Uniform Crime Report (UCR), using data provided by police agencies. This report provides a reasonably accurate count of crimes reported to the police, but excludes all unreported crimes. Beginning in 1973, the Law Enforcement Assistance Administration (LEAA), another agency of the U.S. Department of Justice, began issuing the National Crime Victimization Survey (NCVS). After the abolition of LEAA, the Bureau of Justice Statistics continued to issue this annual report. Using survey data collected from randomly selected households by the Census Bureau, the Bureau of Justice Statistics applies advanced modeling-and-analysis techniques to produce estimates of total crime.

What Is the Real Crime Rate?

A number of authors, particularly those who are highly suspicious of government authority, have made a great deal of the divergence between these two figures.[2] However, a close examination of the discrepancies between the two systems reveals no sinister plan, only different methods of data collection. Additionally, the homicide and general violent-crime rates from the UCR appear to provide a legitimate indicator of trends.[3] The relationship of these two systems to the actual crime rate is best understood as follows. The actual rate, or entire universe of crimes, exists only in the abstract. It remains unknown and unknowable, since surveys and reports will always miss some crimes due to failure of some portion of the population to report these events, even when surveyed. In addition, it is often unclear whether events constitute a crime, several crimes, or no crime at all. Strong evidence supports the conclusion that victims fail to report a large portion of crimes to the police and that some crimes are seriously undercounted, even by using the survey methodology applied to the NCVS.[4] Therefore the NCVS constitutes a subset of the actual universe of crimes, and the UCR a subset of both these numbers.[5]

Murder as a Measure of Violent Crime

Although the NCVS excludes murder for the obvious reason that victims cannot be surveyed, UCR murder rates probably come as close as possible to an accurate count of the real universe of crime.[6] Historical data on murder rates before 1933 are speculative, and estimates for the turn of the century have varied from the very low rate of about 1/100,000, to revised estimates of about 6/100,000.[7] There is wide consensus, however, that the rate peaked in 1933 at approximately 10/100,000.[8] The rate then declined steadily until the middle 1940s; showed a slight increase until after World War II; and then declined again until 1958 (4.5/100,000). The murder rate was actually very nearly flat from about 1940 until about 1965. Beginning in the mid-1960s the murder rate, and crime rates in general, began a rapid rise that reached a plateau in the mid-1970s. Although 1980 was the peak year statistically, rates of 9/100,000 were reached by 1972 and remained near or above that level through 1982.[9]

Although many researchers made optimistic predictions that the crime rate in general and the violent crime rate in particular had begun a long-term decline in the early 1980s, this did not prove to be the case. Murder rates declined from 1980 through 1985, then began to increase in 1986 and again approached 10/100,000 by 1991.[10] By 1994 the rate again began to decline, a trend that has accelerated since. By 1998 the homicide rate declined to 6.3/100,000, down by over 30 percent from the 1991 rate.[11] This trend in murder rates parallels the pattern in overall and reported crime rates.[12] Explanations for this trend abounded. Gun-control advocates credited the Brady Law, while opponents credit the relaxed restrictions on carrying concealed weapons. Mayor Rudy Giuliani of New York attributed the plummeting rate in that city to initiatives by his administration, while California attorney general and 1998 gubernatorial candidate Dan Lungren credited California's Three-Strikes Law. Police chiefs across the country cited innovative strategies by their departments, and President Clinton credited his initiative for funding additional police. Curiously, the trend seems to apply in almost every part of the country as well as Canada, thus raising questions regarding any simple explanation.

The Historically High U.S. Murder Rate

The homicide rate in the United States has historically remained on a magnitude of 4 to 8 times higher than those of Northern European countries and over 10 times higher than Japan's.[13] The homicide rate in England and Wales has remained stable at between about 1 and 1.2 per 100,000 population, of which about 8 percent were committed with firearms during the past two decades.[14] The U.S. homicide rate began the 1990s by being about 7.6 times that of the rate in England and Wales, but had fallen to about 6.2 times the English rate by 1996. However, the rate of gun homicide in the United States remains at almost 75 times that of England's.[15] It has long been noted by opponents of gun control that the rate of nongun-related homicide in the United States far exceeded the total homicide rate in England. As violent crime in the United States dropped during the 1990s, violent crime in England and Wales, with the exception of murder, increased.[16] However, the drop in U.S. rates reduced the U.S./English ratio of nongun homicides by 17 percent, and the ratio of gun-related homicides by 19 percent. Even at this reduced rate, the U.S. rate of homicide with guns remains 50 times that of England and Wales and 7 times that of Canada. The overall Canadian homicide rate has remained between a third and fourth of the U.S. rate for decades.[17] Thus homicide with firearms remains more of an American aberration than does homicide in general. If present trends continue, violent crime in the United States will approximately match the levels common in much of the industrialized world, but firearm homicide will remain much higher. The proportion of homicides committed with firearms in the United States began to increase in the mid-1960s with the upswing in crime, and has remained high. In 1964, firearms accounted for about 55 percent of all homicides; by 1991, over two-thirds of all homicides were attributable to firearms, a level that has continued up to the present.[18] By 1991, about 80 percent of all homicides with firearms involve handguns, a percentage that appears to be stable.[19] This disparity between the United States and other industrialized nations has long fueled the support for gun control.

    Zimring and Hawkins have most recently raised this issue by noting that survey data reflect substantially higher crime rates, even for assault and robbery, in Western European nations than the United States. Yet, homicide rates in these nations remain almost flat, at a fraction of U.S. rates.[20] Kleck has criticized Zimring and Hawkins's conclusions, but not essentially their data, as over-reaching. Kleck argues that Zimring and Hawkins ignored all research on the deterrent effect of guns and exclude a variety of causes other than firearm availability.[21] Kleck also makes a strong case against using cross-national comparisons of crime data, particularly survey data, to draw conclusions.[22]

SELF-DEFENSE: FACTS, FANTASIES, AND SUPPOSITIONS

Much of the philosophical and pragmatic argument regarding the desirability and utility of firearms revolves around their use for self-defense. Beginning with a Cleveland study by four physicians in 1975, the argument that the risk to occupants from the presence of a firearm in the home exceeded any benefit derived from self-defense began to emerge in the public health literature.[23] The general theme of this argument was that guns kept in the home were far more likely to be involved in suicides or accidents than to be used to defend the residents against crimes. The numbers for accidents and suicides were reasonably reliable and not difficult to obtain. The elusive data related to the use of guns in defense against crimes. Although not addressed by the UCR, defensive-use rates can be inferred from the NCVS, where the survey includes questions regarding resistance to crime, once the subject has indicated crime victimization during the past year.

Calculating Defensive Gun Use

The opponents of firearm controls, who viewed the public health argument as essentially supportive of prohibition, have responded aggressively.[24] Their responses generally have accepted the data on accidents and suicides but have challenged the assumptions about the number of defensive gun uses (DGU) as extrapolated from the NCVS. A number of surveys regarding gun issues had also included some questions regarding defensive use, and the results of these surveys appeared to conflict with the NCVS data.[25] The conflict provided a natural question for research. Gary Kleck, who had already established himself as a leading researcher in the firearms field, and Mark Gertz conducted a well-structured telephone survey that used both a large sample group and follow-up questions to provide additional data.[26] Control opponents have embraced the study results and made them the centerpiece of much of their argument regarding firearm utility.

Kleck and Gertz interpret their research as supporting 2.5 million DGUs per year, as opposed to the 64,000 to 85,000 DGUs derived from the NCVS.[27] The obvious question for both advocates and serious scholars was: How could such a wide disparity in results occur? To begin with, both figures are derived from sampling, and then calculated by assuming that what holds true for the sample is reflective of the entire national population. As with all surveys, methodological errors, either inadvertent or intentional, could skew the results. Both of these options appear unlikely in this case. The NCVS has attained wide acceptance from a very knowledgeable audience of social scientists over many years.[28] The National Institute of Justice (NIJ) staff is highly professional, and survey results have not varied with the political leadership of the Department of Justice.[29] Likewise, Kleck is a respected social scientist whose methodology was favorably reviewed by the late Marvin Wolfgang, the dean of American criminologists and an advocate of strong gun control.[30]

The only other options for explaining such significant disparity in survey results are either the variance in the behaviors of the respondents due to differences in questions, or the method of conducting the survey. Those surveyed by the NCVS know that the surveyor is a representative of the government. Although no means exists to use the data to take any sort of action regarding an individual respondent's answers, the respondents may not believe this and thus deliberately withhold information. Kleck and Gertz assume that this is the primary source of the disparity.[31] They postulate that respondents fear that their possession, carrying, or use of a gun may constitute a crime and therefore fail to divulge such information to an official agency of the government. Kleck and Gertz theorize that respondents become more forthcoming for academic researchers in an anonymous, telephone survey. While acknowledging that exaggeration by respondents could also skew results, they discount the likelihood of this. Kleck and Gertz forcefully revisit the assumption that persons defending themselves with guns have reason to underreport; this they do in their 1997 response to a critique by David Hemenway that stated: "DGUs usually involve unlawful possession of a gun by the gun-wielding victim, and sometimes other illegalities as well."[32]

Phillip J. Cook and Jens Ludwig replicated the Kleck and Gertz study for the NIJ and obtained results consistent with it.[33] These authors argue, however, that false positives may in fact have a significant impact on the survey results, a position supported by Hemenway.[34] They point out that a survey of this type is highly susceptible to such distortion. The Kleck and Gertz study recorded 222 cases of respondents or someone else in the household reporting a DGU within the previous five years, out of a survey population of nearly 5,000 subjects. Less than one respondent in a hundred reported a DGU during the preceding year—the responses that Kleck and Gertz characterized as the most reliable. If less than 1 percent of those surveyed falsely responded in the affirmative, the calculated number of DGU could be significantly distorted upward. Of course, the question remains: "Why would respondents respond with false positives?" Kleck and Gertz concluded that respondents have little rational reason to do so, and that any such errors would be more than offset by others concealing DGUs. Such an argument seems logical on its face, but some troubling indicators regarding the accuracy of the responses can be found in Kleck and Gertz's results.

The authors note that respondents reported shooting at adversaries in 15.6 percent of the cases, and claimed to have hit them in 8.3 percent of the cases.

This ratio of hits, questioned even by Kleck and Gertz, far exceeds the rate recorded for criminals who shoot at victims or police who shoot at suspects. More troubling is the fact that 15.7 percent of the respondents reported that the DGU "almost certainly" prevented an attacker from killing them or someone else, and an additional 14.2 percent reported that the DGU "probably" saved their life or the life of another. This implies that firearms were probably used to save over 600,000 lives and almost certainly to save nearly 350,000 lives during a year when the entire nation experienced 23,305 reported homicides.[35] Less than half of all households in the United States possess firearms, and of those persons who own or have access to firearms, not all would be able to avail themselves of a gun for defensive purposes in response to every threat. Thus one must either conclude that the respondents substantially exaggerated the risk that precipitated the DGU, or that their risk of homicide is many times that of the population in general. Even if one assumes that all homicide victims were unarmed, which they were not, and that potential victims were armed one-third of the time, which is questionable at best, armed victims would have to be 30 to 50 times more at risk than their unarmed counterparts.[36] Similar problems exist when other external measures are applied to the responses in the Kleck and Gertz study.[37] Although the small sample of the respondent group increases the chance of random error, the observations strongly imply significant exaggeration on the part of some respondents.

But why would anonymous respondents exaggerate the instances of DGUs? It is not clear that they have; however, it is not beyond comprehension that they might. To understand why would be to understand why people overstate their military service, height, and professional status and understate their age and weight. Defense against a life-threatening adversary validates the decision to possess a readily available firearm and reflects heroically on the part of the respondent. Displaying fear in the face of a nonexistent threat, threatening others with a firearm, or over-reacting to a minor crime demeans or embarrasses a respondent.

The Debate Over Results

Kleck has put forth a well-reasoned argument that the best scientific evidence supports a level of DGUs many times that extrapolated from the NCVS.[38] He points out that all the evidence, with the exception of the NCVS, is consistent with this conclusion.[39] If one assumes replication of findings by multiple researchers as providing the strongest case for validity, Kleck argues from a position of strength. Even the Cook and Ludwig study supports this conclusion. However, *validity* and not *reliability* is the issue. Furthermore, social science differs substantially from physics and chemistry. In this case, the findings depend on the answers received in surveys. The surveys that have produced the higher incidents of DGUs all used similar approaches of directly asking the respondents about DGU, while the NCVS asked first about crime and only afterwards about defensive action. Repetition of the process reduces the probability of random error, and refinement of survey questions can reduce the probability of misunderstanding and inadvertent error. Neither of these would prevent the recurrent skewing of results by cultural influences that were widely dispersed and deeply entrenched in the population. In fact, both Kleck and Cook assume that survey respondents systematically provide false data.[40]

The explanations offered by both Kleck and Cook for the extreme disparity in results between the two methods both depend on assumptions about the nature of respondent distortions. Kleck assumes that underreporting is more likely than exaggeration. In fact, he postulates that DGUs may be several times higher than his conclusions because of the bias for underreporting. Although there is strong evidence that citizens underreport crime, it does not essentially follow that they underreport DGUs. Cook and others, in turn, assume a greater likelihood of exaggeration in reporting of DGUs, an equally unprovable conclusion.

I can offer no new scientific data to resolve this conflict, but I will offer an intuitive critique. I spent 30 years of my life carrying a gun almost daily. I also associated with hundreds of others who did the same. We spent countless days in high crime-rate areas and on surveillance. I never had an occasion to prevent a crime from occurring, although I did make some arrests after crimes occurred.[41] Based on my conversations with many others in law enforcement, I conclude that my experience was not atypical. On the other hand, I did not reside in a poor, inner-city neighborhood nor did I live with a violent and abusive person.[42] I have always made a point of attempting to spot potential trouble in advance and avoid it, unless professional obligation or civic duty mandated otherwise.

I suspect that in any population an unknown number of respondents will inflate the number of DGUs for three reasons. First, some deliberately may attempt to skew the results for political reasons. The controversy over defensive gun-usage has been widely covered in the gun press, and some portion of the population opposed to gun regulation is capable of understanding the potential impact of inflating DGU rates. Based on NRA membership figures, well over 2 percent of the respondents could fall into this category.[43] Second, some portion will invent or exaggerate incidents for the same reason some people lie about other aspects of their lives; they enjoy the attention and want to seem more important than they really are. Although the subject receives no pecuniary benefit from this action, neither do many people who spin yarns for strangers. I have personally observed numerous individuals volunteer false information on criminal activity for no apparent reason except to garner attention and be a part of things. In many instances, these individuals go to great lengths to fabricate stories and will persist in the face of intensive questioning. Finally, some portion of the population will alter or misinterpret the circumstances of an actual DGU to make it more romantic or at least more socially acceptable, such as describing a trespasser as an intruder or failing to include provocations that precipitated a potential assault. In addition to those who intentionally distort circumstances, some portion of the population will misperceive or imagine them. Although this might seem negligible, the widely accepted estimate for the occurrence of schizophrenia in the general population is 1 percent.[44] Hemenway points out that 10 percent of those surveyed by ABC News and the *Washington Post* reported seeing something they believed to be a spacecraft from another planet.[45] The lack of a DGU question in the NCVS removes most of the potential for intentional or unintentional false positives.

To some extent, underreporting by some respondents probably offsets false positives by others for reasons described by Kleck and Gertz. These researchers assume that the intentional underreporting occurs more often than exaggeration or intentional falsification of DGUs, but offer no evidence to substantiate this. My experience with informants and witnesses has convinced me that reconstructing the actual circumstances of any past event is problematic and often subject to distortion. Actions such as self-defense in the face of crime involve stress and self-image, both of which have the potential for distortion. Unfortunately, in-depth, face-to-face interviews of respondents would be costly and might result in the sort of underreporting bias that Kleck and Gertz suspect in the NCVS. Thus the best evidence seems to support a DGU number in excess of that based on the NCVS data, but *how much* in excess remains an open question.[46] Likewise, the NCVS estimates of criminal use of firearms undoubtedly understate the actual number of criminal misuses.

We know very little about the actual nature of uninvestigated events, even when reported in a survey. As examples: A battered spouse might use a firearm to lawfully fend off her abuser on several occasions during the year and also use the same firearm to unlawfully threaten or assault him at other times; a drug dealer might use a firearm regularly to prevent robbery, defend his territory, and collect debts; a fearful homeowner may use a gun to scare away a burglar and threaten a teenager walking across the yard. Thus defensive uses and crimes may be mixed and, in some cases, a single event may fall into both categories, such as an armed drug dealer fending off an assault by a disgruntled customer. For a variety of reasons, therefore, the frequency and nature of DGUs remain controversial.

Policy Implications and Impacts

The fundamental symbolic debate seems to be whether there are more DGUs than criminal gun-uses. Since both figures constitute estimates drawn from survey data and are subject to substantial distortion, the sort of sweeping claims made by advocates on both sides of the gun issue seem questionable.[47] What is reasonably incontrovertible is that guns are used in a significant portion of crimes and in a substantial number of defenses against crime,[48] yet most guns are not used in either way. The American political system has shown little inter-

est in applying social-science research data in other areas, and there is little reason to expect that it will drive policy relating to guns.[49] The research by Kleck
and others has probably had its greatest effect on the policy process by effectively challenging the contention that guns directly increase violent crime. In
the American political system, raising questions about the efficacy of gun control is enough. So long as credible debate exists regarding the influence of guns
on violent crime patterns, the status quo and individual rights prevail by default.

From a political perspective, the importance of guns as a means of self-
defense may be less about preventing actual victimization than about a providing sense of well being. Just as many people do not want to surrender health care
decisions to others, regardless of data about outcomes, many Americans feel
more secure if they possess a means of self-defense. Many other actions, such as
wearing seat belts, exercising regularly, reducing fat intake, stopping smoking,
driving cautiously, avoiding high-risk areas, or terminating an abusive relationship might yield greater safety benefits. However, possession of a firearm may
reduce the sense of helplessness and increase the sense of individual control.

Curiously, advocates, from both sides of the issue, lend support to the perspective that feelings about gun control are largely driven by attitudes toward
individual self-defense. Kates has argued that the core of what is often
described as the "anti-gun" movement primarily seeks to de-legitimate force-
ful self-defense.[50] Political scientist and control advocate Robert J. Spitzer
advances a surprisingly similar analysis of the issue by conceptualizing it as a
component of the argument for international disarmament and peaceful resolution of issues.[51] Self-defense is a visceral issue on both sides. For many gun-
control advocates, the willingness to use deadly force to resist most crime is
incomprehensible.[52] For control opponents, the unwillingness to act in the
defense of oneself, family, or community is equally incomprehensible.[53]

For this reason, research serves primarily to legitimate an argument rooted
in basic cultural values rather than in evaluating the cost and benefit of potential public policy. Ironically, self-defense is quite possible within a highly regulated environment. Only two types of gun regulation have serious implications for self-defense on the macrolevel. Laws that prohibit firearm possession,
or make possession so onerous as to effectively prohibit it, would impair self-
defense. However, self-defense does not require numerous firearms, special
types of firearms, or immediate acquisition of firearms.[54] Laws that restrict the
carrying of handguns also potentially restrict the capacity for self-defense, at
least away from the home or business. Largely as a result of research by John
Lott, liberalized concealed-carry laws became the focus of both the crime
deterrence and policy debates during the late 1990s (see chapter 10).[55]

Interestingly, only between 1 and 4 percent of adults apply for concealed-
weapon permits in those states where issuance is mandatory.[56] Although there
is some evidence that a larger portion of the population may carry a gun on
some occasion,[57] it is not motivated enough to obtain licenses. Among those

who possess licenses, no research has been done to determine when and how often licensees carry guns. If police officers are indicative, most licensees quickly tire of the burdensome nature of gun carrying and limit it to periods of perceived high risk.[58] Apparently, most citizens do not want to carry firearms for self-defense.

MARKETS AND POPULATION

The firearms market has attracted far less attention than the relationship between firearms and crime. Nonetheless, the market constitutes a key component for understanding firearm policy, the reasons for policy stalemate, and the potential for formulating future policy. The most fundamental requirement is to establish the magnitude of the current firearm inventory. Over the past 30 years researchers have offered several estimates regarding the number of guns in the United States, but no precise count exists because neither government nor industry has maintained adequate data.[59] Although the Bureau of Alcohol, Tobacco, and Firearms (ATF) has collected and published production and importation figures since 1974, its reports lump firearms into large categories that do not provide much information other than the number of rifles, shotguns, pistols, and revolvers. Figures for prior years are less-certain estimates from Department of Commerce sources. The Bureau of Alcohol, Tobacco, and Firearms also maintains figures on lawful exports, but no figures exist for firearms that are destroyed, worn out, seized by police, or unlawfully exported.

Estimating the Population

Newton and Zimring estimated a total of 90 million firearms, including 24 million handguns, in private hands as of 1968.[60] Subsequently, there have been periodic estimates by ATF and estimates by Wright, Rossi, and Daly (1983), Vizzard (1993), and Kleck (1997). Because most authors utilize the early estimates as a basis, some examination of the figures and the methodology is useful.[61] Wright et al. offered the most exhaustive and scholarly effort to estimate the number of firearms in private hands in the United States.[62] They critiqued the work on a supply model done by Newton and Zimring as well as developing their own demand-model estimates based primarily on residential survey data. The critique of Newton and Zimring contains errors that reflect the authors' lack of familiarity with the topic rather than any technical shortcomings as researchers.[63] In general, these errors appear to skew the estimates downward.

Although a reading of Wright et al. reveals the authors' limited firsthand knowledge of firearms, their use, and the firearms market, this study is unique in attempting to apply some disciplined methodology to estimating the number of privately held firearms. Two models were presented: The first attempted to improve on previous supply models by estimating the number of firearms removed from private possession through wear and seizure by the police. The second utilized public-survey data to develop a demand model. Both of the models produced lower estimates than ATF or Newton and Zimring. The authors then examined the so-called "fear-and-loathing" explanation for the increase in firearm demand that began in the mid-1960s.[64]

The first Wright et al. model focused on the failure of previous estimates to consider the number of firearms removed from private hands through damage, wear, or seizure by police. This was a legitimate critique, and an accurate calculation of these figures would clearly improve the accuracy of the estimates. Unfortunately, Wright et al. did not have much familiarity with firearm or the firearms market. As a result, their models reflected several practical problems.

The estimate of firearms in private hands in the United States by Wright et al., as of 1978, was 100,000,000 to 140,000,000.[65] By the year 2000 approximately 100,000,000 more firearms had entered the market.[66] Some of these have gone to police or other government agencies, but these agencies have surplused numerous older firearms from their inventories.

The inventory of privately owned firearms did not simply increase by the number of guns manufactured and imported, minus legal exports. Some firearms were seized and destroyed by the police. Although the exact number is not known, the Wright et al. estimate of 260,000 per year would yield an approximate number of 5.5 million during the period between 1978 and 2000, thereby reducing the increase somewhat to under 100 million. Undocumented importation of firearms has not proven to be a significant source of firearms, but illegal export undoubtedly has reduced the domestic supply.[67] Customs and ATF offices near border areas, as well as those in areas with concentrations of recent or illegal immigrants, routinely receive information on the illegal exportation of firearms. It is not unusual to detect substantial purchases of firearms by legal aliens that are clearly meant for export. Examination and traces of firearms seized in Mexico, Central America, the Philippines, Northern Ireland, and other locations with illicit markets have reflected primarily American sources. Because these activities are illegal and often the exporters are individuals who export only a few guns at a time, there is no means of calculating the volume, which probably has involved many thousands of guns per year.[68]

Determining the number of firearms that are worn out or rendered unserviceable each year presents an equal dilemma. Wright et al. did calculations using 30- and 50-year half-lives for firearms, and implied that they considered the 30-year half-life rather generous. If firearms are regularly and often used, the 30-year half-life, in fact, might be reasonable or even generous. For instance, a police sidearm that was fired monthly using ammunition loaded to near the limits of the firearm's stress capacity or a shotgun that was used weekly for skeet or trap shooting might reach the end of its usable life in 10 or 20 years. Even for this type of use, however, some firearms have incredible lifespans.[69]

Most persons do not make the same use of firearms that they do of auto-mobiles, power tools, or lawn mowers, thus extending the life of firearms. Only the most dedicated gun enthusiasts and law-enforcement officers regu-larly shoot firearms that are owned primarily for self-defense. Many hunters fire only a few rounds per year through their rifles, although bird hunters gen-erally fire more rounds through shotguns. Many guns purchased for sport or self-defense simply languish in closets for years. Firearms that are not regularly fired routinely last indefinitely unless destroyed by fire or the elements. In addi-tion, patterns of use tend to extend usable life. Those who shoot regularly and would be most inclined to wear out firearms are the most likely to trade them in for new models or set them aside and buy new firearms for regular use. This has a net effect equivalent to transferring automobiles with a portion of their usable life to persons who seldom drive, own garages, and take meticulous care of them. Cared-for firearms, like hand tools, do not deteriorate with time. Once transferred to a user who is more interested in having rather than using the item, its lifespan will exceed its owner's.[70]

Firearm durability and life have implications beyond theoretical popula-tions. Policy formulation must include the assumption that current stocks of firearms will continue to exist for many years. Thus changes that affect only new firearms will have limited impact. In addition, durability shapes the nature of illicit markets. Because buyers do not consume the product, illicit sellers cannot establish a stable repeat clientele. Therefore they must continually seek out new customers, an action that exposes them to substantial risk of selling to undercover police or informants.

Assuming that a million firearms became unserviceable during the period between 1978 and 2000, the estimate of the year 2000 number, based on the Wright et al. estimates, would have reached between 193 million and 243 mil-lion, minus illegal exports. Since Wright et al. described their original esti-mates as conservative, the current number of guns in the United States most likely exceeds 220 million and grows at a rate of about 4 million per year.[71] As the authors pointed out, the exact number is not as significant for planning and policy purposes as the general magnitude. Wright and other scholars have noted that approximately 50 percent of American households report the pres-ence of a gun. Although this figure appeared to be stable for many years, it has recently begun a significant decline.[72] For the politics and policy of gun con-trol, this figure is probably as important as the number of firearms.

In their effort to critique the Newton and Zimring explanation for the accelerated market demand that began in the 1960s and to create a demand model, Wright et al. become much more speculative than in their supply-side calculations. The authors attempted to calculate the increase in demand gen-erated by new hunters, gun collectors, and shooting-sports enthusiasts to determine if the increase in firearm numbers resulted from fear or normal mar-ket expansion of these activities. Wright et al. concluded that the increased demand emerged largely from an expansion of these recreational activities and *not* from fear and loathing. Here, their lack of familiarity with firearms, the market, and shooting sports resulted in significant errors in the assumptions underlying their model.[73] Subsequent work by other researchers supports the thesis that firearm sales rise in response to perceptions of increased threat of crime.[74]

Still, the sales boom of the 1960s probably owed more to the maturation of baby boomers than to fear of crime. Raised on westerns and stories of World War II, the young males of this generation constituted the first cohort without memory of the Great Depression. Their access to expendable income coincided with a period of rapidly rising consumerism. The firearm market undoubtedly mirrors other consumer markets in the United States. Sales of sport-utility vehicles do not depend on the number of people with a practical need for four-wheel drives, nor do sales of computers depend on the cus-tomers' need for them as tools of a trade. Marketing in America assumes that impulse and image are more important than customer needs. To maintain sales, particularly of a commodity as durable as firearms, manufacturers and dealers must convince customers to purchase far more guns than what they need for either sport or self-defense. Basic firearm function has not changed since the early 1900s,[75] requiring manufacturers and dealers to implement strategies to maintain market demand.

Changes in the Market

An examination of the production and import figures reveals that since 1991, handgun sales have surpassed rifle and shotgun sales. Handgun sales appear to have increased dramatically, beginning in the mid-1960s and quadrupling between 1962 and 1968, while sales of long guns doubled.[76] Observation of the market revealed that handguns suddenly became difficult to obtain in about 1965. For several years thereafter suppliers had difficulty obtaining enough handguns to fill demand. This was especially true of high-quality handguns. Eventually, the manufacturers expanded capacity to meet demand, and, since records have been maintained, handguns have been accounting for an ever-increasing percentage of the market.

In addition to declining as a portion of the total market, the rifle and shot-gun markets have changed markedly. In 1960 the *Gun Digest* listed no long guns other than sporting-type firearms.[77] By 1993 the same publication listed over 100 variations of combat rifles and shotguns.[78] The same results are obtained by examining the shelves of gunshops or their sales records. Although firearms explicitly designed for hunting or target shooting continue to consti-tute the majority of long guns, a significant and increasing number have designs particularly suited for combat.[79] These nonsporting arms do not fall into any single, definable category, although the term "assault weapon" has been applied to a number of them.

Assault Weapons

The concept of the assault weapon derived from the assault rifle, which originally described a short carbine that fired a rifle cartridge of moderate intensity, had a large magazine capacity, and was capable of semi- and full-automatic fire. This weapon was essentially a half-step between the submachine gun—or machine pistol, which fired a pistol cartridge, such as the .45 caliber Thompson or 9mm Sten Gun—and the full-power, semi-automatic rifle such as the M1. The design concept is generally traced to the World War II–era German MKb 42 or later MP44 carbines, although the American M1 carbine was of contemporary design and was essentially a similar firearm.[80] After World War II these smaller, lighter weapons began to replace rifles as the standard infantry weapon, first with the adoption of the AK47 by the Warsaw Pact and the Chinese and later with the adoption of the M16/AR15 by the United States. Today, virtually all the armies of the world use a light, selective-fire infantry weapon chambered for a medium-intensity cartridge. The intermediate cartridges make the weapons easier to fire and allow the individual soldier to carry more ammunition. The smaller size allows for easier exit from armored infantry vehicles and helicopters. These benefits were gained at the expense of range and accuracy, which seem to be of far-lesser concern to modern mechanized armies.

Until the 1960s the idea of selling these firearms to civilians apparently did not occur to manufacturers. By the standards of hunting rifles, these weapons utilized cartridges that were limited in both range and shocking power, and their accuracy was generally below the standards of most hunting firearms. Their large magazine capacities and rapid-fire capabilities were of no particular value for hunting, and they had little or no aesthetic appeal.[81] There seemed little reason to assume that firearms designed more for sustained firefights with determined, multiple opponents than for hunting would appeal to many purchasers. In addition, the original military weapons had been designed as full-automatic and required significant modification to be legally sold in the unrestricted market.

During the 1960s the Director of Civilian Marksmanship distributed World War II–vintage M1 carbines through the NRA. When these firearms proved popular, manufacturers began building this firearm for the civilian market. These M1 carbines demonstrated a market for military-type rifles with little hunting utility, and additional manufacturers began to modify military designs to render them capable of only semi-automatic fire and offer them for sale. Eventually, manufacturers of shotguns such as Remington, Winchester, Mossberg, and Ithaca, began to offer police-type, short-barreled shotguns for civilian sales. Later, manufacturers substituted pistol grips for shoulder stocks on some of these shotgun models, thereby creating shorter, more concealable weapons. In addition, several small manufactures began offering semi-automatic versions of submachine guns, such as the M10 and the KG99 as pistols.[82] Although these handguns provide the purchaser with no unique functional utility and are awkward to shoot or to carry, they have a visual appeal that both attracted customers and repelled gun-control advocates. The large magazine capacity of these so-called "assault" pistols and rifles and their derivation from full-automatic designs made them the favorites for persons desiring to convert legal semi-automatic firearms to full-automatic machine guns. No statistics are maintained as to how many of the long guns currently sold are designed primarily as combat weapons. However, interviews with gunshop owners reveal that sales of these items represent a significant portion of their business. Although some law-enforcement officers noted a trend toward altering certain military-style firearms to fire full-automatic, in addition to the appearance of such weapons in the possession of some criminals,[83] the trend attracted little attention from the public or gun-control advocates until 1989.

The public attention was seized in 1989 by the actions of Patrick Purdy, a mentally disturbed drifter who used an AK-style firearm to randomly shoot down children on the playground of a Stockton, California, elementary school. The California Legislature responded by passing a bill requiring the registration of certain semi-automatic firearms and prohibiting future sales of the same models.[84] The firearms included in the list were selected by a rather arbitrary means that involved appearance and political compromise but paid little attention to function.[85] Later that year, ATF imposed restrictions on the importation of military-style rifles after being urged to action by drug czar William Bennett and given tacit approval by the White House. In this case, specific attributes were used to determine the firearms excluded; however, these attributes, such a bayonet lugs and folding stocks, made no difference in the operation of the firearms. Although the Gun Control Act (GCA) provided authority to take such action on imports, no such authority existed over domestic production. These actions were the first in a series of state and federal initiatives to restrict or ban assault weapons. These efforts eventually resulted in the passage of a federal statute prohibiting specified models of semi-automatic rifles, pistols, and shotguns or semi-automatic firearms with certain specified features.[86]

The ban on the importation of assault rifles temporarily altered the market. Hundreds of thousands of Chinese AK47-type rifles, for which import authority had already been requested, were barred, as well as significant numbers of other weapons. Foreign manufacturers quickly reacted by modifying their firearms slightly, however, and were able to begin imports of essentially identical firearms within months. Domestic manufacturers were not affected and continued to produce assault-type firearms. The subsequent bans on domestic models caused manufacturers to modestly alter their designs. Because these laws did not restrict a basic category of firearm, such as all semi-automatics, they have had only minor impact on markets. To date, the two principal outcomes of federal legislation appear to be cosmetic changes in some firearms and increased sales of existing inventories before the bans took effect.[87] Recent California legislation has extended the federal model by addressing design features such as pistol grips and flash suppressors. This bill became effective on January 1, 2000.

Handguns

Some handguns are primarily designed and utilized for sporting purposes such as target shooting or hunting. An examination of inventories in gun stores quickly dispels any notion, however, that such firearms compose a significant portion of the handguns currently sold. The dominant handguns in the 1990s market have been medium- and large-caliber, semi-automatic pistols designed as combat weapons. Although sporting events for such firearms exist, these events involve only modest numbers of participants. When one combines an examination of the production and import figures with knowledge of what is occurring within the market, it becomes clear that the majority of firearms being sold is no longer primarily for sporting purposes. This does not preclude many firearms being purchased for multiple uses or simply on impulse. Like all consumers in American society, firearm purchasers often buy guns just to have them. Firearm dealers regularly describe many sales as the purchase of "toys."[88] However, whether toys or tools, guns progressively have taken on the appearance of people-killers.

Although firearm sales have occasionally demonstrated a distinct upward movement in response to visible social disorder,[89] the market is shrinking as well as changing.[90] New additions to the market peaked in 1989, with over 6 million units, then began to decline. By 1996 the figure had dropped to fewer than 4 million.[91] Between 1989 and 1996 new handgun sales declined by over half a million, and new rifles and shotguns entering the market decreased by twice that figure. This decline, which has slowed but not ceased, probably results from the extreme durability of firearms as well as the declining opportunity for and interest in shooting sports. Although firearm owners' organizations make substantial efforts to advance hunting and shooting sports, the urbanization of America presents a constant impediment. Some members of the gun community believe the decline in opportunity for shooting is a greater threat than gun-control laws to the future of shooting sports in the United States. They advocate shifting some of the emphasis and resources of the firearm interest groups from opposing gun control to enhancing the opportunities for engaging in shooting sports.[92]

The Illegal Market

Gun-control policy in the United States has been formulated primarily by using the crime-control paradigm. The dominant cultural belief in minimizing government intervention in private behavior and minimizing the burden on "reputable" citizens has led to a strategy focused on denying firearms to high-risk persons—primarily felons, mental incompetents, and minors—with minimum impact on other citizens. For this reason, the movement of firearms from "legitimate owners" to prohibited persons and the leakage of firearms from legitimate commercial channels have been fundamental concerns of policy inquiry. As gun-control opponents have often pointed out, most firearms are never used unlawfully. Even if one uses the conservative estimated figure of 220 million firearms, and increases the Bureau of Justice Statistics estimate of 1.3 million criminal uses of firearms per year to 2.2 million in allowance for underreporting,[93] the resulting estimate of firearms used criminally in a single year remains at 1 percent.

Actually, the number of guns used unlawfully has limited use for policy-making: the proportion of possessors using guns unlawfully has far more importance. It matters little that an individual with ten guns used only one of them unlawfully. To paraphrase an antigun-control slogan, *people commit crimes with guns; guns don't commit crimes*. Although the exact number of gun owners is not known, a reasonable estimate is about 50 million, resulting in an estimate of approximately $2^{1}/_{2}$ percent of gun owners using a gun to commit a crime every year.[94] Of course, this estimate is almost surely skewed upward, because some offenders commit multiple crimes. At the same time, NCVS figures probably understate criminal use as a result of underreporting by victims and the failure to capture criminal uses such as gun carrying by drug traffickers to protect their operations.

The questions of where criminals get their guns and how to prevent them from doing so has occupied several Senate and House hearings. Some persons, who commit crimes with firearms, obtain them lawfully. The source of these crime guns is of little concern when examining illegal markets. Those prohibited from legally obtaining guns most likely obtain firearms from whatever source is most easily available. Two methods have been used to try to construct a picture of the illegal market. Both methods have limitations. The Bureau of Alcohol, Tobacco, and Firearms has conducted several studies of seized firearms traced through its tracing center, as well as all guns seized within specific jurisdictions. This method uses a nonrandom sample and has information limitations and other shortcomings.[95] The alternate methodology uses interviews of persons incarcerated for crimes involving the use of firearms. Subject to all the potential distortions of any sampling methodology, these surveys must depend on subjects who are predictably less honest than randomly selected members of the general population.

Mark Moore conducted an in-depth examination of the illicit handgun market in 1979, using a variety of sources.[96] He categorizes the sources as licensed dealers, "scofflaws" or unlicensed traffickers, private transfers, and theft.[97] Of these, he estimated thefts to be the most significant, with private transfers and licensed dealers roughly equal as secondary sources. However, his estimates display such wide ranges as to place the relative importance of categories into some doubt. In general, all the studies support similar categories of illicit-firearm sources, as does my personal observation and experience.[98] Although well-documented studies are not available for the period prior to 1968 and the passage of the Gun Control Act, congressional testimony from hearings leading up to that Act imply that retail dealers constituted a far-moresignificant direct source of firearms to felons than since the Act was passed.[99]

Surveying Felons

The Florida Department of Justice published the first survey of incarcerated felons regarding their sources of handguns.[100] Similar studies have been conducted by researchers on incarcerated inmates, persons recently arrested, and juvenile offenders.[101] The 1977 study of Florida inmates indicated that legitimate retailers accounted for more of the firearms acquired by the respondents than did theft. Private transactions, which presumably include both legal and illegal purchases, and trades accounted for only 15 percent. This study and subsequent surveys of inmates have been condensed in table 2.1. Because different studies categorized firearm sources in different ways, some merging of categories was necessary to generate the table: Those portions of guns listed as being obtained through borrowing and gifts were consolidated into the source category of friends and family; those obtained by trade were included in private transactions; data separated among nonlicensed sources such as fences, drug dealers, or "on the street" were merged into the single category of private transactions; sources not specified were not included, resulting in some rows adding up to less than 100 percent.

Wright and Rossi conducted the most comprehensive of these studies for the Department of Justice and later published it as a book.[102] They included statistics for a subpopulation that they identified as "handgun predators." Constituting about 17 percent of the surveyed inmate population, this group accounted for almost half of all crimes and the majority of violent crimes reported in the inmate survey. Handgun predators also reported possessing and carrying firearms at a much higher rate than the rest of the inmate population.[103] Figures for the handgun predators have been listed as a separate row in table 2.1.

That some variation appears in these surveys should come as no surprise. Although all the studies surveyed incarcerated populations, these studies lacked any means for matching the demographics of one population to those previously surveyed. Sheley and Wright surveyed juveniles, while all other studies surveyed adult offenders. Because questions were not identical, some interpretation is required to allocate percentages to specific categories. Changes in time and location potentially alter the level of restriction on firearm purchases, since state laws and procedures vary and have the potential for change over time within jurisdictions. The low level of acquisition from licensed dealers for the juvenile offenders and the handgun predators very likely reflects the legal restrictions that these two groups, who by definition were prohibited from making lawful purchases, faced in obtaining firearms from licensed dealers.

Table 2.1
INMATE SURVEYS ON SOURCES OF HANDGUNS

Study	Family and Friends	Private Transaction	Legitimate Dealers	Theft
Burr, FL inmate survey, 1977[a]	.33	.15	.27	.25
Wright and Rossi, inmate survey[b]	.34	.20	.16	.32
Wright and Rossi, handgun predators[c]	not available	.51	.7	.42
Beck et al., inmate survey[d]	.31	.28	.27	.9
Sheley and Wright, incarcerated juveniles[e]	.36	.43	.7	.12
Decker's arrested subjects[f]	<.25	not asked	not asked	.05

[a] Although the original figures were published in D.E.S. Burr, *Handgun Regulation*, the figures here were obtained from Wright and Rossi, 1986, 182.
[b] Wright and Rossi, 1986, 183.
[c] Ibid., 186.
[d] Beck et al., 1991.
[e] Joseph F. Sheley and James D. Wright, "Gun Acquisition and Possession in Selected Juvenile Samples" (Washington, DC: National Institute of Justice, 1993).
[f] Scott H Decker, 1995. This survey did not include the origin of purchases, trades, or gifts. The figure for friends and relatives was obtained by combining percentages for gifts and loans. Presumably some guns were also purchased or obtained in trades from friends or relatives.

Presumably, the other populations contained some individuals who were not prohibited from lawful purchase prior to their current incarceration.

Finally, all the potential problems that emerge in any survey data may exist here. Respondents may lie, either for fear of disclosure or simply to cause mischief. Memories may fail and respondents may answer carelessly. An example of potential problems with data can be found in Decker's reports on arrestees in four locations: Atlanta, Miami, Phoenix, and Washington. The respondents reported a higher percentage of possession of a gun within the past 30 days than they reported in their entire lifetime. In the case of Miami, more respondents (21 percent) reported owning a gun in the past 30 days than during their lives before.[104] Although immersion in a larger pool of data masks these discrepancies, they raise serious questions regarding the care exercised by respondents in answering questions.

Some patterns do emerge, however. Friends and family consistently account for about one-third of all handguns acquired by the surveyed groups, and the combination of friends, family, and private transactions accounts for approximately 50 percent of all acquisitions for every group except juveniles, for whom the percentage exceeds 75 percent. Theft is an important, but not primary, direct source of firearms. However, each of the categories should be viewed with some skepticism.[105] There is no way of knowing, for instance, if guns purchased on the street or obtained from a friend were previously stolen. Likewise, these guns may have been obtained from a licensed dealer through the use of a "straw purchaser." The friend or relative may have provided guns to others and thus be an illicit dealer. Finally, these subjects may make little distinction between borrowing and stealing a firearm from a friend or relative.

The Nature of the Illegal Market

However, nothing in the available studies supports an assumption of a well-structured illicit market in firearms. Transactions appear to be casual and idiosyncratic. My own experience, and that of most other agents I have interviewed, supports an assumption that the majority of sources is very dispersed and casual, and that regular traffickers in firearms to criminals are few. In fact, those who do traffic illegally in arms seldom, if ever, restrict their sales to criminals or prohibited persons. Such action would narrow their customer base and reduce sales. In the numerous unlicensed dealer investigations that I conducted or supervised, no dealer restricted sales to prohibited persons. They simply sold to all buyers without concern for the legality of the transaction.

There is a number of reasons for the lack of a highly structured illicit-firearms market. First, the United States has a massive reservoir of firearms. In every inmate survey cited, the majority of respondents have indicated that they obtained a gun quickly and easily upon release, with friends or relatives constituting the most common potential source. With guns relatively easy to obtain, there is little economic incentive for persons to specialize in the illegal gun trade, although restrictive jurisdictions such as New York may create exceptions. Bureau of Alcohol, Tobacco, and Firearms studies have long documented a flow of handguns from low-control states to New York.

Scholars and advocates generally agree regarding some aspects of the illegitimate market. First, demand usually takes the course of least resistance. Second, demand is adaptive: When one source closes or becomes too costly in either risk or dollars, buyers seek new sources. The primary conflict regarding the nature of the demand side of the market centers on the degree of elasticity.[106] The recurrent refrains of control opponents have been: "If a criminal wants a gun, he will get one" and "when guns are outlawed, only outlaws will have guns." This debate has provided one of the recurring conceptual battles of the gun-control controversy. Unfortunately for control advocates, they have not successfully developed any equally effective slogans. Here the differing worldviews of the two groups have proven decisive in the battle for control of symbolic language. The more complicated, interactive world-vision held by advocates and their potential supporters does not lend itself well to concise explanations and simple description. "When guns are restricted, potential offenders will be marginally less willing to obtain, possess, or carry them" just does not work as a slogan.

The most eloquent arguments regarding the demand characteristics of the market have been made by Daniel D. Polsby, who argues that criminal demand for guns will always be more inelastic than general demand because criminals need guns to survive.[107] Based on this assumption, Polsby argues that gun regulation is destined to fail because criminals will always be more motivated to obtain guns than will more law-abiding citizens. This argument presumes that those who commit crimes constitute a homogeneous class, called *criminals*. Although true by definition, this categorization is also essentially meaningless, as law breaking constitutes the only sure commonality within the population.

Surely, the initiative, resourcefulness, resources, and perseverance of persons vary. The mature career criminal, disciplined enough to participate in an organized criminal enterprise, will certainly differ from the adolescent delinquent. Demand logically would increase with the skill, discipline, resources, and knowledge of the purchaser as well as the purchaser's perceived need for a firearm. On the other hand, some offenders display a very casual and disorganized behavior toward gun acquisition and possession. Cook et al. reported such attitudes among serious juvenile offenders, quoting one offender as stating: "I traded a .22 for a Super Nintendo and some other guns for a VCR and a waterbed"; and another, "I didn't have a gun once for three months because I lent my gun to my cousin to use."[108] In my experience, individual offenders display substantial disparities in organization, focus, and discipline, as well as wide variations in their desire for firearms. Criminals and noncriminals alike carry guns far more often than they use them. In both the criminal and noncriminal world, possession and carrying guns appear to result as much from attitude as from need.

Curiously, the demand side of both the legal and illicit markets is influenced by supply. Wright and Rossi note that perceived need for self-defense and socialization to guns through early association constituted the most significant single factors in the acquisition and carrying of firearms by criminals.[109] As guns become more common in a society, the perception of risk from guns and degree of socialization to guns would both logically increase. Both fear of attack and socialization have been noted as predictors of firearms possession for the general public as well as for criminals.[110] It is also reasonable to assume that criminals and the general population share the trait of impulse acquisition. Thus the presence of more firearms, particularly those designed to appeal to the fantasies of young males, would generate demand among criminals even more effectively than it would among noncriminals.[111] Thus criminal demand, like general demand, most likely increases in response to a large and diverse supply of firearms. In my experience, the interest in and demand for guns by criminals were directly influenced by the general market, and indirectly by the entertainment industry. During the early years of my enforcement career most of the offenders I encountered showed little interest in firearms. Even when they possessed or used firearms, they seemed little concerned with the type or quality. Over time, the quality and numbers of firearms increased and items such as spare ammunition magazines and holsters became more common. Survey data supports the conclusion that this trend has spread to juveniles as well as adults.[112]

Although the role of licensed dealers and unlicensed traffickers in the supply of firearms to prohibited persons has recently come into focus, the primary conceptual conflict remains historically centered around the elasticity of supply. Advocates of gun control have focused less on this area than have opponents. Several possible reasons account for this disparate interest: Primarily, advocates have focused little on the elasticity of supply because presumptions and language favor them in this area. Because the firearms industry is very visible and firearms are manufactured in factories, control advocates assume that alternate sources would not be readily available if the legal industry were restricted. Control advocates differ little from those supporting laws prohibiting prostitution, pornography, or drugs in their failure to examine market response to regulation or prohibition.

Opponents of gun control have argued that tight restrictions on guns would result in their being fashioned in clandestine workshops and illegally imported, mirroring the pattern of drug markets. Some argue that the existing supply is inexhaustible. It is this latter argument that has provided the most concern for policy analysts.[113] Within the United States, the elasticity of supply has never been well tested, except for machine guns and destructive devices. The variation in laws and the ready availability of long guns in almost all jurisdictions have allowed movement across state lines and the substitution of sawed-off shotguns and rifles for handguns with little difficulty.

Control opponents and many scholars have concluded that existing controls have little or no effect on gun availability, because many inmates report that guns are easily obtained. Yet 63 percent of those arrested persons surveyed by Decker reported that it would take them more than a week to obtain a firearm.[114] In Washington, D.C., this figure increased to 78 percent.[115] If compared to the period of time necessary to obtain illegal drugs or an automobile, one might well conclude that existing controls have substantial impact. Kleck has noted that all efforts at controlling violence and criminal behavior face disappointments, unless expectations are scaled down to reasonable levels.[116]

LICENSED DEALERS

The role of licensed dealers as a source of "crime guns" has repeatedly surfaced on the agenda of ATF and occasionally received passing attention on the larger political agenda. Because ATF traces large numbers of guns for police agencies, the agency possesses an available data set for determining the source of firearms seized by police. Since the early 1970s, ATF has conducted periodic trace studies of all firearms seized by police in specified jurisdictions, with the specific objective of identifying sources of unlawfully trafficked guns and guns used in crimes. The level of these studies has been vulnerable to changes in administrations and political climates. They peaked during the Carter administration, then declined significantly during the successive 12 years of Republican administrations, but resurged again during the Clinton years.[117]

The most recent studies have displayed increased sophistication by including data on the time lag between sale of the firearm and its recovery (or the so-called "time to crime") and by providing more detailed analysis of information on the firearm sources and dealer activities.[118] Although the renewed effort at building information on firearm-trafficking patterns began in the mid-1990s, it remained largely out of the public eye until joint announcements regarding it by ATF and the White House in early 2000.[119] The ATF announcement noted that just 1.2 percent of licensed gun dealers originally sold 57 percent of the firearms traced. The president's announcement called for 300 new ATF agents and 200 new ATF inspectors to police the firearm markets and concentrate on illegal trafficking. In addition, the president called for funding for additional state and federal prosecutors to prosecute gun crimes.

Although the 1.2 percent figure seems to imply some unlawful activity on the part of a few dealers, such a conclusion exceeds the information available. The majority of the approximately 100,000 licensed dealers do not actively deal in firearms to the general public[120]—most are hobbyists who sell only to themselves or a few friends. Of those who sell firearms, most sell few. Thus the majority of firearms, and particularly the majority of handguns, is sold at retail by a small percentage of licensed dealers. Therefore a random sample of guns would predictably reflect that a few dealers made the majority of original sales. In addition, location and inventory have potential for creating disproportionate representation. A large-volume dealer, specializing in inexpensive handguns and located in a state with weak restrictions on sales, will inevitably provide more guns used in crime or illegally resold than a dealer who sells more expensive arms or who operates in a restrictive state. Even the dealer's neighborhood will influence the propensity that his guns appear in a trace study.

Although the ATF data offers potential for directing regulatory oversight and in some cases criminal investigation, it does not follow that the identified dealers have violated the law. Even unscrupulous dealers can avoid criminal conduct by following the letter of the law. By making numerous lawful sales to individuals who may lawfully purchase the firearms but who subsequently resell them to prohibited persons or residents of states with restrictive laws, the dealer commits no crime. Only when the dealer knowingly conspires in the illegal activity does he become subject to prosecution. Limits on the number of guns an individual may purchase in a specified time period, such as the one-gun-per-month limit first instituted by Virginia, have attempted to address this problem. However, so long as sales between individuals remain unregulated, no effective mechanism exists for controlling large numbers of resales in the private market. In addition, legislators and regulators must consider that a substantial portion of guns used in crime are never identified, and that many "crime guns" are legally acquired. As in all other aspects of the market, the dispersal of illegal acquisitions among far more numerous legal ones, the large existing inventory, and the capacity of a lawful gun to become a crime gun at any time constitute the greatest barriers to effective market regulation.

Past efforts by ATF to concentrate enforcement efforts on illegal trafficking by licensed and unlicensed dealers resulted in threats to the agency's very existence.[121] Although those efforts reflected the priorities of the existing administration, those who encouraged ATF's efforts proved unwilling to expend political capital in its defense. The current increased interest probably owes much to the primary campaign of 2000, in which presidential candidate Bill Bradley called for more stringent gun control. If past experience provides any guide, ATF will have few defenders if a new hostile environment develops in Congress.

• • •

CHAPTER THREE

CONTROL STRATEGIES AND THE LAW

C ONCEPTUALLY, GUN–CONTROL STRATEGIES divide into five generic categories: restrictions on carrying, storage, and use; restrictions on acquisition and possession by specific classes of persons; market regulation and registration; prohibition of specific types of firearms; and enhanced sentencing. An
alternative approach for classification involves division by the unit of government imposing the policy. In various forms, gun control exists at the federal,
state, and local levels. Although the level of government imposing the policy
and the mechanics of the policy do not correlate exactly, patterns do emerge.
This chapter presents the fundamental conceptual options for gun control and
an examination of the current state of the law in the United States, including
the Second Amendment to the U.S. Constitution.

CARRYING, STORAGE, AND USE

The most common forms of gun control, restrictions on the carrying or discharge of firearms, usually make little or no distinction in the type of firearm
or the background of the possessor. Primarily invoked under authority of state
law or local ordinance, this category includes restrictions on the carrying of
concealed weapons, prohibitions against loaded firearms on public streets,
restrictions against guns on school property or in public buildings, and a variety of restrictions on when and where individuals can discharge firearms. A
number of jurisdictions also restrict the conditions of firearm storage or make
persons liable for injuries resulting from improper storage. Unlike many other
firearm regulations, most violations of these restrictions constitute only misdemeanors or lesser infractions. The majority of states adopted restrictions on the
concealed carrying of firearms in the first half of the twentieth century as an
NRA-backed alternative to restrictions on handgun ownership.[1] These laws
largely remained out of the gun-control policy debate until the mid-1980s.

Since then, the organized opponents of gun control have carried on an active campaign to modify state laws governing the issuance of permits to carry concealed firearms.[2] Prior to this campaign, most states had permissive issuance policies, which allowed local police chiefs and sheriffs to exercise full discretion regarding an applicant's need and suitability.[3] By 1999, 31 states had enacted mandatory issuance laws and Vermont had no law controlling the carrying of firearms.[4] These laws require licensing authorities to issue a license to every applicant that meets specified requirements. Typically, the requirements include a criminal-record check to verify that the applicant has no felony convictions and a minimum competency requirement, such as a training course or test.[5] Ironically, the discretionary model that has become the focus of attack by pro-gun groups evolved directly from the Uniform Revolver Act, a model law advocated for many years by the NRA and other firearm interest groups.[6] California provides a classic example of a discretionary system adopted from the Uniform Revolver Act. Implementation of California's law results in the majority of the concealed-weapon permits being issued by sheriffs in rural or semirural counties while most city police and urban sheriffs issue few permits.[7]

Washington State's 1961 adoption of a permissive concealed-carry permit law, requiring local law-enforcement officials to issue a concealed-carry permit to any applicant without a conviction for a crime of violence,[8] attracted virtually no attention throughout the rest of the nation. However, Florida's 1987 enactment of a very similar law generated national interest and began a trend that has swept through the majority of states. Why the Florida precedent stirred such attention, when Washington's did not, remains an open question. In 1961, gun control did not attract the media attention that it did in the 1980s. No active opposition drew attention to the Washington law, but the national press widely reported the change in Florida. No doubt, a historical bias in the national media toward attaching greater importance to news from East Coast and urban areas over the West and more rural areas played a role. Yet, the controversy generated by gun-control advocates and the national media may have elevated the importance of the Florida precedent.

The NRA has linked the campaign to change state concealed-carry laws to a campaign for state preemption of all firearm regulation. State preemption precludes local governments from legislating in a jurisdictional area once the state preempts that area. Preemption offers the opponents of gun control both political and practical benefits. It allows them to focus attention on the state legislature and avoid costly symbolic fights such as that in Morton Grove, Illinois, which banned private ownership of handguns. For gun owners, preemption reduces the need for complying with a myriad of local ordinances. State uniformity offers particular advantages in a mobile society where many residents cannot identify the political jurisdiction in which they reside.[9]

Controversy over gun-storage restrictions have also heightened in recent years. The public health approach to firearm control includes demands for storage restrictions, safety locks, and new safety innovations in design. Opponents of gun control see these as an attempt to delegitimatize gun ownership in general and possession for self-defense in particular.

RESTRICTING ACCESS BY SPECIFIC CLASSES

The earliest gun laws in the United States prohibited African Americans from possessing firearms.[10] By the early twentieth century, states had shifted from classes based on race to classes based on status. Numerous states adopted versions of the Uniform Revolver Act, which prohibited felons from possession concealable firearms. Over time, most states and the federal government have adopted laws restricting or prohibiting the possession of firearms by minors, drug addicts, the insane, and convicted felons. Although the creation of prohibited categories by federal law in 1968 did not assure uniformity, it created a minimum standard that states could expand on but not reduce. In addition to direct prohibition of possession by specific classes of persons, restrictions on the sales or transfers of guns, point-of-sale record checks, gun-owner identification cards, and owner licensing constitute mechanisms to enforce restrictions on acquisition or possession of firearms by specific classes of individuals.

The general concept of restricting felons enjoys rather wide support even among control opponents, whose opposition generally focuses upon the mechanisms adopted to enforce these restrictions. The greater the impact of a policy on the general population of gun owners or buyers, the greater the opposition from gun-control opponents. Therefore they usually support prohibitions against felons or drug addicts possessing guns but oppose reporting gun sales or licensing gun owners.

REGISTRATION AND MARKET REGULATIONS

Registration and market regulations seek to create information pools or databases that can aid law enforcement in tracing guns and tying them to their owners. Alternately, these policy options can serve as mechanisms for implementing laws restricting access to certain classes of people. Presumably, dealer licensing and records, registration, and reports of sale deter possession by restricted individuals by making transfer to minors, felons, and other restricted classes riskier and easier to detect. Routinely, commentators on gun policy confuse registration with dealer records and reports of sale. The latter systems record or report retail purchasers but require no subsequent reporting of private transfers. True registration requires that all transfers be reported and creates penalties for either failure to report or possession of unregistered guns, or both (see the National Firearms Act). The implementation of registration creates significantly more difficulty than dealer licensing or sales reports.

Registration requires action from significant numbers of citizens, who lack the motivation and knowledge of gun dealers.

RESTRICTED FIREARMS OR CATEGORICAL PROHIBITION

Strategies to reduce or eliminate a specific type of firearm can take several forms: Imposition of very high taxes or onerous controls on storage and transportation of certain firearms can generate such high cost that most persons will avoid possession. National Firearms Act utilized making and transfer taxes to deter the production and distribution of machine guns to private individuals, and California has placed both use and transfer restrictions on the existing stock of registered assault weapons. A prohibition on the future manufacture of certain classes of firearms, without directly restricting the existing population, serves to freeze the number at current levels. A last-minute amendment to the Firearm Owners' Protection Act of 1986 applied such a future restriction to machine guns. Restrictive licensing can be imposed on possession, such as was done in New York for handguns under the Sullivan Law. Of course, prohibiting possession, manufacture, or transfer of a specific class of firearm, or restricting it to public agencies, constitutes the simplest and most direct strategy. Still, even this strategy possesses complexities. To prohibit an item requires a clear and understandable definition. The difficulties encountered in establishing workable definitions of Saturday night specials, assault weapons, and armor-piercing pistol ammunition have demonstrated the complexities inherent in such policy.

ENHANCED SENTENCES

The gun-control policy most favored by the NRA and other organized opponents of the previously cited strategies involves mandatory minimum sentencing or additional sentence enhancement for the use of a firearm in a crime. Gun-control opponents argue that this approach focuses on only those gun possessors who constitute a problem, without imposing any burden on the general population of gun owners. In general, advocates of gun control concur with opponents in support of enhanced sentencing. While gun-control opponents express high levels of confidence in the deterrent potential of such laws, academics, including Kleck, contest this assumption.[11]

THE LAW AS IT EXISTS

The existing law relating to guns in the United States consists of a patchwork of local, state, and federal statutes that utilize all of the approaches previously described. The following section addresses the current state of the law, particularly the federal law, as of the publication of this book. I have deliberately chosen not to address in detail two categories of law: Laws mandating sentencing for the use of guns in crimes exist in all states and at the federal level. Because these laws generate very little controversy and require little explanation, I have largely ignored them. Likewise, I have directed little attention to laws and ordinances regulating the discharge, carrying, and storage of firearms. Although this book addresses both the storage and carrying issue in several sections, these laws are too numerous to chronicle here.

Federal Laws

The federal firearm controls primarily result from four pieces of legislation and the administrative regulations issued to implement these statutes. Originally passed in 1934 under the federal taxing authority, the National Firearms Act (NFA) constituted the first major piece of federal gun legislation. The Gun Control Act of 1968 (GCA) modified the NFA and marked the first significant federal controls on firearms under the interstate commerce authority. The 1986 Firearms Owners' Protection Act (FOPA), often referred to as the McClure-Volkmer Bill, substantially modification of the GCA. The most recent addition to federal law, the Brady Law, passed Congress in 1993. Although I address the political and policy evolution of these laws in subsequent chapters, this chapter outlines the current laws and their patterns of implementation. In addition, this chapter reviews the general pattern of state laws.

THE NATIONAL FIREARMS ACT (NFA): Although the first federal statute aimed at controlling firearms restricted the mailing of pistols and revolvers, this law had little practical impact.[12] The NFA, on the other hand, still constitutes a significant portion of the federal law, having changed little since its passage in 1934. Because of concerns for the constitutionality of a federal gun-control law, Congress modeled the NFA after the Harrison Narcotics Act, which had already withstood a constitutional test in the Supreme Court.[13] The NFA established a $200 tax on the manufacture and transfer of certain categories of firearms, and a $5 tax on the manufacture and transfer of other categories. The $200 tax applied to machine guns, silencers, rifles or shotguns under 26 inches in overall length, shotguns with barrels less than 18 inches, or rifles with barrels less than 16 inches. The law excluded most rifles, shotguns, and handguns but taxed, at $5, the making and transfer of certain unusual firearms such as belt-buckle guns and cane guns. Specifically, the law described this last category as any concealable weapon other than a pistol or revolver. A 1968 amendment to the law added destructive devices, including cannon, bombs, and rockets to the $200 category. Unfortunately, the law's use of the term "firearms" to describe the restricted weapons has the potential for producing significant confusion.

The law allowed dealers and manufacturers to pay a yearly special occupational tax, which exempted manufacturers from the manufacturing or making tax and allowed them to transfer firearms to dealers without tax. Dealers or manufacturers could make tax-exempt sales to government entities, but sales to individuals received no exemption. As a means of administering the tax, the law required registration of all enumerated firearms. With the exception of special occupational taxpayers, hereafter referred to as "manufacturers and dealers," the NFA required the maker of the firearm to first pay the tax and then receive permission from the Secretary of the Treasury or his delegate. The registration of most firearms resulted from reports from manufacturers. The transfer of a legally registered firearm required the permission of the Secretary of the Treasury. To obtain approval, the transferer had to first submit an application accompanied by a tax stamp, a description, photograph and fingerprints of the transferee, and a recommendation of approval by the law-enforcement agency in the transferee's place of residence.[14] Effectively, the passage of the NFA increased the price of machine guns beyond the reach of most buyers.

As originally proposed by Attorney General Homer Cummings, the NFA would have been a significant federal effort to control all firearms, other than traditional sporting arms such as rifles and shotguns.[15] As enacted, however, it had only limited impact as a result of the removal of pistols and revolvers from the final bill passed by Congress. The NFA effectively ended the manufacture of machine guns for private sale and precipitated the assignment of the firearm laws to the Department of Treasury for administration and enforcement, a precedent that endured through the end of the century. Originally assigned to the Bureau of Internal Revenue (IRS), jurisdiction was later redelegated to the Alcohol Tax Unit for enforcement. The jurisdiction remained with IRS under the Alcohol and Tobacco Tax Division (ATTD) and later the Alcohol, Tobacco, and Firearms Division, until the establishment of the Bureau of Alcohol, Tobacco, and Firearms (ATF) in 1972.

In 1967 the Supreme Court ruled in *Haines v. United States* that defendants charged with possession of unregistered firearms could raise a defense of self-incrimination.[16] The *Haines* case was decided in conjunction with two cases under the federal gambling statutes, which probably influenced the outcome of the gun case.[17] The government had never used the registration provisions of the NFA to force self-incrimination. Because the transfer implemented the registration and approval had to precede the transfer, no mechanism existed to generate self-incrimination. On the other hand, the wagering laws required bookmakers, engaged in illegal enterprises in most states, to register and allowed inspection of these registrations by local police. The NFA ruling probably resulted from being lumped with the two wagering tax cases.

Primarily, the ATTD utilized the NFA to charge individual violators with possession of unregistered machine guns and sawed-off shotguns. Many states lacked any statutes controlling these firearms and depended solely on the federal courts for enforcement. The resources devoted to these prosecutions reflected the low priority assigned to firearms enforcement by the federal government. Of approximately 1,000 agents employed by the ATTD, half worked exclusively on liquor violations in the Southeast region. Although agents in other areas pursued some firearm investigations, they devoted the majority of their time to alcohol enforcement.[18]

THE GUN CONTROL ACT (GCA): Congress originally passed Titles IV and VII of the Omnibus Crime Control and Safe Streets Act of 1968 on June 10, 1968. Largely as a result of political pressure that increased after the assassination of Robert Kennedy in June 1968, Congress replaced Title IV with a more comprehensive law, the Gun Control Act (GCA), in October 1968 (see chapter 7). Title VII, which prohibited the receipt and possession of firearms by felons, unlawful aliens, narcotics users, adjudicated mental incompetents, those dishonorably discharged from the military, and those who renounced their citizenship, remained a separate statute until 1986, when it was merged into the GCA.[19]

The GCA actually consisted of two distinct subdivisions or titles, located in different parts of the federal code. The law incorporated the existing NFA with minor additions as Title II of the Act, hereafter referred to as the "NFA."[20] The NFA remained a tax statute, in law if not in fact, and a part of Title 26 of the U.S. Code (the Internal Revenue Code). The larger portion of the GCA, and the one more innovative, constituted Title I of the Act. This portion of the law, relating to the general commerce in firearms, was located in Title 18 of the U.S. Code (the Criminal Code). Title II, or the NFA, retained the same scheme of registration, transfer controls, and taxes on specified firearms. The primary changes to the NFA consisted of the addition of destructive devices to the enumerated firearms, and the termination of authority to register existing NFA firearms after an initial amnesty period. The category of destructive devices included weapons with a bore more than a half inch, explosive and poison-gas bombs, projectiles with explosive warheads, and rockets and missiles.[21]

ATTD policy allowed persons without criminal records to register NFA firearms possessed in violation of the law if the violation were deemed "non-willful" by an investigator. The new law provided for an amnesty period when anyone could register an NFA firearm, regardless of state law or the owner's prior record. All information provided during registration was protected by privilege and could not be released to state authorities or used to prosecute the registrant.[22] The amnesty and nondisclosure provisions served to overcome the defense of self-incrimination established by the *Haines* case. Although this strategy solved the short-term problem of enforcing the NFA, it created a precedent that potentially constrained the form and application of any future firearm-registration system.

The majority of the GCA, Title I of the Act, applied to virtually all firearms and not just those defined in the NFA.[23] Although the GCA provided for no comprehensive system of control or regulation of firearms in the possession of individual citizens, it significantly altered the rules governing commercial firearm transactions. The law mandated that all persons engaged in the business of manufacturing, importing, or dealing in firearms obtain a federal license and maintain records of firearm transactions. The original law virtually prohibited all mail-order and out-of-state purchases of firearms. Subsequent revisions allow individuals to buy long guns outside their states of residence. Manufacturers and importers had to begin identifying every firearm by stamping the name of the manufacturer or importer and a serial number on the receiver. Firearms not suitable for sporting purposes and surplus military firearms were restricted from importation.

The original GCA prohibited dealers from delivering firearms to any person prohibited from possession under Title VII of the Omnibus Crime Control and Safe Streets Act or by state law or to any person under indictment or information for a felony. Subsequent changes have merged the Title VII prohibitions into the GCA and added persons under certain restraining orders and those convicted of misdemeanor domestic violence to the prohibited list. The restriction on transfers to prohibited persons has been extended beyond dealers to any person. The law also prohibited dealers delivering handguns to persons under 21 years of age or long guns to persons under 18. Subsequent additions made handgun possession by, or delivery to, those under 18 years of age a crime.[24]

Two general themes, expressed in the law's preamble, dominated the GCA: Its should serve primarily to provide support to state efforts at firearm regulation and should not burden legitimate firearm users.[25] The first theme appears in the provisions prohibiting delivery of firearms to any person who would be in violation of local or state law by possessing such firearms, and restricting buyers to their states of residence. The second accounted for the original version of the bill allowing procedures for the purchase of long guns in contiguous states, intrastate mail-order, replacement of guns lost or broken on hunting trips, and for collection of curios and relics. To avoid concerns regarding a central registry, dealers retained their records on their premises rather than submitting them to a government agency. While the original law and regulations did allow for future change in record-keeping requirements through administrative regulation, subsequent changes prohibited any central registry (see Gun Owners' Protection Act), and the later reporting requirements of the Brady Law prohibited retention of the reports.

Although the GCA required all persons "engaged in the business of dealing in firearms" to obtain a license, it included no clear definition of this phrase. The government had no discretion in the issuance of licenses if the applicant declared an intention to engage in the business. The Bureau of Alcohol, Tobacco, and Firearms had to issue a license within 45 days if the applicant did not fall into one of the categories of persons prohibited from possessing firearms. Subsequent revisions allow ATF 60 days and authority to verify that the business will comply with state and local law.[26] Originally set at $10 per year, the licensing fee has risen to $200 for the first three years and $90 for each three-year renewal. All violations of the original GCA constituted felonies, but subsequent revisions have reduced false record-keeping by dealers to a misdemeanor.[27]

As with many federal regulatory laws, the administering agency has promulgated regulations under authority of the statute that spells out specific procedures, such as record-keeping, application for licenses, and transfer of NFA firearms.[28] While regulatory agencies can exercise significant discretionary authority through administrative regulations, this has not proven the case for the regulations authorized under the GCA. The regulations restrict themselves to filling-in routine details for activities spelled out in the law. Given the congressional reaction to the only attempt to significantly expand beyond this narrow use of the regulations, their narrow drafting appears to reflect congressional will (see chapter 8).

Thus the GCA serves to set rules for those in the gun business and establish a set of federal standards for persons prohibited from possessing guns. While the NFA applies to only a small portion of the firearm population, the GCA regulates all modern firearms. In most instances, the law makes no distinction regarding the type of firearm. Few acts by most individuals fall under the law, with the exception of restrictions on transfers to prohibited persons and certain gun acquisition outside their home states.

After the passage of the GCA the IRS redesigned its Alcohol and Tobacco Tax Division as the Alcohol, Tobacco, and Firearms Division (ATFD), concurrently increasing its resources and shifting its emphasis toward firearm and later to explosives regulation. Except in a few areas in the Southeastern United States where illegal alcohol production continued, by 1970 ATFD had redirected most of its enforcement resources toward enforcement of the firearm or explosives laws. The majority of criminal investigations targeted felons who acquired or possessed firearms, persons in possession of NFA firearms, and persons suspected of bombings.[29] While these investigations increase the number of criminal prosecutions in the federal courts, they had minimal impact upon the distribution of firearms. The direct purchase of guns from out-of-state dealers probably declined through dealer compliance and termination of mail-order sales, although no data exists to prove this assertion.

The GCA and NFA remain the core federal laws relating to firearms. While the NFA has remained essentially unchanged since 1968, the GCA has been modified on several occasions. The most significant of these modifications have been the Firearms Owners' Protection Act of 1986, the Brady Law of 1993, and the addition of assault-weapon provisions in 1994.

THE FIREARMS OWNERS' PROTECTION ACT (FOPA): In 1972 the Treasury separated the ATFD from IRS by establishing an independent Bureau of Alcohol, Tobacco, and Firearms (ATF). The new bureau transferred responsibility for licensing and inspecting firearm dealers from law enforcement to its regulatory arm. During the next several years, some agents began to pursue cases against unlicensed firearm dealers and licensed dealers who delivered firearms to prohibited persons and falsified their records. Federal law enforcement had long subscribed to a concept of federal interest.[30] Clearly, investigations relating to the trafficking in firearms were more in compliance with the traditional standards for federal interest than cases involving lone felons receiving or possessing firearms. During the Carter administration efforts were initiated by the Justice Department to restrict all prosecutions to a much narrower federal-interest standard. As a result, ATF substantially increased its attention to cases involving firearms trafficking (see chapter 8). Largely in reaction to these cases, the NRA and its allies began a campaign to revoke or significantly limit the GCA. This campaign culminated in 1986 with the passage of the McClure-Volkmer bill, or the Firearms Owners' Protection Act (FOPA). While in chapter 9 I address the details surrounding the adoption of this law, I shall address the content here.

Although the FOPA left those portions of the GCA relating to prohibited persons intact, it made major changes in other portions of the law. The Act removed the prohibition against individuals purchasing long guns outside their state of residence. A specific prohibition in the law forbade the Treasury Department from issuing regulations requiring dealers to submit firearm-sale records to the government or establishing any system of firearm or firearm-owner registration.[31] Inspections of licensed dealers without their consent were limited to one per year.[32]

The most significant changes related directly to the complaints regarding prosecutions of unlicensed and licensed firearm dealers. The law reduced falsification of firearm records by dealers from a felony to a misdemeanor and provided numerous defenses against the charge of engaging in the business without a license. Reduction of record-keeping violations to a misdemeanor greatly complicated prosecutions of licensed firearm dealers. Under the previous law, dealers who sold guns without making records could be charged with a felony for failing to record those transactions. Under the new statute, even the discovery of large numbers of firearms missing from a dealer's inventory can not justify a felony prosecution. Because U.S. Attorneys do not usually entertain misdemeanor prosecutions, this change conveys substantial immunity on most licensed dealers. Investigators can seldom develop a prosecution through third-party witness, because such witness usually consisted of prohibited buyers with little motive to testify and no credibility if they did. Thus prosecution normally requires undercover purchases by an agent or informant. Even this approach presents difficulty. Existing court decisions preclude charging dealers with delivery to prohibited persons for sales to undercover agents posing as felons or other prohibited persons.[33] Therefore investigators must utilize actual felons willing to act as informants and testify at a later date. Controlling such informants and keeping them available through the lengthy federal-justice process often proves difficult.[34]

Changes in the law, meant to protect "collectors" against charges of engaging in firearms, provided unlicensed dealers with almost insurmountable defenses but left the phrase "engaging in the business" as unclear as before. The new definition required a dealer to "devote time, attention, and labor to engaging in such activity as a regular course of trade or business with the principal objective of livelihood and profit."[35] The law went further to exclude those who "make occasional sales, exchanges or purchases of firearms for the enhancement of a personal collection or for a hobby, or who sells part or all of his personal collection."[36] The prosecution's need to disprove any of these defenses beyond a reasonable doubt, without being able to call the defendant or access detailed records virtual elimination charges of engaging in the firearms business without a license.[37]

In addition to changes advocated by the NRA, Congress modified several additional portions of the GCA in conjunction with the GOPA at approximately the same time. These prohibited the manufacture of any additional machine guns for private use and added silencer parts to the NFA restricted firearms.[38] Maximum penalties were raised to 10-years' imprisonment for most felonies under the Act and raised even more for multiconvicted violent felons or drug traffickers convicted of possessing guns. As a result of these changes and changes in federal sentencing guidelines, the sentences for possession of a gun by repeat violent felons or possession of a gun while dealing in narcotics became severe. As an example, the minimum sentence for possession of a firearm by a person with three prior violent or drug-trafficking convictions is 15 years in prison, with the actual time of confinement approaching 14 years with good behavior. For the first offense of being armed with a machine gun while drug trafficking the law imposes a 30-years' imprisonment, in addition to the sentence for the drug offense. Peculiarly, a dealer who knowingly sells a firearm to a felon faces a sentence of about one year under the guidelines, although the felon can receive as much as life imprisonment.[39] Although no common plan nor advocacy existed between the FOPA changes and the increased sentencing for career offenders and armed drug traffickers, both changes proved important in shaping implementation of gun control for the remainder of the Reagan and Bush years.

THE BRADY LAW: Named for former presidential press-secretary James Brady, the Brady Law provided Handgun Control Incorporated its *raison d'être* from the bill's introduction in 1987 until its passage in 1993.[40] Although the five-year struggle to pass the bill generated considerable press attention and exaggerated hyperbole by opponents and supporters alike, its provisions hardly justified the assertions of supporters and foes. As passed, the Law mandated a five-working-day waiting period between the sale of a handgun by a dealer and its delivery.[41] The dealer had to report the identity of the purchaser to the local chief law-enforcement officer (CLEO), who then had to check for criminal records and other evidence of prohibited status.[42] The dealer could deliver the firearm either when notified that the purchaser was eligible or after five working days. The law excepted states with handgun licensing or existing record-check systems.[43] The law limited the information submitted by the dealer to descriptive data about the buyer and prohibited retention of the information by the police agency.[44] Thus a CLEO cannot create a database or registry of purchasers, unless separate authority exists in state law. The Brady Law included a mandate for the creation of a national instant-check system of gun buyers within five years of the Law's passage and a termination of the waiting period concurrent with implementation of the instant check.[45] Beginning in December 1998, procedures for sales by dealers changed in two ways: 1) The requirement for a five-day waiting period ended, and 2) dealers were required to verify purchaser eligibility by telephoning the FBI-operated instant-check center for the sale of both long guns and handguns.[46] Although the waiting period and record checks formed the core of the Brady Law, it contained other provisions. The most important of these raised the firearm dealer license fee to $200 for the initial three-year application, and to $90 for each three-year renewal.

The mandate for CLEOs to check criminal records of gun purchasers faced an immediate legal challenge. Two sheriffs from rural counties in Montana and Arizona, with NRA support, contended that the federal mandate for action by local authorities violated the Tenth Amendment provision reserving undefined rights to the states and the people. In December 1996 the Supreme Court concurred with that argument and nullified the mandate.[47] However, on a voluntary basis most jurisdictions continued to perform the checks. Attorney Stephen Halbrook, who represented the plaintiffs in *Printz v. United States*, brought suit on behalf of the NRA against Attorney General Janet Reno in the U.S. District Court upon initiation of the instant-check system by the FBI in December 1998. The suit sought a preliminary injunction on the grounds that the temporary retention of purchaser identities for up to six months, which the FBI contends is necessary for audit and verification purposes, violates provisions in the Brady Law mandating destruction of all records of purchaser identity.[48] This suit continues a long NRA tradition of opposition to any federal registry of gun owners or purchasers and to any procedure that generates records akin to such a registry.[49] Curiously, gun-control supporters had chosen to have the instant checks conducted by the FBI rather than ATF, on the assumption that opponents and the public would find the FBI's involvement less offensive.[50]

ASSAULT-WEAPON RESTRICTIONS: Less than a year after passing the Brady Law, Congress enacted a ban on the future manufacture or importation of certain semi-automatic assault weapons and ammunition magazines with capacity of more than 10 rounds.[51] The law defined an assault weapon as a semi-automatic pistol, rifle, or shotgun with two or more enumerated features. The list of features included bayonet lugs, flash suppressors, and pistol grips, among others.[52] The practical impact of this law has proven minimal. Manufacturers easily modified existing military-style firearms to be in compliance, since the criteria for inclusion consist primarily of esthetic and not functional features. The restriction on magazine capacity had an immediate effect on new firearms. Manufacturers stopped producing magazines with capacities over ten rounds. However, existing stocks of larger capacity magazines proved adequate to supply any purchaser with the motivation to seek them out. Although the practical impact of the law appears negligible, it may affect change in some long-term markets. The primary appeal of assault weapons appears to lie more in their visual appeal than their practical utility. Thus removing some of the characteristics that create that visual appeal may serve to undercut consumer demand built on spontaneous purchases and image. The short-term result of the law was to fuel market demand for any firearm covered by the law, similar firearms, and large-capacity magazines. In one instance a dealer removed spare pistol magazines that were manufactured before the law and included with the new pistol by the manufacturer, and sold them separately for $100 apiece.[53]

OTHER MODIFICATIONS TO THE GCA: Although routine amendment and correction are common in regulatory law, Congress has made very few changes in the GCA. With the exception of the FOPA and the Brady Law, almost no modification has been made to alter the regulatory structure. Those changes that have occurred predominately share certain characteristics. The three major bills originated outside the bureaucracy and were the result of direct lobbying by interest groups. Other changes reflected the influence of symbolic politics over regulatory process.

The GCA contains a provision for the Secretary of the Treasury or his delegate—ATF—to grant relief from the prohibitions imposed by a felony conviction.[54] From 1969 until 1992 applicants could file a request with ATF, which would conduct a background investigation and subsequently grant or deny relief. The FOPA expanded this provision by adding appeal rights for the applicant. Subsequently, some members of Congress found embarrassing the provision for allowing gun possession by convicted felons. Rather than directly address the politically sensitive question, Congress inserted a provision in the 1993 budget prohibiting ATF from expending funds to restore gun-possession rights,[55] and has continued the restriction in annual appropriations through fiscal year (FY) 2000, effectively nullifying the provision for relief from disability without invoking conflict over a change in the law.

In response to concerns over domestic violence, Congress added persons under restraining orders stemming from domestic violence and persons convicted of misdemeanor domestic violence to the list of prohibited persons.[56] In response to youth violence, Congress prohibited gun possession on school grounds and increased constraints on juveniles obtaining guns.[57] Given the limited investigative and prosecutive resources devoted to enforcement of firearm laws, these changes serve a primarily symbolic function. Because policing rests primarily with local governments, federal laws relating to individual possession of firearms lack the infrastructure to have wide practical impact. The principal federal role remains the regulation of dealers and commerce. However, the extension of restrictions to persons convicted of misdemeanor domestic violence did generate significant policy impact in an area other than gun control: The Lautenberg amendment excluded this prohibition from the blanket exemption granted government entities under the GCA. Thus Congress indirectly precluded persons convicted of misdemeanor domestic-violence charges from employment as police officers and may have prohibited their service in the armed forces. This action appears to be in direct response from feminist lobbying and not be an oversight.[58]

MARKET REGULATION AND DEALER LICENSING: Although the criminal sanctions of the federal firearm laws have attracted the majority of media and public attention, the more obscure regulatory functions have far more impact on most stakeholders, such as licensed dealers. Because a federal firearm license allows the licensee to purchase firearms directly from suppliers in any state with no restrictions, many firearm enthusiasts find it advantageous. With the yearly license fee at only $10, the number of licensed dealers rose steadily from 1968 onward, reaching almost 300,000 by 1994, when the Brady Law increased initial application fees to $200 for three-year licenses. New application procedures also require fingerprints and documentation of compliance with state and local laws and ordinances[59] combined the higher fees, began reducing the number of licensees. By 1999 the total number of dealers had declined to less than 100,000.[60]

Dealer oversight resides with ATF's Office of Compliance Operations. Staffed by approximately 1,000 inspectors, this component of ATF exercises responsibility for oversight of all wineries, distilleries, breweries, wholesale liquor dealers, and the entire explosives and firearms industries from manufacture to retail. In an effort to fulfill their entire range of assigned responsibilities, ATF ceased making personal contacts with applicants for firearms licenses in the early 1970s. ATF's licensing center conducted a computer search to determine if the applicant had a criminal record and conducted a cursory examination of the application. Lacking fingerprints or other positive forms of identification, ATF had no means of assuring eligibility. The use of a false name or date of birth prevented licensing personnel from detecting an applicant's criminal record and they lacked any means to verify that the applicant actually existed. In addition, no automated means of verifying the nature of an address existed; many licensees went years without ever being contacted by an ATF inspector.

Historically, the majority of applicants have wanted the licenses only to obtain discounted prices or facilitate shipment of otherwise legal firearms, but a small number of well-publicized cases demonstrated the vulnerability of the licensing system to fraud.[61] Using a false identity and a mail drop, an applicant could obtain a license by mail, order numerous firearms from wholesalers, sell the guns without records, and disappear without a trace.[62] The new requirements under the Brady Law have mitigated these problems to some extent. With fewer applicants, ATF can conduct more thorough review of applicants and more numerous inspections of existing licensees. The inclusion of finger-print cards in the application package makes the use of false identity more dif-ficult. ATF now verifies that the applicant has obtained the required local and state licenses, which allows local jurisdictions to exercise some control. As of this writing, however, ATF does not verify identity on license renewals.[63]

Even with the reduced number of dealers, most seldom see an inspector, and those that do may still evade detection of serious violations. Since no cen-tral registry of firearm transactions or transfers exists, inspectors have no effec-tive and expedient means for determining what guns a dealer has received. Therefore inspectors cannot verify that the entries in a dealer's records consti-tute all firearms received by that dealer. They *can* detect sloppy record-keep-ing by comparing record entries with existing inventory. However, no means exists for detecting deliberate fraud when unrecorded firearms are not stored on the premises. Only very complex and time-consuming forward-tracing programs from wholesalers can reveal unrecorded firearms. Forward traces require inspectors to randomly select firearms shipped to dealers by whole-salers and send out collateral requests to other ATF offices to verify the receipt of the firearm by the purchasing dealer. If a pattern of failure to record incom-ing firearms becomes apparent, the dealer can then be targeted for intense inspection or criminal investigation. Because this technique consumes signifi-cant time and resources, ATF uses it primarily when substantial evidence of violations already exists.

The current federal system of firearm market regulation depends on author-ity granted ATF by the Gun Control Act as amended by the 1986 Firearms Owners' Protection Act. Policy decisions have concentrated limited resources on individual violent offenders and drug traffickers rather than efforts to control the firearms market. The resulting system makes no pretense of pursuing limits on the size or growth of the civilian firearms population and makes only lim-ited effort to influence the types of firearms available. Although current law pro-hibits acquisition of firearms by certain classes of people, very limited mecha-nisms exist for enforcement of these restrictions. Current law does prohibit the transfer by private citizens of guns to felons and other specified categories of persons and out-of-state residents, no mechanisms exist to control such transac-tions. The law imposes no restrictions on incidental sales between individual and provides no registration, owner licensing, or records-check procedure to filter out sales to prohibited buyers. Although undocumented, the volume of private transaction, both incidental and commercial, is massive.[64]

State and Local Controls

State and local restrictions on firearms vary greatly within the United States. Even without legal variation, dependence on local police for enforcement can

produce significant differences in practice. The exact number of firearm regulations currently on the books in all jurisdictions in the United States is impossible to determine, because, among other reasons, there is no clear line defining a gun regulation. For example, laws controlling the public discharge of
firearms within a city or town might be counted by some and not by others as
a gun regulation. Estimates have consistently run well into the thousands.[65]
The exact number is less important than the existence of many laws at various
levels of jurisdiction. Since local jurisdictions normally lack authority to
impose significant sanctions for violations of their ordinances and no means
exists to control commerce across these boundaries, most of these laws have
limited impact on firearm markets, use, or possession. A number of states have
preempted the firearm-regulation field, thus excluding cities and counties from
enacting local-control ordinances on possession, licensing, sales, carrying, or
other actions.

Unlike local governments, states possess the authority to impose significant regulation, although they lack effective means of restricting the flow of
guns from other states.[66] While state laws display some regional patterns, variations appear even in contiguous states. California prohibits all felons and some
misdemeanants from possessing any firearm, prohibits machine guns, restricts
assault weapons, limits licenses to carry concealed firearms, and requires all
firearm sales to go through licensed dealers and be reported. Arizona allows
many felons to possess firearms, allows registered machine guns, has no law on
assault weapons, issues concealed weapons to all applicants meeting minimum
qualifications, and has no sales controls. Massachusetts requires licenses to carry
a handgun outside one's home or business. Vermont allows the carrying of
firearms, openly or concealed, without any permit. The District of Columbia
effectively prohibits the private possession of handguns and severely restricts
the conditions of possession for long guns—yet adjacent Virginia has few
restrictions on firearms.[67]

All states except Vermont restrict the carrying of concealed firearms in
some way. Six states provide no mechanism for issuing permits to carry concealed weapons. Thirty-one states meet what the NRA describes as the
"right-to-carry" standard by strictly limiting the discretion of issuing authorities and specifying narrow grounds for denial.[68] The 12 remaining states provide for issuance of concealed-carry licenses but grant broad discretion to the
issuing authorities. In most instances such authorities, particularly in urban
areas, issue few permits.[69] A dozen states honor as valid one or more out-of-
state permits to carry guns. Of these, only Idaho, Indiana, Kentucky, and
Michigan universally accept out-of-state permits. Many states prohibit
machine guns, sawed-off shotguns, and silencers. Several states restrict assault
weapons, however, no standard definition of assault weapon exists and thus the
nature of the restriction varies from state to state. The majority of states prohibit felons from possessing firearms, although some state prohibitions apply

only to specified felonies and some states do not apply the restriction to long guns. A few states prohibit persons convicted of certain misdemeanors from possessing firearms.[70]

Among states that prohibit the possession of firearms by felons significant variations in the laws exist. The prohibitions in some states attach only for a specific number of years, others allow for a restoration of rights by application, and some automatically restore rights after a specified period or on release from parole. Between 1968 and 1986 federal law provided substantial consistency for the categories of persons prohibited from possessing firearms. The 1986 revisions of the GCA altered this substantially, however. These revisions recognized state action to reduce, expunge, or restore rights lost due to a felony conviction. Although the general rule in federal law did not recognize state reductions and expungements, firearm laws became the exception in 1986.[71]

Although the variety of state approaches to gun regulation makes classification difficult, I am able to construct four rather loose archetypes. The first of these, exemplified by Vermont, Idaho, and Arizona, I describe as *permissive*. These states allow almost any adult to carry concealed firearms, require no sales reports nor waiting periods, permit private ownership of machine guns, and allow substantial numbers of felons to possess firearms. The second category, which imposes what I call *permissive regulation*, limits concealed-carry permits, requires reporting of sales and waiting periods, prohibits private ownership of machine guns, and generally restrict all felons from possessing firearms. California and Wisconsin provide examples of such states. I would describe the third category, including Michigan, Massachusetts, and New Jersey, as *moderately restrictive*. Although these states impose handgun licensing, they issue licenses to virtually all applicants. The final category, *restrictive*, applies only to New York and the District of Columbia. In the case of New York, New York City more aptly falls into this category than the remainder of the state.[72] Since 1976, the District of Columbia has prohibited the acquisition of any handgun by a private citizen, has registered long guns, and has required all firearm owners to store guns unloaded and disassembled or in locked containers.

States display as much variation in designating licensing authorities as they do in other aspects of gun control. Licensing authorities for concealed-weapon permits include state police, sheriffs, local police, and judges, depending upon the state. While many states have preempted the firearm-regulation field, others such as Virginia allow local jurisdictions wide discretion over all manner of gun regulation. No standard exists for licensing firearm sellers at the state and local levels, and most states have no regulation. Only California has a comprehensive, automated firearms database, and nothing comparable to the standardization of state laws and records on motor-vehicle registration and drivers' licensing exists for firearms.

THE CONSTITUTIONAL QUESTION

When attorney and gun-rights advocate Don Kates emphatically stated that recent scholarship had ended any reasonable debate over the individual-rights interpretation of the Second Amendment, I could only respond that Handgun Control's Dennis Henigan had made the same statement. Yet Kates and Henigan had advanced opposite interpretations of the current state of the law and scholarship. Kates replied that Henigan was simply wrong. As with virtually every aspect of the gun issue, views on the Second Amendment often break along clear fault lines.

The structure and syntax of the Amendment itself contributes to its ambiguity.[73] It begins with a prefatory, dependent phrase supportive of a collectivist or structuralist interpretation: "A well-regulated militia being necessary to the security of a free State," immediately followed by an independent clause far more amenable to an individual rights interpretation: "[T]he right of the people to keep and bear Arms, shall not be infringed." Madison's original text read: "The right of the people to keep and bear arms shall not be infringed; a well-armed and well-regulated militia being the best security of a free country: but no person religiously scrupulous of baring arms shall be compelled to render military service in person."[74] Congress subsequently reversed the clauses and eliminated the reference to religious exemption from militia service in the final version of the Amendment.[75]

Multiple Perspectives

Although most commonly characterized as falling into either a militia-centric interpretation or an individual-rights interpretation, a close review of the literature reveals a more complex and varied body of thought.[76] Still, with every word and phrase in contention, the courts have provided scant clarification.[77] Although current federal court decisions recognize no application of the Second Amendment to an individual's right to possess, carry, or use firearms, the only twentieth-century Supreme Court case, *Miller v. United States*, can be read to imply that guns suitable for use in the militia may be protected.[78] In addition, the courts have yet to recognize any incorporation of the Second Amendment under the Fourteenth Amendment.[79] Since the first ten amendments originally constituted a restriction only on federal authority, incorporation has been necessary to apply them to actions by the states. The current state of the law as established by federal court decisions supports Dennis Henigan's assertion that the issue has been decided in favor of a militia-centric interpretation.

Ironically, the weight of opinion as demonstrated by law review and historical writing favors a broader reading.[80] Although characterized by Henigan and others as merely reflecting an organized effort by Don Kates, Stephen Halbrook, David Kopel, David Hardy, and Robert Cottrol to build a record by recycling the same arguments repeatedly,[81] this body of scholarship is by no means trivial nor limited to works by gun enthusiasts.[82] There seems little doubt about these writers engaging in a conscious effort to build a body of scholarship, which they hope will provide incentive for and guidance to a reexamination of the Second Amendment.[83] One can no more fault this endeavor than similar efforts by civil libertarians, civil-rights advocates, and feminists to expand the applications of the First, Fourth, Fifth, Sixth, and Fourteenth Amendments. The current law governing search and seizure, police interrogation, and representation by counsel all resulted from concentrated efforts to change the existing precedents. The reversal of *Plessey v. Ferguson* resulted from years of effort by attorneys, scholars, and organizations dedicated to eliminating *de jure* racial segregation. Although most Americans may not view the protection of firearms as the moral equivalent of ending racial apartheid, this constitutes a value judgment on outcome and not on process.

I do not seek to resolve the debate over the Second Amendment in these few pages; I seek only to delineate the principal issues and arguments and then move on to their implications for policy formulation. I personally subscribe to historian Don Higginbotham's view that "the rhetoric of the Anti-Federalists and Federalists will never enable us to understand fully what the members of the First Congress intended by the language of the Second Amendment."[84] My own agnostic view of the meaning reflects not what I want the Amendment to say but acceptance that a variety of well-reasoned arguments on various views and a lack of Supreme Court precedents allows the court wide latitude in any future decisions. More significantly, few likely interpretations would inhibit adoption of any policy that could conceivably obtain political support in the United States.[85] The real importance for policy formulation can be found in the Amendment's symbolic power and not in its legal constraint.

A Well-Regulated Militia

Controversy regarding the Amendment begins with the meaning of the "well-regulated militia." Although arcane and rooted in early English and colonial and postcolonial American history, the arguments group into three fundamental positions: 1) The first position contends that "militia" refers to the general militia or the entire enfranchised population who have a right to arm themselves in defense of themselves against all perceived threats, including the state itself.[86] This position, supported by the modern militia movement, essentially ignores the modifier "well regulated." It is the argument that warms the hearts of gun-control advocates, who believe that this extreme position will alienate most judges, who will find it as anathema.[87] 2) The second position also assumes reference to a general militia, but emphasizes the individual's right to arms and self-defense while discounting or deemphasizing any right to organize military units without state authorization.[88] In this interpretation "well regulated" means that the states assure that the militia is armed and available.[89] Making the transition from the general militia to individual self-defense presents at least two difficulties: Individual self-defense does not involve any state-sanctioning organization, and a general militia presumes homogeneity and organization against an external threat. 3) The third position essentially argues that the general militia never functioned in reality and that the term refers to the organized or select militia already addressed in Article I of the Constitution.[90] This militia essentially ceased to exist with the creation of the National Guard.[91]

Conflicts over the second clause begin with a debate regarding its relationship to the first. In the 1939 decision, *Miller v. United States*, the Supreme Court reversed a lower court finding that Miller's conviction for interstate transportation of a sawed-off shotgun violated the Second Amendment, stating that there was an "absence of any evidence tending to show that possession or use [of a sawed-off shotgun] has some reasonable relationship to the preservation or efficiency of a well-regulated militia." The court failed to clarify the issue with clear language relating to the relationship between the weapon, militia service, and constitutional protection. The decision simply states that "[I]t is not within judicial notice that this weapon is any part of the ordinary military equipment or that its use could contribute to the common defense."[92] Thus the court made clear that, in its opinion, the first clause was a modifier on the rights granted in the second, but did not clearly specify the relationship. The Supreme Court has denied *certiorari* in all subsequent Second Amendment cases, and the circuit courts have consistently declined to recognize an individual right.[93] Most recently, the Ninth Circuit Court of Appeals held in *Hickman v. Block et al.* that the Second Amendment is a right of the states and does not apply to private citizens.[94]

Who Are "the People" and What Are "Arms"?

The meanings of both "the people" and "to keep and bear arms" are also both contested. Individual-rights advocates interpret "the people" as referring to citizens as individuals,[95] while collective-rights theorists contend that "the people" refers to the collective body, as in *the American people*.[96] The terms "keep and bear" are interpreted by individual-rights theorists as the retention of personal arms in the home and the carrying of such arms elsewhere,[97] as opposed to the collective-rights interpretation as keeping and bearing in a military sense.[98] To add to the confusion, a number of scholars argue that the Amendment should be read as both a collective and individual guarantee.[99]

Underlying each of the positions are assumptions about the purpose of the Amendment. At one extreme is what Henigan has characterized as the "insurrectionist" interpretation. This presumes that the Amendment grew out of Lockeian social-contract theory and was meant to preserve an armed populace as a counter-balance to government power.[100] Akhill Amar has argued that all ten of the Amendments originally were intended to function structurally in shaping the nature of government,[101] and David C. Williams has argued that the Second Amendment in particular served a structural purpose.[102] Hardy and others argue for a dual purpose of protecting individual rights and assuring the preservation of the general militia.[103] Finally, collective-rights theorists contend that the purpose of the Amendment was to preserve the status of the organized militia.[104] The most recent addition to this argument comes from Carl Bogus, who contends that the Amendment was written to pacify opposition from Southerners, who feared that the central government would attack slavery by neglecting and weakening state militias, the primary defense against slave revolt. Since Article I specified that the federal government would be responsible for organizing, arming, and disciplining the militia, the Amendment guaranteed an alternative means of arming the militia if Congress chose to let the militia system wither.[105]

All of these interpretations assume some consensus on the meaning of the text of the Amendment. A distinct alternative, implicitly recognized in some arguments but not fully developed, is that its purpose was political and its meaning purposefully ambiguous to facilitate that end. As Richard Stillman and others argue, the Constitution itself was a compromise document that sought to merge conflicting intellectual doctrines.[106] Written in response to Anti-Federalist efforts to prevent ratification and adoption of the Constitution, the Amendments were a continuation of the drafting process in an even more complex context.[107] Presumably, Madison intended to neutralize opposition and attain ratification with the amendments. The classic strategy in such situations is to assuage the concerns of as many ambivalent voters as possible, without engendering new concerns within one's existing base of support. Ambiguity provides a useful tool in such an endeavor. Members of Congress and delegates to state-ratification conventions probably subscribed to a variety of interpretations regarding the meaning of the Second Amendment, and many may have given it little consideration. In this case, as is generally true in deciphering law, scholars seek to impose reconstructed logic to evolving, dynamic environments of logic presently in use.[108] Most recently, constitutional scholars Laurence Tribe and Akhill Amar took the position that "the Second Amendment reference to the people's right to be armed cannot be trumped by the Amendment's preamble."[109]

Incorporation

Because the limitations of the first ten amendments originally applied only to the federal and not state governments, the Second Amendment has no relevance to state laws unless incorporated as a fundamental right of due process by the Fourteenth Amendment.[110] Although the Supreme Court has not addressed the incorporation question during the twentieth century, it did so twice during the nineteenth in the *Cruikshank* and *Presser* cases.[111] Not surprisingly, the court found that the Second Amendment did not apply to the actions by state governments. Since that time, the court has vastly expanded its interpretation of the constraints on state action of the equal-protection and due-process clauses of the Fourteenth Amendment. Although the court has incorporated most of the protections enumerated in the Bill of Rights, it has refused to consider a Second Amendment incorporation case during the twentieth century.[112] However, the issue has been addressed at the circuit-court level. The lower courts have refused to recognize any incorporation, citing *Cruikshank* and *Presser*.[113] As with other Second Amendment issues, the individual-rights advocates have offered extensive arguments as to why these rulings are in error.[114]

Practical Implications

Although the individual-rights interpretation of the Amendment has made little headway in the federal courts during the twentieth century,[115] the routine allusions to such a right by officeholders demonstrate its wide acceptance.[116] Thus the Second Amendment most likely serves as a very real constraint on gun-control policy options. The assumption by the majority of citizens that a right to possess firearms exists, combined with an individual guarantee in a number of state constitutions, serves as a powerful symbolic barrier to prohibition or restrictive-licensing options. In fact, for the NRA and other opponents of firearm restrictions, the risks of a Supreme Court hearing might greatly outweigh potential benefits.

The court might follow the pattern of lower courts, most recently the ninth circuit in *Hickman v. Block et al.*,[117] and find no application of the Amendment to individuals. Such a ruling would severely damage the symbolic importance of the Second Amendment, at least among the general public. Even if the court recognized an individual right, it might not be practically strengthened. Core supporters already take the individual-rights position as a given and can be energized by a perceived threat of prohibition or quasi-prohibition. Recognition of an individual right might undercut the ability of the NRA and other organizations to energize and activate their base by invoking a slippery-slope argument. Even if the court ruled that the Amendment constrains Congress, it might also rule against incorporation of those restrains. Thus the states would be free to pass any laws they chose, without even a symbolic restriction from the Second Amendment. The court could also find an individual right, but only in conjunction with the existence of a well-regulated militia.

Even if the court found for an individual right to keep and bear arms, it might well accept a wide variety of limits. Even scholarly advocates of an individual-rights interpretation have recognized that a variety of gun controls would probably be constitutional, including registration and permissive licensing.[118] The court would also have to define "arms." In fact, this might well constitute the most vexing task in crafting an individual-rights opinion. If a primary purpose of the law is to allow individuals to effectively oppose a tyrannical government, the court could hardly limit arms to pistols and rifles. Ironically, advocates for an individual-rights interpretation have labored long and hard on theories to limit the definition of arms. Although argument for the limitation is not typical of advocates for other rights, gun-rights advocates undoubtedly assume that no court would ever contemplate granting a right to Stinger missiles, TOW antitank weapons, and machine guns, not to mention nerve gas, cruise missiles, tanks, and fighter planes. Thus recognition of the right depends upon its reasonable limitation.[119]

The arguments for limitation usually contend that the Amendment protects only common handguns, rifles, and shotguns. Advocates of this position justify the limitation on conclusions that the right extends only to the types of arms possessed at home by the militia,[120] that are portable or able to be borne,[121] that are suitable for self-defense,[122] or that are not capable of terrorizing fellow citizens.[123] Although a limitation on the nature of arms, protected by the Second Amendment, is very likely a necessary component of any finding of an individual right, much of the existing scholarship undercuts such a conclusion. Virtually all authors who argue for an individual right, and some who do not, contend that the Amendment is rooted in either Republican or social-contract theory.[124] If the Amendment exists to facilitate resistance against corrupt and tyrannical government by the populace, how can one support its excluding the weapons necessary to accomplish such a task? Like incorporation, the issue of limiting the definition of arms has never entered the public awareness, but is very much a focus of gun-rights advocates because of its practical implications for policy. The final irony of the Second Amendment is that virtually all writers on all sides of the issue concur that its purpose was the preservation of a strong militia system in preference to a standing army, yet this primary intent appears to be of no interest to contemporary scholars.

The dismissal of the Second Amendment as a red herring by writers such as Spitzer and Edel seems far from justified. At minimum, it will remain a powerful symbol for opponents. With one court decision it could radically modify the policy environment.

CHAPTER FOUR

INTEREST GROUPS AND PUBLIC ATTITUDES

INTEREST GROUPS, BOTH FORMAL AND INFORMAL, have played a key role in the American political process. For a time, scholars viewed these groups as mechanisms for enhancing participative democracy. More recently, scholars have begun to view pluralist theory as more descriptive than normative. Some have characterized interest-group theory as lacking adequate descriptive power for some aspects of the political process.[1] The history of gun-control policy offers strong support for the descriptive value of interest-group theory, but little reason to embrace its normative value. Although not engaged in a traditional fight for limited resources, interest groups have played significant roles in the shaping of specific gun-control policies and in the development of public perceptions, including the framing of the issue.

OPPONENTS

The National Rifle Association (NRA)

The oldest and most influential of interest groups in support of a laissez-faire policy toward firearms is the National Rifle Association (NRA). Founded in New York after the Civil War to advance marksmanship, the NRA first lobbied against firearm laws when it opposed the 1911 passage of New York's Sullivan Law, which required permits for possession of pistols and revolvers.[2] By 1934, when Attorney General Cummings proposed the most sweeping firearms legislation ever considered by Congress, the NRA had become an active force in opposition to the bill. Their opposition was largely responsible for removing pistols and revolvers from the bill, thus altering it significantly.[3] Subsequently, the NRA resisted a second effort by Cummings to pass a bill that would significantly control commerce in firearms, and finally agreed to the largely ineffective Federal Firearms Act, which the NRA authored.[4]

For many years the NRA was the only organization focused upon the issue of gun control, although its primary activity remained the promotion of shooting sports and membership service. With the rise in interest in firearm legislation in the early 1960s, the NRA began to increase its focus on this area. Although NRA officials did not universally oppose all proposed firearm legislation in testimony before Congress, its official organ, *The American Rifleman*, consistently editorialized against all proposals and encouraged members to do likewise.[5]

After the passage of the Gun Control Act in 1968, internal conflict within the NRA began to increase: A bifurcation within the organization between those interested only in the recreational aspects of firearms and those who desired a more active political role in support of what they interpreted as a long-existing, absolute constitutional right to bear arms. The leaders of this latter faction included Representative John Dingell (D-Mich.), firearms writer and publisher Neal Knox, and former Border Patrol Director Harlon Carter.[6] This group gained significant ground with the 1971 shooting of Kenyon Bellew during the service of a search warrant by ATF agents and Montgomery County police in Silver Springs, Maryland. Agents obtained a warrant to search Bellew's apartment for unregistered NFA firearms based on information from a local police informant. The agents and police broke down the door after—allegedly announcing their identity and purpose—being denied entry. Hearing his wife scream, Bellew rushed out with a revolver and confronted the agents and police, who shot and paralyzed him for life. Some empty grenade hulls and powder were seized from his apartment, but no other illegal firearms were found. As both a life member of the NRA and an employee of the *Washington Post*, Bellew received considerable attention from the press and the opponents of gun control.[7]

This raid and its tragic results owed more to rapid expansion of federal law enforcement and the emerging antidrug tactics emulated by ATF than to overzealous enforcement of gun laws. In fact, those opposing the drug laws often cited such tactics as arguments against these laws, but the NRA and gun owners constituted a far more organized and effective interest block than did drug-law opponents. Although sometimes characterized as a key event in changing the perception of NRA membership and leadership regarding the impact of gun laws, the Bellew case more likely served as an opportunity for hard-liners than a wake-up call for moderates.[8]

The American Rifleman immediately began a long series of articles and editorials on the Bellew case and the general dangers to gun owners from the GCA and overzealous enforcement by ATF.[9] However, the majority of those in the NRA leadership apparently continued to view the organization's primary role as one of advancing shooting sports. Although the leadership did not favor gun control and was committed to opposing most gun-control proposals, it did not operate on an assumption that the infidels were at the gates or that gun prohibition was imminent. A minority of insiders, including Carter, Knox, and Dingell, strongly dissented from this view.[10] As the internal conflict in the NRA continued to escalate during the 1970s, the leadership was in the process of planning a move of their headquarters from Washington to Colorado Springs, as well as the building of a massive outdoor recreational complex in New Mexico. These moves, along with other actions that signaled a lack of interest in political issues and a desire to focus only on recreational firearms, precipitated an organized revolt.[11]

At the 1977 convention in Cincinnati, the dissenters, led by Carter and Knox, executed a well-organized coup and seized control of the board of directors. The coup required a relatively small number of supporters because only life members present at the convention could vote, and those members dedicated enough to attend the convention were supportive of a politically active organization. Elected chief operating officer, executive vice president Carter selected Knox as the director of the Institute for Legislative Action (ILA), the political arm of the NRA.[12] The NRA then began a systematic attack on the existing federal law and its enforcers, which led to a series of oversight hearings of ATF. These hearings formed the opening salvo in an attack on the GCA, which would shift the momentum of public and congressional focus away from new controls and onto the costs of enforcing gun-control laws.[13]

The campaign centered around the McClure-Volkmer bill. Beginning in the early 1970s, petitions circulated through gun shops around the country calling for the revocation of the entire GCA. The McClure-Volkmer bill did not revoke the entire GCA, but weakened it in many areas related to firearm dealing and trafficking. By the time a watered-down version of the bill finally became law in 1986, fractures had appeared in the coalition of true believers, resulting in firing of Neal Knox from his position as ILA director and his subsequent removal from the NRA board of directors.[14] During his tenure at the ILA, Knox mentored and promoted two lobbyists, Wayne LaPierre and Tanya Metaska, who would play major roles in the NRA and Knox's own future.[15]

In 1982 a more moderate J. Warren Cassidy replaced Knox as director of the ILA.[16] Following Carter's retirement, G. Ray Arnett briefly occupied the executive vice president position. Arnett arrived in Washington from California with the Reagan administration as an assistant secretary of the Department of Interior. Characterized by many insiders as more interested in the benefits than the duties of the position, Arnett's tenure proved both brief and controversial. With Arnett's departure, Cassidy assumed the position of executive vice president, only to be forced out by those who considered him too weak.[17] Upon Cassidy's departure, Wayne LaPierre assumed the executive vice president position.

A consummate Washington insider, LaPierre resembles more the profile of the urbanite advocate of control than that of a rural gun devotee.[18] Although LaPierre does not carry Knox's credentials as a firearm authority, he has become well known and widely supported by the general membership and members of Congress.[19] His book, *Guns, Crime, and Freedom*, has been widely distributed and read among control opponents, and he is prominent on numerous NRA pamphlets and publications.[20] One of these pamphlets, which described ATF agents as jackbooted thugs, generated substantial reaction in the aftermath of the Oklahoma City federal-building bombing, including the res-ignation of George Bush from the NRA.[21]

Knox waged war on the NRA leadership for several years after his 1982 removal as ILA Director. His public criticism of compromises in the evolving McClure-Volkmer bill eventually resulted in his 1984 removal from the board by the NRA leadership.[22] By the early 1990s, however, the indomitable Knox had returned to the NRA board of directors and appeared to have gained con-trol of a majority of the votes on that body.[23] The director of the ILA, James Baker, allegedly departed the organization as a result of frustration with Knox's constant efforts at intervention.[24] Knox's former protégé, Tanya Metaska, whose reputation for combativeness and zealous advocacy of gun rights rivaled Knox's, replaced Baker.[25] Although Metaska's selection was allegedly meant to appease Knox, he continued to pursue control of the organization.[26]

By 1997 Knox had ascended to second vice president. Normal progres-sion would have taken him to the position of first vice president and heir ap-parent to the presidency.[27] LaPierre, Metaska, and the existing leadership apparently decided that Knox could not be pacified or co-opted. They made their move at the 1997 Seattle convention by advancing actor Charlton Heston, rather than Knox, for the position of first vice president. In a close vote the LaPierre slate and Heston won. One year later, with much national attention and fanfare, Heston ascended to the presidency. Insiders characterize the conflict as one between pragmatists and purist, rather than between mod-erates and radicals, although Heston publicly advocated concentration on improving the organization's image.[28]

Six months later, Metaska resigned as director of the ILA, ostensibly to spend more time with her grandchildren.[29] Insiders reported that Metaska's replacement by James Baker owed more to personality clashes with Republi-can leaders in Congress. "She was to be replaced after the first of the year, but she had a blow up with Newt Gingrich," confided one source. Apparently Metaska's downfall did not arise from an unwillingness to compromise or negotiate, as had Knox's, but from an abrasive personality. By contrast, Baker, who returned to the ILA position from the Sports Arms and Ammunition Institute, seems the quintessential Washington insider. He projects an image both charming and calculated, more befitting a corporate counsel than an ide-ologue. With LaPierre and Baker firmly in control of the NRA leadership, at least for the time being, the organization most likely will remain on a cautious path while polishing its image. There is little chance that these two veteran lobbyists will turn the NRA away from politics and back to a primary focus on shooting sports, but they will *pick* their fights, with an eye towards both internal constituencies and public image. They will also solidify the natural allegiance between the present Republican majority in Congress and their organization.

In the early 1990s the public defection of former supporters such as Representative Les AuCoin (R–Ore.) and Senator Dennis DeConcini (D–Ariz.)[30] appeared to represent a visible blow to the NRA's symbolic power in Congress. The subsequent election of Bill Clinton, who successfully pursued congressional approval of the Brady Law and the assault-weapons legislation, seemed to confirm a general decline in NRA influence. But the 1994 midterm elections and success at obtaining permissive concealed-carry laws at the state level undercut such a conclusion.[31] The long-term effect of a flurry of negative publicity regarding a fundraising letter from LaPierre that characterized ATF agents as "jackbooted government thugs" and the subsequent resignation of former President George Bush from his NRA membership remains unclear.[32] The subsequent election of Charlton Heston appears to indicate an effort by the existing leadership to distance itself from some of the more radical fringe elements associated with the militia movement and to portray the NRA as a mainstream organization.[33] However, ILA Director Baker displayed no new spirit of compromise in personal conversation.[34]

The NRA remains able to contribute sizable sums to its friends in Congress and state legislatures and influence the actions and voting of both members and others that are influenced by members.[35] Its current politically sophisticated leadership appears to enjoy wide member support. If past history provides any guide, however, the Neal Knox faction will again challenge the leadership at first opportunity. Keeping the militants at bay and maintaining leadership among firearm organizations require the NRA leadership to maintain a very hard line on legislation. Compromise threatens their position in two ways: 1) Militant factions will use any perceived weakness to justify another coup or to build more militant organizations, and 2) more moderate members might perceive compromise as a sign of reduced threat to gun ownership and therefore drift away from the organization.

Other Firearms Interest Groups

In addition to the NRA, several special-interest groups focus exclusively on opposing gun control. Among these are the Citizens' Committee for the Right to Keep and Bear Arms, the Second Amendment Foundation, and the Gun Owners of America. These groups pursue exclusively political agendas without the member services and sponsorship of shooting sports provided by the NRA.

Formed by *Gun Week* editor Joseph Tartaro, former NRA employee Robert Kukla, and gun-activist Allan Gotleib, the Citizen's Committee has included among its advisory-council members Dan Quayle, Dick Cheney, and

Jack Kemp. Former California State Senator H. L. Richardson constituted the moving force behind the formation of Gun Owners of America, and Allan Gotleib served the same role for the Second Amendment Foundation.[36] With small but militant memberships, these groups exercise more influence on the policy process by keeping pressure on the NRA than by their own direct influence. Any move by the NRA to compromise on the issue of gun laws will surely bring an attack by these organizations.

A variety of lesser-known organizations, ranging from the National Firearms Association (advocating legal machine-gun ownership) to the American Pistol and Rifle Association, actively oppose firearm-control laws. These organizations are not, however, significant participants in the policy process, although firearm-recreation groups probably provide an infrastructure of personal association for opponents. The very small Scholars for the Second Amendment may constitute something of an exception to the rule in small organizations having little policy influence. Dependent primarily on the efforts of attorney and author Don Kates and law professor Joseph Olson, it has actively advanced arguments among academics favoring an individual-rights interpretation of the Second Amendment and opposing gun control.[37] Although cause and effect are difficult to establish, the tenor of academic writing on gun control has progressively shifted to a more skeptical position throughout the 1990s, and articles supportive of an individual-rights interpretation of the Second Amendment increasingly dominate the law reviews.[38]

Although industry and business routinely form the core of many interest groups, the pattern differs for firearm-interest groups. Manufacturers are represented by the Shooting Sports Council, which has played only a minor role in shaping firearms legislation.[39] Commercial dealers also have associated as the National Alliance of Stocking Gun Dealers Association. A well-regulated market benefits commercial dealers by eliminating competition from unlicensed dealers and hobbyists with licenses. Commercial dealers must comply with all waiting periods, reporting, and record-keeping requirements as well as pay taxes and maintain commercial premises. These dealers have long been caught in a crisis of conscience. Primarily gun enthusiasts, they are predisposed towards hostility and fear of gun regulation and are fed a steady diet of horror stories about ATF enforcement of gun laws against dealers by the NRA and other organizations. Gunshops have traditionally been a meeting place for gun enthusiasts and served an important function of dispersing information and facilitating organization. For years, ATF agents and inspectors have received complaints from commercial dealers regarding the activities of unlicensed and home dealers, yet these same dealers could not bring themselves to take a public position on regulation of these competitors.[40] Recent interviews with staff of the California legislature confirm that a significant number of these dealers have responded to self-interest and acquiesced to laws that regulate the market.[41]

CONTROL ADVOCATES

Handgun Control Incorporated (HCI)

By far the most visible of the gun-control advocacy groups is Handgun Control Incorporated (HCI), founded in 1974. Soon after its formation, HCI came under the leadership of Nelson T. "Pete" Shields, a moderate Republican and hunter, whose son was murdered with a handgun. Shields retired from active leadership of the organization in the early 1990s, dying a short time later. Shields's ability to raise funds and his mainstream background put his organization in the forefront of the pro-control groups. HCI claims a million members, although this number probably includes known supporters not currently paying dues.[42]

After several years of frustration in pursuit of comprehensive national handgun legislation, HCI shifted to a strategy of passing some kind of national bill, even if the results were of questionable utility. This decision reflected the realities of opinion polls taken in the late 1970s, Shields's penchant for seeking reasonable compromise, frustration with the repeated failure of proposed federal legislation, and the defeat of Proposition 15 in California.[43] Ultimately, the process resulted in the organization focusing all its resources on a single objective, passage of the Brady Law. After Shields's retirement and death, Sarah Brady, wife of former White House Press Secretary James Brady, assumed the presidency of HCI. Her interest in gun control arose after her husband was shot during an assassination attempt on President Reagan. Daily operational control of HCI has rested in a series of executive directors, with former Republican congressional staffer Bob Walker being the most recent. Initially, HCI conceptualized the gun-control issue primarily as a crime-control problem, but it has progressively shifted during the 1990s toward invoking the paradigms and language of public health. It has experimented with a variety of symbols to develop public support and recast the issue. Among these have been "Saturday night specials," "cop-killer bullets," "plastic guns," and "assault weapons." Since the early 1980s it has consistently avoided any discussion of handgun prohibition.[44]

The passage of the Brady Law left HCI without a unifying core objective. It has proposed a broader agenda of licensing and registration but this has gained little public attention, and HCI leadership seems more concerned with locating targets of opportunity.[45] Opponents of gun control routinely characterize HCI as advocating gun prohibition. Although the organization began with a prohibitionist agenda toward handguns,[46] the current official position and literature of the organization provide little support for that characterization.

Other Control-Advocacy Groups

The other significant control-advocacy group, the Coalition to End Handgun Violence, has operated under the direction of Michael Beard since its formation nearly 30 years ago as the Coalition to Ban Handguns. Neither Beard nor the Coalition reflect the Washington-insider image currently in evidence at HCI or the NRA. The Coalition appears more like a public-interest lobby with employees who pride themselves on their knowledge of guns and the gun issue. Relations between the Coalition and HCI have been, on occasions, strained. The Coalition advocates attacking on multiple fronts and openly pursues an agenda of prohibiting the private ownership of handguns. While the leadership of HCI, predominately drawn from the ranks of moderate Republicans, has sometimes characterized the Coalition as a group of "bomb throwers," current relations appear more congenial.[47]

A third organization committed to firearm regulation is the Violence Policy Center, which for some time consisted primarily of Josh Sugarmann and Kristen Rand. Sugarmann and his small staff routinely challenge the agenda of HCI, which they characterize as accommodationist.

The most recent entry into the field operates under the title of The Bell Campaign. Director of Policy Eric Gorovitz characterizes the group as more broad based in its policy focus than HCI, with an agenda of registration and licensing for all guns and gun owners.[48] The group seeks to build a grass-roots structure to rival the NRA's by organizing victims and families of victims of gun crimes, accidents, and suicides.

Although the opponents of gun control regularly characterize these proponents as advocates of confiscation and prohibition of all firearms, an examination of the agendas of the organized groups provides scant support for this argument. No doubt, some members favor ridding society of all firearms, but no such proposal appears in the organizational literature or writings of the leaderships. The Violence Policy Center *does* openly advocate the prohibition of private handgun ownership, as has the Coalition for some years. This lack of a significant extremist-fringe organization constitutes one of the most notable characteristics of the organized proponents of gun control, although the HCI leadership views Sugarmann and the Violence Policy Center as the militant voices in the field.[49] Unlike the opponents of control, HCI and the Coalition have little need to pacify a militant populist constituency within their organizations or fend-off militant competitors. Their primary problem seems to be maintaining the support and attention of a sympathetic but tepid constituency.

Beginning in the mid-1980s, law-enforcement organizations began to take an active interest in firearm laws at the national level. Previously, managers of large urban law-enforcement organizations expressed substantial support for gun-control laws, but managers of rural and suburban agencies and rank-and-file officers displayed little support. Although rural police still tend toward hostility to gun control, attitudes among the majority of urban police appear to have shifted around the issue of armor-piercing ammunition controls and later to have coalesced around the Brady Law, which was supported by virtually every major law-enforcement organization.[50] In both the 1982 California Proposition 15 campaign and the 1997 Washington State Initiative 667 campaign, the failure to develop police support proved disastrous for advocates.

THE PUBLIC

Proponents of gun control have consistently cited opinion surveys as evidence of special interests thwarting the public will.[51] Given the evidence of consistent support for proposals such as licensing and permits to purchase or own firearms, this seems a reasonable conclusion.[52] But this simple characterization proves far less useful than it might at first seem. At least three scholars—Kleck, Harding, and Spitzer—have attempted in-depth analyses of public opinion on gun control.[53] I commend all three to serious readers. All three authors address the failure of apparently wide and continuing support for numerous gun-control provisions to translate into legislation, although Harding notes that increased public support coincided with the passage of restrictions on armor-piercing ammunition and assault weapons as well as the passage of the Brady Law but fails to address the passage of the Firearms Owners' Protection Act. These authors, and others, have attempted to explain this failure to translate apparently enduring support into legislation with a variety of theories.

Kleck has speculated that gun-control support lacks intensity. In his view, the public expresses support in surveys for options that it perceives as having little cost, but knows and cares little about the details of gun control.[54] In support of this position, he cites polls reflecting that most Americans do not view gun control as a principal means of controlling crime and that there is vacillation in aggregate support levels for specific gun-control options. Harding critiques Kleck, noting that volatility in individual, not aggregate, opinions demonstrates a lack of commitment to a position. Harding also notes that although belief in the efficacy of gun restrictions as crime-control measures lags behind general support for gun control, one cannot assume that this constitutes evidence of weak support for gun control. Although Harding raises a valid criticism regarding Kleck's use of volatility in aggregate support as evidence, nothing in his critique disproves Kleck's conclusion. Lacking a panel study that tracks changes in individual support, the source of volatility remains open to question. Still, the fact remains that such volatility has occurred and individual vacillation offers as reasonable an explanation as any. With regard to Harding's other critique, Kleck himself makes the point that a significant portion of the public supports gun control in spite of reservations regarding its utility as a crime-control measure.[55] Although such a position does not essentially translate into weaker support, lack of faith in the efficacy of a policy requires an individual to support the policy on moral or symbolic grounds. Given the role that pragmatic self-interest plays in support of legislation, Kleck's conclusion seems legitimate.

Schuman and Presser found that intensity levels appeared to be similar for opponents and advocates of control and theorized that the difference between opponents and advocates was the greater organization of the former.[56] However, a simple review of such indicators as letters to the editor, letters to legislators, or book reviews on Amazon.com will reveal substantial evidence of the intensity and openness of commitment of opponents.

In his extensive study of gun-control attitudes over time, Smith found great consistency in attitudes. Although he found no pattern by birth cohort, he found that sex, region, race, and community type all related consistently to attitudes about gun control, with opposition concentrated most highly among white Protestant males from Southern or Western rural communities,[57] a finding that supports a cultural explanation for gun-control views. On the other hand, Kleck found that only gun ownership, hunting, and region proved reliable predictors of position on gun registration.[58] Although Kleck's findings remain compatible with a cultural explanation, they suggest a narrower cultural profile.

Most scholars have advanced the view that a solid core of opposition to most gun-control measures exists among a sizable minority of Americans. Although Harding suggests that this opposition may grow out of fundamental distrust of government or a sovereignty paradigm, the majority of these opponents appear to share in the gun culture, although not essentially in hunting or sport shooting.[59] If one assumes the existence of a stable, culturally motivated core of gun-control supporters, gun control looks much like the rest of American politics, with two, strong, polar-interests blocks competing for a largely independent and often disinterested center. If this be the case, the argument that much of the public has expressed support for gun-control provisions while concurrently lacking knowledge of existing policy, failing to actively support new policies, and entertaining serious reservations regarding the practical utility of both, seems reasonable.

Clearly, something has prevented the support evidenced in the polls from translating into comprehensive legislative action. Scholars have ignored a telling demonstration of the differing nature of involvement between advocates and opponents. The failure of gun-control advocates to punish members of Congress, particularly Democrats, for their support of the Firearm Owners' Protection Act reflects a lack of either organization, intensity, or interest (see chapter 8). While controversy exists over the degree to which gun-control opponents contributed to the defeat of such prominent members of Congress as Senator Joseph Tydings (D-Md.) and Representative Jack Brooks (D-Tex.), no comparable situations appear to exist for gun-control proponents. Liberal Democrat John Dingell of Michigan has never had to repel an attack from gun-control advocates. Although HCI may back successful candidates, I am unable to find any evidence that incumbents fear its wrath or that any incumbent has been turned out of office for refusing to support gun control. Control advocates have also demonstrated a poor history of delivering the vote in state referendums.

Still, lest gun-control opponents assume that past is prelude, signs of change have appeared on the horizon. Historically, few Americans listed gun control as an issue of primary political importance.[60] But, the June and September 1999 Harris polls report 9 percent of the respondents citing gun control as the most important problem facing the nation.[61] Likewise, the September 17, 1999 Gallup poll reports a significant increase in the number of respondents (65 percent) who consider it important that Congress pass gun-control legislation. Further support for this trend appears in the Field poll of California residents, issued on September 2, 1999, which reflects a significant increase—from 54 to 61 percent—in those viewing gun control as very or somewhat effective in reducing violent crime.

Public support for comprehensive control measures decreased slightly in the late 1970s and early 1980s, but rebounded by the early 1990s. Support for handgun registration remained between 74 and 80 percent during the 1970s, dropped to 66 percent in the 1982 Gallup poll, then rebounded to 81 percent by 1990.[62] While support for registration of all guns remained somewhat lower, it followed the same pattern of resurgent support in the early 1990s.[63] In the wake of highly visible mass shootings in schools, a surge of gun-control sentiment during the spring and summer of 1999 brought support for registration of all guns to the 79 percent level.[64]

There can be little question that a large majority of the American public gives at least tacit support to more comprehensive gun control. But opinion-poll results do not reflect the depth of commitment, degree of interest, or depth of knowledge regarding a policy area. Spitzer argues that a lack of knowledge on the part of the public differs little from other policy areas and provides legislators with a clear mandate for action.[65] But Harding points out that Spitzer never specifies how legislators can interpret public mandates if the public knows little about the existing policy or details of proposed policy.

Surveys regarding gun control routinely fail to specify policies with enough detail to allow respondents to give meaningful answers, nor do they examine awareness of or attitudes toward implementation costs. Surveys often ask questions that make little face-value sense, such as the respondents position on banning mail-order gun sales, which have been prohibited since 1968. Another common question relates to increasing or decreasing the current level of control, without specifying the current level or determining whether the respondent has any knowledge of it. Thus respondents may be under- or overstating their desired level of control. They may also support a specific action such as registration, but not support the mechanisms necessary to implement it.

Unfortunately, most polls ask only superficial question, which often appear to have been drafted by someone with little or no knowledge of the topic. More in-depth survey research requires substantial funding, and such funding usually comes only from interest groups.

Both advocates and opponents of gun control have attempted to use polls to increase the legitimacy and credibility of their positions, although advocates have generally enjoyed the advantage. Two studies conducted in 1978, and often cited thereafter, typify the effort to use opinion research to shape the gun-control debate. One study, commissioned by the NRA, was conducted by Decision Making Information Inc. (DMI). The second, commissioned by HCI's Center for the Study and Prevention of Handgun Violence, was conducted by Patrick Cadell. These two studies obviously had differing biases.[66] The DMI report reflected very strong support for gun-control measures (with the exception of prohibiting private ownership of handguns), with 88 percent "strongly" or "somewhat" favoring waiting periods, 82 percent favoring licenses to purchase, and 74 percent favoring licenses to own a handgun. Although the poll results reflect strong support for gun control, that support declined significantly as measures became more stringent and intrusive.[67]

The DMI poll focused on the perceived efficacy of firearm laws and the expected compliance. The survey revealed public reservations regarding the capacity of firearm laws to reduce crime or alter criminal conduct. Opponents have interpreted this skepticism to mean that the public has little faith in or support for the idea of firearms laws.

Several questions might well be answered by an in-depth but less ideologically motivated poll. For instance, all polls reflect lower levels of support for gun control among gun owners, but no poll has provided adequate information to determine the support for specific control options among them.[68] There is some reason to believe that owner licensing that incorporated competency testing might be rather widely accepted, even by gun owners.[69] Better research might also determine the level of intrusion and cost that the public would accept to implement firearm laws, as well as preferences for the means of financing any registration or licensing. A final survey that would be useful to scholars and policy-makers would be focused on the level of knowledge of existing law demonstrated by the public and corresponding views on specific policies.[70]

Although opinion surveys consistently have reflected support for licensing and registration above the 70 percent level, they also reflect reservations regarding prohibition.[71] Handgun prohibition consistently has received only minority support in a variety of surveys, and a general ban on firearm ownership has been even less palatable[72]—facts that probably have moderated the strategy of gun-control advocates. Any strategy perceived as advancing prohibition of "ordinary" firearms risks alarming the majority of voters. Thus control advocates must differentiate between "evil" guns—such as assault weapons and Saturday night specials—and "good" guns. Support for prohibition consistently rises when the focus is restricted to one of these two categories of firearms. However, no common definition exists for either item. Thus the question makes little sense. Some Saturday-night-special bills have included virtually all handguns, while others have been considerably narrower (see chapter 7).

Two other aspects of opinion data potentially constrain firearm-policy options. A majority of Americans believe that the Second Amendment is a protection of the individual right to own a firearm, and a majority of both gun owners and nonowners believe that stricter gun laws will lead to prohibition.[73] Thus a significant number of Americans might logically oppose otherwise-acceptable policy proposals solely on the assumption that these policies will lead to future broader policies that they perceive as being unacceptable or unconstitutional. The second area of difficulty results from perceptions of efficacy and compliance. Apparently most Americans have questions regarding the probability of compliance with more strict statutes and the impact of the laws on crime. Presumably these two concerns are related; the assumption being that those most likely to misuse firearms are the ones most likely to violate firearm laws.[74]

Although both sides have attempted to use opinion polls to support their positions, elections ultimately count far more than polls. To date, control advocates have not translated their apparent advantage in polls into comprehensive legislation. Significant handgun-control initiatives have faced decisive defeats in Massachusetts in 1976, in California in 1982, and in Washington State in 1997. Only in California did the initiative obtain more than 30 percent of the vote. In each case, the polls showed the initiative winning in the early polling.[75] In the face of such events, politicians demonstrate little willingness to take on a determined, organized, and well-funded minority deeply committed to opposing gun control.

OPINION AND WORLDVIEW

Although the majority of activists for and against gun controls may, respectively, display cosmopolitan and traditionalist perspectives, the majority of gun owners fit into no clear category. Exposure to guns in early life appears to be the most significant predictor of gun ownership. Relative to nonowners, self-reported gun owners are more likely to be male, Protestant, rural, Southern, affluent, and middle class.[76] Wright, Rossi, and Daly characterized recreational owners as outnumbering others by three to one;[77] however, the patterns of gun ownership have shifted steadily away from this profile as hunting has declined and the market shifted progressively to handguns.[78] They also argued that the profiles do not apply to nonrecreational owners.[79] Given the current trends in the firearms market, nonrecreational owners will eventually predominate.[80] The dominance of nonsporting firearm sales calls the older profile, built on sporting use, into question. In addition, middle-class gun owners may be over represented in sampling due to willingness to admit gun ownership.[81]

Affluence and middle-class status probably facilitate gun ownership by enhancing the ability to purchase and hold material items of significant value. People with these characteristics are more able to afford shooting sports, to purchase firearms, and to have permanent residences that lend themselves to retention of personal property for extended periods. The question not answered by any research to date is the profile of the future gun owner. No doubt ownership will remain high among Americans with rural and small-town roots, particularly in the South and West. Does this group account for the majority of current gun purchases? This appears to be a question as yet unanswered.

Although opposition to gun control remains most concentrated among rural residents of the South and West, the leadership of opposition groups displays a more cosmopolitan profile,[82] and the NRA can trace its roots to New York. Most likely, strong partisans develop their positions as a result of a combination of factors. For instance, persons who profit financially from commerce in guns appear almost universally to oppose any regulation that they view as a threat to their activities. Persons actively involved in shooting sports—likely to be inconvenienced by regulation—generally appear to oppose it. Likewise, association with persons opposed to firearm regulation or government regulation in general would predictably increase the likelihood that one would oppose firearm regulation.

Most gun-control activists appear to come from urban backgrounds in which gun ownership invokes negative cultural images; a few seem motivated by a personal tragedy involving a firearm. Nelson Shields and Sarah Brady of HCI, arguably the two most visible advocates of gun control during the 1980s and 1990s, both came to the issue as the result of a family member being shot. As an issue offering neither economic nor personal benefits for advocates, gun control lacks the institutional base enjoyed by opponents, who benefit from shooter, dealer, and collector networks and organizations. Although gun control may derive some benefit from general "good government" efforts and political opportunism, commitment to the issue probably requires either a strong personal distaste for guns or a personal triggering event.

That personal interest, ideology, and worldview influence attitudes should come as no surprise. These elements provide the intellectual structure for human interpretation of information and experience. The presence of these characteristics neither furthers nor disproves an instrumentalist view of positions on gun control. In all likelihood, symbolism and utility are mixed for both advocates and opponents. Some people apparently feel comfort in the presence of a firearm, regardless of the evidence of its utility; others feel threatened by a firearm's presence, even when it presents little or no threat. In a nation that concurrently experiences the highest level of firearm violence in the industrialized world and has millions of firearm owners and users, the merger of myth, culture, and utility in shaping opinion seems inevitable.

CHAPTER FIVE

THE EVOLVING POLITICS OF GUN CONTROL

D URING THE DECADE of the 1990s gun control progressively has become
more deeply imbedded in partisan politics. Identified as a Democratic
issue since the election of 1968, gun control has assumed a more prominent
place on the Democratic political agenda as party realignment has stripped it
of support in the South and West. This geographic realignment, combined
with the increase in Republican support among men and social conservatives,
has reduced the political costs of supporting gun control for most Democrats.
Concurrently, the rise of Republican strength in the South and West and loss
of power in the Northeast has pushed the Republicans toward a more socially
conservative position that depends on constituencies hostile to gun control.
Prominent Democratic opponents of gun control, such as Representatives Jack
Brooks (D-Tex.) and Tom Foley (D-Wash.), have gone down to defeat,
although John Dingell (D-Mich.) remains in office. With the death of Senator
John Chafee (R-R.I.), Republican advocates of strict gun control have virtually disappeared from the national scene. In the House, the critically important
House Judiciary Committee has become the core of social conservatism in
official Washington. With each incremental move toward single-party identification with a position on gun control, the issue becomes politically safer for
both parties.

However, some members of both parties still perceive risk in becoming
identified too strongly with either advocacy or opposition to gun control.
Among Democrats, the few remaining members of Congress from conservative districts still fear association with virtually any gun-control measure.
Representative Charles Wilson (D-Tex.) compared his voting for gun control
with a Brooklyn congressman's voting against Israel.[1] Conversely, conservative
writer Christopher Caldwell has described the NRA as constituting a political

liability that symbolically ties the GOP to extreme libertarianism, much like the ACLU symbolically tied the Democratic party to civil disorder in previous years.[2]

THE ELECTIONS OF THE 1990s

Until the election of 1992, no presidential candidate had risked using gun control as a domestic issue. Even when Republicans implemented a well-orchestrated characterization of Democrat Michael Dukakis as weak on crime during the 1988 campaign, he refrained from using the gun-control issue to attack the Reagan–Bush crime-control record. Republicans had characterized Democratic presidential candidates as "soft on crime" in every election since 1964, often with substantial success.[3] In 1992 Bill Clinton countered this strategy by openly endorsing the death penalty and by using both the Brady Law and assault-weapon legislation to characterize the Republicans as weak on crime. Although this strategy presented some difficulty for individual Democrats in Congress by associating the national party with gun control, it apparently worked nationally for Clinton. Once in office, Clinton successfully supported both Brady and assault-weapon legislation, both of which passed before the 1994 mid-term election. While this strategy offered potential benefit for the Democrats in a national election, it energized the NRA base[4] and apparently contributed significantly to the loss of Democratic control of Congress in the 1994 election.[5]

Thus the political legacy of the Brady Law and assault-weapon legislation appears mixed: Beneficial for presidential politics but costly for individual congressional Democrats in marginal districts and for the party's control of Congress. Clinton again used gun control to blunt Republican attacks on crime and drug policy in 1996, while Republican candidate Bob Dole generally downplayed the issue, disassociating himself from efforts to revoke the assault-weapon ban.[6] Neither candidate focused on the issue, and Clinton addressed it only when it served a short-term tactical advantage. Although the 1998 election eroded the Republican strength in Congress, gun control did not appear to play a significant direct role. However, gains among Democrats in the suburbs and with women may result from an image problem among conservatives that is driven by a number of issues. If this is the case, gun control may contribute to an increasing perception among moderate voters that Republicans hold extreme ideological positions that generate a sense of uneasiness. The one arena where gun control appeared to play a significant role was in the California state elections, which are covered later in this chapter.

WACO, OKLAHOMA CITY, AND MILITIAS

Although one might expect a Republican Congress dominated by social conservatives to attempt repealing recently enacted gun laws, this did not prove to be the case. Essentially, gun-control legislation never entered the Congress agenda between 1995 and 1999, with the exception of the House passage of a bill revoking the assault-weapon ban. Even the modest knowledge accumulated by congressional staffs dissipated with the shift from Democratic to Republican control.[7] Few incentives exist for policy expertise in gun legislation. The issue appears only intermittently on legislative agendas, and then in the form of very limited policy initiatives. Legislative positions appear to derive primarily from political interest or ideology, thus generating little need for analysis or information.[8]

While the new Republican Congress made no serious effort to repeal existing gun control law, it did attempt to placate gun interests in a move that proved beneficial to Bill Clinton and the Democrats. On February 28, 1993, shortly after Clinton took office, a large force of ATF agents attempted to serve search-and-arrest warrants on the residential compound of the Branch Davidians, a small religious sect located near Waco, Texas.[9] The warrants charged the Davidians and their leader, Vernon Wayne Howell (aka David Koresh), with possession of unregistered machine guns and hand grenades in violation of the NFA. Although an undercover agent warned ATF managers that word of the raid had leaked to the Davidians, the managers proceeded on the mistaken belief that the Davidians would not forcefully oppose such a large and well-identified group of law-enforcement officers. The Davidians *did* resist, using machine guns and grenades. In the ensuing gun battle four agents and several members of the Branch Davidians died, and many members of both groups received serious injuries. The Davidians refused to surrender and an extended siege began. Two days later, the FBI's Hostage Rescue Team (HRT) assumed control of the scene from ATF. Negotiations continued for almost two months. Although negotiators obtained the release of several children in the early stages of the siege and promises from Koresh to surrender, Koresh remained in the compound with a large group of adults and children. On April 19, 1993, after receiving reluctant authorization from Clinton's new attorney general, Janet Reno, the HRT assaulted the compound with massive amounts of tear gas and began collapsing portions of the compound with armored vehicles. Ignoring the repeated requests to surrender, the Davidians ignited fires at several locations within the wooden structure and committed mass suicide.

Although the events at Waco appeared to have little impact on the public at large, they intensely affected a core group of libertarians and gun-rights activists. Numerous individuals and groups had long viewed the federal government, and particularly ATF and IRS, as hostile and dangerous; Waco and earlier events at the home of Randy Weaver in northern Idaho validated and focused their beliefs.[10] Weaver and his wife, both believers in Christian Identity, had moved to Idaho from Iowa in 1983 and established residence with their children in a remote cabin. As followers of Christian Identity, the Weavers believed that whites descended from Adam and were God's chosen people, while Jews and all nonwhite peoples descended from Satan.[11] Identity theology predicted a coming conflict between these two groups, and it was in preparation for this conflict that the Weavers moved to Idaho.

Both the FBI and ATF concentrated investigative efforts on the northern Idaho area, which had become a focal point for a variety of white racist and anti-Semitic groups. Several of the more militant of them engaged in violent activity, including murders and bombings, and numerous others advocated violence. Though not a member of these groups, Randy Weaver associated with a variety of other white separatists and racists. In an effort to recruit Weaver as an informant, ATF agents directed an informant, who had previously discussed gun purchases with Weaver, to buy sawed-off shotguns from him. Agents then used the threat of prosecution to gain Weaver's cooperation. When Weaver rejected their efforts to recruit him, the agents forwarded the case to the U.S. Attorney, who presented the case to a grand jury. Although, by a ruse, ATF agents arrested Weaver without serious incident, both he and his wife were armed and had to be physically subdued. After being released on bail, Weaver refused to appear in court and armed his entire family.

Once Weaver had appeared before a magistrate, jurisdiction passed to the U.S. Marshal's Service (USMS). After months of negotiation, a USMS tactical team began clandestine surveillance of Weaver's cabin. On the second day of the surveillance, Weaver, accompanied by his 12-year-old son and a friend, accidentally encountered the marshals. Weaver's party, all armed, had followed the son's dog, apparently in the belief that it had detected a deer or elk. The marshals retreated, believing they were being pursued. The exact sequence of events remains in controversy; however, the subsequent encounter resulted in the deaths of a marshal, Weaver's son, and the dog.[12]

As would later occur in Waco, the FBI HRT assumed control of the scene. In this case, FBI managers issued an order to shoot armed adults on sight. An HRT sniper shot and killed Weaver's wife as she opened the cabin door for Weaver's friend Kevin Harris, who was fleeing the snipers bullets. As with the original shooting, considerable controversy exists regarding the exact sequence of events and intention of the actors, in spite of civil suits and investigations by the FBI, local and state authorities, and a Senate committee.

These two events merged symbolically and mythically for those who viewed central government as the real and immediate menace. Because both cases evolved from enforcement of gun-control laws, the NRA could not resist capitalizing on these events to intensify fear of gun control and the ATF. This put the NRA in common cause with more extreme elements on the libertarian and racist right. In particular, these events energized the militia movement, which advocated the creation of armed, volunteer militias as a counterbalance to government authority.[13] The nation has a long history of libertarian rightist organizations, some racist and others not, that include the Minute Men, Posse Commitatus, the Aryan Nation, and numerous antitax groups. Virtually all of them share a hatred of gun control and those who enforce the gun laws. Thus Randy Weaver and the Branch Davidians proved far more important than cases involving laws, such as drugs.

Although libertarian and antigovernment groups used the Weaver and Branch Davidian cases to legitimatize fear of the government and expand their membership, a few individuals ultimately went further. On April 19, 1995, two years after the final events at Waco, Timothy McVeigh, a young former soldier with a love of guns and deep hostility for government, parked a rented truck filled with explosives adjacent to the federal building in Oklahoma City and left the scene. A short time later the truck exploded, destroying the building and killing 168 people. In an ironic twist of fate, a gun charge contributed directly to the solution of the bombing. Shortly after the bombing, an Oklahoma trooper stopped McVeigh for driving without a license plate on his car and arrested him after discovering a concealed pistol on his person. Subsequently, FBI agents developed information linking McVeigh to the truck rental. A computer search revealed the concealed-weapons arrest and his car and clothes produced significant evidence.[14] Investigation revealed that McVeigh's life centered around guns and militant libertarianism. Although he had attended militia meetings in Michigan, his only confederates appear to have been two former army buddies with similar predilections.[15]

Although the bombing shocked the nation and turned public attention towards the militia movement and extremist groups, the newly elected majority in the House reacted with stunning political ineptness. Rather than examine the implications of militias, militant separatists, or armed libertarian extremists, the House formed a joint committee from Judiciary and Government Operations to investigate ATF and FBI activities at Waco.[16] The hearings appeared to focus primarily upon political objectives,[17] but failed either to link the administration to the events at Waco or to garner public support. The administration characterized the hearings as anti-law enforcement and supportive of radical paramilitary groups, a theme picked up by House Democrats.[18] Republican credibility suffered when Democrats revealed that the majority staff had links to the NRA and that NRA staff members identified themselves as working for the committee and contacting potential witnesses.[19] The committee majority found itself completely routed when the Democrats put 14-year-old Keri Jewel before the committee to testify that sect-leader Howell (Koresh) raped her at the age of 10 with the consent of her mother.[20]

Unable to tie the decisions regarding Waco to the White House and saddled with "victims" who encouraged child rape, stockpiled machine guns, discussed mass-murder plans, and killed four federal agents, the committee majority succeeded only in characterizing themselves as extremists at worst and pandering to extremists at best. Many of the same Judiciary Committee members who played such a visible role in this hearing would appear again during the Clinton impeachment hearings with an equal lack of success.

In addition to being seen as orchestrating the House hearings, the NRA lost political ground in other ways during this period. Although it did not intentionally associate itself with violent or illegal groups, the NRA did attempt to capitalize on Waco in order to intensify fear of gun control, which resulted in the pamphlet describing ATF agents as "jackbooted thugs." Although Representative John Dingell and others in the NRA had similarly described ATF agents during the 1970s, nobody noticed. In the aftermath of Oklahoma City, public and media attention focused on anyone seen as encouraging or aiding extremists and this generated substantial reaction, including the resignation of former President George Bush from his lifetime NRA membership.[21]

1998 ELECTION

In spite of these missteps, the NRA retained more-than-adequate influence to prevent any gun legislation from passing Congress, and proved able to move permissive carry bills through numerous legislatures (see chapter 10). Although the 1998 election reduced the Republican margin in Congress, it had little impact on the politics of gun control at the national level. In California, however, Democrats used the issue very effectively in their sweep of statewide offices.[22] This marked a significant change in California politics, where gun control had never before constituted a serious issue in campaigns. Although this trend had gathered strength since the Stockton massacre, 1998 seems to mark the point at which gun control moved from an issue for limited numbers of urban Democrats to a fundamental principle of the party's identity.[23]

To date, the outcome of the 1998 election seems to be a competition by various members of the California Legislature in pursuing individual pieces of gun-control legislation, with little attention to either their integration into a comprehensive policy or to implementation. Although members of the legislature, legislative staff, and political consultants all concur regarding the increased interest in gun control as a political issue, they also concede that there is limited interest in the actual details of the legislation.[24] Apparently, few if any incentives yet exist for becoming involved in the details of gun control or following through to determine the outcome of legislation. It would appear that gun-control advocacy has become a critical symbolic issue for California Democrats, much like family-values legislation has for Republicans. Ironically, while the California legislature debates such marginal issues as trigger locks and one-gun-per-month purchase limits, it has ignored the failure of the state to enforce its existing controls on the transfer of firearms between private individuals.[25] For a decade, California law has required private individuals selling firearms to deliver the arms to transfer agents, who must report the sales, and wait the required waiting period.[26] All new residents must register their handguns with the California Department of Justice upon moving to the state. These requirements, although unenforced, prohibit virtually all casual sales of firearms and come close to establishing a state-registration requirement for handguns.[27]

Although the legislature enacted this law, it provided no funding to assure its implementation and charged no state agency with ass The California Department of Justice performs the recc and maintains the gun records, but lacks an enforceme pliance with state laws.[28] Although local agencies have law at gun shows, the state has made no effort to publ for reporting private gun sales and most citizens rema tence.[29] California, with its large and diverse population for the future of gun-control politics. If so, the curre imply that accomplishing comprehensive, well-crafted, mented policy may require more than simply overcom sition of the NRA.

SCHOOL SHOOTINGS AS FOCUSING EVENTS

Although spectacular acts of violence involving firearms, such as the assassinations of John and Robert Kennedy and Martin Luther King and the mass killing of school children by Patrick Purdy in Stockton, California, have sometimes functioned as what Birkland calls "focusing events,"[30] equally spectacular shootings have failed to place gun control on either the political or media agenda. The murder of musician John Lennon and the attempted assassination of President Reagan generated little public interest in gun control, and the House defeated an assault-weapon ban immediately after the murder of 22 people in a Killeen, Texas, cafeteria by a man with a semi-automatic pistol.[31] Why the policy window opens after one event and not another most likely depends on a wide variety of variables, including the level of interest in competing issues, the presence of "policy entrepreneurs," and the context of the event. Birkland theorizes that focusing events will produce the least impact on the political agenda when the policy issue proves contentious and the policy community consists of two distinct and ideologically opposed groups.[32] Gun control confirms his thesis. The shootings that have recently focused media and political attention on gun control seem to fit primarily into what Birkland classifies as "new focusing events" because of their unique nature.[33]

The April 20, 1999 shooting spree by students Dylan Klebold and Eric Harris at a Littleton, Colorado, high school provides an example of just such an event. Armed with a semi-automatic carbine, a semi-automatic pistol, two sawed-off shotguns, and homemade bombs, the two students methodically murdered 12 students and a teacher, wounded 23 others, and committed suicide when surrounded by police.[34] The shooting culminated an 18-month period in which mass shootings by students in Mississippi, Kentucky, Arkansas, and Oregon had resulted in 15 deaths and scores of injuries.[35] All of these shootings involved young, white males with no serious history of crime or violence. None resulted from any direct provocation. Still, the Columbine High School shooting of April 20, 1999 captured public and media attention as none of the others had.[36]

Most likely, political reaction to the Columbine shootings resulted from a confluence of events. With both Congress and the presidency to be contested in the 2000 election, both parties feared alienating even a portion of suburban swing voters.[37] The Republican Party had misjudged the politics of impeachment, and the congressional leadership appears to have perceived a need to protect its flank with moderate voters. In addition, Senator Orin Hatch (R-Utah) had long nurtured a juvenile justice bill in his Judiciary Committee that seemed the appropriate political vehicle to capitalize on public interest. The Democrats had several modest gun bills available that no one expected to pass. When the Littleton shooting radically altered the political dynamics,[38] the Republican leadership in the Senate could hardly advance their juvenile justice bill while blocking the gun proposals. This proved particularly true of legislation applying Brady-type checking of purchasers at gun shows, when investigation revealed that the Littleton shooters had illegally obtained guns at such a show.[39]

During a two-week period that witnessed Senate Republicans struggling to regain control of the political agenda, the Senate first voted down mandatory purchaser checks at gun shows, then passed a Republican bill that required a one-day waiting period and purchaser check, which Democrats characterized as ineffectual.[40] One week later, a more restrictive Democratic bill passed on the tie-breaking vote by Vice President Al Gore, after a 50–50 tie vote.[41] In addition to the gun-show issue, the Senate passed bills mandating the supplying of trigger locks when guns are sold and prohibiting the importation of firearm magazines with a capacity of over 10 rounds. However, predictions of an altered political landscape proved premature. Although Speaker Dennis Hastert (R-Ill.) predicted House passage of a gun bill and other House Republicans voiced support for record checks at gun shows, trigger locks, and other marginal issues, the politics of the issue shifted again.[42] As significant Republican opposition developed to the Senate-passed provisions, Hastert shifted to a neutral position. The gun proposals became entangled with other social legislation and the House fractured into supporters of the Senate's bill, supporters of more restricted legislation, and opponents of any legislation.[43] Ultimately, long-time gun-control opponent John Dingell provided the Republican leadership with a way out by offering a proposal endorsed by the NRA.[44] Although Dingell's proposal easily passed with overwhelming Republican support, it resulted in Democrats and some northern Republicans opposing the final bill as inadequate. With aid from conservatives, who refused to vote for any gun control, the liberals and moderates prevailed and the Dingell bill died.[45] Although House members of both parties probably breathed a sigh of relief at not having to face the unpredictable fallout from a gun bill during the coming election, the

Democrats clearly intended to utilize the issue to position themselves with female and suburban voters.[46]

The political events of May and June 1999 did not produce any clear winners, although Democrats may have profited by widening the gender gap. Caught off guard, the NRA lost some of its apparent air of invincibility it had exuded since 1994, but it was able to quickly recover. Republicans appeared to be as disorganized and fractured as they had in the earlier impeachment hearings, but emerged without serious damage. The confusion of issues allowed individual members to portray their actions in virtually any way they chose during the campaign. The most interesting insight into the policy process emerges less from what participants *did* than from what they *did not* do. A review of the rather extensive news coverage reveals very little attention to the actual content of policy initiatives and virtually no analysis of potential impact. In addition, the rather limited nature of the policy initiatives offered by gun-control advocates reveals how unprepared they were for the policy window to open. That this flurry of activity related far more to the next election than to gun-control policy seems quite clear. The media attention generated by the school shootings was revived and extended by the July 1999 shootings in Georgia, Indiana, and Illinois and an August attack on a Jewish day school in Los Angeles.[47]

As the 2000 election took shape, gun control emerged as an issue primarily in the race for the Democratic presidential nomination. Bill Bradley advanced licensing and registration proposals, albeit without much detail or emphasis, forcing reaction by Vice President Al Gore and the Clinton administration. Clinton's proposal for additional ATF personnel and intensified enforcement of existing law responded to both Bradley's challenge and accusations by the NRA that existing laws were not being enforced. This move facilitated Gore's presidential strategy without placing marginal members of Congress at increased risk. With his nomination assured, Gore continued to keep the gun-control issue alive with vague proposals for licensing future purchasers and requiring trigger locks. George W. Bush has largely avoided becoming embroiled in the issue during the early stages of the campaign.

LAWSUITS

The decade of the 1990s closed with one new component in the firearm-policy mix that may prove more significant than the flurry of activity in response to the Littleton shooting. Following the pattern established by state and local government suits against the tobacco industry for the health cost of smoking-related illnesses, numerous cities filed suits against gun manufacturers for the costs of gunshot injuries.[48] The strategy began with New Orleans and Chicago but soon spread to numerous other cities. In May 1999, eight California cities and counties filed a joint lawsuit, charging unfair business practices.[49] Although none of the suits by local governments have come to trial, one suit by New York victims and families did reach a verdict in February 1999. That case, filed in federal court, charged gun manufacturers with saturating Southern states with handguns that predictably would find their way to New York by way of illegal traffickers.[50] Although the jury rejected damages for all but one of the plaintiffs and found only some of the gun manufacturers liable in a verdict devoid of any notable logic, the case accentuated the potential risk for the gun industry.[51]

The NRA has responded to the rash of lawsuits with a drive to pass state and federal legislation prohibiting the suits.[52] Although 12 states have passed legislation to prohibit local government suits, the federal bill did not succeed. Without federal legislation, the state laws do little to protect the gun industry from the threat of costly litigation.

The circumstances surrounding the firearm suits differ from those relating to tobacco in several significant ways: First, the gun industry's resources do not begin to approach those of the tobacco industry. The latter industry, comprised of only a few manufacturers, constitutes one of the richest businesses in the country. By contrast, the gun industry is small, not particularly rich, and fragmented among numerous small manufacturers. Because of its resources, size, and stability, the tobacco industry had conducted extensive testing on its product. It had also spent huge sums to distract the public from the risks of cigarettes. The dangerous nature of guns has never been at issue. Thus the gun industry has no record of deceptive marketing of its products. Finally, the lawsuits against the gun industry lack the intellectual cohesion, at least to date, of the tobacco suits. Plaintiffs have proceeded on different theories, including product liability for failure to include safety devices and public nuisance for selling quantities in excess of an area's capacity.[53] The lack of organization and diversity of legal theory present individual gun manufacturers with obstacles in organizing a systematic defense. They enjoy certain advantages, however. Current legal theories require a jury to find a manufacturer liable for injuries to persons in a political subdivision under one of two general conditions: In one case, liability would result from not implementing unproven safety technologies that would significantly increase the cost and decrease the marketability of their products. Although some inventors have claimed development of workable safety devices,[54] none have yet proven effective.[55] An alternative cause of action charges manufacturers with liability for having legally sold guns to dealers, who later sold these guns, legally or illegally, to traffickers, who, in turn, transported them unlawfully into the affected jurisdiction.

These suits have opened up a new arena for the gun-control issue. Although gun-control opponents have embraced this new strategy as a means of breaking the current deadlock,[56] its long-term impact remains unclear. Moving the policy conflict from the legislative arena to the courts has the potential to break the stalemate. As an interest group engaged in defending the status quo, the NRA fears and opposes any change that redefines the policy conflict.[57] More specifically, the litigation appears to exacerbate differences between the gun industry and the NRA.[58] Gun manufacturers have an economic interest in preserving a stable market and limiting costs and risks. To do so, they might support certain market regulations in exchange for protection against unlimited liability. Dealers have also demonstrated more independence in recent years through the National Alliance of Stocking Gun Dealers. Full-time dealers would benefit from tighter regulation of gun shows, unlicensed dealers, and casual sales.[59] Most manufacturers would not suffer significant injury from any of these approaches, and might accept any one of them if it were linked with liability protection.

On the other hand, a trend toward unpredictable risk or mandated changes in firearm design, significantly increasing manufacturing cost or decreased firearm functionality, would seriously threaten the industry and force it closer to the NRA. The NRA has laid the groundwork for a close alliance by pursuing liability protection for gun manufacturers in Congress and state legislatures. The NRA and the industry may find powerful allies among other manufacturing interests, who fear the potential precedents from these suits. The reckless use of automobiles kills and injures far more Americans every year than do gun accidents. One could even imagine future suits against cellphone manufacturers for injuries caused by distracted drivers. Thus the class-action lawsuit strategy constitutes a roll of the dice by frustrated control advocates and innovative trial lawyers. By moving the policy question from the legislatures to the courts the suits have altered its dynamics, but in ways no one can predict or likely control.

DECADE OF CHANGE OR MORE OF THE SAME?

The 1990s produced no surprises in the history of gun policy. Although the Brady Law and assault-weapon restrictions passed Congress, neither constituted a significant policy shift. And, as had occurred after the passage of the GCA in 1968 and passage of the Firearms Owners' Protection Act in 1986, the enactment of a modest policy change signaled the culmination of a period of activity rather than the opening salvo in a campaign. Success by pro-control forces contributed directly to the 1994 Republican-majority election and a Congress hostile to passage of new control legislation. Whether the 1999 House defeat of gun-show legislation will contribute to a reaction and another shift in power remains a question, but the stalemated nature of the issue persisted throughout the 1990s.

The strategy of pursuing limited initiatives, selected more for their political acceptability and symbolic appeal than for their utility, continued. HCI, the most powerful of the gun-control advocates, barely makes a pretense of advancing comprehensive policy, and most control advocates in Congress seem never to have actually considered the concept. Debate now centers around child safety, minor expansions on the Brady Law, and definitions of assault weapons. This pursuit of modest, politically attractive, and largely ineffective proposals has been ingrained in advocates during the past two decades. Although this pattern emerged from repeated failures to pursue more comprehensive policy, recent trends in California suggest that liberal, Democratic politicians may continue the pattern, even when they hold a significant majority. The recent behavior of legislators in that state implies more interest in gun control as a symbol for shaping elections than as a substantive policy issue. If this trend persists it will constitute as much of an obstacle to comprehensive gun policy as does NRA opposition.

A few trends have emerged with the potential for changing the politics of gun control in the long term. The expansion of permissive carry laws has changed the nature of gun laws in almost half the states and may eventually redefine the gun-control argument. Already it has created a structure for licensing gun owners and legitimatized armed self-defense in public space. At the same time, lawsuits against gun manufacturers threaten the economics of the gun industry and hold the potential for accentuating differences between the gun industry and the ideological opponents of gun control. In the political arena, the Democratic losses in the South and West appear to have permanently altered political calculations and placed gun control firmly on the agenda of the national party. Although about 40 House Democrats remain vulnerable,[60] continuation of this party realignment will eventually remove effective opposition to gun control in the Democratic Party. At some point in this process, the ability of control opponents to build coalitions between conservative, rural Democrats and the majority of Republicans will end, radically changing the balance of political forces in a Democratic Congress.

Several long-term trends that have yet to significantly influence the politics of gun policy may also prove critical in the long term. Although some authorities contest the validity of the figures, the number of gun owners, households with guns, and persons with gun experience appears to be declining.[61] Even more significant, gun ownership decreases significantly as people age.[62] This trend, interacting with a decreasing interest in and exposure to guns, may foreshadow long-term problems for gun interests. In both the 1992 and 1996 elections the long-predicted gender gap finally materialized. Virtually every poll ever conducted on firearms has reflected substantially lower proportions of women claiming possession of firearms and higher proportions favoring gun control.[63] Overshadowing these specific trends is the continuing urbanization of the nation. While an increasingly independent women's vote may translate directly into support for gun control, the other trends threaten gun interests more indirectly. They potentially undercut the broad base of support that has provided a key component of the NRA's political strength. Although the majority of gun owners do not belong to the NRA or other gun-interest groups, they *do* provide a reservoir of potential supporters. Equally as important, they constitute a huge body of stakeholders and thereby complicate any effort at gun policy.[64]

Part Two

HOW WE GOT HERE

CHAPTER SIX

EARLY HISTORY

ALTHOUGH LOCAL ORDINANCES may have constituted the initial gun laws, the first state gun-control laws in the nation appear to have been restrictions on possession of firearms by both free blacks and slaves.[1] After the Civil War a number of Southern states continued to restrict firearm possession by African Americans, later shifting to restrictions on possession of all but the most expensive handguns, the so-called army-and-navy revolvers.[2] The latter strategy avoided conflict with the equal-protection clause of the Fourteenth Amendment and effectively denied most blacks from acquiring handguns because of escalating costs. A number of Southern and Western states also prohibited the carrying of concealed weapons of all types.[3]

THE SULLIVAN LAW

In 1911 the state of New York passed the Sullivan Law, which requires a police permit to possess a handgun. Almost a century later, New York remains the only state that significantly restricts private ownership of handguns.[4] The context in which the Sullivan Law was enacted differed from those surrounding subsequent efforts to pass firearm legislation in other jurisdictions. First, from the middle of the nineteenth century the City of New York outstripped all other American cities in urbanization. This urbanization existed as much in attitudes and self-perception as in buildings and population. By the turn of the century New York had produced a generation of opinion-makers and leaders who had come to maturity without exposure to a rural, gun-oriented culture. The Civil War generation had largely passed from power, and the following one had not experienced military service. This generation fostered the "good-government" movement of the early 1900s, urban progressivism that advocated improved public services, parks, child-labor laws, and prohibition. In addition, a large immigrant population probably facilitated passage of the

Sullivan Law by generating concern among the established power structure over radical political doctrines and high crime rates among new immigrants.[5] Tammany Hall, the primary political power in opposition to the good-government movement, had little reason to contest the gun issue. Tammany Hall's power rested largely on new immigrants. Lacking socialization to firearm ownership as an inherent right in addition to experience with firearms, Tammany's constituency had little motivation to oppose the law.

In fact, little effective opposition emerged to obstruct the passage of the Sullivan Law.[6] Although the NRA opposed it, it lacked the political experience, resources, and organization that would become its hallmark in later years. Contrasted with subsequent conflicts over firearms legislation, the Sullivan Law's passage provides a very curious contrast. Clearly, the political and social dynamics necessary for passage of strict firearm control has failed to come together in other political venues.

OTHER STATES

Although several other states more or less emulated New York, none of these enforced their laws in fact, and a number repealed them after years of non-enforcement.[7] Little solid research is available, but anecdotal evidence is that gun laws were not actively enforced in most states.[8] After the wave of firearm statutes passed during the 1920s, the general trend appeared to have been inaction or retreat from control until the 1970s.[9] Although the New York law failed to initiate a wave of state restrictions, it proved important for another reason: For the opponents of gun control, the New York precedent was a constant reminder of "what they want to do." This effect was exacerbated by the administration of the law in the City of New York. The New York City Police Department clearly implemented the law as a means of denying citizens access to handguns, except under unusual circumstances.[10] A reading of Congressional hearings or discussions with opponents of firearm legislation regularly reveals that the Sullivan Law was an example of its opponents' ultimate fear.[11]

THE FEDERAL GOVERNMENT ENTERS THE FIELD

The 1920s and early 1930s witnessed significant change in the federal government's policy toward exercise of police power. During this period the federal government provide the primary force behind enforcement of Prohibition. The Federal Bureau of Investigation, Federal Bureau of Narcotics, and the U.S. Border Patrol were all formed during this period. Although 1933 marked the end of the "noble experiment" of Prohibition, it did not witness a collateral decline in the general involvement of the federal government in law enforcement.

In 1927, Congress, after several years of debate, passed the first national firearm-control legislation when it banned the shipment by mail of handguns to individuals.[12] The issue of mail-order sales of handguns would continue for another 41 years, as Congress did not address the question of shipment by common carriers. Although this was clear at the time, Congress was willing to settle for a largely symbolic action.[13] This pattern of debate, followed by action characterized by its advocates as inadequate to solve the alleged problem but the best that could be accomplished at the time, would repeat itself for years to come.

The National Firearms Act (NFA)

With the election of the Roosevelt administration came the first executive initiatives to pursue gun control at the federal level. Franklin Roosevelt had previously demonstrated a predilection to support gun control as the governor of New York, where he vetoed a bill to rescind the Sullivan Law and supported the prohibition of private ownership of machine guns.[14] The Department of Justice, under the direction of Attorney General Homer Cummings, began a concerted effort to pursue serious federal legislation.[15] Cummings's proposal was modeled on the Harrison Narcotics Act and utilized the federal taxing power as a mechanism of control. Under his proposal, transfers of handguns over .22 caliber between individuals would be taxed at a rate of $1 and would require approval by the Secretary of the Treasury. The making or transfer of "gangster weapons," including machine guns, silencers, and sawed-off rifles and sawed-off shotguns, invoked a $200 tax. The law exempted transfers to government and dealers, who obtained a special occupational tax.[16]

Hearings were held concurrently in the Senate to consider two bills introduced by Senator Royal Copeland of New York, along with the administration's proposal. Copeland's proposals were based on the interstate-commerce authority and proposed: 1) limiting the shipment of concealable firearms across state lines to licensed dealers, 2) prohibiting the interstate shipment of machine guns, and 3) requiring a library of bullets from all new firearms.[17]

Opposition to the proposed legislation focused principally on the inclusion of handguns and primarily came from the firearms industry, sport and hunting groups, and the NRA.[18] Both the NRA and the firearms industry had responded to past legislation with improved organization.[19] The opposition achieved the removal of handguns from the proposed act before it was reported out of both the House and Senate committees.[20] Additionally, the committee rejected a definition of machine guns that included semi-automatic firearms with 10-round magazines, a definition that would have included modern assault weapons.[21] The resulting bill was quickly passed by Congress and signed by the president.

During the 1934 hearings, the crime-control paradigm clearly dominated the testimony of both advocates and opponents.[22] Advocates alluded to the low violent-crime rates of Britain and the NRA argued that laws could not prevent criminals from obtaining firearms. One unusual characteristic that appeared in the Senate hearings, particularly as they related to Senator Copeland's bills, was the focus on gun-control laws as a mechanism for law enforcement. Although Copeland's proposals for manufacturers' retaining sample bullets and for marking bullets were not practical, they represented an attempt to utilize firearm laws in aiding police. Later hearings would largely ignore such concepts and focus exclusively on the efficacy of denying criminals access to firearms. The NRA was not impressed with the concept of firearm laws being a useful mechanism to aid law enforcement.[23]

The Federal Firearms Act (FFA)

The passage of the NFA did not end the discussion of firearm legislation by Congress or the efforts of the Justice Department to pursue more strict legislation. In 1937 the Justice Department again proposed the placement of handguns into the National Firearms Act.[24] The resulting compromise, largely written by the NRA, utilized the interstate-commerce authority for jurisdiction. Passed in 1938, the new law was titled, the Federal Firearms Act (FFA).[25] It applied to all firearms but provided only limited controls. Persons dealing in firearms in interstate commerce were required to obtain a $1 license, but the fingerprints, photograph, and police reference required for NFA registration were not required for a license. Some restrictions were placed on the shipment of firearms into states in violation of state law but no mechanisms were provided for enforcement. Dealers were required to maintain records but no viable penalties were provided to sanction failures to comply. In essence, FFA proved to be a symbolic effort, with little practical effectiveness.[26]

Curiously, the original legislation proposed the Department of Commerce to be the agency of jurisdiction. During the hearings it was pointed out that the Department of State already had jurisdiction over international commerce, and Treasury over the NFA. The NRA proposed consolidation of jurisdiction in the Department of Commerce, a department with no law-enforcement structure. A compromise granted jurisdiction over both the NFA and FFA to Treasury. There was no discussion of the structure or resources necessary to enforce the law, thus giving the distinct impression that not much enforcement was contemplated.[27]

By the time of the 1937 hearings, the NRA emerged as the primary force in opposition to firearms legislation. The NRA had adopted the tactic of endorsing alternate legislation whenever legislation capable of significant impact on unrestricted possession of and commerce in firearms threatened. In addition to the FFA, the NRA had cooperated in the drafting of a uniform handgun act for adoption by states.[28] Ironically, this model legislation introduced the concept of the waiting period for handgun purchasers. Over half-a-century later, the NRA would be at the center of opposition to the Brady Law, which imposed a national waiting period and purchaser screening. Even at the time when the NRA advocated such legislation as a compromise, it apparently had little faith in its usefulness.[29]

Although the passage of the Federal Firearms Act marks the end of a cycle of interest in firearm legislation, the momentum probably dissipated as of 1934. The Roosevelt administration clearly had many higher priority interests and the forces of opposition had proven themselves capable of forcing compromises that would prevent policy from impacting the majority of firearms and firearm owners. Moreover, the murder rate and crime rate in general had taken a sudden downturn during the middle 1930s.[30] As a confirmation of the thesis that gun control was primarily viewed in a crime-control paradigm, the issue would not get serious national attention again for 30 years, when crime rates again began to rise steeply. For all practical purposes, the issue of gun control lay dormant until after the assassination of President Kennedy in 1963.

THE DYNAMICS OF THE FIRST WAVE

Between 1934 to 1938 gun control was on the congressional agenda, although comprehensive policy was rejected at the earliest stages. The political dynamics that have since dominated the issue were already largely in place during that period. The initiative for control came from a few key legislators, the current administration, and some private organizations with peripheral interests.[31] The opposition was led by the NRA and included sportsmen's organizations and the firearm industry. The opposition possessed several advantages that would remain intact for years to come. It was, in fact, broad based: NRA membership grew substantially during this period, and far more opponents than advocates of gun control wrote their congressmen.[32] At the time, the opposition demonstrated organization and focus, both of which were apparent from the testimony of NRA representatives and the degree of consensus exhibited by witnesses in opposition. A final element—perhaps more important than any other—was the deep-seated belief among some members of Congress that unrestricted access to firearms was natural and desirable.[33]

The crime-control paradigm dominated the consciousness of both the advocates and opponents, who primarily framed their arguments in these terms. However, the worldview and sovereignty paradigms were present below the surface. This was particularly true of the opponents, who focused on the wholesome nature of shooting sports, the moral quality of gun owners and shooters, and the constitutional right of citizens to possess arms. Opposition to including handguns in the NFA reflected all three paradigms and focused on three premises: The first was that handguns should not be associated in the law with "gangster" weapons such as machine guns, because handguns were wholesome firearms owned by honest citizens; the second was the "slippery-slope" assumption that would be a key element in all opposition to future gun control; and the third was that firearm laws do not affect criminals but only the law abiding.[34]

Gun-control opponents eventually accepted controls on a few "bad" or abnormal guns if "normal" guns were not included in the law. In 1934 this argument reflected the desire to separate gun owners in general from the crime focus of the day, the gangster. The other two premises would form the basis of opposition in every future battle, along with the constitutional arguments.

The slippery-slope argument, combined with constitutional arguments, reflected a sovereignty paradigm and incrementalist assumptions. It seeks to establish the legitimacy of the individual right to firearms over the state's sovereign power to control them. In later years these arguments would be seen as being weakened by the acceptance of even a small category of "bad" guns for which controls were legitimate. This concern appeared as early as the 1930s when the NRA advocated repealing the NFA and substituting the FFA.[35] The arguments relating to efficacy were clearly focused on the crime-control paradigm.

THE ISSUE BECALMED

Although the 1920s and 1930s had been a period of some activity in the field of firearm regulation, the next two decades would not be so. Both the NFA and FFA were assigned to the Treasury Department for administration and enforcement, where they received little attention and few resources.[36] In 1958 the Treasury Department proposed new regulations that would have strengthened the FFA, but these were significantly watered down. The proposal to require serial numbers on all firearms was, for instance, modified to exempt .22 rifles and shotguns.[37] Congress also made minor changes in the Law, extending interstate-transportation prohibitions to all felons and not just those convicted of violent crimes, and modifying the definition of short-barreled rifles. State laws changed little, although some handgun controls were repealed. The next round of activity in the gun-control field would not come until the violent crime rate ceased its long decline and again began a rapid ascent with the coming of age of the baby-boom generation.

• • •

CHAPTER SEVEN

THE GUN CONTROL ACT OF 1968

FOR THREE DECADES, the Gun Control Act of 1968 (GCA) has formed the legal core of national gun policy in the United States. The congressional deliberations leading to the passage of the GCA and companion legislation extended over five years and involved the Departments of Justice and Treasury, the White House, firearm-interest groups, and both houses of Congress. At no time before or since has Congress addressed gun-control policy with as much breadth or depth.[1] Although the National Firearms Act (NFA) of 1934 imposed strict federal regulation on machine guns and other "gangster" firearms[2] by using taxation legislation, the 1938 Federal Firearms Act (FFA) had proven ineffectual in asserting even minimal federal controls over interstate commerce in ordinary handguns, shotguns, and rifles.[3] The structure of the GCA emerged largely from observed weaknesses in the existing FFA.[4]

THE DODD HEARINGS

In early 1958 Senator John Kennedy of Massachusetts introduced legislation to control the importation of surplus military firearms.[5] Clearly protectionist, the legislation targeted the increase in imported firearms, the great majority of which were military surplus.[6] Congress acted only to ban the importation of previously exported U.S. military firearms.[7] The flood of imports continued, fueled by surplus World War II firearms and inexpensive pistols and revolvers.[8]

Upon assuming the chairmanship of the Juvenile Justice Subcommittee of the Senate Judiciary Committee in 1961, Senator Thomas Dodd (D-Conn.) directed the staff to conduct a study of mail-order sales of firearms. After two years of staff study, Senator Dodd introduced his first gun bill (S.1975) and held hearings to generate public interest in the gun issue.[9] The bill required mail-order purchasers of handguns to provide the seller a notarized affidavit stating that they were over 18 years of age and legally entitled to purchase the firearm, and additionally restricted the importation of surplus military firearms.[10] This bill had input from the Treasury Department and received support from both the firearms industry and the NRA.[11]

After the assassination of President Kennedy with a mail-order, surplus military rifle, Senator Dodd amended his bill to include long guns under the mail-order restrictions.[12] The bill died in the Senate Commerce Committee in 1964, but Senator Dodd reintroduced it as S.14 in January of 1965. Two months later, he introduced a more restrictive bill (S.1592) at the request of the administration and the political battle over gun control began.[13] Although various members of Congress introduced a variety of gun bills during the period between 1964 and 1968, the Dodd bill became a generic description for all pending legislation, particularly among opponents of firearm-control legislation. Between 1938 and 1965 Congress displayed little discernable interest in gun-control legislation; however, external events, administration interest, and public opinion altered the policy dynamics within Congress over the next four years and opened up the policy window.[14] Events during this period also foreshadowed the form and dynamics of the gun issue for years to come.

The shift by the leadership of the NRA, from cautious support for the original Dodd bill to modest opposition of S.1592, foreshadowed the most significant and lasting change in the dynamics of gun-control policy to occur in the twentieth century. The NRA and firearm manufacturers had supported Dodd's original bill and the subsequent addition of interstate controls on long guns.[15] Although the official organ of the NRA, *The American Rifleman*, indicated otherwise, the NRA leadership displayed some willingness to compromise with Dodd as late as 1965.[16] Negative response by the membership precipitated a subsequent reversal of direction by the NRA leadership.[17] This uprising by a significant portion of the NRA membership owed much to the development of a specialized gun press that catered to the most avid of gun enthusiasts.[18] The editorial staffs of magazines such as *Guns, Guns and Ammo*, and *Gun Week* adamantly opposed gun control in any form and benefited from heightened interest in gun issues.[19] By 1965 the leadership and membership of the NRA divided along a fault line separating those tolerant of moderate increases in gun control from those opposed to any significant change in the law.[20] Although the NRA leadership responded to this internal pressure with increased opposition to new legislation, its policy shift failed to satisfy a powerful segment within the membership. This internal dissatisfaction within the NRA provided the impetus for a 1977 coup by the libertarian faction within the organization and the ouster of the more moderate old guard.[21] Although the relations between Chairman Dodd and the NRA witnesses remained marginally cordial during the 1965 hearings, the atmosphere had begun to chill. Any hope of compromise between advocates of stricter gun control and the NRA ended after 1965.

The 1965 hearings also shaped the future dynamics of the subcommittee. Over the next three years Dodd assumed the role of spokesman for a series of progressively more restrictive bills drafted by the administration. Relations between Dodd and ranking minority member Roman Hruska (R-Neb.) became progressively strained on personal rather than ideological grounds.[22] Although his rural constituency and conservative view of the federal role predisposed Hruska toward a skeptical view of gun control, he lacked any ties to the gun lobby or any personal stake in the gun issue.[23] Apparently the personal relationship between them directly influenced committee dynamics and the formulation of policy.[24]

Both the House and Senate conducted hearings on a number of proposed pieces of gun legislation between 1963 and 1968. Although these various bills bore different designations during different sessions of Congress, they can be somewhat simplified. The original Dodd proposal (S.1975) would have restricted the importation of surplus military firearms and required sworn affidavits of eligibility to purchase handguns by mail. The seller would have been required to mail the affidavit to the chief law-enforcement officer of the purchaser's jurisdiction. Dodd reintroduced this bill as S.14 in 1965, and Hruska again introduced essentially the same bill as S.1853 in 1967.[25] Although Dodd introduced S.14, he soon shifted his support and the attention of his subcommittee hearings to S.1592, a bill that was largely drafted by the administration. The majority of the 1965 gun-control hearings concerned this bill, which: prohibited interstate mail-order sales and interstate over-the-counter sales of handguns to individuals; increased dealer fees from $1 to $100; extended controls to ammunition; restricted destructive devices; and prohibited sales by dealers to minors.[26] Existing law already prohibited sales by dealers to felons and certain other classes of persons.

THE ADMINISTRATION UPS THE ANTE

In 1967 Senator Dodd reintroduced S.1592 as S.1, but soon introduced Amendment 90 to S.1 (hereafter "S.1 as amended") in response to administration proposals. Rather than amending the existing Federal Firearms Act, S.1 as amended replaced the FFA with a new law. It also extended the interstate prohibition on mail-order sales of handguns to all guns, and prohibited interstate transactions between individuals. S.1 as amended also reduced proposed dealer license fees to $25 and removed controls on ammunition.[27] A companion bill (S.1854) placed destructive devices under the NFA as items requiring registration and tax payment.[28] Senator Hruska had advanced this approach for some time in lieu of placing such items in the FFA.

Senator Hruska's reintroduction of the original Dodd bill as S.1853 provided a compromise position for senators fearing constituencies on both ends of the gun issue. With strong NRA opposition to S.1 as amended and an alternative bill to divide support, the probability of passing a comprehensive gun bill appeared low. External events suddenly altered the policy agenda. The assassination of Dr. Martin Luther King opened up the policy window and altered the political dynamics in the Judiciary Committee.[29] On April 29, 1968 the Senate Judiciary Committee reported out a bill resembling Dodd's S.1 as amended—with the exception of a ban on interstate sales of long guns—as Title IV (hereafter "T-IV") of the Omnibus Crime Control and Safe Streets Act.[30] On May 23, 1968 the full Senate amended the Omnibus bill by adding Title VII (hereafter "T-VII"), which prohibited felons and certain other classes of individuals from receiving, possessing, or transporting a firearm in or affecting commerce.[31] The Senate passed S.917 as amended, the Omnibus bill, on May 24, 1968 and sent it to the House.[32] The policy window had opened in the Senate, but the House remained a potential obstacle.

BREAKTHROUGH

A second assassination further pried open the policy window and assured House passage. On June 5, 1968 an assassin murdered presidential-candidate Senator Robert Kennedy. The following day the House passed the Omnibus Crime Control and Safe Streets Act, including T-IV and T-VII.[33] Ironically, after years in formulation, T-IV never became effective. Before its effective date of implementation, Congress passed the somewhat more comprehensive GCA.[34] This Act extended interstate restrictions to all firearms and also included ammunition.[35] It also revised the NFA by adding destructive devices to the restricted categories and by restricting future registrations of firearms made or transferred in violation of the law.[36]

Although T-IV of the Omnibus bill and the later GCA reflected extensive hearings and staff work, T-VII benefited from no such history. At the last minute the Senate inserted T-VII into its version of the Omnibus Crime Control and Safe Streets Act by voice vote.[37] Proposed by Senator Russell Long (D-La.) and considered without hearings, the bill suffered from poor drafting that would bedevil its enforcers and confound the courts.[38] T-VII addressed simple firearm possession for the first time at the federal level. The bill included a finding that strongly implied such intent,[39] and Senator Long's statements on the Senate floor likewise support such an interpretation.[40] Apparently this bill—intended to significantly alter federal policy—became law with little analysis largely as a political favor to improve its author's image as being tough on crime.[41]

The new momentum generated by the Robert Kennedy assassination continued to alter the political dynamics of the gun-control issue through the summer and fall of 1968. In earlier years, congressional mail, dominated by gun-control opponents, generated fear even among many liberal members of supporting significant legislation.[42] Although opinion polls reflected broad-based support for stricter controls on firearms, this support failed to translate into constituent demand.[43] After the 1968 assassinations of Robert Kennedy and Martin Luther King, a groundswell of visible support for more decisive federal action temporarily materialized.[44]

During the summer of 1968 gun-control advocates in Congress tested the limits of the new policy dynamics with the introduction of bills calling for registration and licensing of firearms.[45] Senator Joseph Tydings (D-Md.), who replaced Senator Dodd as the most visible congressional proponent of gun control over the next two years,[46] introduced one of four major bills relating to registration and licensing. His S.3634 would have established national firearm registration and required a license issued by the Secretary of Treasury to possess a firearm. The bill allowed the states to substitute state licensing for federal. The administration advanced S.3691, which mandated federal licensing if the states failed to act.[47] The administration proposed the use of licensed, federal firearm dealers as licensing agents, following the pattern of hunting and fishing licenses.[48] The administration's bill contained two cumbersome requirements: That applicants provide certification from a doctor regarding their mental state, and certification from the local police regarding their residence and lack of criminal record. Similar in structure and intent, S.3634 and S.3691 both allowed and encouraged the states to develop firearms owner licensing, but mandated federal licensing if the states failed to act.[49]

Senator Edward Brooke (R-Mass.) and Senator Dodd also introduced registration bills, but of less sweeping proportions. Brooke's bill, S.3637, required registration through local police authorities, but not a license to possess a firearm. Likewise Dodd's S.3604 required registration but contained no licensing provision.

Following the passage of the Omnibus Crime Control and Safe Streets Act, the Dodd subcommittee continued gun-control hearings focused almost exclusively on these registration and licensing bills.[50] Although the summer of 1968 was the high-water mark for gun control on the national policy agenda, none of the registration bills came close to passage. In October, Congress passed the GCA to replace T-IV of the Omnibus Act after a spirited debate in both the House and Senate and a flurry of motions by both supporters and opponents of gun control.[51] The GCA constituted the last major gun-control bill to pass Congress until the Firearms Owners' Protection Act of 1986, which reduced a number of the controls imposed by GCA.[52] Not until the Brady Law of 1994 would Congress again pass significant gun-control legislation.[53] The final bill constituted only a modest revision of the already-passed T-IV of the Omnibus Act.

THE LAW

The GCA actually consisted of two distinct subdivisions or titles, located in different titles of the federal code.[54] In addition, T-VII of the Omnibus Act was the functional equivalent of a third subdivision of the GCA, although it constituted a separate piece of legislation.[55] The majority of the GCA—Title I (hereafter "the GCA")—regulated all firearms and was located in Title 18 of the U.S. Code (the Criminal Code), as was T-VII. Title II (hereafter "the NFA") incorporated the existing National Firearms Act (NFA), with minor additions. The NFA remained a tax statute, in law if not in fact, within Title 26 of the U.S. Code (the Internal Revenue Code). It retained the existing scheme of registration to enforce the making, transfer taxes, and special occupational taxes required by the 1934 Act.[56] The primary changes to the NFA consisted of the addition of destructive devices to the previously enumerated categories of so-called gangster weapons, and the termination of authority to register existing NFA firearms after an initial amnesty period.[57] The category of destructive devices included weapons with a bore exceeding $1/2$ inch in diameter, explosive and poison gas bombs, projectiles with explosive warheads, and rockets and missiles.[58] While this change attracted little attention at the time, it conferred upon the Bureau of Alcohol, Tobacco, and Firearms (ATF) jurisdiction over the primary federal law relating to bombing.[59] Although future legislation expanded the jurisdiction of the FBI over bombings, ATF retained joint jurisdiction in this area, and later extended that jurisdiction into commercial arson.[60]

Between 1934 and 1968 Treasury Department policy allowed persons without criminal records to register NFA firearms possessed in technical violation of the law when: 1) the violation was not willful, and 2) the firearm was legal under state law.[61] The new law provided for a 30-day amnesty period during which time any person possessing an NFA firearm could register it without restrictions.[62] No information provided in furtherance of registration could be released to state authorities or used to prosecute the registrant for any crime other than false statements in the registration application.[63] The amnesty and nondisclosure provisions overcame the defense of self-incrimination established by *Haynes v. United States*.[64] While this legal strategy served to eliminate a short-term impediment to enforcing the registration provisions of the NFA, it established a precedent that may prove troublesome in any future effort to pursue general registration or licensing of firearms.[65]

Although the GCA created no comprehensive system of control or regulation of firearms in the possession of individual citizens, it significantly altered the rules governing commercial firearm transactions. It prohibited engaging in the business of manufacturing, importing, or dealing in firearms without first obtaining a federal license.[66] Licensees were prohibited from selling firearms to out-of-state residents, minors, felons, persons under indictment for felonies, fugitives, and certain other categories of persons[67] and required the maintaining of records of all sales.[68] The law prohibited interstate mail order sales and tightly restricted intrastate mail-order sales.[69] Manufacturers and importers had to begin identifying every firearm by stamping the name of the manufacturer or importer and a serial number on the receiver.[70] Firearms not suitable for sporting purposes and surplus military firearms were restricted from importation.[71]

The GCA prohibited dealers from delivering firearms to felons and several other categories of persons and those same classes of persons from receiving firearms that had moved in commerce,[72] but failed to address the question of possession by these persons. The GCA also ignored transfers by individuals to felons and other restricted categories, while prohibiting transfers to out-of-state residents.[73] T-VII prohibited felons and certain other categories of persons from receiving, possessing, or transporting firearms in commerce; however, the categories enumerated by T-VII differed slightly from those in the GCA.[74] In addition, the question of whether T-VII applied to simple possession remained unanswered for several years. Following the passage of T-VII, the Departments of Treasury and Justice assumed a very cautious posture toward the prosecution of felons for possession of firearms. Until the 1971 decision in *United States v. Bass* (hereafter "*Bass*"),[75] policy virtually precluded federal prosecution of felons for possession of firearms except in cases where the government could directly prove interstate transportation or receipt by the defendant.[76] Even after *Bass*, prosecutive policy remained conservative until 1977, when the Supreme Court affirmed that prior interstate movement of a firearm fulfilled the "in or effecting commerce" element of possession.[77]

Although subsequent statutory changes merged into the GCA the prohibitions against possession of firearms "in or affecting commerce" by felons and others,[78] T-VII provided the only functional federal restriction on possession for almost a decade. Even the incorporation of the prohibition into the GCA did not address the complexities raised by the need for proof of the interstate nexus. Section 922(g) simply incorporated the same "possession in or affecting commerce" language that previously existed in Section 1202(a). Thus the requirement to establish the interstate nexus in every case, adopted as a result of *Bass*, remained. Although evidence of prior interstate shipment ordinarily fills the "affecting commerce" requirement, firearms seized in their state of manufacture constitute an exception.[79] The ambiguous syntax of the original T-VII and the failure of its congressional finding to satisfy the interstate requirement have resulted in law that neither restricts its reach to true commerce nor efficiently addresses all possession. The perpetuation and incorporation of the possession restriction demonstrates an apparent congressional intent to establish a federal prohibition against firearm possession by felons and certain other high-risk offenders, but this intent has not translated into corrective legislation to address the faults incorporated in the 1968 law.[80]

In addition to not directly addressing the possession of firearms by high-risk classes, the GCA provided no authorization for an oversight mechanism to ensure that licensed dealers did not transfer firearms to such persons.

Although required to maintain a record of gun disposition and obtain identification and a signed certification of eligibility from the purchaser, dealers had no means for determining eligibility.[81] While the original GCA required dealers to submit such reports as the secretary might require, the Treasury Department made no effort to include a reporting requirement on sales in its implementation of regulations.[82] The Firearms Owners' Protection Act of 1986 specifically prohibited such a requirement,[83] and the Brady Law of 1994 instituted required reporting for the sole purpose of screening buyers.[84]

The preamble to the GCA defined its purpose as providing support to state efforts at firearm regulation without placing a burden on legitimate firearm users.[85] These themes dominated the entire law. The first theme appeared in the provisions prohibiting acquisition outside one's state of residence, interstate mail-order sales, and delivery to out-of-state residents or persons who would be in violation of local or state law by possessing such firearms. The second theme appears in a number of provisions, including exemptions for purchase of guns in contiguous states, provisions for intrastate mail-order sales by dealers, and provision for replacement of guns that are lost or broken by nonresidents on hunting trips. Presumably this concern about placing burdens on individuals accounts for the lack of controls on transactions *between* individuals. Concerns about the burdens of licensing on small, rural businesses manifested themselves in the $10 yearly license fee, and concerns for collectors resulted in the collector license for curios and relics.[86]

STRUCTURAL ISSUES

A fundamental deficiency in the law resulted from the failure to define the term "engaged in the business of dealing in firearms." Although the law required any person engaged in this activity to obtain a license and provided for felony penalties for failure to do so,[87] it included no definition or statutory presumption to clarify this crucial term. This lack of definition underlaid much of the subsequent conflict over the implementation of the law and generated considerable difficulties for gun enthusiasts and law enforcers.[88] The ambiguity resulting from a failure to define "engaging in the business" interfaced with other structural shortcomings to generate years of conflict over the entire licensing process.[89] The law required the issuance of a dealer license within 45 days to any applicant declaring an intention to engage in the business from a premise, unless the applicant was under 21 years of age or fell into the one of the categories of persons prohibited from possessing firearms.[90] These minimal criteria, combined with a license fee of only $10 annually, ensured issuance of licenses to numerous individuals desiring the convenience of licenses but lacking actual intent to engage in legitimate business enterprises.[91] Because Congress granted no discretion in the issuance of licenses, the ATF could address this issue only after an inspection had revealed a failure to engage in the business. This placed ATF in the awkward position of revoking or denying renewal of a license for failing to engage in the business rather than for some intentional violation of the law or regulations.[92]

Although many license applicants had no intent of carrying on a commercial enterprise, many persons who actually sold firearms commercially resisted licensing and its requirements to conduct business from a fixed premises and maintain records of purchasers.[93] Thus ATF found itself concurrently prosecuting unlicensed dealers for what appeared to be casual sales, while encouraging other casual sellers to surrender their licenses. The results proved disastrous for ATF, although the contradictions existed more in appearances than fact.[94] These problems could easily have been avoided with higher dealer fees, a definition of "engaging in business" based on the number of sales or offers per year, modest licensing discretion, and elimination of the requirement that licensees engage in the business.[95] Efforts at minimizing the burden on licensees and restriction of bureaucratic discretion generated serious implementation problems.

As with many federal regulatory statutes, the GCA granted authority to the implementing agency, ATF, to promulgate regulations spelling out specific procedures under the law.[96] While regulatory agencies may exercise significant discretionary authority through administrative regulations, this has not proven the case for the regulations authorized under the GCA. The regulations are restricted to filling in routine details for activities spelled out in the law. In light of the hostile congressional reaction to the only effort at utilizing the regulations to increase the reach of the statute, the narrow drafting appears to reflect congressional will.[97]

Thus the GCA and T-VII imposed procedures on persons in the gun business and established classifications for persons ineligible to receive and possess firearms from dealers or in interstate commerce. With the exception of the NFA restrictions on machine guns and certain other unusual firearms, the law applied equally to all modern firearms.[98] Individuals other than felons and certain other prohibited persons were little affected by the law. Although most persons could not acquire a firearm outside their state of residence, only a small minority of persons probably desired to do so.[99] The law terminated the nation's totally laissez-faire policy on gun commerce. Although proceeded by extensive hearings, the law generated numerous implementation problems.

IN RETROSPECT

Events surrounding the passage of the GCA provide some insight into the policy process and nature of gun control as an issue. From the interest-group perspective, the events present a rather straightforward and well-defined scenario, with the groups divided into two fairly distinct camps. The events differed from a classic clash of interest groups only in that the pro-control advocates included neither a broad-based organization specifically committed to gun control or any other organization with an economic stake. The only organized special-interest group solely devoted to gun control—the National Council for Responsible Firearms Policy—consisted of only about 50 prominent, though not essentially powerful, citizens.[100] Although the pro-control position received some support from groups with more widespread membership such as the International Association of Chiefs of Police (IACP) and the American Bar Association, these groups pursued a variety of interests and issues other than firearms.[101] The pro-control forces did enjoy two key sources of support: The Johnson administration consistently supported a more comprehensive federal gun statute, although the Justice Department provided more support than did the Treasury Department. Justice lawyers drafted the most restrictive proposals and Justice officials testified in their support. Although less active on policy formulation, Treasury officials consistently supported the administration position.[102] The advocates of control also enjoyed widespread support in most of the national media.[103]

The opponents more closely approached the classic interest group model. First among equals, the NRA benefited directly from the heightened interest generated by the legislative hearings and debates. Its membership rose rapidly during this period, reaching 700,000 by 1965 and 1 million by 1968.[104] Although it supported Senator Hruska's bill as an alternative to more-restrictive legislation, the NRA solidified its position of leadership in opposition to all other control proposals, with support from associations of arms collectors, manufacturers, and shooters. The membership of these groups overlapped substantially; in fact, most members of these other groups were most likely NRA members.[105] Although some have characterized the opposition as a classic economic-interest group with the NRA acting as a front for arms manufacturers, the record provides little support for this interpretation.[106]

In the case of gun control during the 1960s, the interest groups (or "factions" in Madison's words) did not resemble the general concept of interest groups based on economic interest, class interest, geography, or ethnicity. Control advocates consisted of a loosely organized elite, focused on a perceived public-interest issue with support from the administration and presumably from much of the public. Although principally composed of narrow special-interest groups, control opponents enjoyed a very broad-based support that did not grow primarily from economic self-interest. While this support was mostly concentrated in rural areas, it spanned class and geography.

Advocates for both positions utilized similar strategies to prevail. Political-theorist E. E. Schattschneider characterized advocates in the American political system as expanding political conflicts by attempting to bring the audience into the conflict.[107] Both sides followed this pattern. The advocates used the press and the hearings themselves to create demand for legislation. The opposition utilized the special-interest press and direct mailings for the same purpose, often at times characterizing the proposed legislation as being far more restrictive than it in fact actually was.[108]

The crime–control paradigm dominated and framed the policy discussion. In the early hearings, the impact on crime of sales to out-of-state residents by mail order and over-the-counter transactions received considerable attention in the hearings.[109] As the hearings progressed, advocates repeatedly stressed the number of killings with guns and rising crime rates. The evidence most cited was the low crime rates in nations with strong gun-control laws and the relatively low homicide rate in New York and other high-control environments as compared to Houston, Phoenix, and other low-control cities.[110] Advocates also raised sovereignty and social-order arguments when addressing militant groups and the riots.[111] The examination of the interstate movement of firearms to thwart state restrictions more closely approximated policy analysis than did other testimony to the various committees.

Destructive devices and machine guns received substantial attention in the 1965 Senate hearings, even though there was very little controversy about controlling the former, the latter being already under federal legal control.[112] After the reports of sniping during the Newark and Detroit riots, the focus shifted far more to social order.[113] On occasions, proponents challenged the most sacred sovereignty argument of opponents by questioning their interpretation of the Second Amendment as an absolute, individual right.[114] They did not, however, rely heavily upon a sovereignty argument, even when opponents continually cited the potential impact on hypothetical individuals. Advocates showed little interest in challenging the legitimacy of applying individual-level analysis to public policy or the language of individual rights. Instead, they generally attempted to minimize the potential impact of proposals on individuals. No doubt, this reflected the discomfort most Americans feel with regard to collective rights and state authority.

Gun-control opponents also addressed the crime-control paradigm with arguments that criminals would never comply with any gun law and cited the low homicide rate in low-control cities such as Milwaukee.[115] But opponents proved far more willing than advocates to shift from crime control to other conceptual frameworks. Their favorite was the sovereignty/individual-rights paradigm. Although opponents occasionally used self-defense as a means of invoking this context, they more often addressed individual rights. Repeatedly, opponents characterized the impact of proposed legislation as denying rights to individual gun owners.[116] In addition, opponents argued that the federal government would be intruding into the sovereignty of the states.[117] Curiously, some opponents concurrently advocated HR6137, a bill that would have made virtually every violent crime involving a firearm a federal offense.[118] For opponents, several key symbols were clearly of paramount importance: New York's Sullivan Law provided the ultimate symbol of evil.[119] It took on added importance during the period, when New Jersey passed a permissive licensing law that covered both long guns and handguns.[120] Opponents repeatedly invoked the symbols of freedom, individual rights, and the Constitution. During the 1965 hearings advocates displayed destructive devices such as rocket launchers, presumably in an effort to symbolically demonize the firearm trade.

No clear winner emerged from the gun-control policy battle of the 1960s. Control advocates succeeded in passing the GCA, largely due to events external to the policy arena. Upon first inspection the law appears to constitute a significant policy shift. Measured by impact, however, the policy shift appears more incremental than radical. At the law's passage, control advocates expressed concern with the fact that over 100,000 individuals and corporations held federal firearms licenses, and that at least a quarter of these licensees were not legitimately engaged in business.[121] Almost three decades later the number of dealer licenses had increased nearly threefold, with the majority still issued to persons not legitimately engaged in business.[122] The volume of firearm sales continued to increase after the passage of the law,[123] and few effective restrictions were placed on unlicensed traffickers in firearms.[124] Although activity by both advocates and opponents declined briefly with the passage of the GCA, both sides soon renewed their activities.

The failure to pass more restrictive and comprehensive legislation, despite the alignment of public opinion, a sympathetic press, and active administration support, raises a most interesting policy question. Although many have attributed this result entirely to the institutional power of the NRA, the record suggests more complex answers. At the Senate subcommittee level, personal conflicts between the ranking minority and majority members prevented compromise.[125] The full committee split evenly between support and opposition, but the chairman opposed gun control.[126] Since the primary momentum for action resided in the Senate, this severely reduced the probability of a more restrictive bill emerging from committee.

The Senate presented particular structural problems for gun-control legislation. The issue broke down largely on rural versus urban lines. The structure of the Senate provided rural legislators with disproportionate power to prevent passage of strict controls. A review of the hearings reveals that numerous senators and House members from rural states felt a need to not only oppose the Dodd and administration bills, but also to testify in committee against them.[127] The intense personal opposition of a few key members, such as John Dingell and Robert Sikes, reinforced the existing ideological and political reservations of their rural and conservative cohorts.[128] An additional center of resistance formed around ideological conservatives such as Strom Thurmond and Roman Hruska, who opposed the prevailing view that the interstate commerce clause could be interpreted to give the federal government power over acts within states.[129]

None of these obstacles might have proven insurmountable if public opinion had been translated into a focused demand for action, but it did not. With the exception of the short period after the Robert Kennedy assassination, the public displayed little active interest in the issue. Because opposition crossed party lines, party discipline proved ineffective for advancing control legislation, as it has until the early 1990s.[130] Much as with civil rights before the 1960s, a few key Democrats from Southern and rural areas proved critical to the opposition, even when the administration strongly supported the bill.

The lack of preparation and organization on the part of policy advocates, the administration, and the bureaucracy doubtless played a significant role in limiting their policy success. Political scientist Nelson Polsby cited the failure to pass more significant firearms legislation in 1968 as a classic example of failure of a policy initiative due to inadequate preparation by advocates.[131] The advocates lacked organization, and Vietnam and the War on Poverty occupied the majority of the administration's interest and resources. The jurisdictional split between Treasury and Justice exacerbated the lack of preparation and policy coordination by the bureaucracy.

That the passage of the GCA did not mark the beginning of an incremental process of increasing control seems less surprising in retrospect than many would have believed at the time. In many ways, 1968 marked the official end of an era. The election of Richard Nixon signaled the reversal of a trend toward an expanded federal role in domestic social policy that began with the 1932 election of Franklin Roosevelt. Although Nixon's rhetoric on decentralizing domestic policy-making and reversing the federal government's activism may have exceeded his actions, momentum had shifted. After a caretaker Ford administration, Jimmy Carter attained the presidency by campaigning against the Washington bureaucracy, only to be defeated four years later by the ultimate symbol of decentralization, Ronald Reagan. The 1970s brought the abolition of federal controls over airline fares and service, shipping rates, and saving-and-loan operations. Scholars began to question the assumptions of interest-group liberalism, and, by the end of the decade, many embraced public-choice theory.

Rather than the next incremental steps in gun control, the decade of the 1970s would witness the emphasis of government shift toward implementation of existing law, while interest groups, on both sides, solidified and intensified their positions.[132] If the measure of policy change is the degree to which it changes social behavior, then the policy changes of 1968 were modest.

• • •

CHAPTER EIGHT

A BUREAUCRACY UNPREPARED

THE GUN CONTROL ACT (GCA) became effective on December 16, 1968. Before the Alcohol and Tobacco Tax Division (ATTD) of the Internal Revenue Service (IRS) could implement the new law, it faced a number of administrative obstacles. The GCA mandated an amnesty period for registration of NFA firearms. Any person possessing a machine gun, sawed-off shotgun or rifle, silencer, destructive device, or certain other unusual firearms, could register it without tax payment or questions during the amnesty. In addition, ATTD, soon to be redesignated the Alcohol, Tobacco, and Firearms Division (ATF) had to contact all dealers licensed under the old Federal Firearms Act, both to educate them regarding the new law and to determine if they had valid business premises, while training and expanding its own staff.

Although the ATTD had a regulatory branch that licensed and supervised the alcohol industry, its law-enforcement component exercised responsibility over firearm dealer licensing and compliance as well as the registrations under the NFA.[1] Prior to 1969, IRS simply mailed out licenses to all applicants without review or investigation; thus ATTD possessed little licensing experience or apparatus with which to implement the new law. The majority of special investigators, later titled "special agents," possessed little knowledge of the firearm laws or licensing procedures. Composed primarily of former police officers, state troopers, state liquor agents, or border-patrol agents attracted by higher salaries and an opportunity to work outdoors, investigators were primarily assigned to the Southeastern region and adjacent states, where they concentrated on raiding stills and arresting moonshiners. The division's unusual structure combined this enforcement component with a regulatory component that differed in function, culture, and mission.[2] Thus ATTD possessed a unique structure. Although the investigators viewed themselves as a part of the federal law-enforcement establishment, the organization differed significantly from those other federal law-enforcement agencies lacking significant regulatory missions such as the Secret Service and Federal Bureau of Investigation (FBI). Even when compared to other agencies exercising enforcement and regulatory roles, the ATTD proved unique. In regulatory agencies with enforcement functions such as the Environmental Protection Agency, or an enforcement agency with regulatory functions such as the Drug Enforcement Administration, one culture and function dominated the agency. ATTD lacked a dominate function and thus a dominate organizational culture.[3]

Although nominally a division of the Internal Revenue Service, ATTD exercised substantial autonomy. The national office, or headquarters, set standards for hiring, training, and equipment. Operating control resided in the hands of the assistant regional commissioners for the Alcohol and Tobacco Tax Division, who worked directly for the regional commissioner of IRS. Unlike other IRS functions, ATTD employees did not come under the control of the powerful district directors of Internal Revenue. Thus the ATTD depended on IRS for general administrative support, but its field operations remained separate and distinct and its employees did not identify with the larger agency. The unique relationship with IRS also produced significant decentralization and fragmentation. Each region operated with great autonomy and different priorities.[4] This decentralized structure did not facilitate uniform implementation of the new law.

The ATTD generally benefited from good relations between its investigators and the majority of gun dealers, who primarily operated small hardware and sporting-goods stores. Most dealers willingly complied with the law, and the investigators often shared the dealers' interest in firearms, hunting, and fishing. The investigators viewed the dealer contacts as a temporary diversion and had no reason to be officious.[5] Thus most inspections proved to be a positive experience for most of the investigators and many of the dealers, fostering a number of personal friendships.[6] Although the inspection and education of dealers proved largely successful, the establishment of licensing sections at the regional offices did not. No support existed for computerization of records. Although IRS possessed vast experience and expertise in records control and management, the semi-autonomous status of the ATTD and the low priority of firearm-dealer licensing in an agency focused on revenue collection prevented application of this expertise to it.

Although the ATTD grew substantially between 1968 and 1972, little changed in its structure. The addition of jurisdiction jointly with FBI over the Explosive Control Act in 1970 accelerated a slow but steady shift of agency personnel from rural to urban areas. Still, the rural roots and Southern powerbase of the agency remained largely intact as evidenced by the fact of there being more agents in Georgia than in California.[7] In 1972 the Nixon administration removed the agency from IRS and designated it as the Bureau of Alcohol, Tobacco, and Firearms (ATF).[8] The administration cited management reasons, and conventional wisdom at the time assumed that IRS officials wanted to distance themselves from the controversial area of gun enforcement. However, the best available evidence indicates that the administration acted primarily for the purpose of creating a position for White House aid and former New York Police officer John Caufield.[9] Caufield served briefly as assistant director of ATF, but resigned after he became publicly linked with Watergate.[10]

Upon becoming an independent bureau in 1972, ATF transferred the firearm and explosive licensing functions from its law enforcement to its regulatory division. Although it was a rational division of labor from a management perspective, this change fractured the relationship between special agents and firearm dealers that had evolved from their routine contacts and inspections. Over the next several years ATF concentrated most of its law-enforcement resources on the prosecution of felons who acquired firearms in violation of the law, bombers, and possessors and makers of NFA firearms. Primarily focused on street criminals, these cases created little controversy and attracted little attention. However, ATF pursued some cases against unlicensed firearm traffickers and licensed firearm dealers. Beginning in 1977, the Justice Department issued prosecutive guidelines restricting federal prosecutions to cases involving federal interest.[11] This required ATF to focus its resources on investigation of violations that were not subject to local enforcement action. ATF interpreted this to mean bombing, arson fraud, organized crime, and illegal firearms trafficking. Although these cases never constituted the totality of ATF prosecutions, their impact on future policy proved significant.

The existing structure and resources, barely adequate to implement the GCA, could not have supported implementation of a more sweeping law—had one passed. ATF lacked the experience and resource base—both human and structural—to administer and enforce anything as significant as owner licensing or general gun registration.[12] Within the federal bureaucracy, few models existed that could be emulated. Both the IRS and Social Security Administration processed numbers of transactions similar to what a national gun licensing or registration would have required, but these agencies developed their operations progressively over many years and had accumulated massive resources. Both of these programs received extensive support from the private sector in the form of information from employers, and both experienced their greatest noncompliance among small-business operators and individuals. Virtually all retail firearm transactions involved small businesses or individuals. Citizens routinely fail to report income from casual transactions among individuals—the very type of transaction that occurs when one person sells or gives a gun to someone else. Likewise, illegal immigration and the employment of undocumented workers demonstrate the difficulty of controlling numerous individual actions, particularly in a country such as the United States that lacks a tradition of bureaucratic central administration and regulation of individual behavior. As examples, Congress has never considered, nor has any national politician advocated, a European-style national identity system nor has Congress implemented national health care.

RENEWED LEGISLATIVE ACTIVITY

Between the 1968 election and 1974 appointment of Edward Levi as attorney general, neither the Nixon nor Ford administrations displayed any interest in additional gun legislation.[13] Apparently assuming that Democratic support for gun control contributed to the growing alienation of white, blue-collar Democrats, particularly in the South and West, the Nixon administration focused its federal "war on crime" on drug enforcement, maintaining a low profile regarding gun control.[14] However, continuing reports and recommendations by national commissions on crime and violence kept the issue in the public arena, with repeated recommendations for more-stringent firearm-control laws.[15]

Even without encouragement from the administration, some in Congress actively pursued new legislation. In 1972 the Senate passed a bill restricting the manufacture of "Saturday night specials," but it failed to pass the House.[16] The legislation grew naturally out of a contradiction in the GCA, which prohibited the importation of firearms found "not suitable for sporting purposes" but failed to address the domestic manufacture of the same firearms. In order to implement the mandate, ATF established factoring criteria, which assigned points for specific features such as barrel length, adjustable sights, and safety devices. These criteria function, in fact, to exclude small, poorly-made handguns, sometimes called "Saturday night specials." ATF applied the criteria only to handguns, and accepted all long guns as suitable for sporting uses. Overseas manufacturers responded with minor design changes or by importing the parts and assembling the firearms in the United States.

The market availability of small, inexpensive handguns changed very little. Some in Congress believed that the importation of parts constituted a circumvention of the law and responded with a bill that applied the same "suitable for sporting purposes" standard to domestically manufactured firearms. The concept of minimum-quality standards for firearms had once received rather wide support in the pro-gun community.[17] The majority of firearm enthusiasts did not buy these inexpensive firearms, and tended to look upon them and their buyers with disdain. Some form of the Saturday-night-special legislation would very likely have passed, along with other minor modifications to the GCA, but for the emergence of a more militantly libertarian component within the NRA and overreach by some gun-control advocates. The NRA leadership began to feel pressure from its more libertarian wing, which viewed firearms control primarily as a sovereignty issue, and strictly subscribed to the slippery-slope argument that all firearms legislation constituted a step toward prohibition.[18] This argument gained legitimacy by the occasional pronouncements from a few highly visible control advocates.[19]

The Saturday-night-special effort marked the beginning of a new approach by control advocates to advance their agenda by reformulating and narrowing the issues. As bills evolved, the definition of Saturday night specials became progressively more inclusive, and the controls moved from manufacture to possession and transfer. In 1975 Senator Edward Kennedy introduced S.1447, which would have, in the senator's words, "banned the manufacture and possession of over 99.9 percent of all handguns."[20] Gun-control opponents had legitimate reason to believe that the advocates of Saturday-night-special legislation intended to eventually encompass restrictions on all handguns, which further reinforced the position of the libertarian faction of the NRA.

In 1975, shortly after his appointment, Attorney General Levi proposed a scheme that would have invoked federal restrictions on handgun sales and possession of handguns outside the home. The original proposal contained a peculiar and probably unworkable feature: The proposed restrictions would apply only in metropolitan areas that had specific levels of reported street crime.[21] Levi apparently offered this unprecedented proposal—a federal criminal law applicable to only certain communities—in the hope of avoiding the rural opposition to firearm controls while responding to the urban demand for such controls.[22] By the time a proposal reached Congress the administration had removed the regional prohibition concept.[23] The administration's bill—S.1880—increased controls and raised licensing fees for dealers, mandated a waiting period for handgun deliveries by dealers, and prohibited the manufacture of small handguns. Again, the term "Saturday night special" was used, but the definition applied to far-fewer guns than would have come under Senator Kennedy's bill.[24]

Levi's original proposal for restrictions applying only to high crime areas provides a stark example of policy advocates crafting legislation for compromise, even at the cost of internal consistency and rationality. The bill, as proposed to Congress, retained much of this character. Although it mandated a waiting period, it contained no system for checking buyers' criminal records during this period. The administration apparently hoped that the states would take advantage of the period and initiate purchaser screening. However, the states needed no federal action to institute purchaser screening or waiting periods, and many had shown no inclination to do so. Even the prohibition on small handguns begged the issue: The barrel length, set at four inches, would have prohibited handguns easily carried in a pocket, but not handguns easily concealed under a jacket. As with the NFA, GCA, and successive proposals, efforts to make the bill more politically palatable served to undermine its rationality, consistency, and utility.

Two proposals of the era failed to follow the pattern of compromise. Senator Philip Hart's (D-Mich.) S.750 prohibited the manufacture, importation, sale, and ownership of handguns except for a few categories of persons such as the police and organized competitive shooters.[25] Alternately, S.141, offered by Senator James McClure (R-Idaho), revoked the Gun Control Act of 1968 in its entirety.[26] Although neither of these bills came close to passing, they clearly staked out the intellectual parameters of the issue during the mid-1970s. Clearly, Senator Hart grounded his proposal on crime control[27]; Senator McClure, on the other hand, primarily invoked a sovereignty paradigm.[28]

None of the firearm legislation proposed during this period passed. Even relatively innocuous provisions failed for increasing control of licensed dealers and for differentiating between various types of dealers such as handgun, long gun, gunsmith, and ammunition with differing fees. The stiffening resistance of the gun lobby and its key supporters in Congress contributed significantly to this phenomenon. The failure to pass any bill in spite of administration support and a Democratic Congress probably owes much to the weak leadership of House subcommittee chairman John Conyers (D-Mich.).[29] By 1976, President Gerald Ford, facing a strong challenge for the presidential nomination from Ronald Reagan, began to shore up his image with conservatives and terminated all advocacy of gun legislation and closed the policy window.

FOCUS ON ENFORCEMENT

Driven by rising crime rates and increased national concerns about crime and violence, the Ford administration initiated a shift in implementation strategy of the existing gun laws. In the spring of 1975 Ford proposed adding 500 new ATF agents to 11 major metropolitan areas. These agents would focus entirely on firearm enforcement, with the goal of reducing the availability of firearms and the incidence of armed crime. Although it had minimal input in the details of the original policy proposal, ATF enthusiastically began planning for a massive expansion.[30] It appears the initiative derived from the perceived need to take visible action on crime before the 1976 elections, combined with aspects of Attorney General Levi's concept of focus on key metropolitan areas and the research and writing of Frank Zimring.[31]

The White House and Congress significantly reduced the resources for the proposed program between the time of the announcement and implementation. The reduced plan funded tests in 3 cities rather than the 11 cities originally proposed and added 180 ATF agents rather than the original 500. Washington, Chicago, and Boston were designated as test cites in this program, the Project Consolidated Urban Enforcement (CUE). In both Washington and Chicago, involuntary transfers from the Southeast region composed the majority of additional agents.[32] A decline in liquor violations had created an excess of agents in the South and CUE offered an easy solution. The agents primarily came from rural Southern backgrounds and expected to spend the rest of their lives in that setting. Many, resentful of their forced transfers to high-cost urban environments, responded by doing very little.[33] Lacking a coherent plan and limited by a weak law and inadequate resources, those agents who *did* apply themselves primarily pursued the only available strategy: They associated with local police and investigated routine gun cases against street criminals.[34] Because the project lacked any additional prosecutorial resources, even these routine cases often failed to reach the courts, and those that did often resulted in probationary sentences. Although ATF managed to obtain a favorable evaluation from an independent consulting firm, the project produced little discernable impact on violent crime,[35] but did have significant organizational impact on ATF. CUE marked the end of domination by the Southeast region, seven years after the agency had shifted from liquor to firearm enforcement.[36]

The high-profile application of resources for the enforcement of existing law did not signal a radical policy shift. With crime at record levels and a difficult campaign looming, the gun laws provided the administration with one of the few jurisdictions for a federal initiative against violent crime. Application of resources towards enforcing existing law offered the opportunity for visible action without expending political resources in a fight for new legislation. This allowed the administration to act decisively without becoming challenged or hindered by the legislative process. Even such long-time opponents of expanded federal jurisdiction as Senator Hruska supported increased enforcement of the existing statutes, and since liberal Democrats had generally lined up in support of gun control, their support was likely.[37] Unable to achieve consensus with new legislative approaches and new language, the administration tried shifting the focus to resource allocation and implementation. Given the administration's willingness to reduce resources applied to CUE after the presidential announcement and before implementation, one might even conclude that the announcement itself and *not* the program constituted the primary objective.

ADVOCACY INTENSIFIED

At the same time that some in Congress and the administration pursued a new consensus on gun control, external events further reduced the likelihood of achieving even a modest compromise. The emergence of two gun-control advocacy groups convinced both advocates and opponents alike that new national regulation of firearms probably loomed in the near future.[38] For many in the NRA, the emergence of these interest groups, combined with the 1974 congressional and 1976 presidential elections, fanned fears that all gun control constituted a step on the slippery slope toward gun prohibition. Ironically, a growing trend toward suspicion and hostility to government in general and federal expansion in particular actually favored opponents of gun control over advocates, but neither group perceived this at the time. The resulting rise in expectations among advocates and fears among opponents ensured increased conflict over gun policy—a conflict shaped and intensified by the administration's rather benign proposal to expanded ATF enforcement resources and shift its focus to urban crime.

The emergence of advocacy groups focused solely on promoting the elimination or strict control of privately owned handguns. Combined with legislation such as Senator Kennedy's sweeping Saturday-night-special bill and Senator Hart's handgun-prohibition bill, the new groups energized and legitimated the opponents of gun control. NRA membership, which had increased greatly during the Dodd hearings, again accelerated.[39] The NRA established an official lobbying arm and dropped all pretense of seeking compromise. In 1977 a militant, libertarian faction led by Neal Knox and Harlon Carter seized control of the NRA at the Cincinnati convention (see chapter 4). A core group of board members, led by John Dingell and Harlon Carter, had pushed the NRA to increase its opposition to both new and existing legislation and the implementation of the GCA.[40] Although the leadership of the NRA had long held reservations about gun control, the pre-1977 leadership was not primarily libertarian; most had served as civil servants or military officers for many years before coming to the NRA. The new consensus in the NRA formed around categorical opposition to all gun regulation.[41]

The libertarian purists viewed gun control primarily in the context of individual sovereignty. In the words of Neal Knox, "gun control is about power, the person with the guns has the power."[42] This paradigm interlocked closely with a worldview or cultural paradigm that had long dominated the NRA. In its more benign form this paradigm extolled the values of outdoor life, shooting, and hunting. This worldview took on a harder edge as it merged with the radical libertarian sovereignty paradigm in an environment of paranoia. The resulting process mirrored the aftermath of a disruption in the balance of power between coexisting but competitive cultures. The world became divided into allies and opponents, with opponents' every action viewed as hostile and sinister and any call for compromise or conciliation viewed as weakness. In such an environment, leadership must harness the fear and cultural hostility or lose control. In the case of the NRA, the leadership lost control and was replaced. As the internal structure of the NRA shifted toward an emphasis on conflict, ATF and the gun-control-lobby activities fueled the fires of paranoia.

In classic bureaucratic form, ATF management sought widespread publicity of their expanded enforcement activities in pursuit of an improved public image that would translate into organizational legitimacy and support.[43] Gun-control opponents mistakenly interpreted this publicity as one component in a coordinated campaign by ATF and the administration to pass restrictive legislation and ultimately to prohibit private ownership of firearms.[44] In fact, ATF managers had far more modest objectives; neither the Ford nor Carter administrations had any willingness to expend political resources on gun control, and ATF management never had access to major policy-makers in either administration.

Concurrently, the pro-control groups assumed a high profile that attracted far more attention than their numbers justified. Even experienced politicians mistakenly read the development of these groups as a major shift in the political dynamics of gun control.[45] Apparently, both opponents and advocates misread the nature and implications of the "Watergate Congress." Neal Knox reported that many in the NRA interpreted the 1974 election as a precursor for strict gun control, a view shared by control-advocate Michael Beard.[46] In retrospect, Watergate exacerbated suspicion of government action far more than it encouraged liberal activism. The popular media seems to have sensed this before the politicians and responded with accounts of conspiracy in high places in films and books such as *The Three Days of the Condor*. Rather than pursuing new social legislation, the post-1974 Congress began to focus more and more on its oversight function.[47]

The 1976 election of Jimmy Carter signaled growing public distrust of official Washington as much as it did a mandate for the Democratic party agenda of social action. Carter campaigned as an outsider to Washington, intent on fixing ineffective government. Viewed from this perspective, Carter's election becomes another step in the conservative political trend that began with the 1968 election and culminated in the election of Ronald Reagan in 1980. Unfortunately for ATF and the advocates of gun control, they misread or ignored the signs. Although the opponents of gun control also misinterpreted the 1974 and 1976 elections, their response served to strengthen their position. Motivated toward conflict without compromise, the new NRA leadership capitalized on the perceived liberal shift in Congress and the administration, the advocacy of the new gun-control organizations, and the elevated profile of ATF to energize its base, expand its membership, and consolidate its leadership. The more attention the activities of ATF and proposals for control received, the stronger and more intransigent the NRA became.[48]

Neither ATF nor Ford and Carter political appointees appreciated the intensity of the developing opposition in the NRA and among its public supporters. Few in the administrations had much knowledge or interest in the NRA, and ATF managers concerned themselves primarily with seeking wider public attention as a means of expanding their status and resources. ATF relations with the NRA began to deteriorate after the passage of the GCA, a trend made apparent by the increased criticism of ATF in *The American Rifleman* after the Kenyon Bellew incident. Still, ATF Director Rex Davis and his successor G. R. Dickerson both believed they could negotiate with the NRA.[49] A long history of amicable relations with the liquor industry had produced an organizational culture in ATF favoring accommodation and harmonious relationships with interest groups.[50] Dickerson lacked an ATF background but had worked for many years as a regulator in the Customs Service, which also enjoyed harmonious relations with commercial interests. Although the gun lobby differed substantially in structure and purpose from the liquor lobby,

ATF's predecessors had maintained reasonably harmonious relations for many years with the NRA.[51] In spite of failing to understand the magnitude of the coming conflict with the gun lobby, ATF and Treasury leadership displayed more caution than did their counterparts in the Department of Justice, who openly advocated Saturday-night-special legislation and appeared to be cavalier in their attitude toward gun interests.[52]

AN END RUN WITH REGULATIONS

In January 1977 the incoming Carter administration faced demands for action both from the gun-control lobby and from the failure of twice-Senate-passed Saturday-night-special legislation to pass the House. Rather than make a repeated attempt at new legislation, the Carter administration opted for the alternative tactic of expanding the regulations authorized under the GCA and promulgated by the Department of Treasury. Initiative for this action apparently came from the White House, presumably as a less-risky means of achieving some visible movement in policy.[53] Clearly, navigating a bill through both houses of Congress posed significant problems. While offering less potential for comprehensive action, change by administrative decree undoubtedly appeared far easier. Although the impetus to take action came from the White House, the form of the proposals was crafted at the Treasury Department, with heavy input from ATF.[54]

Deliberately crafted to arouse minimal resistance, the proposals required manufactures to identify all new firearms with unique serial numbers that included coding identifying the manufacturer and model of the gun, similar to the system already in use for automobiles. They also required military personnel to obtain prior authority to bring firearms into the United States when returning from foreign tours, and required licensed dealers and manufactures to report gun thefts to ATF. The most controversial proposal required licensees to file quarterly reports of all firearm transactions.[55] In an effort to minimize controversy, the reports of firearms dispositions specifically excluded any information on names or addresses of the retail buyers and thus would contain only the identity of dealers receiving firearms.[56]

No one in the administration or ATF foresaw that such a limited and conservative set of proposals would provoke significant reaction.[57] Agencies proposing changes in federal regulations must first publish the proposed changes and solicit public comment. The NRA utilized this period to mount an active campaign of opposition in which the regulations were portrayed as a "centralized national firearms registration system."[58] During the initial comment period, ATF received over 175,000 letters overwhelmingly in opposition to the regulations.[59] The comment period was extended and ATF ultimately received 350,000 letters, which ran 38 to 1 against the regulations.[60] Examination of the letters revealed that the majority of opponents phrased their objections in terms of confiscation, registration, or violation of the Second Amendment rather than in response to the specifics of the proposals.[61] Apparently the response had far more to do with the gun lobby's ability to marshal up constituents and symbolic opposition to gun control than the actual proposals themselves, a point not lost on the NRA.[62]

The opposition focused on reporting of transactions by licensed firearm dealers. The GCA required licensees to maintain such records as prescribed by the secretary and to make such reports on those records as the secretary might prescribe by regulation.[63] This section theoretically allowed ATF to invoke by regulation a report-of-sale system and waiting period, although it never contemplated such a bold action.[64]

The libertarian perspective of gun-control opponents made suspicion of regulatory discretion almost inevitable, a concern that surfaced during the Dodd hearings.[65] Although the proposed regulations would not have required the reporting of buyers' names, they would have established a precedent for requiring reports from dealers. ATF linked the regulations to a plan for computerizing transfers of firearms between dealers, which it justified primarily as a means for improving gun tracing. Although ATF's proposed database would not have contained the identity of most buyers, it would have contained some individual names from gun-trace information, imports, and out-of-business records. By computerizing the information, ATF could begin gun traces with the retail seller of the gun and not the manufacturer, thus saving time and guarding against gaps caused by dealers who had gone out of business.[66] Secondarily, to facilitate audits ATF would have had an automated record of a dealer's acquisitions.[67] Unfortunately for ATF, opponents used the agency's past claims of tracing success as a means of contesting the need for the regulations.[68] As repeatedly was proven the case, ATF efforts to develop public support and legitimacy though publicizing its enforcement activities was detrimental to any effort to strengthen gun-control legislation.

Control opponents interpreted the proposed regulations and the resulting computer database as the "camel's nose in the tent," and some believed the regulations constituted the first phase of a comprehensive ATF–Carter administration plan for gun registration—a position still held by Knox.[69] Knox has told me that memoranda between Director Davis and the Treasury Department documented the plan in detail, an assertion made by Representative John Ashbrook (R-Ohio) to Former Assistant Secretary Rex Davis in 1978. Davis stated that Ashbrook held up a copy(-ies) of the alleged memorandum(a) but refused to show it to Davis.[70] Both Rex Davis and Richard Davis denied the existence of any such plan or memoranda in their interviews. During my years at ATF headquarters and in later research and interviews, I have located neither evidence of such a plan nor any person who can confirm its existence. I am personally convinced that no comprehensive plan existed in ATF. ATF management never demonstrated any interest in long-term policy planning nor did it display a willingness to take risky positions. What probably happened was that some advocates in Treasury or the White House saw the proposals as a means of testing the political waters for more comprehensive action. Under the GCA, ATF possessed authority to require dealers to submit copies of their ATF Form 4473s, which identified the gun sold and the buyer, but national registration would have required legislation. This is not a distinction without a difference. Registration would require gun owners to register the firearms already in their possession and that private individuals report all transfers.

Energized by the fight over regulations, the NRA began to develop an active strategy of rolling back the GCA and not just opposing new legislation.[71] The opposition to new regulations constituted the first battle in an extended campaign. When ATF Director Rex Davis testified in appropriations hearings that the computerization of the data would cost $4.2 million, which ATF would take from its existing budget, the subcommittee, following the direction of Chairman Tom Steed, cut $4.2 million from ATF's budget for the next fiscal year.[72] The committee's action transmitted a clear message that was not lost on ATF. For years afterwards the agency avoided even discussing computers in public and lagged far behind other agencies in the automation of information.[73] Congress included language in fiscal year (FY) 1979 appropriations legislation blocking implementation of the regulations, which the administration subsequently abandoned. As a result of these events both ATF and Treasury for years avoided any association with new regulations or legislation. Previously, ATF management had avoided close association with gun-control proposals. After this experience it became compulsive about disassociating itself from the political process or new legislation.

Although he assumed leadership of ATF at the height of the NRA attack, NRA life member G. R. Dickerson believed he could reach a reasonable accommodation with the NRA.[74] In spite of its retreat from offering new legislation or administrative regulations related to guns,[75] other administration policies continued to inadvertently exacerbate the conflict with the gun lobby. Jimmy Carter built his campaign on rationalizing management of the federal government. The cornerstone of the rationalization effort was to be a massive reorganization and simplification of the government structure. The administration got as far as a comprehensive study of federal agencies and their functions, which would have transferred the responsibility for firearm enforcement to the Department of Justice, but failed to implement virtually any of the reorganization proposals as a result of congressional opposition.[76] Although the administration failed at large-scale reorganization and rationalization, it had more success in changing policy within existing agencies.

Ironically, a classic conservative policy initiative most aggravated the relations with the gun lobby.[77] In its efforts to limit the scope and size of the federal role, the administration mandated that federal law-enforcement agencies and prosecutors restrict their efforts to cases that met a test of "federal interest." The concept of federal interest had long existed. In law enforcement, it had once restricted federal law enforcement to suppressing counterfeiting, tax fraud, and treason. The concept had been greatly expanded during the 1930s with new federal jurisdiction, and again during the Nixon administration, when emphasis was placed on violent crime and street-level drug trafficking. Beginning in 1977, directives ordered all U.S. Attorneys to set clear guidelines and stay within them. The Office of Management and Budget utilized the budget process to enforce policy guidelines on all federal law-enforcement agencies. The administration terminated Project CUE and mandated that ATF develop a comprehensive plan.

Because historically ATF had concentrated on street criminals—who did not meet the administration's criteria of organized crime, public corruption, major drug trafficking, or white-collar crime—the agency had limited options. ATF responded by concentrating on commercial fraud arsons, bombings, possession of guns by organized crime members, and a firearm strategy termed "interdiction." The latter consisted of efforts to interdict the flow of guns to criminals. Although CUE had been conceptualized as such an effort, most of the work done by agents assigned to the CUE test cities involved felons with guns, bombers, and illegal possessors of sawed-off shotguns and automatic weapons. This time the administration made clear that business as usual would not suffice. Unfortunately for ATF, the traffic in firearms did not divide into distinct lines of legal and illegal: Illegal transactions sometimes did not involve criminals, and guns used in crime could often be legally obtained. Even the illegal sales to persons intent on illegal uses were usually co-mingled with numerous less-nefarious transactions. Any effort to restrict the access by criminals to firearms required efforts directed at unlicensed and licensed dealers.

CHALLENGING OLD ASSUMPTIONS

For the issue of gun control, the 10 years beginning in 1968 started with apparent momentum and high expectations from advocates. It ended with advocates on the defensive and the opponents emboldened and empowered. The expected incremental model had not materialized. Implementation strategies had increased opposition, while efforts at breaking the impasse through regulation or redefinition increased conflict. Apparently, Congress interpreted the use of administrative regulations as an effort to bypass congressional legislative prerogatives and therefore responded with hostility. Lacking adequate constituencies in the administration, Congress, and the public to prevail, the proposed regulations served only to escalate fear among stakeholders and empower opponents. The attempt to pursue a political goal without adequate political resources had weakened the movement, not strengthened it. In particular, the administration displayed little willingness to pursue gun control at political cost. All of these conclusions must be examined in the context of the period. A retrospective knowledge of the changing political tide that would carry to ascendancy Ronald Reagan and the libertarian wing of the Republican party provides us with insights denied to advocates and policymakers at the time.

Yet, many of the patterns of the 1970s have reoccurred. As proposals moved from abstract concepts to specific proposals with potential impacts on real people, support ebbed and opposition stiffened, a pattern observable in later state initiatives in California and Washington.[78] Although the Clinton administration finally broke the pattern of avoiding new control proposals, the bureaucracy has remained timid in its participation. Opponents continue to view all control initiatives as part of an incremental move toward prohibition, and the existence of advocacy groups in support of gun control has failed to shift the balance of power in Congress. The leadership of the NRA and other opponents used the existence of pro-control advocacy groups, legislative and administrative control initiatives, and heightened enforcement of existing law to strengthen and legitimatize their positions and solidify their base. This same pattern continued as evidenced by the reaction to the Brady Law and the Waco raid.

• • •

CHAPTER NINE

REACTION

I MPLEMENTATION OF THE GUN-CONTROL ACT (GCA) and political efforts to incrementally expand on the GCA toward more extensive gun regulation upset the equilibrium of prior years at a time when the public trust in government, particularly federal government, solutions to social problems experienced a rapid decline. The interaction of these emerging public attitudes with forces triggered by bureaucratic implementation of the GCA and political pursuit of the "next incremental step" in gun regulation generated reactions that dominated the next wave of events relating to gun control.

THE BUREAUCRACY EVOLVES

In 1976 ATF eliminated its regional law-enforcement structure and the position of regional director. Although the agency retained some regulatory and administrative functions at the regional level, it now centralized policy-making in its Washington headquarters. While this reorganization marked a shift in management style from decentralized regionalism to centralized, rational bureaucracy, real change came slowly. Many agents perceived the new policy of interdiction and earlier Project CUE as one continuous process designed to destroy their old way of life. CUE, the first national policy initiative of the new bureau, had closed small offices in the Southeast region and adjacent states and reassigned agents to urban areas. Just as this process had been completed, the new interdiction policy mandated that agents shift from work on individual criminal violators to firearm-trafficking operations.

In some parts of the country the earlier transition from liquor to firearms and explosives enforcement had gone smoothly. Good relations with local police and U.S. Attorney's offices had allowed the agents to shift their efforts to street-level criminals with relative ease. The new shift to interdiction (chapter 8) proved another matter. While Project CUE primarily affected offices in the Southeast, interdiction altered priorities and operations nationwide. Throughout the late 1970s ATF continued to close offices in less-populated areas and move agents to larger metropolitan areas or firearm "source states." These states with few or no gun regulations provided illegal traffickers with an easy means for buying guns to transport into more restrictive states. ATF traces of guns seized in restrictive states and other nations repeatedly revealed retail dealers in Ohio, Virginia, Florida, the Carolinas, and Texas as origins of the guns. ATF concentrated much of its effort on dealers in these source states, who appeared to be engaged in supplying guns to interstate or international traffickers. This change in priorities—from cases involving felons with firearms or sawed-off shotguns to gun dealers—undercut the agency's close alliance with local police in firearm-source states, who cared little about problems that materialized in another state or the nation at large. These local officials had little interest in the actions of gun dealers, with whom they usually had good relations and from whom they often received discounts on firearms and shooting supplies. Local law enforcement, particularly in the South and border states, had come to depend upon ATF assistance in prosecuting street criminals, particularly violent offenders. This dependence grew out of a shortage of resources on the part of local agencies and a lack of gun laws at the state level. In some areas the federal courts and prosecutors had devoted substantial time to the prosecution of illicit liquor cases and made the transition to firearms when moonshine began to decline. U.S. Attorneys often prosecuted ordinary street criminals for federal gun charges in lieu of state prosecutions for more substantive crimes, and ATF investigative resources often aided in the investigations of a variety of state crimes. Ironically, gun-control opponents characterized the shift to investigation of gun trafficking as evidence of the ATF's hostility toward gun ownership. In reality, the vast majority of agents viewed themselves as police officers and preferred to work on cases that enhanced their relations with local police and their image as crime fighters; few had any position on gun control.[1]

In spite of reservations by most agents and significant internal opposition, ATF changed its way of doing business during the Carter administration, particularly in relation to firearm enforcement. Agents directed most of their efforts either at arson or explosives cases or investigation of illegal transactions by licensed dealers, trafficking by unlicensed dealers, stolen gun trafficking, and international trafficking in firearms. Investigations of felons for firearm possession or possession of illegal firearms primarily involved defendants associated with other illegal enterprises who were deemed worthy of federal interest such as drug-trafficking organizations, organized crime, or criminal gangs.[2] Storefront sting operations directed at stolen guns and concentrating on gangs and organized crime created very little controversy. On the other hand, investigations of licensed and unlicensed dealers, particularly unlicensed dealers operating at guns shows, exacerbated gun-owner fears and provided the NRA and associated groups with clear "evidence" of the evolving attack on gun ownership.

Primarily white, middle-aged, and long-time residents of rural or suburban communities, the defendants in trafficking cases seldom had serious prior criminal records. Almost all belonged to the NRA, and many belonged to more strident organizations such as the Second Amendment Foundation. They benefited from both public empathy and organized interest-group support. The nature of the violations did little to demonize the defendants and added to the controversy. The most intense reaction by gun-control opponents centered on two issues: the definition of "engaging in the business," and a practice known as "straw purchase."[3]

The GCA included no precise definition of "engaging in the business." Historically, the courts had defined it as devoting time and attention for profit. ATF and state liquor agencies with very little controversy had interpreted any sale of alcoholic beverage for profit in this manner. Although the firearm and liquor control might appear similar, ATF found that the alcohol precedent provided a poor guide for predicting reaction to enforcement of gun laws. Gun enthusiasts had freely bought and sold guns for many years in much the same way that others bought and sold antiques and other collectibles. No clear line existed between avocation and vocation, nor between collectors' items and other firearms. As the gun market grew during the 1960s and 1970s, gun shows evolved from events for collectors to display and trade rare and unusual guns into swap meets for guns and associated items. Gun shows became magnets for unlicensed firearm dealers. Although many innocent transactions took place at these events, they provided cover for large-scale unlicensed dealers and provided an easy source of untraceable firearms for criminals and violent militants. Agents repeatedly traced guns to gun shows, where the trail ended, and militant publications even recommended purchasing guns at gun shows to avoid detection.[4]

The administrative controls for liquor differed in several ways from those created under the GCA for firearms. Alcohol beverage regulation and enforcement primarily resided with the states, which granted the licensing agencies substantial discretion on issuance of licenses. The states largely ignored firearms dealing. All alcohol sales were normally restricted exclusively to licensees, although law or tradition usually allowed special exceptions for one-day events. Neither federal nor most state laws controlled incidental sales of firearms among unlicensed individuals. Liquor licenses served primarily to restrict the location and circumstances of sales, but did not impose any record-keeping requirements on sellers. Thus, liquor licenses were generally valued assets to be coveted and protected. The GCA provided no restrictions on the number or location of firearms licenses, granted no discretion to ATF on the issuance of licenses, and imposed significant record-keeping requirements on licensees. Thus firearm-dealer licenses did not become a valuable commodity, since selling without a license reduced restrictions and overhead, and dealers could obtain a license at any time the need arose. A license allowed the dealer to order new guns from wholesalers and to deal openly from a public premises[5]; on the other hand, an unlicensed dealer enjoyed certain advantages over licensed dealers, including the avoidance of sales taxes, record keeping, and local and state waiting periods. Many buyers sought out unlicensed dealers for these reasons.

The law required ATF to issue a license to virtually any adult applicant other than felons or other firearm-prohibited categories so long as the applicant declared an intention to engage in the firearms business from a premises. Since no means existed to confirm an applicant's intent in advance, ATF attempted to implement this requirement retroactively by refusing to renew licenses when an inspection revealed that the licensee did not carry on a regular volume of sales nor had a business premises. In some cases, ATF refused to renew licenses because a dealer made only two or three sales, usually to friends or relatives. This put ATF in the position of denying license renewal because a dealer made only two or three sales, while concurrently prosecuting unlicensed dealers who sold two or three firearms to undercover agents. Although not actually the contradiction they appeared to be, these concurrent activities set ATF up for severe criticism. In fact, unlicensed dealers did not sell just two or three firearms, but regularly offered many more for sale. Undercover agents would make a single purchase from the firearms offered and then repeat this practice several times to demonstrate a continuing enterprise. Limits on the availability of investigative funds and undercover agents usually constrained the agents to limit purchases to the minimum number necessary (commonly three or four) to show a pattern.

Opponents regularly cited these cases as examples of ATF using three sales to "make someone a dealer." Defendants routinely denied selling any guns other than those purchased by undercover agents. Although prosecutors could introduce evidence of defendants' offers of additional guns to refute this defense, gun-control opponents could omit such evidence from their descriptions of the cases without committing any falsehood. Undoubtedly, some overzealous agents pursued marginal cases and in some cases may have come close to the practice of entrapment. However, this did not constitute either policy or prevailing practice.[6] In addition to management controls, the U.S. Attorneys acted as a very effective level of review, refusing to prosecute cases that did not appear to have jury appeal. Agents knew that the cost of "burning" an assistant U.S. Attorney with a bad case would be a loss of credibility and the rejection of future cases.

In addition to the controversy over criminal prosecutions, seizure of firearms offered for sale became a focus of gun-lobby concern. Under the existing law, any item "used or intended to be used" in violation of the law was subject to civil seizure and forfeiture. Thus any firearm offered for sale by an unlicensed dealer or any firearm offered for sale without proper record keeping by a licensed dealer could be seized and forfeited. Preponderance of the evidence, rather than just "beyond a reasonable doubt," constituted the standard of proof for civil forfeiture. Thus a not-guilty verdict or failure to prosecute did not preclude the forfeiture of guns offered for sale under the lesser standard of proof. Seizures often involved thousands of dollars worth of guns and generated accusations that ATF was seizing entire gun collections.

The "straw-purchase" issue also resulted primarily from poorly crafted legislation. Sales by dealers to certain categories of people such as felons and minors constituted a crime. Nothing, however, prevented buyers from giving or selling the gun to a prohibited person.[7] The dealer could not be held liable for the actions of the purchaser, and the law's authority did not extend to the purchaser—a loophole recognized during congressional hearings but unresolved due to unwillingness to address private transactions.[8]

However, a dealer who participated in the agreement became a party to a criminal conspiracy and was criminally liable. In aggravated cases, out-of-state purchasers would contact a dealer in order to purchase multiple handguns, and the dealer would provide someone to execute the forms, thus effecting a "straw purchase." Knowing that the buyer of record served only to facilitate a false record, the dealer conspired to make delivery to an out-of-state resident and to falsify his records. More often, the buyer brought his or her own straw purchaser to the dealer. In such instances, successful prosecution of a dealer depended upon convincing a jury that the dealer knew the actual nature of the transaction. The government could often demonstrate that the dealer falsified his or her records, even when it could not prove that the dealer knew of the recipient's prohibited status as a felon or out-of-state resident. Recording the straw purchaser in the records as the buyer when knowing the third-party recipient to be the buyer in fact, completed the crime without any showing that the dealer knew or believed the recipient to be in a prohibited status. As with unlicensed dealer cases, some agents pursued cases that probably did not warrant prosecution, but assistant U.S. Attorneys and sympathetic local juries mediated against this. The extensive publicity given to straw-purchaser cases by the NRA and other organizations convinced substantial numbers of dealers that ATF undercover agents routinely approached dealers at random in an effort to entrap them in an illegal transaction. In reality, very few dealers were actually approached.[9] It is likely that NRA rhetoric accomplished a higher level of compliance with the law than ATF ever could have done.

The NRA did not focus attention on these alleged abuses of ATF in order to ensure compliance with the existing law. The accusations against ATF provided a key component in a general attack on the GCA. The emerging NRA leadership intended to reverse the trend toward federal gun control by accomplishing the revocation of the GCA. Congressional opponents of gun control, including Representatives Ashbrook and Dingell and Senator McClure, had advocated the repeal of the GCA for several years. A steady decline in public and congressional trust of the bureaucracy in the aftermath of Watergate and the Vietnam War provided a favorable milieu. The shift in congressional focus from legislation to oversight and an aroused body of gun enthusiasts energized by fear opened the policy window. The 1978 elections had signaled a continuing conservative move in the voting public, and ATF's prosecution of licensed and unlicensed dealers had provided a visible "victim" of gun control. Individual victims play a crucial role in the policy process by allowing the development of a narrative, a morality play, which humanizes the issue as no theoretical or statistical argument can. In this morality play, ATF assumed the critical role of villain.

OVERSIGHT AS THEATER

The stage for the coming drama was to be the congressional oversight hearings. The new director, G. R. "Bob" Dickerson, arrived on the scene with the battle already joined. He immediately assumed a strategy of reasonable compromise, assuming he could pacify ATF's critics by admitting past errors and guaranteeing future corrections.[10] He became the victim of his own strategy. By 1979 the Carter administration exercised little influence in Congress, even among Democrats. Individual members pursued strategies of survival with little concern for the administration. Ironically, Senator Dennis DeConcini (D-Ariz.) chaired the first in a series of hearings in 1979. A former state attorney general and county prosecutor, DeConcini had long shown an interest in Treasury enforcement agencies and eventually became ATF's greatest advocate and protector on the "Hill."[11]

The NRA devoted considerable resources to preparing its case against ATF. In addition to lobbying individual members of Congress and generating constituent input, it hired a retired assistant commissioner of customs, Mike Acree, and his investigative staff to review ATF cases in several Eastern states and render an opinion on the propriety of ATF operations.[12] It had also retained Phoenix attorney David Hardy, who produced a monograph titled *BATF's War on Civil Liberties: The Assault on Gun Owners.*[13] Both Acree and Hardy engaged in advocacy research. In addition to reviewing cases over a nine-year period, they solicited input and reports from any person who felt abused by ATF. They sought evidence of ATF misconduct, with particular focus on firearm cases in which the defendants were found not guilty or a judge either dismissed the action or expressed displeasure with the government's case or tactics. The examinations made no effort to compare ATF actions with those of other agencies nor to obtain ATF's version of events or examine cases in which ATF acted properly.[14]

In much the same way that gun-control advocates used individual acts of violence to demonize gun ownership and guns, the NRA and other gun-control opponents used individual acts by ATF to demonize the gun laws.[15] By

depending on the accounts of defendants and seeking out negative information and interpretations, they produced a record of questionable reliability and
zero balance.[16] This pattern began with the Bellew incident in 1971 and has
continued since.[17] Characterizations of ATF and the gun laws as threats to civil
liberties routinely avoid any comparison with other enforcement activities.
Even a cursory examination reveals that the civil liberties' implications of drug
enforcement dwarfs those of firearm enforcement by any measure.

During the hearings of 1979 and 1980—just as in later years—ATF had
only a supporting role in the morality play. Critics reserved their greatest wrath
for the GCA, which they characterized as an evil and ambiguous law that
guaranteed the entrapment and persecution of innocent citizens.[18] ATF and
the Department of Treasury assumed a largely passive role during the hearings.
Much to the consternation of the majority of ATF employees, Dickerson
assumed a strategy of avoiding direct confrontation over the facts and promis-
ing that such problems would not occur in the future. Treasury and the rest of
the administration showed little interest in alienating NRA allies in Congress
over ATF or gun control. Thus the record consisted primarily of accusations
against ATF, with little response or explanation. As an example, Acree's conclusions about the proportion of ATF cases directed at felons receiving firearms
and the typical defendant in a firearm case reveal either incompetence or dis-
honesty, yet received little response.[19]

Although evidence of direct attitudinal change in individual members of
Congress remains elusive, several outcomes appear to be directly attributable
to the hearings and the NRA campaign associated with them. They energized
the NRA's core constituency, solidified its primary position in the gun lobby,
and aided in increasing its membership to almost two million by 1980.[20] In
addition, the hearings established an "official record" of abuse by ATF that
would be repeatedly cited.[21] This "record" created "victims" of gun control
with human faces and provided cover for any congressman voting to weaken
the GCA, laying the groundwork for the NRA to pursue its legislative goal,
the Firearm Owners' Protection Act or the McClure-Volkmer bill. Unlike
previous bills sponsored by Representative Volkmer and Senator McClure, this
one would not revoke the GCA, but would only render it impotent.

MOVING WITH THE TIDE

The 1980 election clearly demonstrated a continuing rightward movement of
the American electorate. A Republican coalition built on strong defense, low
taxes, and social conservatism in control of the White House and Senate hardly
boded well for gun control. In the Senate, the push for the McClure-Volkmer
bill became much more intense and the administration immediately began to
review the status of ATF. During the campaign Ronald Reagan had expressed
concern for ATF "entrapment" of legitimate gun owners and received NRA

support.[22] Conventional wisdom in Washington after the 1980 election was that ATF would be abolished as an agency.[23] In an effort to preserve most of ATF's trained personnel, Treasury officials from past and future administrations advanced a plan to merge ATF's law-enforcement functions and personnel with the U.S. Secret Service.[24] The White House approved the proposal, no doubt believing it would pacify the gun lobby while avoiding the hostility of law enforcement.

Presumably the merger would reduce the visibility of the controversial firearm-enforcement function, while it approximately doubled the law-enforcement staff and expanded the investigative jurisdiction of the Secret Service. The Secret Service would benefit both from enhanced jurisdiction and a greatly enlarged pool of agents during the peak demands of campaign years. The two agencies had a long history of close association, and ATF provided the Secret Service with substantial manpower during campaign years. Thus, the management of Secret Service supported the plan; with its leadership in disarray, ATF offered little initial resistance to it.[25]

Because the merger required no specific statutory authorization, the Secretary issued a directive without any consultation with Congress and active planning for the merger began.[26] At first, the firearms lobby appeared to be somewhat confused regarding an appropriate response. It had called for the end of ATF and been successful beyond its expectations; yet, the loss of ATF meant the loss of an important symbol. The gun lobby had expended extensive resources demonizing ATF and convincing constituents that the agency posed a threat to their civil liberties. ATF's continued existence had become more important to the NRA than to the majority of ATF's employees.[27] The NRA avoided public reaction for several weeks and the merger seemed assured. In all likelihood the merger would have occurred but for the intervention of the liquor lobby, which immediately brought great pressure to bear on Congress to stop it.[28] Senate hearings were quickly called for under the chairmanship of James Abnor of South Dakota. Once the hearings began, the firearms lobby recovered its composure and opposed the merger on the grounds that nothing would change if the law remained.

The administration dropped the merger plan after Congress included specific language prohibiting it in the fiscal year (FY) 1982 budget authorization. Subsequently the gun lobby pushed forth a plan to reduce ATF to a mere token agency, but neither Congress nor the administration showed great enthusiasm for it. The administration and Congress did reduce ATF staffing somewhat in the aftermath of the merger, but in a strange turnaround, Senator Abnor, an NRA favorite and congressional advisor to the Second Amendment Foundation, assumed the role of ATF patron.[29] By the end of the Bush administration ATF had rebuilt to an all-time high staffing level, and enjoyed more support and attention than at any time in its short history.[30]

PROPOSITION 15

The other event that influenced the evolution of firearm-control policy significantly during the early 1980s occurred not in Washington but in California. Once again, misinterpretation of the political climate proved critical. This time, the pro-control forces did the misreading. A small group of California liberal activists led by John Phillips, a Los Angeles attorney, and Victor Palmieri, a well-connected entrepreneur, hatched the concept for Proposition 15, which they qualified for the November 1982 ballot with little or no help from gun-control organizations.[31] Largely modeled on a 1976 Washington, DC, law, the initiative would have frozen the number of handguns in California, allowing those who had guns to keep them but denying the acquisition of new handguns. The NRA, with financial support from the firearms industry, employed political consultant George Young, who framed the issue in terms of self-defense and equity. The opponents expended massive financial resources to the defeat of the initiative, which lost by a 63-to-37 percent margin.[32]

Most long-time gun-control advocates considered the defeat of Proposition 15 as being devastating to their cause.[33] For years the advocates of gun control had cited polls that indicated broad-based and consistent support for stronger gun-control laws.[34] This allowed the advocates to invoke democratic values as a powerful argument for gun-control enactment. An initiative to virtually ban private handgun ownership in Massachusetts failed in 1976, although the state already had rather strict gun laws. Now the voters of the most populous and politically important state in the nation had soundly defeated a ban on new handgun acquisition.[35] The press interpreted these defeats as signaling a lack of public interest in the topic; morale in gun-control organizations waned and the remaining political momentum for control evaporated.

Gun-control advocates seemed to be far more affected by the loss of Proposition 15 than by the congressional hearings and other assaults on ATF and the GCA. This can probably be explained by their lack of contact with opponents of gun control or with ATF. ATF had assiduously avoided contact with the gun-control organizations, who, in turn, showed little concern for ATF.[36] Centered in urban areas and surrounded by cosmopolitan populations, gun-control advocates failed to appreciate the political impact of the NRA's campaign on gun owners in the rest of the country. On the other hand, the loss of Proposition 15 influenced the urban press and political elite.

A key element in the defeat appeared to be the failure to obtain the support of police and sheriffs from rural and suburban areas, a lesson not lost on the gun-control advocates.[37] More importantly, the dynamics of the initiative process do not favor issues like gun control. Initiatives are far easier to defeat than to pass, particularly if they face an organized and well-funded opposition.[38] Opponents need only to raise questions regarding the drafting of an initiative in order to deter most voters. Gun control enjoys broad but shallow support and faces passionate opposition. Supporters do not provide funds, nor do they walk precincts. This pattern repeated itself in the unsuccessful 1997 Washington State Initiative 676. As with Proposition 15, early polls showed strong support, but the support evaporated in the face of a well-funded opposition campaign.[39]

The Proposition 15 defeat, combined with continuing frustration over lack of success at passing a national handgun-control bill, heightened the developing fissure in the gun-control movement. This division increased when neither the murder of singer John Lennon nor the shooting of President Reagan succeeded in generating significant visible support for new gun-control initiatives.[40] For some time HCI and Pete Shields had been gaining the dominant position among advocates, particularly in terms of press visibility and fundraising. HCI favored the advocacy of handgun regulation rather than prohibition, although the differences may have related to tactics as much as objectives.[41] Many in both groups favored a ban on private ownership of handguns and permissive licensing of long guns. Shields and HCI concluded that public advocacy of handgun prohibition was politically dysfunctional, and that the immediate need was to build a lobby to match the NRA's. Beard and the Coalition continued to openly advocate handgun prohibition on the theory that to deny this objective would undermine their legitimacy.

After Proposition 15, the split became more public. HCI concentrated on building membership and finding wedge issues that would undermine the NRA. The Coalition continued to advocate banning handguns and thus fell into a distant second place in visibility, press coverage, and fundraising. The failure to generate widespread law-enforcement support for Proposition 15 proved critical. Historically, big-city chiefs had supported gun control, as had the International Association of Chiefs of Police. Rank-and-file police and executives of smaller departments had remained uninvolved or in some cases openly hostile to gun control. Successful gun control apparently required the symbolism of strong law-enforcement support. A split in law-enforcement opinion robbed advocates of that symbolism. Supporters needed a wedge issue to define the NRA and its allies as opponents of the police and law and order.[42] The issue would be "cop-killer bullets."

COP-KILLER BULLETS

Beginning in the mid-1970s, bullet-resistant vests became standard equipment for most of the uniformed police in the nation. The vests became practical with the development of Kevlar, a synthetic fabric that when layered could resist penetration by bullets. The rising violent crime rate of the period ensured demand. None of the vests would stop the penetration of rifle bullets without the addition of heavy metal or ceramic plates that made the vests too cumbersome for routine wear. Vests adequate to protect against most handgun and shotgun projectiles could be worn under the officer's uniform shirt on a regular basis. Armor-piercing handgun rounds had existed for many years, but failed to gain any popularity with police or civilians. Dealers seldom stocked the ammunition and few buyers showed any interest in ordering it. Interest in pistol ammunition had primarily focused on development of effective soft-point handgun ammunition that increased trauma.[43] Armor-piercing ammunition had a sharp-pointed bullet that reduced trauma in the target. Since the bullet resistance of soft body armor resulted from the number of layers of fabric and the penetration characteristics of various cartridges, one cannot rationally define an absolute point at which a cartridge becomes armor-piercing. The issue of armor-piercing bullets and body armor reflects the historically shifting balance between offensive and defensive weapons.[44] The penetration of a bullet depends on mass, velocity, shape, and composition, thus producing a continuum of capacity to penetrate soft body armor or any other medium. However, when a small ammunition company marketed Teflon-coated pistol bullets, capable of penetrating soft body armor, the symbolism generated widespread attention, particularly among the police.[45]

In 1981 Representative Mario Biaggi (D–N.Y.), a former New York police officer, became the visible advocate of federal legislation to outlaw "cop-killer bullets." A dispute exists over the actual originator of the strategy to use armor-piercing ammunition as a wedge issue, but HCI clearly assumed the lead role in advancing it.[46] The strategy called for pursuing a ban on the ammunition with police support, thereby forcing the NRA to either give tacit support to a gun-control measure or oppose it and alienate law enforcement and the public. The NRA rose to the bait, attempting to invoke a new paradigm: technology. Cop-killer bullets clearly constituted a symbolic rather than substantive policy issue.[47] Unfortunately for the NRA, its effort to invoke a rational technological paradigm in relation to this symbolic conflict proved unsuccessful. The issue defined it as unwilling to accept reasonable compromise on even the smallest issue.[48] The wedge had been set, but the NRA would now drive it much deeper.[49] The cop-killer bullet controversy was soon followed by the "plastic gun" controversy. Again the NRA held the technical high ground, but lost the public-relations battle.[50]

THE McCLURE-VOLKMER BILL

The McClure-Volkmer bill, introduced in 1981, became the centerpiece of the NRA strategy, crafted by Neal Knox and Harlon Carter. Unlike McClure's earlier bills to abolish the GCA in toto, this bill targeted specific portions of the law that had become the focus of the ATF oversight hearings.[51] Between 1981 and 1986 NRA directed the majority of its efforts and attention toward passage of McClure-Volkmer. Ironically, Neal Knox, a primary architect of the NRA strategy, lost his position as director of the ILA in 1982 and was replaced

by the more conciliatory J. Warren Cassidy. Two years later, Knox lost his position on the board of directors as a result of his efforts to resist Harlon Carter's
control of the organization.[52] Knox's aggressive lobbying and unwillingness to
compromise apparently led to his isolation. Much like true believers in the
American Civil Liberties Union, Operation Rescue, the feminist movement,
and other causes, Knox proved the good soldier in battle but unwilling to
compromise, a character trait that is antithetical to Washington culture.[53]

Unable to pass the McClure-Volkmer bill in its original form, the NRA
agreed to a revised and less-offensive version of it. Knox's public opposition to
these compromises led to his removal from the board.[54] The administration
refused to oppose the bill but did allow ATF to offer suggestions for changes
to specific provisions that presented it with the greatest problems.[55] McClure-
Volkmer and gun control became a component in the Republican strategy to
define the Democratic Party as liberal and marginal, while holding onto its
own right-wing. The administration avoided the issue officially but provided
aid and support to the bill's supporters in Congress and outside of it.[56] The
issue provided benefits for the Republican leadership in Congress by cutting
across party lines and thereby weakening Democratic loyalty.

In all likelihood McClure-Volkmer might never have passed but for House
Judiciary Committee Chairman Peter Rodino, who had a reputation for arbi-
trarily bottling-up legislation he opposed in committee.[57] One former staff
member stated that Rodino's declaration that the bill was "dead on arrival"
and the decision to hold hearings in the liberal strongholds of New York and
San Francisco proved to be key tactical errors that resulted in a discharge peti-
tion from the Judiciary Committee.[58] Once discharged, the bill passed the full
House and was signed by the president.[59] Although the passed bill constituted
a far less-radical retreat than the original proposal, the Democratic House had
allowed a major reversal in the trend toward stricter firearm regulation.
However, as if to signify a coming shift in political dynamics, a last-minute
amendment from the House floor attached a prohibition on the future possession of machine guns. Although primarily offered in an effort to frustrate the
advocates of the bill, the amendment passed, thus becoming the first federal
ban on possession of any type of firearm.[60] Without this last-minute amendment to McClure-Volkmer, machine-gun sales would almost assuredly have
become more commonplace. Half the states allowed machine-gun possession
and the NFA only imposed a $200 transfer tax. Only the unwillingness of
major manufacturers to sell to the public had prevented a market from developing. Small manufacturers had already begun to produce machine guns for
private consumption in 1986.

The passage of the McClure-Volkmer bill in many ways proved to be a
tactical defeat for the NRA. It redefined and altered the law in the two areas
that had created the most concern about the GCA—engaging in the business
and false record-keeping[61]—thus denying the NRA these issues in the future.

It also exacerbated the growing rift between the NRA and police. Even advocates of McClure-Volkmer realized that the bill could not have passed after 1986,[62] and the NRA might have been better served if it had died.

SHIFTING POWER

The fourth wave in the evolution of gun-control policy lasted from the NRA's 1978 defeat of proposed regulations to the passage of McClure-Volkmer. Although gun-control opponents appeared to be at the peak of power, the tide had already turned. HCI had utilized the cop-killer bullet issue and McClure-Volkmer to drive a wedge between the police and the NRA, thus laying the groundwork for a significant shift in the NRA's important symbolic position as supporter of "law and order." In a period when public concern about crime had produced historically favorable attitudes toward police, this constituted a significant tactical loss for the NRA and associated forces. In addition, violent crime rates again turned upward in the mid-1980s, and the two-decade trend toward support for decentralization and deregulation by government appeared to lose momentum. Once again, the initiative had shifted to the pro-control forces.

• • •

CHAPTER TEN

BRADY AND BEYOND

T HE ABILITY TO CONCEPTUALIZE gun control in the context of protecting individual rights faded after the passage of the FOPA, and the initiative shifted back to the controllers. Just as McClure–Volkmer had provided a tangible focus to energize and direct the NRA and its supporters and allies for almost a decade, the Brady Bill later served a similar function for HCI and the advocates of gun control. After being severely wounded and permanently disabled in the 1981 assassination attempt on President Reagan, White House Press Secretary James Brady became an activist for gun control. Brady's wife Sarah became president of HCI, and the national media anointed them as the primary spokespersons for and authorities on the topic. Brady's severe injuries, resultant disabilities, and subsequent courage provided the gun-control movement with both a visible victim and hero. The Bradys' conspicuous Republican credentials constituted an additional asset. Like HCI founder Pete Shields, the Bradys enjoyed substantial protection from characterization as wild-eyed liberals. Their association with the HCI-drafted bill provided credibility, gave the movement a human face, and solidified the HCI position as the dominate gun-control interest group.

Although the Brady bill continued the cautious HCI strategy of pursuing limited objectives, it advanced a more substantive policy issue than cop-killer bullets or plastic guns: a national waiting period for gun buyers. Twenty-four states already required waiting periods and/or reporting when individuals purchased handguns from dealers. Ironically, these laws evolved from the Uniform Revolver Act, which had once been advocated by the NRA.[1] The standard model required dealers to report identifying information about the purchasers and allowed a specified period for local police, state police, or state departments of justice to verify that the purchaser had no prior felony convictions or other impediments to gun ownership. These systems varied widely—from New York's restrictive licensing requirements to states with waiting periods but no mandatory system for background checks. Some states such as California used the reporting to build a registry of gun purchasers, which fell short of a true registration system but provided information for firearms tracing.[2]

The Brady bill proposed a seven-day national waiting period and mandatory record checks on all purchasers of handguns from licensed dealers. Although the NRA and other allied groups vigorously opposed the bill as radical and burdensome, HCI had crafted it specifically to undercut such arguments. In so doing, HCI also limited the potential utility of the bill: It applied only to handguns sold by federally licensed dealers, thus avoiding the issue of waiting periods on rifles and shotguns and excluding private sales of all firearms. This greatly reduced any potential inconvenience to the vast majority of gun owners, but also created a massive hole in the buyer-screening system. The bill also mandated that dealers send sale reports to local police rather than to a federal agency. This reduced the potential for exacerbating fears of an expanding federal power, but dispersed the checks among thousands of agencies that the federal government had neither the authority nor means for supervising.[3] Finally, the Brady bill prohibited the retention of information resulting from dealer reports. This precluded the argument that it constituted a de facto system of registration of gun owners, but removed the potentially most valuable result of purchaser reporting. California's Automated Firearms System, which contains purchaser identities and gun descriptions, provides law enforcement with firearm-tracing information much more quickly and efficiently than the primitive gun tracing provided by ATF.[4] Equally as important, a database of purchasers and guns provides a source of information to identify illegal gun traffickers who purchase large quantities of guns from dealers, and it aids in dealer oversight by creating a permanent record outside the dealer's control (see chapter 11). Thus those charged with administering and enforcing firearm laws viewed the bill as modest indeed.[5]

Introduced in both the House and Senate in 1987, the Brady bill managed to reach the House floor by September 1988. Massive NRA opposition and the use of hostile amendments defeated it, in spite of rather visible support from police organizations. Continuing the trend that began with the cop-killer bullet controversy, police groups gathered under the Law Enforcement Steering Committee to support the bill's passage. In spite of visible law-enforcement support that included uniformed officers lobbying House members, the House substituted an amendment by Bill McCullum (R–Fla.) to study an instant check system for the Brady waiting period and record checks.[6]

Two years later, Congress again voted on the bill. This time, both houses passed versions of it but not before opponents, seeing the trend of support for the bill, offered an alternative one. Representative Harley Staggers (D–W.V.) proposed mandating an instant background check that would eliminate the need for the Brady bill and its waiting period. Gun-control advocates responded that existing criminal-records systems had not reached a point of automation and accuracy to support such a system, and the Staggers amendment went down to defeat.[7]

Unfortunately for the supporters of the bill, the Senate and House versions differed: the Senate bill required only a five-day waiting period and was included in a large omnibus crime bill. Although a conference committee produced a single crime bill with a five-day waiting period that passed the House, opponents filibustered it in the Senate. With Republicans unwilling to support cloture, the bill died.[8] Without administration support or evidence of significant public outrage, advocates again lacked the leverage to move the Brady bill through Congress. Although it had again failed, it had served to solidify the position of HCI as the principal gun-control interest group. It also solidified links between HCI and the police, while casting the NRA as a powerful special-interest lobby in a time when such groups had become the focus of public hostility.

Ironically, the NRA's earlier success at passing McClure-Volkmer served to undercut its political position during the latter part of the 1980s and early 1990s. A combination of the legal impediments imposed by McClure-Volkmer and the political pressure resultant from the NRA campaign to enact it by demonizing ATF's enforcement activities resulted in ATF shifting investigative efforts away from firearm-trafficking investigations.[9] All investigations of licensed dealers by ATF agents required advance approval from bureau headquarters, as did any investigation involving a gun show or flea market.[10] By the late 1980s, investigations of criminal activities by licensed dealers had dwindled to only a handful and prosecutions of unlicensed dealers virtually ceased.[11] The Bush administration reinforced this trend with Operation Triggerlock, which mandated that U.S. Attorneys aggressively prosecute firearm violations involving convicted felons and drug traffickers. ATF reveled in this newfound support and eagerly responded with vigorous pursuit of cases against illegal gun possessors. This policy shift noticeably increased ATF's case output, but virtually denied the NRA the sort of middle-class "victims" of gun control who had proven so useful during the campaign for McClure-Volkmer.[12]

With the 1992 election of Bill Clinton, the advocates of gun control enjoyed open support from the White House for the first time in 12 years, although that support proved more symbolic than political.[13] Advocates again advanced the Brady bill, now with a five-day waiting period. A change in political climate became clear when Democrats managed to separate the Brady bill from a larger crime bill, with the reluctant acquiescence of House Judiciary Chairman Jack Brooks (D-Tex.). Although Brooks tried to redeem himself with gun-control opponents by offering amendments on the floor, the amendments failed and the bill passed by 238 to 189 in a vote by the full House.[14] Control opponents did not forget, and Brooks, one of the few remaining Southern Democrats in Congress, faced opposition and defeat in the next election.[15]

The Brady bill still faced the less hospitable environment of the Senate, where opponents enjoyed two advantages: proportionate representation by state and the filibuster. Because gun-control opposition centers in rural Southern and Western states, the Constitution's allocation of two senators per state favors gun-control opponents, who can neutralize California's two votes with Wyoming's. This advantage proves greatest when rural interests oppose legislation. Senate rules require 60 votes to invoke cloture and end a filibuster. In theory, this allows the senators representing a small minority of the population to block any bill. In practice, states such as Delaware and Rhode Island culturally and politically align with urban states, and Texas aligns with rural Southern and Western states. Thus region and culture come closer to defining the fault line than does state population.

The combination of administration support, the successful use of gun control by Bill Clinton as an issue in the 1992 election, and the building public awareness of the bill proved to be adequate political incentive to facilitate a compromise between the leadership of the two parties. Democrats allowed a floor vote on two Republican amendments. One prohibited state waiting periods and substituted the five-day Brady waiting period. Opposed by the bill's backers, this amendment raised practical, political, and constitutional issues: Prohibiting state regulation of firearm sales most likely exceeded Congress's authority under the commerce clause and directly contradicted the established Republican doctrine of deferring to state authority. This amendment was defeated.

A second amendment imposed a five-year sunset provision on Brady's waiting period, by which time all background checks would be conducted instantly. This amendment passed and became a part of the final bill. Although faced with another potential filibuster and Republican Senate Majority Leader Robert Dole's (R-Kan.) desire to build credibility with the conservative wing of his party, the bill eventually passed the Senate. Within less than a week, a House–Senate conference committee produced a final version of the bill, which passed both houses and was signed into law on November 30, 1993.[16]

In spite of the characterizations by advocates and opponents of gun control to the contrary, the Brady Law did not constitute a significant policy change. The law modestly increased the fees for a firearm-dealer license to $200 for the first three years, and $90 for each three-year renewal. Although the $200 initial fee deterred some frivolous applicants, the increase failed to restore license fees to even their 1968 level of $10 per year, taking inflation into account. The fees also fell far short of compensating the government for the cost of issuing licenses and overseeing licensee operations.

The law did impose a mandatory waiting period and records check (see chapter 3) for handgun buyers. Although the majority of populous states already had some similar process, this did establish a national standard. Still, the bill failed to take advantage of the reporting process to establish a national gun-sales registry. While even strong advocates of gun control recognized the bill's significance as being more symbolic than real,[17] its passage challenged the myth of NRA invincibility that had begun with the defeat of Senator Joseph Tydings and had gained strength for more than a decade.

ASSAULT WEAPONS BILLS

Although some law-enforcement officers—particularly ATF agents, narcotics officers, and gang investigators—began to note the emergence of the "assault weapon" and the conversion of these weapons to fully automatic machine guns during the 1970s, gun-control activists took little note.[18] The market for paramilitary firearms with limited sporting uses began to develop in the early 1960s with the marketing of M1 carbines (see chapter 2) and continued to slowly expand for more than a decade. The market expanded rapidly in the late 1970s with the emergence of several new manufacturers, and later with the importation of inexpensive Chinese rifles. The most visible domestic contributor to the trend was a large semi-automatic pistol known at different times as the "MAC-10," "M-10," or "M-11." Originally designed as a small machine pistol and marketed in a semi-automatic version by a succession of companies, this aesthetically and mechanically crude firearm possessed only two attributes: a low cost and the ease of conversion to full-automatic fire. Eventually the manufacturer began selling parts kits for these guns by mail. Purchasers could buy these kits—allegedly replacement parts for machine guns, which are not prohibited under the NFA—and obtain the receivers separately. The most common method of obtaining receivers was to purchase a "flat," consisting of a pre-drilled piece of flat metal with a template for machining and bending into a receiver. Other manufacturers began offering a variety of paramilitary semi-automatic firearms in response to the apparent demand.

However, none of the domestic manufacturers influenced supply with anything near the impact of Chinese imports. The Chinese began to flood the United States with inexpensive semi-automatic versions of the AK47 assault rifle. These weapons sold for a fraction of the cost of the domestically produced Colt AR15 that had previously dominated the assault-rifle market. The Chinese imports eliminated the largest barrier to market expansion—cost.

Neither the GCA nor state laws recognized any legal distinction between a semi-automatic rifle or pistol with military characteristics and any other rifle or pistol. Although the technical category of assault rifle had long been used to describe small military rifles or carbines firing cartridges of mid-range intensity (see chapter 2), no corresponding legal category existed. The GCA classified military-assault rifles—which merged the submachine-gun characteristics of full-automatic fire, compact size, and large magazine capacity with rifle accuracy and velocity—as machine guns.

In technical jargon, "machine gun" describes a heavy, crew-served, full-automatic weapon, and does not apply to assault rifles or submachine guns. In legal usage, however, "machine gun" describes any full-automatic weapon. These new semi-automatic firearms bore the appearance of their full-automatic cousins, but lacked the crucial functional characteristic of expelling multiple shots with a single pull of the trigger. Occasionally, small producers of semi-automatic "knockoffs" of full-automatic firearms would fail to make adequate design changes in the semi-automatic version, and ATF would rule the firearm a machine gun. However, the law requires no advance approval of new domestic designs and ATF never applied the sporting-use requirement to imported long guns before 1989.[19] Thus the marketing of military-style firearms faced only two minor legal constraints: Manufacturers might face an after-the-fact ruling that the gun was a machine gun if their design was poorly executed; they also could not duplicate the appearance of most submachine guns. Because most submachine guns have shoulder stocks and barrels less than 16 inches in length, a semi-automatic version would constitute a "short-barreled rifle" under the GCA. Manufacturers solved this legal problem by removing the shoulder stocks to create the so-called "assault pistols." Although the resulting pistols proved awkward and difficult to shoot, the law classified them as handguns.[20]

Among the owners of gun shops and shooters alike, the new wave of firearms became known as "toys."[21] These new products, through their appearance, served to stimulate a new demand for guns. Many young males with little or no interest in hunting or shooting sports displayed interest in these firearms—no doubt intensified by the wave of action films and television programs such as *Rambo* and *Miami Vice* that featured their full-automatic cousins. Although this sort of market change might have alarmed the conservative firearms community of the 1950s, the politicized firearms community of the 1980s showed no such concern. Likewise, HCI continued to concentrate its efforts on the Brady bill.

MASSACRE AT STOCKTON

The political dynamics changed suddenly in January 1989 when Patrick Purdy, a mentally disturbed drifter, opened fire with a Chinese-made semi-automatic rifle on children playing in an elementary schoolyard in Stockton, California, killing 5 and wounding 29. The legally imported 7.62mm AKM-56S used a detachable 30-round magazine and had an external appearance that is virtually identical to that of the Soviet and Chinese AK-47 assault rifles.[22] Although the country and California had previously experienced random mass shootings, this deliberate murder of schoolchildren captured the attention of the nation in ways that earlier shootings had not.[23]

The efforts of a small group of California law-enforcement officers to lobby the legislature for a bill to control the military firearms had produced little response prior to the Stockton shooting.[24] Immediately after the shootings, the California attorney general and leaders of the legislature embarked upon a crash program to develop legislation.[25] Although offered an opportunity to participate in drafting the legislation, the NRA adopted a tactic of total opposition.[26] Very little gun legislation had moved through the California legislature for a number of years. The California Department of Justice took little active role in enforcing the state's gun laws, and legislative staffs had paid little attention to gun issues. Driven by a desire to take quick and dramatic action, the legislature did not benefit from the usual sources of expertise; the NRA and other gun organizations had excluded themselves from the process, and the bureaucratic and legislative staffs lacked specific knowledge and experience. Ironically, most of the technical advice supplied to the legislature and attorney general came from California's Assistant Director of Law Enforcement, Steven Helsley,[27] who subsequently left to become the NRA's chief California lobbyist.[28]

The combination of a legislative desire for fast and visible action, the limited available policy expertise, and a disengaged opposition shaped the resultant bill. Rather than developing a permissive licensing or registration system, the legislature modeled the bill on California's existing machine-gun law. Although those owning affected firearms could register and retain their weapons, the law prohibited new acquisitions by California residents and transfer of registered firearms to other California residents.[29] To ensure passage of the legislation, advocates narrowed its application to firearms with little legitimate constituency. Rather than attempting to define functional assault weapons, the legislature adopted a list of specific firearms chosen primarily on appearance.[30] This strategy of naming specific firearm models generated both practical and conceptual problems. In its haste to pass a law, the legislature listed firearm models incorrectly.[31] The naming of models also allowed manufacturers to simply rename their firearms.[32] Although the law applied to certain "series"— specifically the AK and AR15 series—and variations on the prohibited models, the state failed to effectively apply the law to similar firearms for a decade.[33] The approach of using appearance created legitimacy problems as well: Firearms, functionally identical to those on the restricted list, remained legal, raising serious questions regarding the purpose and equity of the law.

Although the assault-weapon bill attracted most of the attention, the political shift that it precipitated resulted in the California legislature passing several other gun bills. The legislature extended the prohibition on gun possession by felons to include all firearms rather than just handguns. In addition, bills requiring reporting and waiting periods on all gun transfers by dealers and private individuals became law. Although some other states eventually followed California's precedent, the trend did not sweep the nation.[34]

FEDERAL REACTION

Although President Bush initially attempted to avoid the controversy by stating that the assault-weapon issue would best be dealt with at the state level,[35] he soon shifted his position. Apparently as a result of lobbying by drug czar William Bennett and Mrs. Bush, the president directed ATF to impose the "suitable-for-sporting-purposes" test to imported assault weapons.[36] The order to apply the standard to imported assault weapons came with no input from ATF, although the agency had to devise a means of applying the sporting standard to long guns. Within ATF, the technical staff bristled at the entire undertaking on the grounds that no reasonable and workable definition was possible.[37] But in the end ATF produced standards that considered such characteristics as bayonets, bayonet lugs, flash suppressors, and pistol grips. Although this approach constituted a more generic standard than naming models, it still depended primarily on appearance and not function. The new standards temporarily halted a massive wave of pending imports, but manufacturers soon adapted by making minor modifications to their firearms. The ATF restrictions may have had some minor dampening effect on market demand by reducing the visual appeal of the imported firearms. However, the federal action also apparently stimulated demand by convincing numerous potential buyers that the firearms would soon become unavailable.[38]

Handgun Control Incorporated quickly recognized the assault-weapon issue as symbolically and politically significant and modified its agenda to include assault-weapon legislation as a companion to the Brady bill. By the spring of 1991, Brady had passed in the House as a result of substantial police and constituent pressure. *Congressional Quarterly* described a "sea change" in members' attitudes on gun issues.[39] Caught between constituent demand to oppose Brady and assault-weapons restriction and his own members' demand for a vote, House Speaker Tom Foley (D–Wash.) faced serious political consequences.[40] In July the Senate passed a crime-control bill (S1241) with a version of the Brady bill and a ban on nine specific assault weapons by a 45 vote margin.[41] In October the House stripped the assault weapon ban from the crime bill by a 70-vote margin, in spite of the mass murder of 22 people in a restaurant in Killeen, Texas, by a demented man armed with a semi-automatic pistol.[42]

The 1992 election of President Bill Clinton signaled an improving political environment for gun-control legislation. In addition to using Republican opposition to the Brady bill and assault-weapon legislation to counter the proven Republican strategy of attacking Democratic candidates as soft on crime, Clinton signaled support early in his presidency when he included the subject of handgun control in his February 17, 1993 economic address.[43] Still, assault-weapon legislation faced numerous daunting hurdles, including the opposition of Speaker of the House Foley and House Judiciary Chairman Brooks,[44] the perception that the bill offered little substance,[45] and the intense lobbying by the NRA.[46] In addition, inclusion of the assault-weapon legislation in the larger crime bill would have entangled it in the internal Democratic fight over death-penalty legislation, which was also included in the bill.[47] By October, Brooks had allowed Brady to proceed as stand-alone legislation, but the assault-weapon bill remained a part of the larger House crime bill.[48]

In the Senate, Diane Feinstein (D-Calif.) began assuming the lead in assault-weapon legislation in the fall of 1993, when she successfully crafted a compromise between Senator Dennis DeConcini's (D-Ariz.) earlier bill and a more encompassing ban offered by Senator Howard Metzenbaum (D-Ohio).[49] The crime bill, with Feinstein's ban on 19 specific assault weapons and their derivatives, passed the Senate in November, after an effort to table the assault-weapon bill failed by one vote.[50]

Throughout 1994 House and Senate versions of the crime bill varied, with the assault-weapon ban remaining the most difficult issue to resolve in the House.[51] Although Judiciary Chairman Brooks voted against the assault-weapon ban, he did allow a vote that moved the bill out of committee. Brooks continued to work against the Feinstein amendment in conference committee by proposing less-restrictive legislation, but lost the argument with Senate counterparts.[52] Conflicts among Democratic factions and between the House and Senate appeared to doom the crime bill. But last-minute lobbying by the White House, congressional perceptions of public support, and Republican fear of being branded obstructionist in the upcoming election combined to push forward a compromise crime bill containing an assault-weapon restriction through both Houses by the end of August.[53]

The final bill banned future production or importation of specific semi-automatic rifles, pistols, and shotguns. In addition, it applied the restrictions to copies of these banned firearms and other semi-automatic arms with two or more designated characteristics.[54] It also prohibited ammunition magazines with a capacity of over ten rounds, but exempted firearms and magazines legally possessed at the time of the law's enactment. Although heralded as a victory for Clinton, the Democrats, and advocates of gun control, the assault-weapon bill took a major political toll. Forty-seven House Democrats opposed the crime bill solely because of the assault-weapon ban,[55] and the NRA base was energized for the next election. Just how much the bill cost would become evident in the November 1994 congressional elections.

The bill exempted those firearms and magazines already in circulation at the time of its passage.[56] While this reduced the potential effect of the law, it greatly simplified passage by removing large numbers of stakeholders and avoiding the implementation problems inherent in retroactively controlling firearms legally purchased and dispersed through the population. In addition to exempting firearms legally possessed at the time of the law's passage, it included an extensive list of exempt firearms that some have characterized as having weakened the law.[57] However, an examination of the exempted list quickly reveals that few of these firearms are even semi-automatics, and less than half-a-dozen could even be characterized as military-style rifles.[58]

In July 1999 California revised its definition of assault weapons by adopting a more generic approach that encompassed most of the guns designed to avoid the earlier ban.[59] However, even this new extension failed to include all designs.[60] The law also prohibited the sale or exchange of magazines with a capacity of over 10 rounds, but allowed the retention of those possessed at the law's enactment. This change in the law will not end the cycle of action and reaction that has continued since 1979. In all likelihood, manufacturers will soon market both a semi-automatic rifle that accepts the 30-round AK-47 magazine and a modified rear stock for the existing AK-47–style weapons. Without a folding stock or pistol grip, semi-automatic rifles meet California and federal standards and could be sold with a 10-round magazine; purchasers could obtain with ease 30-round magazines at gun shows.

SUBSTANTIVE ISSUE OR TEMPEST IN A TEAPOT?

Does assault-weapon legislation address a new and serious policy issue, or does it simply provide gun-control groups with a new target for hysteria? I would suggest that it provides a little of each. As critics readily point out, so-called assault weapons defy technical definition.[61] The fact that the firearms covered by the law do not fit the technical category of assault rifle matters little. The technical and legal definitions of "machine gun" differ, yet the law works reasonably well. The problem lies in the inability to develop a politically acceptable definition of an assault weapon, a problem neither side shows interest in addressing.

To include all the weapons at issue, avoid confusion, and prevent efforts to circumvent the law, the definition would have to include all semi-automatic firearms, with either a detachable magazine or a fixed magazine exceeding a specific capacity such as five (or six or eight) rounds. Alternatively, the definition could encompass all semi-automatic firearms, an approach used by Canada, Australia, and Great Britain. The latter approach could allow for the licensing of certain existing firearms such as .22 rimfire rifles without attempting to create broad exclusions. Advocates have avoided proposing such a definition because the former would encompass every semi-automatic pistol in existence, and the latter would additionally encompass a number of popular rifles and shotguns. In either case, far too many stakeholders would be drawn into the conflict. Without such an approach, one must justify outlawing a large clumsy and awkward "assault pistol," while ignoring a smaller but move effective pistol that fires the same cartridge. This places advocates in an ethically and rationally indefensible position. The restrictions by federal and California law on magazines with capacities over ten rounds constitute attempts to accomplish the same objective, while circumventing much of the political conflict.

This solution appears to offer a simple and expedient solution upon first examination; however, the huge existing stock of magazines remains legal.[62] With no means available to determine the manufacture date of a magazine and no records or serial numbers, commerce in large-capacity magazines will thrive for many years. Magazines, consisting of thin stamped metal and springs, constitute the most easily fabricated part of a firearm. Once produced, no investigator can establish the date of manufacture. Although California law prohibits sales and transfers of magazines, they remain legal in other states and lend themselves easily to illegal trafficking.

Opponents of gun control have gone beyond the definition argument, arguing that assault weapons are seldom used in crimes, pose no unique threat to the public or police, have valuable sporting and self-defense uses, and are constitutionally protected.[63] On the crime score, the evidence favors their argument. Although assault weapons show up more often in trace requests made to ATF than in crime, they constitute a small minority of the firearms in each category.[64]

On the issue of potential threat, the argument seems to be more disingenuous. Morgan and Kopel contend that assault weapons fire no more projectiles than conventional weapons. Of course, this depends on the definitions of "assault weapons" and "convention weapons," but they use the example of a semi-automatic AK-type rifle in comparison with a 12-gauge shotgun, firing buckshot. They fail to explain that the projectiles from the shotgun, though multiple, disperse at random and quickly lose energy. Unless fired into a closely packed group of individuals, the shotgun does not have the capacity for inflicting lethal wounds on nearly as many individuals as does the AK.[65] In addition, the shotgun takes much more time to reload after its six rounds are expended than does the AK when its 30 rounds are expended. Coincidentally, Morgan and Kopel, who rightfully point out the blatant use of symbolism by gun-control advocates, chose to picture in their publication an ancient Winchester M97 shotgun with a 30-inch barrel rather than a more menacing police riot gun.

Morgan and Kopel also note that assault weapons do not fire particularly powerful cartridges, and that murders of policemen failed to escalate as the numbers of assault weapons rose. Although valid, these assertions ignore some concerns. Assault-weapon cartridges, particularly the popular 7.62×39 and .223, produce less energy and have less penetration than most commercial hunting-rifle cartridges. However, the compact size of assault rifles, particularly those with folding stocks, and their popularity with young urban males greatly increases the potential for their use against police.[66] Any rifle cartridge will easily penetrate soft body armor, car doors, plasterboard walls, and glass, the principal means of defense used by police when they encounter an armed subject. In addition, the accuracy, range, and firepower of semi-automatic assault rifles puts police with handguns at a marked disadvantage in any confrontation.[67]

The potential becomes apparent in anecdotal evidence from such well-publicized incidents as the killing of two FBI agents and the wounding of several more by Miami bank robbers armed with a Ruger Mini-14, and the stand-off between scores of Los Angeles police and two bank robbers armed with assault rifles, wearing body armor. The fact that urban criminals have only occasionally utilized assault weapons against police does not ensure that this pattern will continue. Handgun inventories escalated rapidly from the mid-1960s onwards, yet use of handguns by young urban offenders did not rise rapidly until the mid-1980s.[68] Utilization of available implements depends on a variety of social, economic, and learning factors and may lag availability. In addition, police must respond to potential as well as actual threats. The presence of significant numbers of assault rifles forces police to alter tactics, increase armaments, and become more militarized and remote from the population.[69]

Morgan and Kopel as well as many other gun-rights advocates describe the utility of assault weapons for hunting, target shooting, and self-defense. The hunting argument hardly deserves a response. Although usable for hunting, these arms do not offer any unique advantages; other firearms offer more accuracy, equal durability, better cartridge choices, and easier scope mounting than the popular assault rifles. Some forms of rifle competition require the use of military-type arms, but these arbitrary rules imposed by shooters could be changed at will. Designed primarily to kill people, these weapons do work as effective instruments of self-defense. If one expects his home or business to be invaded by a group of armed individuals, an assault rifle might prove superior to any other weapon. For up to three opponents, a repeating shotgun offers equal utility for defense. The one exception to this scenario involves the defense against opponents with body armor, but this does not constitute a threat for even a miniscule portion of the population.

Unlike the Brady Law, which has begun to fade as a political issue, assault weapons remain on the policy agenda. In April 1998 President Clinton ordered ATF to permanently impose import restrictions against 58 models of firearms of semi-automatic firearms as being not suitable for sporting purposes.[70]

EXPANDING PROHIBITIONS

In addition to the assault-weapon ban, the 1994 crime bill expanded the "prohibited persons" definition in the GCA to include those under court-restraining orders to cease stalking, harassing, or threatening an intimate partner. It also prohibited the possession of handguns by and the transfer of handguns to juveniles, tightened firearm-dealer application procedures, and implemented other minor changes in the gun laws.

Although the restraining-order provision and a later expansion of the prohibited-person category to include those convicted of domestic-violence misdemeanors created little stir with the gun lobby or conservative members of

Congress, their long-term policy implications may exceed those of the assault-weapon ban. The addition of persons under restraining order has generated a serious Second Amendment legal challenge in the northern district of Texas,[71] and the inclusion of misdemeanor domestic-violence convictions to the GCA's prohibited classes has significantly extended federal gun prohibitions. In addition, these categories have proven particularly difficult for those attempting to determine eligibility for firearm purchasers.[72] Determining one's status in relation to mental problems, drug addiction, and illegal immigration has long proven to be problematic due to poor documentation and difficult identification. Likewise, misdemeanor convictions often lack clarity in criminal-records systems. Courts routinely indicate that convictions constitute a felony, a category well established in law and buttressed by fingerprinting and criminal-identification records. Although some misdemeanors appear on face value as domestic violence crimes, many acts of domestic violence result in convictions for crimes such as battery and assault. These can only be definitively resolved through investigation and remain open to interpretation. Restraining orders offer even greater difficulty, since they are seldom accompanied by fingerprinting or other positive identification, and the status is transitory. The due-process standards for issuance of such orders fall far below the requirements for a criminal conviction, and experienced family-law attorneys report that many judges issue such orders routinely with little or no evidence. Expansion of possession prohibitions to ambiguous groups—not well defined in official records—generates significant future implementation problems, particularly for actively enforced licensing and registration laws

CONCEALED-CARRY LAWS

While the initiative in Washington swung in favor of gun-control advocates after passage of FOPA, the NRA and its allies took the initiative at the state level. Although several states passed assault-weapon bills and both Maryland and Virginia adopted other modest legislation,[73] liberalized concealed-carry laws constituted the principal issue before state legislatures between the mid-1980s and mid-1990s. With little or no national attention, Washington State liberalized its concealed-carry law in 1961, allowing virtually all adults, other than specified felons, to obtain a concealed-weapon permit on demand. Vermont has no restrictions on carrying guns concealed or openly, and a number of other states never restricted the open carrying of guns. But the issue attracted little national attention until Florida passed a permissive carry law in 1987. Virginia followed Florida's precedent in 1988, with Oregon, Pennsylvania, and Georgia following a year later.[74] By 1998 32 states, including Vermont, allowed virtually any adult other than felons to carry a concealed firearm, although 31 of those states required permits and some charged substantial application fees.[75]

This rather sweeping national trend owes much to active lobbying by the NRA and to the research and publications of economist John Lott.[76] A classic public-choice economist, Lott lacks the cultural ties to the gun community displayed by Kleck, Kates, and Hardy. By applying regression to county-level crime data, Lott has produced a series of papers and a book that report evidence of decreased rape and murder rates in conjunction with the adoption of permissive license to carry laws. In addition, Lott has contended that adoption of such laws would reduce murders by over 1,500 per year and reduce mass killings.[77] Lott's methods and conclusions have been challenged by other methodologists, and policy advocates on both sides have gravitated to the scholars most supportive of their own position.[78] Both Lott's methodology and the critiques by his critics exceed the technical comprehension of most readers. His results constitute only a modest statistical inference rather than the scientific proof characterized by many gun-control opponents,[79] and recent crime trends have not followed the patterns one would expect from Lott's conclusions. For instance, between 1991 and 1998 homicide rates in New York and California—states with restrictive carry laws—declined by 63 and 51 percent respectively, while the rates in Florida and Virginia, states with permissive concealed-carry laws, decreased by 30 and 33 percent respectively. Although Texas showed a significant drop in homicide over the same period, most of the decline occurred before the liberalization of that state's concealed-carry laws.[80]

Gun-control advocates responded to the trend toward liberalized concealed-carry laws with predictions of an upsurge in gun violence.[81] Gun-control opponents repeatedly cited a drop in Florida's murder rate and later invoked Lott's research as proof that concealed-carry reduces crime. Both sides have dueled over the viability of research by McDowall, Loftin, and Wiersema that contested the conclusions about Florida.[82] Although the crime effects of liberalized concealed-carry laws remain a controversy, one conclusion seems clear: In the short and intermediate runs any impact on the crime rate remains modest, and the rhetoric of both camps most likely overstates the effect. Thus the concealed-carry debate may revolve more around culture and sovereignty than around crime.

By 2000 the concealed-carry trend seems to have paused, if not stalled. Bills have failed in California, Colorado, Illinois, Kansas, Missouri, and New Mexico.[83] In Missouri, a 1999 initiative to institute a shall-issue system failed, in spite of the massive grass-roots support from the NRA and the four-to-one funding advantage enjoyed by supporters.[84] Although Colorado appeared to be on the verge of passing a permissive carry law in April of 1999, it was quickly shelved in the aftermath of the Columbine High School shooting.[85]

Although the relationship between increased concealed carrying of firearms and crime may remain controversial, other aspects of the issue appear less so. Changes in concealed-carry laws do not appear to significantly change gun-carrying behavior, at least in the short run. Survey research by Kleck and

Gertz indicates that nearly 9 percent of the national population report having carried a gun for self-defense during the previous year.[86] Of these, slightly more than half carried the gun exclusively in a vehicle.[87] The mean number of days carried ranged from 38 to 40.[88] The proportion of the population applying for and receiving concealed-carry permits in shall-issue states has consistently remained between 1 and 4 percent.[89] As an example, Florida reported approximately 230,000 permit holders in an estimated population of over 15 million as of July 1999.[90] Assuming that some portion of the permit holders seldom or never carry a firearm on their persons,[91] some portion of the population apparently continues to carry guns unlawfully, even when permits become available. In addition, some significant portion of those obtaining a permit probably carried a firearm unlawfully before the law allowed them to obtain the permit. If so, permissive issuance of concealed-carry permits may simply legitimatize behavior that already occurs rather than alter behavior patterns.

The trends in Florida and Washington do not indicate that demand for permits increases over time. This implies only that a small portion of the population demonstrates a clear desire to carry a firearm on their persons—a fact that is not surprising. Carrying a firearm on one's person is uncomfortable, constricts one's mode of dress, and can prove socially awkward. In light of the low probability of becoming a victim of violent crime on any given occasion, the immediate cost outweighs the theoretical benefit for most people.[92]

In spite of the difficulties imposed by gun carrying, Kleck and Gertz found that 27.3 percent of gun owners reported carrying a firearm for protection at some time during the previous year. Assuming that handgun owners constituted an unknown subset of this population, gun carrying, at least in vehicles, appears to be fairly common among handgun owners. This should come as no surprise, since handguns are primarily designed for ease of portability and concealment. Although usable for some hunting and competitive target shooting, most handguns are primarily designed for use against humans at close range. Because rifles and shotguns provide greater accuracy and striking force as hunting and anti-personnel weapons, a knowledgeable user chooses a handgun only when circumstances preclude using a long gun. Presumably, some handgun buyers do not conduct a rational analysis of their needs and buy handguns based on impulse. Still, presuming that most people acquire an implement for use as designed does not seem to be an irrational assumption. Thus many handgun buyers must acquire these weapons with the intent of carrying them, at least on some occasions. Ironically, more people carry guns in their vehicles than on their persons. This practice affords convenience but leaves the gun vulnerable to theft and provides the owner no protection when out of the vehicle.

The recent push by pro-gun forces to liberalize handgun carry laws may have pushed Americans closer to facing the internal contradictions of a national policy that allowed virtually unlimited access to handguns, but generally prohibited their use as designed. Assuming that people buy handguns to carry seems far more reasonable than the alternative. Does a national policy of easy access to handguns not imply tacit acceptance of carrying these guns? Public policy often lacks internal consistency. The United States restricts immigration, but tolerates massive numbers of illegal immigrant workers. Likewise, traffic-safety laws limit speed but make no effort to limit the speed capability of automobiles. The laws of virtually all the states prohibit prostitution and gambling, but both exist openly in every American city. Ironically, the NRA has pushed Americans a step closer towards facing the contradiction and hypocrisy of existing gun policy by demanding legal acceptance of the status quo. Emboldened and legitimated by the research of Kleck and Lott, gun-rights advocates have abandoned arguments based on the sporting use of firearms and have framed the gun issue almost exclusively in terms of armed self-defense. One need only examine the writings of those who constitute the intellectual core of the gun-rights movement—Blackman, Hardy, Lott, Kopel, Kates, Polsby, and Snyder—to understand the centrality of self-defense to their positions. The public policy of Britain, which rejects all use of arms by citizens for self-defense, constitutes their greatest nightmare.[93] This trend has hardened the edges of the debate and denies moderates the opportunity to frame the issue around the sporting use of firearms.

How this policy trend will play out in the long run remains unclear. Ultimately, the states could apply the structures and procedures established for concealed-carry licensing to gun-owner licensing. Recognizing this, the Gun Owners of America (GOA) has opposed the permissive carry laws and called for application of the Vermont model, which allows any citizen to carry a gun at any time without a permit.[94] Grounds might conceivably exist for compromise between interest groups by extending concealed-carry rights to all licensed handgun owners, and requiring all handgun owners to obtain a license. This policy addresses the reality that government can do little to stop the carrying of a handgun once a person possesses it. In shall-issue states, any person eligible to own a handgun can obtain a permit; thus such a policy would probably have minimal impact on gun carrying. At the same time, gun interests have recognized the right of the state to establish standards for and license gun carrying. Therefore neither side would give up much in shall-issue states if all handgun owners obtained licenses and could then carry their firearms. However, both sides would most likely reject such a policy for political and symbolic reasons.

TRIGGER LOCKS AND GUN SAFETY

Gun-control advocates and a number of politicians have recently focused on the issue of trigger locks, gun storage, and safer gun design. In addition, design-safety issues have played a major role in class-action suits against gun manufacturers (see chapter 5). In particular, accidental deaths of young children who discovered loaded and unsecured firearms have been the focus. Although the proper storage of firearms and child safety are legitimate issues, their relationship to gun-control policy is tenuous at best. The rate of accidental deaths from all firearms is less than one-thirtieth that from automobiles, and moreover has been falling for decades.[95] Of the accidental deaths that *do* occur, less than 15 percent occur to those under 14 years of age.[96] Kleck makes a strong case that firearm accidents primarily occur among persons who have access to firearms and generally display reckless behavior.

Although the potential benefits from reducing firearm accidents are limited by the relatively small number of accidents, ensuring that those handling guns have adequate knowledge to safely do so should constitute an issue that appeals to all sides: The NRA has long sponsored safety training; providing such training offers potential profit for dealers; and gun-control advocates have already made safety training an issue. Whether control advocates can refrain from attempting to use safety proposals as barriers to gun ownership and whether opponents can bring themselves to support any gun-control measure remain open questions.

Part Three

WHERE WE ARE GOING

• • •

CHAPTER ELEVEN

WHAT COULD BE DONE AND WHY IT WON'T BE

T HE SHEER NUMBERS of the honest, law-abiding gun owners have long constituted one of the principal obstacles to strict gun control in the United States. Even if the number of households containing a firearm has fallen below 40 percent, gun owners still number in the tens of millions. By any calculation, only a small minority of gun owners possesses or uses firearms illegally. Thus gun regulation potentially impacts the interests, if not the rights, of a large portion of the public.

The size of the affected interest group, if not the Second Amendment, precludes prohibition as a politically viable gun policy for the foreseeable future. Even if a majority of Americans favored prohibition, that majority would have to possess an adequate commitment to prioritize gun control over other issues on a limited political agenda. Still, polls have consistently shown that the issue ranks low on surveys of issue importance.[1] In our political system, a highly committed minority can easily overcome passive support from a much larger but less focused majority.

The number of gun owners and the size of the existing inventory constitute as large an obstacle for implementation of gun control as for enactment—an issue little examined or discussed by advocates. Over a quarter-century ago, political scientists Jeffrey Pressman and Aaron Wildavsky warned that policy formulated without concern for implementation has little chance for success.[2] Unfortunately, crafting policy for implementation offers no political advantage for advocates. Enactment of policy requires skill in manipulating symbols, communicating a simplified and appealing message, developing constituencies, and bargaining. Crafting policy that accomplishes a desired result requires defined objectives, understanding the implementation environment and available incentives, recognition of limitations on implementation, and acceptance of the need for repeated adaptation. Policies that impose restrictions or requirements on a very large, dispersed, and diverse population pose special

153

problems. Unlike the regulation of some commercial class such as pharmacists or alcoholic-beverage dealers, the regulation of guns must apply to a large and dispersed population that includes persons with limited intellectual capacity, limited sources of information, limited incentives for compliance, and no central organization.

To date, neither the majority of state legislatures nor Congress have displayed the political will to seriously address gun regulations that mandate action by the majority of gun owners.[3] Even when legislatures have enacted such requirements, as with California's requirement to process all firearm transfers through a dealer and observe the 15-day waiting period, neither the executive nor legislative branches have aggressively pursued compliance.

Unless gun-control supporters focus on substantive policy options, the issue will remain little more than a battle over cultural symbols. The opponents routinely cite the plethora of gun laws in the United States and the lack of enforcement of existing laws when opposing new legislation with the slogan: "We don't need any more laws, we only need to enforce those we already have." Although these complaints ignore the role gun interests have played in both conditions,[4] the argument has substantial validity. Regardless of one's position on gun control, the number of laws is indefensible. America needs *better* gun laws, not *more* gun laws. The key to successful implementation of regulatory law rests on widespread, voluntary compliance. Compliance requires understanding, which, in turn, requires simplicity. Thus simplicity, standardization, and the ease of compliance should characterize any requirements imposed by regulatory law on a large population. Increasing the number of laws accomplishes none of these goals.

Although any level of government can, in theory, pass firearm regulations, local regulations serve only to complicate the issue. Local jurisdictional lines in the United States follow no rational pattern. Daily, citizens can and do pass totally unaware across city and county boundaries within metropolitan areas. Mobile populations move across these boundaries without taking notice. Citizens would not tolerate requirements to obtain a new driver's license or vehicle registration as they passed from one municipal jurisdiction to another. Likewise, local regulation of gun ownership and transportation would seem to defy logic. Advocates of control do enjoy political advantages within core cites dominated by urban, Democratic voters. However, the passage of highly restrictive handgun laws in Chicago and Washington, D.C., have not led to changes in surrounding jurisdictions. They have provided the opponents of gun control with legitimacy in their pronouncements that *all* gun control will lead to prohibition. Pursuit of gun control at the municipal level may provide control advocates with a sense of satisfaction, but it does little to advance us toward a consistent and uniform policy.

Although addressing guns at the state level involves some of the problems raised by a local approach, the federal system establishes duel sovereigns. Thus gun-control policy in the United States will continue as an amalgam of state and federal law. The laws and regulations in many policy areas such as transportation, welfare, public health, and environmental protection reflect extensive state and federal integration. With the exception of a few provisions in the GCA to restrict the interstate flow of arms and provisions for the substitution of more stringent state procedures for Brady checks, gun laws reflect little effort at integrating state and federal action. Nor have states developed the sort of mutual reciprocity that prevails in such diverse areas as driver licensing, vehicle registration, marriage, and education. Policy initiatives, which addressed some of these issues, offer two advantages: They potentially undercut opposition among gun owners, who have something to gain from uniformity and simplicity; and they potentially lead to more uniform and standardize laws, which facilitates compliance.

The incremental model has failed to move the agenda. Modest, symbolic legislation has not led to significant, comprehensive control policies. If gun-control advocates desire real policy change they must move the agenda beyond the current piecemeal, guerrilla-warfare approach, in which they advance discreet initiatives selected primarily for political appeal, to a more comprehensive policy approach. Although control advocates have little hope of reaching compromise with the core of control opponents, they *can* craft legislation that recognizes the legitimate interests of the vast majority of gun owners and dealers in an effort to divide them from the militant core. Standardization and uniformity can benefit gun owners and dealers without undercutting gun regulation. Four strategies exist for increasing standardization and uniformity: 1) Legislatures can preempt the firearm field and preclude local legislation. They can also consolidate and simplify existing state laws. 2) States can offer reciprocity and pursue compatibility with the laws of other states. 3) The federal government can take the lead by encouraging state uniformity and reciprocity. 4) Most of all, policy advocates at all levels can continually ask: "Can average citizens understand and comply with these laws?"

In addition to uniformity and simplicity, policy should pursue rational utility. Restrictive legislation that fails to meet this standard reinforces the perception that control advocates will use any means to burden gun owners, without concern for the policy's purpose or efficacy. As an example, repeated efforts to establish a class of prohibited firearms based on questionable criteria, as has occurred with assault-weapon and Saturday-night-special legislation, may make political sense, but it reinforces the belief among gun owners that control advocates seek incremental prohibition through demonization. Even laws that initially appear to be rational can prove otherwise in application. The regulation of large-capacity ammunition magazines provides an example: Although this concept seemed to offer a way around the difficult issue of defining assault weapons, it offers little practical utility (see chapter 9).

Options for modest but useful improvements exist. At the federal level, Congress could enact a clear definition of "engaging in the business of dealing in firearms." The simplest definition would define a dealer as a person offering more than a specified number of guns, such as six, for sale during a 12-month period. The law could include provisions for a limited license or other means of allowing a person to dispose of a collection. Such a change would eliminate ambiguity for sellers, enforcement agents, and courts. A simple definition would eliminate anxiety for gun owners and weaken the NRA's ability to generate fear of arbitrary enforcement action by ATF.

In conjunction, Congress should raise the cost of a dealer license to a level adequate to reimburse the government for the cost of the licensing and inspection of gun dealers and eliminate the requirement that a licensee be engaged in the firearms business. This would allow persons to obtain a license if they chose to sell more firearms, but would remove the burden for licensing costs from the general taxpayer.

In combination, these changes would channel most legal sales through licensed dealers, reducing the unregulated secondary market. Although some unlicensed dealers would continue to violate the law, they would have far greater difficulty in blending in with collectors and hobbyists. Significant trafficking at gun shows would become impossible. Prosecution of those engaged in unlicensed dealing would become far easier for two reasons: Defendants could no longer invoke the defenses established by the FOPA nor could they claim confusion regarding the need for a license. Those who wished to sell more guns than the prescribed maximum could obtain a license and keep records. Sales volume constitutes a far more rational criterion for regulation than commercial intent.

Congress could also restore the felony statute for willful falsification of firearm-dealer records. The 1986 reduction of this offense to a misdemeanor by the FOPA severely hampers the prosecution of licensed dealers who transferred guns to prohibited persons and unlicensed traffickers.[5] Congress could also act to ensure dealer compliance by requiring dealers to report all transfers to other dealers. In addition to expediting the tracing process, this proposal, which generated such controversy in 1978 (see chapter 8), would significantly aid in detecting the small portion of dealers who purchase guns from wholesalers, sell them illegally, and never make any record of the transaction.

Congress could entirely eliminate the need for the current cumbersome and inefficient tracing process and improve information support for police by requiring that Brady checks include a complete description of the firearm and that the information on the gun and purchaser be retained and computerized. Although an observer unfamiliar with gun-control politics in the United States might find adoption of this procedure, already in effect in states like California, a modest proposal, gun-control opponents would characterize it as gun registration and respond with a firestorm of opposition. Given this political reality, control advocates have little reason not to simply pursue owner licensing and gun registration, looking to recorded Brady checks as a worst-case compromise.

LICENSING AND REGISTRATION

Traditionally, arguments for firearm licensing and registration have rested on one of two presumptions: That firearms are dangerous and, therefore, should be controlled; or that the population of firearms and firearm owners should be restricted to a narrow class of people. Restrictive licensing assumes that guns are dangerous items and that the government should restrict their possession to a few individuals. The criteria for allowing firearm possession can vary: Government can implement racial, class, or political criteria or make an even-handed effort to restrict firearms only to those with a significant need. Regardless of the criteria, such systems run counter to the populist traditions of the nation and have not been widely enacted, with the notable exception of New York's licensing of handgun owners. Gun owners fear this discretionary licensing almost as much as outright prohibition. New York City's long history of restricting handgun permits to a select few and the progressive movement of British and Canadian licensing toward prohibition have exacerbated and legitimized these fears.

The attitude of many gun owners towards licensing changes significantly when licensing becomes mandatory for all applicants meeting specified qualifications.[6] Therefore permissive licensing offers control advocates a policy alternative that could develop significant support, even among gun owners, if crafted around the acceptance of their legitimate interests and designed to minimize cost and bureaucracy. But would a permissive system provide the required utility or simply impose a useless regulation?

Most gun regulation in the United States has sought to prevent certain narrow classes of individuals—such as felons, the mentally disturbed, and children—from acquiring firearms. Although gun-control opponents routinely characterize as ineffectual laws prohibiting acquisition and the possession of firearms by such persons, they have long supported these laws.[7] Clearly, passing a law that prohibits a class of individuals from obtaining or possessing guns will not in itself ensure that those persons do not possess firearms. Effective policy requires the evaluation of the effectiveness of available enforcement mechanisms, the identification of weaknesses in those mechanisms, and efforts at correction.

Unfortunately, scholars, regulators, and legislative staffs have devoted little attention to the nature of firearm markets and the potential means for regulating them.[8] The entire body of published literature consists of a handful of articles and a few government reports.[9] In spite of this limited research, a reasonably clear picture emerges of the market in macrocosm. Cook et al. characterized the market as two interrelated markets, which they called *primary* and *secondary*.[10] Although I previously addressed legal and illegal markets (chapter 2), the Cook characterization offers an equally accurate perspective with a different emphasis. The primary market consists of licensed dealers, primarily selling new guns, while the secondary market includes all other sources. These secondary sources provide firearms previously sold in the primary market. Both markets involve legal and illegal transactions. This division of the market has assumed more descriptive power with the advent of the Brady Law requirement for the screening of all buyers in the primary market.

Cook et al. concluded that most individuals, including those prohibited from acquiring firearms, prefer the primary market for its ability to supply specific firearms.[11] In my own experience this holds true for those who care about guns and desire a particular type. Some individuals have little interest in firearms and desire them only as a tool for a specific purpose, although this population seems to have declined over the past quarter-century.[12] Cook et al. also argue that blocking access to primary markets will shift buyers to secondary markets, which, they theorize, are equal in volume to the primary market. Unlike many products, guns have two characteristics that ideally suit them for sale in a secondary market: They have great durability, and their technology has changed very slowly. Cook et al. also concluded that active offenders, particularly young offenders, must continually renew their supply of firearms as a result of seizures, losses, and new offenders entering the scene.[13] Thus the secondary market requires constant replenishing from the primary market, primarily in the form of semi-automatic handguns.

REGULATING MARKETS

Cook et al. argue that market regulations designed to tighten control on the primary market will generate benefits by reducing the flow of firearms from the primary to the secondary market. For many years, ATF and others have proceeded as though two markets existed, one legal and the other illegal. Experienced agents have long known that the two markets constituted the extreme ends of a continuum and not discrete entities. Virtually no seller restricts himself to prohibited buyers or persons with illegal intent. Unlicensed dealers routinely sell to law-abiding citizens who can lawfully possess firearms. The most recent ATF document on firearm trafficking recognizes the illegal market as a complex mix of commercial and private sources, providing new and used guns acquired by both legal and illegal purchases and by theft.[14] However, even this more sophisticated view fails to adequately discuss the integrated nature of legal and illegal markets.

While Cook et al. advocate tighter controls on the primary market, they provide few specific details beyond increasing ATF scrutiny of applicants and cracking down on those not legitimately in the business. Although Cook and others seem enamored with the idea of eliminating dealers not actively engaged in the business, they provide no documentation that these dealers significantly contribute to the flow of arms to gun traffickers or that these dealers constitute a major source of firearms to prohibited persons. My own experience convinces me that the majority of these "kitchen table" dealers do very little, other than buying guns for themselves at a discount. This does not imply that they do not create impediments to effectively administering and enforcing the firearm laws: Their sheer numbers strain regulatory resources and provide cover for the small minority of illegal traffickers among their ranks. Despite this, efforts to deny licenses to persons not actively selling firearms has generated immense hostility toward gun laws and ATF, while producing little benefit (see chapter 8). The increase in the license fee to $200 for an initial application, combined with requirements for fingerprints and more detailed application information, reduced the number of licensees by two-thirds and demonstrated the inelastic nature of license demand.

By simply setting dealer license fees at a level adequate to compensate the government for the cost of administering the licensing and compliance functions, Congress could further reduce the number of licensees to a more manageable level without generating additional regulatory burden or conflict between the regulators and regulated.[15] The use of costs to establish license fees would provide two advantages: By reimbursing the government for the cost of administration, the fees would place the burden on the beneficiaries and not the taxpayers. This would ensure symbolic fairness and counter the characterization of higher fees as an anti-gun strategy. Combining higher fees with the restoration of a felony section for a dealer's willful falsification or failure to maintain records and a requirement to report all gun transfers between dealers would lead to a smaller and much more compliant primary market.

As the number of marginal dealers declined, full-time dealers would benefit economically. This would increase both the value of a license and the marginal cost of losing a license, thus further discouraging violations of laws or regulations. This strategy of differentiating between dealers and nondealers would further benefit from a clear and concise definition of what activity constituted "engaging in the business." By defining "engaging in the business" as the offering of a finite number of guns, the line between dealers and others would become much clearer. Even if the number of guns was kept at a level below ten guns per year (I recommend six), most gun owners would not feel its effects. Although those unfamiliar with gun markets may find six guns per year overly lenient, it would prove more than adequate to control unlicensed traffickers, who often stock dozens and sometimes hundreds of guns, while allowing gun owners the right to sell a gun every other month.

The final component—reporting gun and purchaser information on Brady sales—would ensure that dealers could not destroy records to cover unlawful transactions and would provide a means for identifying persons who purchase firearms in the primary market for unlawful resale. In combination, these policy changes would create a structure that facilitates quick detection of violations and ensures the existence of documentation, allowing the substantiation of detected violations. Even though most dealers remain law-abiding in the current market, in spite of dysfunctional policies and inadequate oversight, a single unscrupulous dealer can flood the illegal market with thousands of firearms before detection. Equally as important as any improvements in detection and prosecution of illegal action by dealers would be the changes these policies cause in the market environment. Dealers, who perceive their licenses as valued assets endangered by violation of the laws and regulations, have great incentive for compliance with them. In an environment where violations seldom occur, both the visibility of violations and the likelihood of official sanction in response to those violations increases. Conversely, the perception that violations are common and carry little risk of detection, prosecution, or regulatory action encourages illegal activity. In such an environment, even otherwise law-abiding individuals may view cutting corners as a means of keeping up with the competition. Well-crafted gun policy should not result in a high level of enforcement and regulatory actions against licensees, but in low rates of licensee violations.

James Jacobs and Kimberly Potter responded to the Cook et al. article with a detailed examination of the weak points in the existing Brady procedure and a critique of the problems inherent in any potential remedies.[16] As attorneys, they focused substantially on potential evidentiary issues arising from specific policies. This attention to the mechanics of enforcement, so often absent from policy analysis, constituted the core and most important contribution of their work. Although their article provides valuable insight into the problems inherent in gun control and market regulation, the authors devoted no attention to potential solutions.

Jacobs and Potter critique both the weaknesses in the federal licensing system and the gaps in current data systems used to detect prohibited persons. Much of their critique of licensing coincides with other critics and the earlier discussion in this book. They correctly identify gaps in available record systems as a limit on Brady checks, particularly with regard to prohibited persons other than felons. While improved record systems will likely reduce this gap over time, it will never disappear. Jacobs and Potter do identify owner licensing, which they reject for other reasons, as a means of addressing this problem. They also address a number of gaps in the Brady procedures that allows sales to prohibited persons to pass undetected or allows guns to migrate to the secondary market, where no Brady checks occur. These gaps result from the ability of purchasers to use false identities and straw purchasers as a means of avoiding detection.

The false identity problem creates an additional difficulty not addressed by Jacobs and Potter. Unscrupulous dealers can create false identities and enter them in the gun records to cover illegal sales. Determining whether the false identity originated with a purchaser or the dealer presents a difficult problem for investigators. A system of gun-owner licensing supported by fingerprints would address both problems. The dealer's report could be verified against a current license. Combining this system of verification with a requirement for dealers to obtain a thumbprint from the buyer would make the use of false identities by either dealers or buyers extremely risky.[17] No equally direct strategy exists for attacking the straw-purchaser problem.

As Jacobs and Potter point out, proving that a straw purchaser transferred the gun to the ultimate recipient constitutes a difficult evidentiary problem in that neither participant in the transaction need respond to questions. Firearm registration more directly addresses the issue than does licensing by narrowing potential explanations and defenses. A straw purchaser who has made multiple transfers faces a strong circumstantial case in the absence of an explanation. Straw purchasers can claim that a transfer to a prohibited or unlicensed person occurred in the erroneous belief that the recipient could lawfully possess the firearm. A requirement to report and obtain prior authorization of a transfer precludes this error defense. Registration and a requirement for prior approval of transfers denies virtually all explanations for transferring a gun to a prohibited recipient, leaving the straw purchaser with no available explanation except that someone took the firearm without his knowledge or consent. This becomes a very weak defense in cases of multiple transfers. Although some would continue to make straw purchases, a registration system should deter the risk-averse and inform the ignorant, leaving only those with specific criminal intent, on whom enforcement efforts should be concentrated.

Jacobs and Potter argue that the lack of Brady checks on private transactions allows a giant gap in the Brady procedures. Cook et al., who call for extending Brady to private transactions, agree. In fact, the conclusion seems obvious. Jacobs and Potter go beyond Cook, however, and argue that the extension of Brady checks to private transactions, called for by Cook, will fail and generate a further call for more restrictive legislation. I largely agree. Mandated checks, without a system of registration to document the transfers, would prove difficult to enforce. Recording the transfers, including the gun description and the identity of both the buyer and seller, would provide significantly better mechanisms for enforcement. However, California's experience has revealed that even these requirements will not generate compliance without some education and enforcement effort. True registration, unlike an extension of Brady, would subject illegally transferred guns to seizure and forfeiture. This would provide a powerful incentive for the law-abiding to comply. Once compliance became routine, those violating the law would become more conspicuous and easier to prosecute. Although the prosecution of incidental violators, without criminal histories, would probably remain difficult, those who transferred guns to prohibited persons or for specific criminal purposes in violation of registration could no longer use the defense of simple error or oversight. The deliberate bypassing of a required procedure would provide strong evidence of specific criminal intent and aid prosecution for the more serious charge of furnishing a firearm to a prohibited person or aiding and abetting a crime.

A well-designed registration system would place tremendous pressure on both the illegal market and the casual transfers, which undercut the screening of purchasers in the primary market. Registration records would allow investigators to track every gun to its last legal owner. This alone would deter most gun owners from making an illegal transfer. Even persons who routinely violate other laws would have reason to avoid illegal gun transfers. They do not welcome police attention and thus would have reason to avoid transferring guns registered to them.

Enforcers would face a massive task in obtaining registration of all the existing inventory of firearms. Some otherwise law-abiding gun owners would simply refuse to comply, and most criminals would ignore the requirements. Over time, the first group would probably realize that unregistered firearms, which could not be legally sold, lacked value and that registration had not led to confiscation. Obtaining the compliance of this group would require adaptive strategies and experimentation. For those who did not comply, seizure and forfeiture would provide a far better remedy than prosecution. Many who refused to comply would hide some or all of their guns away. Because such action would remove most of these guns from the market and from risk of theft, it poses little problem for enforcers. Any national registration policy should emphasize gentle persuasion and patience for those whose violations lack specific commercial or criminal intent. Serious enforcement efforts should be reserved for those with serious criminal histories and for those who possess or use firearms unlawfully.

Jacobs and Potter make a cursory examination of licensing and reject it on the grounds that it would require a massive bureaucracy, face widespread non-compliance, and fail to reduce crime. Although these all constitute legitimate policy concerns, Jacobs and Potter assert all three, without detailed analysis. The need for a massive new bureaucracy assumes that existing institutions could not adapt to the issuance of gun-owner licensing and gun registration. However, every state has a motor-vehicle agency that accomplishes just such tasks for drivers and vehicles. The existing procedures for concealed-carry permits in shall-issue states provide an excellent model for licensing procedures: Licensing entities must issue a license to any applicant upon completion of a background verification and a safety course or test, unless the applicant falls into a narrowly defined group of prohibited persons.[18]

Although a universal registration and licensing system could only come about under a federal mandate, that does not require direct federal implementation. States have both the experience and structure to better perform the task than has the federal government. Constitutionally constrained from mandating state action, Congress could pursue state cooperation through a variety of approaches, including providing financial incentives, mandating federal licensing and registration with a waver for citizens in states with equivalent systems, and prohibiting the issuance of federal firearm licenses in states without registration and licensing systems. Although license and transfer fees should cover the cost of such a system and avoid placing the financial burden on the general population, fees should not exceed these costs. The system should pursue convenience, economy, and service, with the goal of widespread voluntary cooperation. Current computer technology would allow the issuance of licenses for extended periods, since computers can detect a change in eligibility status. Interfacing the indexes for criminal records and gun licenses, as an example, would allow detection of new criminal convictions and automatic notifications to revoke licenses, although mental patients, misdemeanor domestic-violence convictions and restraining orders pose more difficult problems.

Although many gun owners perceive owner licensing as a burden, and even a threat, it would undercut any justification for waiting periods. A single, in-depth inquiry could occur at the time of licensing. Any subsequent firearm purchase would only require verification that the license remained valid. Licensing and registration would remove all ambiguity and liability for gun sellers by providing a required procedure and prescreening licensees. These procedures would also place significant pressures on those possessing or trafficking in stolen firearms, and aid in the recovery of stolen firearms. Currently, a person apprehended while possessing a stolen gun or while offering one for sale can claim ignorance of the theft. The possession of an unregistered stolen gun, or the offering of a stolen gun, without complying with transfer procedures would constitute a strong circumstantial evidence of knowledge and intent. In addition, registration would allow police to determine the serial number on virtually every stolen firearm and trace recovered arms back to their owners. Currently, many owners fail to retain serial numbers and cannot provide them to the police with theft reports.

A well-crafted licensing and registration system would probably prove both a burden and boon to gun owners. It would raise the cost of guns somewhat and would impose new procedural burdens in states that do not currently regulate private transfers. But it would simplify the Brady process, distinguish legitimate owners from illegal traffickers, clarify transfer procedures, and place new pressures on gun thieves and those who traffic in stolen guns. Jacobs and Potter suggest that such a system would face massive noncompliance. They cite the difficulty in controlling unlicensed drivers, but ignore the overwhelming compliance with driver licensing and vehicle-registration laws. No system can obtain total compliance, but much of the noncompliance among gun owners would involve hiding guns away to avoid registration. Such a response removes the gun from commerce, reduces theft risk, and generates little need for government response.[19] I suggest that a simple, uniform system maximizes the potential for compliance and serves to differentiate the criminally intent from the careless and the ignorant. The regulation of guns will remain a volatile issue for years to come. Acceptance of regulation will not improve through the gradual enactment of numerous confusing and inadequate requirements, each followed by a call for new requirements. Control advocates should determine what constitutes their desired level of regulation, considering both utility and the interests of gun owners, then pursue that goal. Gun owners have a right to know the ultimate objective and its costs. An open pursuit of registration and licensing could hardly increase their fears.

GUN CONTROL AND THE PREDATORY CAREER CRIMINAL

To date, most of the justification for presale checks, registration, and the licensing of firearms has rested on efforts to deny guns to high-risk persons, primarily convicted felons. Opponents have long argued that highly motivated persons will simply adapt to restrictions and acquire their firearms by other means.[20] This assumes that all criminals have a high level of motivation and remain focused on objectives. My own experience convinces me that most lower-level street criminals display neither of these traits; in fact, the failure to focus on anything but immediate gratification constitutes a common trait among this group. Interviews tend to confirm that the desire for a firearm competes with other objectives and may not prevail.[21] Thus these laws may reduce the level of arms among street criminals, especially the young and poorly organized. By reducing the flow of guns from the primary to the secondary market, and by constricting sales in the secondary market, these changes would reduce the opportunities for bypassing control procedures. However, the argument that highly motivated criminals will still obtain guns remains a valid critique. Of course, experience with drug prohibition provides overwhelming evidence that drug laws do not prevent determined users from obtaining drugs. In fact, some portion of the population violates every law. Still, we have not seriously considered revoking drug laws or any of the multitude of other laws widely violated. The current debate ignores addressing the utility of gun laws for purposes other than preventing felons and other prohibited persons from obtaining guns.

For over a decade, American criminal-justice policy has primarily pursued the strategy of identifying and removing high-risk and repeat offenders from society. The assumption that a small number of active offenders commits a large portion of street crime—the conceptual basis for the three-strikes laws widely enacted in recent years[22]—has significant support from research. James D. Wright and Peter Rossi's survey of inmates in 11 prisons in 10 states provides the most extensive research available. Fortuitously, the Wright and Rossi study obtained extensive information on firearm acquisition and possession as well as on criminal activity. The results provide important information regarding gun possession and criminal activity.

Wright and Rossi designated approximately 20 percent of their sample as being firearm predators. This subgroup reported committing about half of all the crimes admitted by inmates and most of the violent crimes.[23] Interestingly, this group also reported habitually obtaining, owning, and carrying firearms.[24] Based on the Wright and Rossi data, the coalescence among active criminals between high levels of criminal activity, particularly violent activity, and gun possession and carrying seems striking. Although this study has received significant attention from the opponents of gun control, who view it as proving that violent offenders will obtain guns by some means, the correlation between armed felons and high levels of criminal activity has remained largely unexamined. However, the discovery that active violent offenders have an affinity for guns comes as no surprise to experienced law-enforcement officers and moreover is supported by other research.[25]

This propensity toward firearm possession among the very group that criminal-justice policy has attempted to target offers a unique opportunity to utilize firearm laws to great effect. Rather than assume that the laws will deter active felons from acquiring firearms, I suggest we accept that they often will not. Policy-makers, police, and prosecutors should use gun laws as a means of removing these active offenders from society—a gun policy that even the NRA endorses.[26] In addition to providing a mechanism for removing repeat offenders from society, rigorous enforcement, coupled with the harsh sentencing of repeat offenders for gun possession, would sharply increase the risks associated with gun carrying for anyone in this group. An examination of the habits of career offenders reveals both opportunistic crime and rash behavior.[27] Any deterrent that reduced the casual carrying of firearms—so common among repeat offenders—should reduce both crimes of opportunity and spontaneous armed assaults.

Currently, only California includes possession of a firearm by a convicted felon among the predicate offenses that trigger mandatory sentencing on a second or third strike.[28] California included the offense not through deliberate consideration but by the questionable decision to include all felonies as predicate crimes.[29] A somewhat parallel federal law imposing a minimum 15-year sentence on felons with three prior violent or serious drug-trafficking convictions for possession of a firearm exists largely because gun laws provided one of the few vehicles for Congress to "get tough" on street criminals.[30] Although numerous arguments may exist for limiting what crimes qualify as a second or third strike, the Wright and Rossi research argues against excluding possession of a firearm by a felon.

A number of practical considerations also support the use of this statute as a mechanism for removing active offenders from society. With the exception of two articles (which I published), these practical utilities have received virtually no attention in the criminal justice or legal literature, presumably because academics and legal scholars have little experience with the mechanics of street-level law enforcement.[31]

Although the nature of the practical advantages differs for reactive and proactive policing, it exists for both. Most arrests for firearm possession result from reactive police action. Patrol officers inadvertently discover a gun during a car stop, while making an arrest, or during a field interrogation. Investigators often discover firearms while serving a search warrant for other evidence. Reactive discoveries of firearms provide police with two advantages: By discovering the firearm themselves, the police become the primary prosecution witness. This eliminates dependence on citizen witnesses, who may not appear or who may perform poorly on the witness stand. Issues of identity seldom arise. When the felon has the firearm on his person, the only hope for defense lies in suppressing the search. The courts have granted the police authority to "pat down" persons for weapons on mere suspicion, which is more discretion than the police possess in virtually any other search.[32] Therefore few legal defenses exist in these cases and the cases do not require elaborate preparation, although they become more difficult when police discover the firearm in a vehicle, residence, or other location. In these instances, investigators must develop evidence to link the gun and the suspect.

An example of such a case and its utility involved two convicted murderers, both with other violent felony convictions, who were stopped by California highway patrol officers for speeding. The officers observed blood on the subjects' clothing and searched the vehicle. In the trunk they discovered clothing soaked with human blood, an assault rifle, and a pistol. Imbedded in the frame of the pistol were bits of human flesh. Although subsequent investigation by homicide investigators and ATF agents, working under my supervision, never located a victim, both subjects received sentences of approximately 20 years in federal prison for firearm possession.

Police have developed proactive career-criminal programs in recent years to target the very type of individuals that Wright and Rossi identified as firearm predators. In combination with parole and probation officers, special career-criminal squads have conducted surveillance on selected suspects in hopes of apprehending them during a criminal act. They have also attempted to develop informants to determine the nature, time, and place of future criminal acts by these targeted offenders. Police justify the time and effort required by these efforts with the presumption that one active offender can generate numerous crimes, each of which produces both a societal cost and a demand on police resources. Although an apprehension might require a number of officers to spend days or even weeks investigating and observing one suspect, the apprehension can save immense police resources and societal cost. Of course, this logic presumes the ability to apprehend the suspects in a significant number of cases.

Law-enforcement officers, who conduct surveillance and proactive investigation, soon find that catching an experienced offender in the process of committing a crime is no easy task. Offender wariness and caution peak immediately before and during criminal acts, making them difficult to follow and observe. Career offenders often have no regular employment, schedules, or places of residence. Even an active criminal spends most of his time engaged in other activities and usually habituates areas in which residents quickly note even a discreet police presence. In addition, the development of informants willing to risk the wrath of violent career offenders proves very difficult. These offenders have learned circumspection regarding their specific criminal activities. Thus potential informants often cannot obtain information regarding the offender's future activities; those who do often know that its disclosure would focus the offender's attention on themselves as the source, placing them in jeopardy. In addition to the problems associated with surveillance and information, catching the offender in the act raises tactical and ethical problems. Arresting offenders before they complete the crime may preclude later prosecution. Waiting until the act is in progress or has been completed not only subjects innocent parties to risk but subjects police to liability and public outrage. Apprehension after the crime risks flight and precludes exercising control over the arrest setting.

Proactive pursuit of gun violations allows several advantages over attempts to apprehend the offender in the act of a crime. Many more people know about an offender's gun possession than about the specifics of upcoming crimes. The nature of firearms and their possession and storage allow investigators numerous advantages in obtaining search warrants for firearms,[33] and parole searches can often eliminate the need for a warrant. Suppression of evidence obtained with a search warrant has become virtually impossible.[34] Timing an arrest of an armed felon, though problematic, offers far fewer problems than apprehension during a robbery or burglary. Police can control both the time and place of the arrest.

Given this litany of legal, tactical, and investigative advantages, one would expect police and prosecutors to pursue with zeal firearm investigations and prosecutions against convicted felons. This has not proven to be the case, although pilot efforts have produced encouraging results. A coordinated effort between local, state, and federal agencies to attack gun trafficking and illegal gun possession appears to have significantly contributed to a sharp drop in armed violence in Boston.[35] In Richmond, Virginia, a combined effort by police, local prosecutors, ATF, and the U.S. Attorney—termed Project Exile— appears to be contributing to a precipitous drop in the city's murder rate— down 30 percent in the last year.[36] In both of these cases, interviews with gang members and other offenders indicate an increased wariness regarding the carrying of firearms. This fear seems to relate directly to the intensive prosecution and lengthy sentences, which have been widely publicized.[37] While such efforts enjoy the support of both the NRA and HCI, they depend heavily on the federal courts for prosecution. Federal judges in Richmond express open hostility to the project, and the federal courts lack the capacity to handle massive numbers of felons with firearm cases nationwide.[38] The strategy also raises serious questions regarding the federalization of crime. The states could largely address

these issues by incorporating possession of a firearm by a felon into the predicate crimes for mandatory sentencing. In addition, most local police and prosecutors would have to revise their attitudes and approaches toward this offense.

WHY GUN LAWS ARE AN UNDERUTILIZED LAW-ENFORCEMENT TOOL

In my years in law enforcement I conducted investigations in six states and
many more cities. I worked with and trained federal, state, and local investigators from all parts of the country.[39] I have found that most police and prosecutors have long ignored firearm violations. While virtually every police
agency of 25 or more officers has a narcotic-enforcement unit and a swat team,
even most large departments lack a firearm-investigation unit. Likewise, prosecutors devote little time and attention to these violations, and few offices
assign specific responsibility for their prosecution. Although these observations
may seem to raise questions regarding the potential utility of pursuing firearm
violations, an examination of the history of these violations provides another
explanation. For many years firearm convictions invoked very lenient sentences. Viewing these violations as status crimes, judges routinely imposed
short sentences. Routinely, prosecutors dropped charges in favor of parole violations or agreed to lenient sentences to obtain guilty pleas.[40] Even in federal
court before 1986, a felon convicted of firearm possession served no more than
eight months in custody, regardless of the number or nature of prior criminal
convictions.[41] Under these circumstances, defendants routinely pleaded guilty
to gun charges or prosecutors dismissed the gun charges if defendants pleaded
to other charges.

Since the sentence serves as a de facto indicator of a crime's importance,
police and prosecutors did not place a high priority on gun cases. They also
saw little need for investigation or trial preparation of cases that would probably result in plea bargains, and that seldom went to trial in any case. In some
instances, police filed misdemeanor concealed-weapons charges rather than
felony charges of a felon in possession of weapons, because no one bothered
to check the prior criminal record. More often, they failed to obtain certified
proof of the prior convictions or to verify that the gun possessor's fingerprints
matched those of the person previously convicted. Police routinely failed to
properly handle or process firearms as evidence, take statements from witnesses
regarding possession of the firearm, or collect important evidentiary items such
as holsters, ammunition, or receipts. None of these oversights appeared to be
important so long as cases never went to trial, and police passed on these procedures from one generation to the next. Only ATF agents, forced by jurisdiction to focus on firearm violations, differed as a group from this pattern.[42]

Unfortunately, as gun violations take on the severe sentencing imposed by
three-strikes legislation or by the federal armed-career-criminal provisions,

defendants cease pleading guilty. Faced with potential sentences of 25 years to life in California courts, or 15 to life in federal court, career offenders have every motivation to fight conviction with every available means. In cases where police recover the firearm from their person, defendants have little hope beyond suppressing the search. When police recover the firearm from a vehicle, residence, or other location, the defense most-often attempts to raise doubt regarding their possession of the gun with a claim of ownership by a third party, usually a relative or close friend. When the defendant disposes of the gun during pursuit, the defense usually consists of simple denial.

INVESTIGATIVE UTILITY OF SPECIFIC GUN LAWS

Just as the utility of laws requiring records of sale, registration, and licensing in preventing and prosecuting illegal gun trafficking has received little attention, the advantages that these laws offer investigators and prosecutors in possession cases have remained little understood. I supervised two cases in which suspects with multiple violent convictions, including murder, fled the police and discarded firearms in the process. In both cases, investigators significantly shored up marginal circumstantial cases by tracing the recovered revolvers to associates of the suspects. Both gun owners testified that the guns had disappeared when the suspects had access to their houses. Although this testimony may have served to cover up a voluntary transfer of the gun by the owner to the felon, the records served to establish the link. I have also conducted and supervised many cases in which the trail ends with an owner selling the firearm to a person they cannot identify. Gun shows provide one of the most common forums for such untraceable sales, as buyers and sellers seldom know each other.

Although most gun-control advocates have argued for the extension of the Brady process to screen individual buyers, this change offers little utility without a requirement for the full reporting of purchaser identity and gun description and the retention of that information in a readily retrievable system. A reporting system that does not capture transfer information involves virtually all the expense for far less than half the benefit. Not only does a record of transfers facilitate tracing, it also greatly increases pressure on individuals to comply with reporting and transfer requirements by ensuring a permanent record. Investigators could always determine whether a gun had been transferred properly. True registration, which renders as contraband an unregistered gun, would significantly increase the pressure beyond a simple record of transfer.

Both registration and licensing create difficulty for the common defense that another person placed the gun in the defendant's vehicle, room, or other location without the defendant's knowledge. Juries sometimes reject such testimony, as when the girlfriend of a defendant, accused of throwing a gun out the window as agents came through the door, testified that she had placed the loaded, cocked revolver in her yard to keep it away from her young child. But more plausible stories can raise serious doubts for a jury. Such stories become more risky and difficult when the witnesses must explain their failure to obtain permits or acquire the guns through proper transfer procedures. Witnesses usually agree to offer such testimony in the belief that they face little or no risk of prosecution because their possession of the gun constitutes no crime and no documentation exists to prove perjury. Of course, when the gun truly belongs to a third party the record would aid the defense, as it should.

By constricting the secondary market, registration and licensing would increase the marginal value of every firearm a felon could obtain. This should produce two results: The overall quality of firearms used by criminals should decline, as they settle for what they can get. More importantly, from an investigator's perspective, criminals would become less willing to discard a firearm for fear of not finding a suitable replacement. This would benefit investigators in any crime involving ballistic evidence. Ballistic technology has advanced markedly in the past decade as a result of development sponsored by ATF and the FBI. Current technology allows scanning and digitizing the unique characteristics of fired bullets and casings and storing the resultant profile in a computer database. Investigators can now conduct a search for matches between recovered bullets or cases and available samples. To date, the databases consist of scannings from crime scenes and recovered firearms, but the potential utility is staggering. We stand on the threshold of the ability to catalog bullet and cartridge-case markings from every firearm manufactured and then search that database for matches with samples recovered from crime scenes. Similar technology has already revolutionized the investigative utility of latent fingerprints and is in the process of revolutionizing the utility of blood, semen, and hair samples. Implementation of this technology now depends more upon policy decisions regarding information collection than upon technological development.

WHY REGISTRATION AND LICENSING?

We could develop a national system of gun registration, administered at the state or federal level, without owner licensing, but we should not. Identity constitutes a key element in a registration system. Without requiring fingerprints, the system cannot verify identity. In a system that requires verification of identity by fingerprints, licensing ceases to impose an additional requirement and becomes a means of expediting verification. Even without registration, the current Brady system requires repeating the checking process every time a person makes a new purchase. By establishing a file of licensed individuals, regulators can instantly check a status with assurance of identity. If information indicating a change in status becomes known to the licensing entity, as with a first felony conviction, the agency can revoke the license, notify the individual, and take action to ensure that existing firearms are surrendered. Registration and licensing provide mutually supportive structures in which licensing ensures identity and eligibility and registration ensures that legal transfers only go to licensed individuals.

Licensing and registration requirements should apply to long guns as well as handguns. Although the National Crime Victimization Survey data indicates that 85 percent of gun crimes involve handguns, effective restriction of handguns would most likely result in the substitution of long guns.[43] Sheley and Wright report that 51 percent of surveyed juvenile inmates reported having possessed a sawed-off shotgun, and 38 percent reported having possessed a semi-automatic rifle.[44] In addition to the substitution issue, trying to define specific classes of firearms for regulation adds confusion and complexity—one need only examine the income-tax system to understand the cost in complexity generated by a policy of exclusions.

WHY EVERYONE NEEDS TO COMPROMISE

I recognize that the foregoing proposals constitute only an outline for policy development. I also recognize that policy formulation only constitutes a first step in the policy process. Successful policy requires effective implementation, followed by evaluation, feedback, and ultimately reformulation and adaptation. The devil remains in the details, and policy-makers must address the details of such mundane issues as the temporary loan or storage of registered firearms. Stakeholders, interest groups, and politicians must compromise to hammer out such details, and revisit those details periodically in light of implementation experience. Given the history of gun policy to date, even the modest degree of specificity offered here probably overreaches reasonable expectation. Still, within these outlines the nation could shape a workable gun policy that recognizes our unique political and social realities and protects the rights of gun owners, while significantly improving regulation of the marketplace and providing law enforcement with powerful tools for attacking illegal trafficking and illegal gun possession.

The advocates of regulation would have to abandon regulation for its own sake and accept that guns will remain a part of American culture for at least the foreseeable future. Opponents would have to work at ensuring the consideration of the interests of gun owners and dealers by helping to craft legislation, rather than opposing every proposal. Politicians would have to address the details of legislation rather than using it solely for symbolic political purposes. The state and federal governments would have to work out policies dividing responsibility for general areas of regulation and implementation and ensure continuity. All government entities would have to accept simplicity and uniformity as the primary objectives of any policy. The current environment has not produced the incentives for these behaviors.

CHAPTER TWELVE

GUN CONTROL AND
THE POLICY PROCESS

IN A 1995 *PUBLIC ADMINISTRATION REVIEW* article on gun-control policy, I suggested that the inability to reach consensus on policy involving so little potential for economic and cultural change did not bode well for weightier issues.[1] Although recommending publication of the article, one reviewer took sharp exception to this conclusion, pointing out that one could hardly extend conclusions drawn from the case of gun control to more weighty issues such as health care. Ironically, the review came to me as President Clinton's health-care initiatives dissolved in the face of opposition, which successfully utilized symbolism to tap public concern regarding implementation.

I restate my case. Our political structure favors policy deadlock by providing numerous mechanisms for obstruction, including allocation of senators by state, bicameral legislatures, separation of powers, presidential vetoes, and weak party structures. Combined with our immense size and diversity, our preference for individual rather than collective perspectives, and our populist fears of elites and institutions, these structural characteristics have left little choice but to embrace an incrementalist model. Because a pluralist system affords determined minorities numerous means for obstructing policy change, advocates of change frequently compromise-away key components of the policy in order to move it through the legislative process. Believing that even an ineffectual and symbolic move in the chosen direction will lead to meaningful change allows policy advocates to maintain legitimacy and self-respect and preserves belief in the efficacy of the system.

As Lowi and Spitzer have argued, policies requiring direct government coercion of individual citizens generate the widest resistance.[2] Thus policies requiring the imposition of controls on the conduct of large numbers of citizens become the most dependent upon incremental enactment. Policy advocates must assume that resistance will fade, as the population becomes more familiar and comfortable with the existence of controls on specific behavior.

But all policy advocates do not begin with equal advantage. Drug prohibition, for instance, constitutes national policy in the United States, while gun control flounders. Existing drug laws, passed in the absence of organized resistance, constitute the status quo; therefore supporters of drug control possess all the advantages of a system structured to favor opposition to change. Furthermore, drug users and dealers have been widely demonized, delegitimizing their claims to equal protection with much of the public. Increasing the punishment for criminal conduct enjoys the same advantage over any opposition. Traffic-safety advocates enjoy a different sort of advantage: Opponents of mandatory seat-belt laws had no hope of convincing the general public that these laws constituted the first step in an incremental assault on driving. Smoking restrictions offer a third example of successful advocacy of a regulatory policy: Perhaps the most analogous to the gun issue, this effort seems to have successfully rallied wide public support with a public-health argument, although the daily irritation of exposure to smoke may have played a larger role than public-health data. In addition, the objectives of the antismoking lobby— higher taxes and expanded nonsmoking areas—constitute modest objectives.

Although the foregoing examples confirm the capacity of our system to sometimes enact regulatory policy affecting significant numbers of people, the need to pursue an incremental strategy presents several problems: By failing to take decisive action, while threatening future action, incrementalism encourages growth in the number of opposition stakeholders. This has proven to be the case with gun control, most recently with assault-weapon regulation. The belief that the sale of assault weapons will eventually be prohibited pushes large numbers of potential purchasers to buy them, increasing demand that further accelerates buying. While the acceptance of the concept of regulation may build over time among the general public, the number of stakeholders requiring accommodation concurrently increases. A parallel example exists in land-use policy, where an extended incremental movement toward preservation accelerates development by those seeking to gain their objectives before implementation of the final policy.

The incremental strategy also encourages policy advocates to compromise proposals before introduction in an effort towards reducing fear and opposition. Because the ultimate policy goal usually exceeds the early proposals, opponents can readily invoke a slippery-slope argument against any proposal. This strategy has worked repeatedly with gun control; in fact, it has constituted the single most-important element in the successful opposition to change in gun policy. By characterizing every proposal as the first step toward prohibition, opponents have successfully determined the policy agenda. Discussion remains focused year after year on inconsequential issues of marginal utility such as cop-killer bullets and the definition of an assault weapon. In spite of perennial predictions of the imminence of repressive legislation, gun-control opponents have never had to seriously address gun owner licensing or gun registration as national policies.[3]

ACCESSING THE POLICY AGENDA

For policy change to occur, substantive proposals must first gain access to the policy agenda, and pluralism offers no assurance of such access. Cobb and Elder characterized pluralism as favoring the maintenance of stability between interests over decision-making and innovation and, therefore, open to policy change only at the margins.[4] In their model, policies reach the systemic policy agenda only when a significant portion of the public perceives the underlying issue as a significant problem of legitimate public concern, amenable to government action.[5] In Kingdon's model of agenda-setting in the pluralist state, the occasional convergence of policy entrepreneurs and policy streams results in the opening of what Kingdon calls the "policy window"; this model of periodic attention fits well with Baumgartner and Jones's episodic disruption model and Birkland's study of focusing events.[6] All these models characterize agenda-access as being difficult and fleeting, often the result of an uncontrolled symbolic event.[7] As Birkland predicts, events are least likely to move issues onto the policy agenda when the policy community consists of contentious elements. This has proven to be the case for gun control, where policy advocates on both sides have failed to move the agenda after such visible events as the Waco raid and the Littleton shooting.

In such an environment, policy advocates have strong incentives for crafting policy initiatives to capture fleeting public attention and capitalize on current symbolic concerns, but have few incentives for devoting resources to building expertise in policy implementation or outcomes. In fact, incorporating into the process policy experts without political expertise or motivation could easily reduce flexibility; subject-matter experts tend to ignore the issues and opportunities of the moment and encumber policy formulation with discussions about details.

INFORMATION, IDEOLOGY, INTEREST, AND GUN-CONTROL POLICY

Scholars and academics routinely recommend additional research to resolve policy dilemmas and deadlocks. In the case of gun control (and probably many other issues), there seems little reason to assume that any outcome from research would alter the public's awareness or characterization of the issue adequately so as to alter the political situation. Although the work of Kleck, Lott, and others may fall short of proving a crime-deterrent effect from the presence of guns, it raises serious doubts regarding the probability of any research disclosing a direct causative link between guns and violent crime. Although one can never predict future research findings with assurance, the lack of correlation between gun ownership and violent crime rates does not imply a close, direct linkage. Although more sophisticated models such as Spitzer's arming for defense generating fear in others and responsive arming that facilitates violence might help to explain the increase in armed violence among urban youth that began in the mid-1980s, it does not explain its subsequent decline.[8] In fact, drawing long-term policy conclusions from social science is always problematic.

Humans respond to change—thus the short-term results of a policy change may differ greatly from the intermediate- or long-term results. As an example, increased gun carrying might initially reduce certain crimes such as robbery, until robbers adapted to the change. At that point it might raise homicides as robbers increased their armament and altered their tactics to preclude the use of guns in self-defense. In turn, potential victims might react to this trend in a variety of ways. Ultimately, the only way to determine the efficacy and unintended consequences of a policy remains trial and error. Even then, the outcomes may evolve over time in response to social, economic, or demographic changes.

It seems unlikely that social-science research will make any significant changes in the political dynamics of gun control. In her 1982 examination of congressional policy decisions, Carolyn Weiss found that three primary influences shaped policy positions: interest, ideology, and information. Only when interest and ideology directly conflicted did she find information to constitute the deciding factor.[9] Because geography usually predicts both ideology and interest in the gun-control issue, policy-makers have little reason to turn to information—the information available provides no simple answer. In addition to the alignment of interest and ideology, legislators appear unwilling to accept gun control as a serious policy issue worthy of study. Veteran Democrat State Senator Leroy Greene, in an interview shortly before his 1998 retirement from the California Senate, expressed the opinion to me that gun control did not matter at all. Although those facing re-election seldom speak with such candor, staff interviews support the conclusion that most legislators devote little thought to the issue.[10] Because the policy process seldom or never addresses gun control as a systemic issue, legislators view it as an arena for political, rather than subject, expertise. Reflecting the views of their employers, legislative staffs in Congress and the states have devoted little time and attention to gun control as a systemic issue.

Neither the advocacy groups nor the bureaucracy has done much to fill the gaps in legislative expertise. While legislative staff members often cite the NRA as possessing expertise in gun issues, they usually include the caveat that the NRA seldom helps in the drafting of any gun law.[11] HCI and other supporters of gun control have developed some knowledge regarding the size and nature of gun markets and current litigation, but legislative staffs report that control supporters possess only limited expertise. Staff members report similar frustrations with members of state and federal bureaucracies.[12]

Although lobbyist and advocacy groups often constitute a primary source of information for legislators and their staffs, gun control lacks the incentives and structure to produce this support. Neither interest group operates with the sort of economic incentive that drives many other lobbies. HCI lacks adequate resources to amass a large staff and mostly concentrates on building public support for gun control rather than addressing the details of policy. The NRA *does* possess a large staff, but has no motive to pursue better policy. Essentially, the NRA has incentives only to pursue negative information regarding gun control and to avoid addressing the details of any substantive proposals so long as it can keep them off the public agenda. In addition, lobbies respond to the demand of legislators, and legislators want symbolic and political analysis of gun issues to defend their existing positions.

The bureaucracy has little reason to address policy initiatives with no realistic chance for enactment, and every reason to avoid close identification with gun control.[13] ATF has learned from long years of experience that gun-control opponents will capitalize on every opportunity to characterize the agency as "gun grabbers." Unlike many other federal agencies, ATF does not even offer routine cleanup bills for fear they will invoke the wrath of gun-control opponents.[14] This avoidance of any association with gun legislation began with the congressional hostility over the proposed changes in GCA regulations in the late 1970s; it increased with Reagan administration proposals to abolish the agency and became policy during the 12 years of the Reagan and Bush administrations. Although the political changes of 1992 produced an environment in Washington that was more accepting of gun control, the election of 1994 quickly reversed that trend in Congress. A policy area as contentious and politically stalemated as gun control offers no incentives for developing the sort of topic expertise that would facilitate effective policy.

THE ABSENCE OF POLICY

This book began with the statement that most people I encounter seem to discuss gun control without ever defining or clearly understanding what they mean by the term. This same lack of clarity infects existing gun policy in the United States. Only three general-policy aims seem to emerge from the existing hodgepodge of federal, state, and local laws: 1) denying general access to implements of war, 2) denying felons and other high-risk persons access to all firearms, and 3) limiting the carrying of concealed weapons to licensed persons. However, even these objectives do not enjoy universal support. Not only do some states' laws not contain these restrictions, but the definition of "felons" varies with the law of each state. If the examination of policy extends beyond legal prohibitions to mechanisms for enforcement, even these limited objectives come into doubt.

Essentially, we have declined to formulate any policy on gun commerce or to examine the regulatory structure necessary to maximize our policy of denying guns to specified classes of individuals. However, the failure of policymakers to address an issue does not *remove* the issue. In the words of Benjamin

Barber: "Without public judgments, private action will always prevail."[15] Although policy-makers have often avoided addressing contentious issues, the issues persist and often become more intractable. One hundred years of avoidance did not simplify the civil-rights issue or reduce conflict. Civil-rights change did not occur until the courts and, ultimately, Congress and the administration accepted confrontation and allowed the issue to be put on the agenda. As already noted, the practical difficulties of regulation can actually increase as the issue simmers on the sidelines of public policy, encouraging potential stakeholders to act before policy changes. Any future effort to address urban sprawl must face the reality of post–World War II suburban development.

The failure to address fundamental gun policy in 1934 and 1968 has allowed a massive unregulated increase in the gun population. Although some argue in favor of a laissez-faire market and view this population growth with approval, few can characterize it as a conscious policy choice. This outcome, which now constrains policy options, resulted more from decision avoidance than from conscious decision-making. Political scientist Charles Lindblom characterized pluralist democracies, or "polyarchies," as having a preference for epiphenomenal action in the face of interest conflict.[16] Faced with a structure that affords policy opponents the advantage of numerous blocking points, governments shift decisions to the market mechanisms by avoiding substantive policy decisions, a practice that Lindblom viewed as dangerous to the future of democracy.[17] Likewise, Barber points out that "inaction will inevitably result in other actions taking their natural course."[18] Gun control provides a classic example for the case that the failure to agree on the nature of regulation or on effective mechanisms for its implementation constitutes a decision *not* to regulate.

The enactment of substantive policy in our system requires either a lack of opposition or public support adequate to force compromise on the opposition. To reach that level against organized opposition, support must be more than mere acquiescence—it requires a depth of commitment and endurance. Even when support exists for policy in the abstract, it may not prove to be adequate to support effective implementation policies that impose costs and hardships on real people. This has largely proven to be the case with immigration, where Congress has imposed restrictions on it but refused to effectively address the key component of employment.[19] Even imposing the implementation of the metric system—an action taken by virtually every nation in the world— has frustrated American policy-makers.

Policies intended to generate widely dispersed societal benefits over the long term, rather than individual short-term benefits, lack self-interest constituencies and run counter to the American cultural bias towards individualism, which is hostile to collective solutions. To develop broad public interest and support, policy advocates can attempt to link the policy to powerful symbols or exaggerate the immediate nature of the problem and the probability of its immediate solution through adoption of the advocated policy. They can also attempt to undercut opposition by demonizing or compromising with opponents. In any case, they must move rapidly whenever external events focus public attention and open up the policy window. These factors have combined to favor symbolism over efficacy, isolated initiatives over comprehensive proposals, political skill over policy expertise, and rapid action over careful deliberation. Ironically, as gun control demonstrates, such haste ensures that the issue will remain unresolved.

American political theory has long included the concept of the "iron triangle," consisting of legislators, regulators, and economic interest. Over time, a symbiotic relationship forms around their mutual interest in maintaining a stable environment, and excludes larger public interest. Gun control displays an interesting variation on this theme: Continuing conflict without substantive action has allowed both conservative and liberal politicians to use gun control to shore up their bases. Periodic policy proposals, exaggerated in importance by advocates and opponents, allow interest groups on both sides of the issue to maintain support and membership. Finally, the bureaucracy has developed a successful strategy of avoiding association with any policy proposals. All three elements have learned to live successfully with indecision; in fact, they have built a presumption of indecision into their routine behavior. Interests behave as though future policy discussions will center primarily on symbolism and efforts to control the rhetoric of the issue and not on the substance of policy proposals.

WHAT THE FUTURE HOLDS

Without a change in the political environment, the gun-control issue will remain indefinitely stalemated. Little or no evidence exists that a natural, incremental process will eventually resolve the issue or bring about comprehensive policy. Political environments *do* change. Between the mid-1960s and 1980s, American politics shifted decidedly to the right. Following that shift, power began to devolve back toward the states. In spite of this significant shift in politics, the Firearms Owners' Protection Act of 1986 appears to mark the limits of the gun-control opponents' ability to move the country toward an openly libertarian gun policy. Any push to shift the agenda further to the right would most likely energize the gun-control movement to levels not yet experienced. Therefore control opponents will likely remain in a defensive posture.

Current demographic trends favor pro-control forces over the long term. As urbanization increases and experience with firearms declines, the NRA's support-base erodes and the number of people who are uncomfortable with firearms rises. Party realignment also favors control proponents over time. Republican gains in the South and West have strengthened the position of control opponents in the Republican party. Conversely, Democratic losses in those areas free the Democrats to pursue gun control as a congressional issue. If the present trend continues, a Democratic majority in Congress in conjunction with a Democrat in the White House would eventually assure significant gun control legislation. Only opposition by a minority of primarily rural Southern and Western Democrats has precluded such an event.

Both of these trends constitute long-, not short-term threats. Opponents can fight an effective holding action for some time to come. The danger for gun interests lies in the nature of a potential loss. As a well-organized and committed minority it can successfully resist a much larger majority, even if that majority increases its interest in and support of additional gun controls. To maintain the commitment of its constituency, the NRA must convince it that all initiatives will lead to prohibition. This has two inherent risks: First, the constituency will not tolerate compromise. Therefore if the time comes that compromise becomes necessary, constituents may not allow negotiation. Second, the ability to hold back action with a minority may result in the opposition building up such strength before a break in the deadlock that the opposition has no need to compromise. Of course, neither of these may occur, and chief NRA lobbyist James Baker believes that there would always be an opportunity for negotiation, if it became necessary.[20]

Conceivably, gun advocates could alter the demographic trend by inducing more people to become interested in firearm ownership and shooting sports. Although the NRA professes interest in these objectives, one sees little evidence of its success. If current crime trends continue the fear of crime will continue to decline, reducing the likelihood of individuals buying guns solely for protection. Lacking a cultural link to firearms, many of those who acquired guns for this reason will probably lose interest in guns and the gun issue. While the NRA promotes and supports shooting sports, these efforts appear to have the effect of solidifying, but not expanding, its base. The NRA has devoted few of its precious political resources to the pursuit of public shooting facilities.

The courts remain an incalculable element in the gun–control issue. The current wave of litigation against gun manufacturers and Second Amendment challenges to existing laws both have the potential for altering the political landscape in ways difficult to predict. Control advocates have long expected public reaction to some horrific event, committed with a firearm, to alter the political landscape and open the policy window. However, this has not proven to be the case since 1968. Even then, its effect proved transitory and inadequate to pass the sort of broad systemic policy desired by the administration.[21]

If gun–control advocates wish to accelerate the rate of change in the political dynamics of gun control beyond what will result from natural demographic evolution, they either must win additional converts to their cause or reduce the opposition's core support. Control advocates' early strategy of supporting systemic control failed for lack of a committed constituency support. They then shifted to a strategy of pursuing limited objectives with strong symbolic appeal but little utility. Although this has produced limited victories, these have not evolved into committed support. In my opinion, the key to winning additional supporters lies in convincing citizens of the utility and efficacy of gun control. This would require building proposals around specific, well-defined objectives. The linkages between means and ends must be clear and defensible and the arguments consistent. Rank-and-file police and prosecutors constitute the most important potential constituency. If they are convinced that specific gun regulations would provide them with useful tools for pursuing high-risk, repeat offenders and for investigating and prosecuting violent crime, they would become a powerful force for winning over the general public.

Reducing opposition to gun control presents a more challenging task— few fervent opponents will likely become supporters. For those opposed for ideological reasons rooted in a sovereignty paradigm, no approach offers much hope for conversion. For those whose cultural or economic life depends upon the ability to freely transfer guns at will without regulation, no grounds for compromise exist. Moreover, for most gun owners the fear of prohibition provides the tie that binds them to the NRA and motivates their opposition to all gun-control proposals. If control advocates can reduce this fear, which rests on a firm acceptance of the slippery-slope argument, they will succeed in reducing gun-owner support for the NRA. If advocates wish to reduce this fear they must repudiate prohibition as an objective, avoid rhetoric that demonizes gun owners, and avoid support for control initiatives that do not further their avowed goals. Because some supporters *do* support prohibition and favor any restriction on guns without regard for the measures utility, advocacy groups probably forgo these approaches in deference to their most committed base. However, they may have some success in co-opting elements within the firearm industry, who come to view market stability as worth the cost of additional regulation.

The case of gun control illustrates a dilemma present in the American policy process. Policy-making is an intensely political process in which language, symbols, and culture play a critical role. In this process, the advantage belongs to the opponents of comprehensive policy and the opponents of change. The structural bias of the system therefore favors nondecisions over decisions, and symbolic action over substantive action. To overcome these natural advantages, policy advocates must marshal overwhelming and sustained support or nullify opposition. Thus the system favors political skills over substantive policy knowledge. Political battles often revolve around symbolism and efforts to define the nature of the issue. As a result, policy issues remain unresolved for extended periods, with participants having little incentive to develop substantive knowledge regarding details of the policy or its implementation.

• • •

Afterword:
Background and Literature

UNFORTUNATELY, MANY OF THOSE who have written on the issue of firearms have failed to understand the limitations resulting from significant gaps in their knowledge of some basic components of the issue. Advocates of regulation have routinely displayed a woeful lack of knowledge of the very nature of firearms themselves.[1] In the main, both advocates and opponents of firearm control display only limited knowledge of the mechanics of regulation and enforcement. That being said, there exists a growing body of serious literature relating to gun-control policy with which any student of the issue should be familiar.

Primarily written since 1970, much of the gun-control literature consists of advocacy pieces for or against the control of firearms as a government policy, although it often takes the form of history or policy analysis. Historian Richard Hofstadter argued that there is an American "gun culture" that grew out of the frontier myth.[2] In their social history *The Gun in America: The Origins of an American Dilemma*, Lee Kennett and James Anderson chronicled the history of guns in America in what is one of the least ideological pieces available. They theorized that support for gun control centered in what they characterize as the "cosmopolitan population." Defined as being more educated and primarily urban, the cosmopolitans shared a worldview more compatible with Western Europe than with Middle America. They supported collective planning and favored government intervention in solving social problems. The opponents, on the other hand, were characterized as being primarily rural or newly suburbanized and suspicious of both planning and government intervention.[3]

Sociologist Barry Bruce-Briggs's 1976 essay analyzed gun control in terms of its social dynamics and the worldviews of proponents and opponents. Like Kennett and Anderson, Bruce-Briggs theorized that reaction to gun control closely parallels one's orientation on social issues. Those persons disposed toward collective explanations and remedies to social problems favor gun control, and those who view individual causes and solutions oppose it.[4] Sociologist William R. Tonso built on this theory and elevated it to an almost conspiratorial level in his attacks on what he characterizes as an elitist effort to impose its values on America. Tonso's early work primarily consisted of a critique of what he characterized as hypocrisy in academia, but he has progressively moved toward a libertarian populist view of gun control as an elitist conspiracy.[5]

While offering insight into the cultural history of gun control, these social analyses do little to link social history with the policy process. Gun-control advocate Josh Sugarmann and journalist Osha Davidson have both produced histories of the National Rifle Association (NRA) that offer more practical insight into the mechanics of gun politics.[6] Although openly ideological, Sugarmann's work provides some insight into the evolution of the NRA and to the motivation and reward structure for policy outcomes within this key organization. Davidson's more impartial study provides rich detail regarding the political history of the issue during the 1980s.

Journalist and writer Robert Sherrill integrated a theory of self-interest by all parties concerned with cultural explanations in his 1973 history of gun-control policy efforts.[7] Sherrill presented a picture of advocates who had cynically used the issue without commitment, opponents who valued economic interests over ethics, bureaucrats that were incompetent and opportunistic, and a public that was really not concerned. In an analysis akin to that of Bruce-Briggs, Tonso, and Kennett and Anderson, Sherrill described the American social character as being incompatible with gun control and theorized that gun control could not be made to function in the social and political systems of the United States.[8] Lawyer and gun-control opponent David Kopel's extensive cross-cultural study *The Samurai, the Mountie, and the Cowboy* advances much the same argument in its examination of guns, crime, and culture.[9] Conversely, political scientists Robert J. Spitzer and Wilbur Edel both have produced comprehensive policy studies with an emphasis on interest-group theory.[10] Although both of these works provide useful histories, the authors appear to lack detailed knowledge of either firearms or firearm regulation. Both authors favor a pro-control position and lean toward an interpretation of the history of gun policy as an organized minority imposing its will on the majority.

Carol S. Leff and Mark H. Leff produced a very thorough piece of historical scholarship relating to congressional action on gun-control policy in the early part of the century.[11] Surprisingly, although the Gun Control Act of 1968 constitutes the most extensive piece of federal firearm legislation ever passed, no detailed histories of its enactment have been published.[12] Kennett and Anderson's general history has a section on the evolution of the bill, and legal scholar Frank Zimring has done one in-depth article on the law that includes some information on its evolution.[13] The most detailed discussion of the law's adoption and implementation can be found in my earlier writing.[14]

A group of researchers at the University of Massachusetts—James Wright, Peter Rossi, and Kathleen Daly—initiated a major effort at firearm-policy analysis in the early 1980s under a grant from the National Institute of Justice (NIJ). This study was structured in classic social-science format, which attempts to ignore all political ramifications and quantify results and outcomes. In addition to the report for NIJ, this work resulted in a book and several articles.[15] The authors' impartiality appears to have eroded somewhat as they became convinced that the problem was more difficult than they originally envisioned and could not be significantly reduced through restrictive policy without impacting a large number of law-abiding citizens.[16] In this, it was a harbinger of future work by social scientists, particularly Gary Kleck. The work of these authors remains, however, one of the few available book-length efforts at policy analysis of gun control. Wright has also made two other important contributions to the literature: He and co-author Peter Rossi surveyed convicted felons in 11 prisons in 10 states regarding patterns of behavior relating to crime and guns.[17] Subsequently Wright and Joseph Sheley conducted and published similar research with juvenile offenders.[18]

Four other authors have contributed consistently to the serious literature on gun control over an extended period of time: University of California law professor Frank Zimring; Florida State University criminologist Gary Kleck; attorney and civil-rights activist Don Kates; and Duke University public-policy professor Phillip J. Cook. Zimring and Hawkins's 1987 response to Wright et al. was both a critique of methodology and an advocacy piece in its own right.[19] Zimring's earlier work focused on the analysis of Chicago police records to determine the impact of firearms on the outcome of assaults.[20] From this study he theorized that the presence of firearms aggravates the outcomes of many assaults. This theory contends that many attacks result from momentary impulses and not a determination to kill, and that the lethality of firearms greatly increases the likelihood of death. Zimring has continued to write about gun control, but with little new research until his most recent work with Gordon Hawkins.[21]

In many ways the early work of both Kates and Kleck constituted responses to arguments by Zimring and others that the presence of firearms aggravates violent crime and increases the likelihood of serious injury or death. Kleck has become the dominant social scientist in the field of guns and crime, while Kates has primarily pursued issues of law and the Constitution. Zimring has continued to pursue the central theme that guns alter the nature of crime in the United States. Most recently, Zimring and Hawkins have argued that the high level of lethal violence in the United States relative to other G7 nations, which now exhibit equal or higher overall crime rates, primarily results from the availability of guns.[22]

Although both Kates and Kleck describe themselves as liberals, their approaches differ significantly. Kates admits a strong attachment to firearms and engages in unabashed advocacy. On the other hand, Kleck displays far more interest in social science methodology than in guns. He focuses primarily on countering what he characterizes as poor-quality research and careless conclusions. Although more concerned with basic research than policy, Kleck characterizes highly restrictive or prohibitionist gun-control laws as ineffective, costly, and undemocratic.[23] He bases this conclusion on the difficulty of isolating and controlling the small portion of firearms used for criminal purposes and on research findings relating to the influence of guns on overall violent-crime rates.[24] In recent years Kleck has become best known for his survey research on the defensive use of firearms to thwart crimes. He supports moderate control policies, which he believes would receive public support and be cost effective.[25] He theorizes that the failure to implement strict gun control in the United States results from a lack of intensity of public support,[26] which he attributes to the public's lack of faith in the efficacy of gun control.[27]

Kates has characterized gun-control proposals as unconstitutional, ineffective, and antidemocratic.[28] Although a long-time advocate of a basic right to possess and use arms in self-defense, Kates concedes that a wide variety of gun-control laws are constitutional.[29] He further contends that the unwillingness of control advocates to recognize a right to possess or use arms for self-defense exacerbates fears of incremental prohibition among gun owners and aids the NRA and its allies in opposing all controls.[30] While both Kleck and Kates are associated with the argument that guns can reduce crime through self-defense, Professor Phillip Cook has long been associated with the position that the presence of firearms *does* exacerbate violent crime.[31]

Cook has critiqued Kleck's research on the deterrent effect of guns[32] and responded to the structural policy analysis by University of Chicago Law Professor Daniel Polsby and others, who argue that incentives for bypassing controls will always render them ineffective.[33] He is also one of the few authors, along with New York University law professor James B. Jacobs and David Kennedy and Mark Moore of Harvard, who has examined the specific details of firearm markets and their regulation, an area largely neglected in the literature.[34]

The most recent controversy in the academic literature derives from the application of complex regression analysis to cross-sectional, county-level, time-series data by economists John Lott and David Mustard. Their analysis shows a positive correlation between liberalized concealed-carry laws and reduced crime.[35] Lott's work has generated an extensive critique of his methodology and assumptions, both of which have been challenged.[36] In spite of these, Lott's work has generated a sharp challenge to the presumption that the mere presence of firearms generates risk and it has significantly influenced public policy at the state level (see chapter 10).

NOTES

INTRODUCTION

1. For those seeking a comprehensive review of research, I recommend Gary Kleck's *Point Blank: Guns and Violence in America* (Hawthorne, NY: Aldine de Gruyter, 1991) and his more recent paperback version, *Targeting Guns: Firearms and Their Control* (Hawthorne, NY: Aldine de Gruyter, 1997).
2. Roger W. Cobb and Marc H. Ross, *Cultural Strategies of Agenda Denial* (Lawrence: University of Kansas Press, 1997), 205.
3. Frank R. Baumgartner and Bryan D. Jones, *Agendas and Instability in American Politics* (Chicago: University of Chicago Press, 1993), 4–9.
4. Aaron B. Wildavsky, *Speaking Truth to Power: The Art and Craft of Policy Analysis* (New York: Little, Brown, 1979), 83.
5. Robert J. Spitzer, *The Politics of Gun Control* (Chatham, NY: Chatham House, 1995), 4.
6. Theodore Lowi, "Four Systems of Policy, Politics, and Choice," *Public Administration Review* 32 (July/August 1972): 298–310.
7. William J. Vizzard, "The Evolution of Gun Control Policy in the United States: Accessing the Public Agenda." DPA dissertation, University of Southern California, School of Public Administration (Los Angeles, 1993).
8. Ibid. The Gun Control Act of 1968 addressed all types of firearms and had some impact on individual possession and all commercial sales. The Brady Law approached this standard by regulating all handgun sales by dealers.
9. Roger W. Cobb and Charles D. Elder, *Participation in American Politics: The Dynamics of Agenda-Building* (Baltimore: Johns Hopkins University Press, 1972), 14–16.
10. Ibid., 44–51.
11. Ibid., 85–87.
12. Cobb and Ross, 7.
13. John W. Kingdon, *Agendas, Alternatives, and Public Policy* (New York: HarperCollins, 1984), 188–200.
14. Thomas A. Birkland, *After Disaster: Agenda Setting, Public Policy, and Focusing Events* (Washington, DC: Georgetown University Press, 1997), 1–20.
15. Examples of legislation passed by one House of Congress and rejected by another include Saturday-night-special legislation and the Firearm Owners Protection Act; see Vizzard, 1993.
16. William J. Vizzard, *In the Crossfire: A Political History of the Bureau of Alcohol, Tobacco, and Firearms* (Boulder, CO: Lynne Rienner, 1997), 70–71.

17. William J. Vizzard, "The Impact of Agenda Conflict on Policy Formulation and Implementation: The Case of Gun Control," *Public Administration Review* 55, no. 4 (July/August 1995): 341–47.

18. William J. Vizzard, "A Systematic Approach to Controlling Firearm Markets," *Journal of Firearms and Public Policy* 11 (fall 1999): 177–220.

CHAPTER ONE

1. *Sacramento Bee*, "Family Targeted by Invaders in Deadly Attack" (January 6, 2000): A4.

2. Deborah Stone, *Policy Paradox* (New York: W.W. Norton, 1997), 1–13.

3. William J. Vizzard, 1993; 1995; and 1997, 20–24.

4. Robert Reich, ed., *The Power of Public Ideas* (Cambridge, MA: Ballinger, 1988), 1–13. In the introduction Reich postulates that ideas about the nature of man, human behavior, and what is desirable for society are often more important in the development of public policy than the process of balancing and compromising competing interests.

5. Kleck, 1997, 222; also see Kleck, 1991, 205, for a summary of studies. The concept of a triggering effect of a gun on individuals is virtually impossible to establish empirically. Although anecdotal evidence suggests such an event is possible, measuring its societal impact is beyond our capacity.

6. See George D. Newton and Franklin E. Zimring, *Firearms and Violence in American Life: A Staff Report Submitted to the National Commission on the Causes and Prevention of Violence* (Washington, DC: National Commission on the Causes and Prevention of Violence, 1969); Franklin E. Zimring and Gordon Hawkins, *A Citizen's Guide to Gun Control* (New York: Macmillan, 1987); and Phillip J. Cook, "The Effect of Gun Availability on Violent Crime Patterns," *Annals of the American Academy of Political and Social Science* 455 (May 1981): 63–79.

7. The Coalition Against Handgun Violence and Hand Gun Control Incorporated have focused their effort almost entirely on handguns, although "assault weapons" have become part of the agenda during the past decade.

8. The citation of 20,000 laws is a virtual mantra with opponents of gun control. It is cited repeatedly by Hardy and Kopel as well as in publications of the National Rifle Association. The 20,000 existing laws are primarily ordinances on carrying and use, see chapter 4 for more detail.

9. The exception to this pattern is opposition to prohibition proposals, where the cost falls on all potential owners. An example can be seen in the attack on Saturday night special legislation as discriminatory against the poor.

10. The work of Kleck and Lott is covered in chapters 2 and 10.

11. Barry Bruce-Briggs, "The Great American Gun War," *Public Interest* no. 45 (fall 1976): 37–62; and Lee Kennett and James Anderson, *The Gun in America: The Origins of an American Dilemma* (Westport, CT: Greenwood Press, 1975), 254–55.

12. Osha Gray Davidson, *Under Fire: The NRA and the Battle for Gun Control* (Washington, DC: National Press Books, 1992), 168–69.

13. William R. Tonso, "Social Problems and Sagecraft: Gun Control as a Case in Point," in ed. Don B. Kates, Jr., *Firearms and Violence* (San Francisco: Pacific Institute for Public Policy Research, 1984).

14. John Kaplan, "The Wisdom of Gun Prohibition," *Annals of the American Academy of Political and Social Science* 455 (May 1981): 11–21. Although Kaplan primarily characterizes the advocates of gun control as utilizing the issue to define the opponents as less worthy, a review of the rhetoric by both camps seems to produce similar results. The most extreme advocates characterize gun owners as violent, unsocialized dullards and

ask rhetorical questions such as "why would anyone ever want a gun?" At the other extreme, opponents characterize control advocates as wimps, cowards, elitists, and, occasionally, traitors; see Jeffrey R. Snyder, "A Nation of Cowards," *Public Interest* 113 (fall 1993): 40–55.

15. Don B. Kates, "Bigotry, Symbolism, and Ideology in the Battle Over Gun Control," *Public Interest Law Review* (1992): 31–46.

16. Spitzer, chapter 6.

17. Zimring and Hawkins, 159–69.

18. Richard Hofstadter, "America as a Gun Culture," in ed. Richard Hofstadter and Michael Wallace, *American Violence: A Documentary History* (New York: Knopf, 1970), 25–34.

19. Robert Dahl, *Dilemmas of Pluralist Democracy* (New Haven, CT: Yale University Press, 1982), 176–78.

20. Benjamin Barber, *Strong Democracy* (Berkeley: University of California Press, 1984), 14–16.

21. Ibid.

22. John C. McWilliams, *The Protectors: Harry J. Anslinger and the Federal Bureau of Narcotics, 1930–1962* (Newark: University of Delaware Press, 1990), 46–52.

23. Carl Bogus, "The Hidden History of the Second Amendment," *University of California Davis Law Review* 31, no. 2 (winter 1998): 309–408. Second Amendment issues are covered in depth in chapter 2.

24. Kleck, 1997, 38–41.

25. Gun-rights purist Neal Knox began his discussion with this writer with the statement that, "gun control is about power." This same theme runs through the publications of such groups as the Gun Owners of America and the Second Amendment Foundation. It can be seen on bumper stickers available in most gun shops declaring: "The Czechs registered their guns," or associating the swastika and hammer and sickle with gun control.

26. Don B. Kates, Jr., *Restricting Handguns: The Liberal Skeptics Speak Out* (Croton-on-Hudson, NY: North River Press, 1979); and Robert J. Cottrol and Raymond T. Diamond, "The Second Amendment: Toward an Afro-Americanist Reconsideration," *Georgetown Law Review* 80 (1991): 309–61.

27. Sanford Levinson, "The Embarrassing Second Amendment," *Yale Law Journal* 99 (1989): 637–59.

28. See, for example, *The Federalist Papers*, numbers 29 and 46.

29. John A. Rohr, "Ethical Issues in French Public Administration: A Comparative Study," *Public Administration Review* 51, no. 4 (July/August 1991): 283–98.

30. In my 27 years of enforcing firearm laws, I had many opportunities to observe the behavior and attitudes of prosecutors at both the state and federal level as well as jurors and judges. The pattern of reluctance to prosecute for violations that are not perceived as related to other "evil" behavior is common, often from those characterized as liberal and likely to support controls.

31. Levinson.

32. See James G. Haughton, "Doctors Should be Fighting to Ban Guns," *Medical Economics* 66, no. 16 (August 21, 1989): 24–27; Jaurie Jones, "MD Groups Support Semiautomatic Gun Ban," *American Medical News* 33, no. 8 (February 23, 1990): 11; Daniel Webster et al., "Reducing Firearms Injuries," *Issues in Science and Technology* 7, no. 3 (spring 1991): 73–80; Bijou Yang and David Lester, "The Effects of Gun Availability on Suicide Rates," *Atlantic Economic Journal* 19, no. 2 (June 1991): 74; James Price, Sharon Desmond, and Daisy Smith, "A Preliminary Investigation of Inner-City Ado-

lescents' Perceptions of Guns," *Journal of School Health* 61, no. 6 (August 1991): 255–60; Colin Loftin et al., "Effects of Restrictive Licensing of Handguns on Homicide and Suicide in the District of Columbia," *New England Journal of Medicine* 325, no. 23 (December 5, 1991): 1615–21; John Sloan et al., "Handgun Regulations, Crime, Assaults and Homicide: A Tale of Two Cities," *New England Journal of Medicine* 319, no. 19 (November 10, 1988): 1256–63; Arthur Kellermann and Donald Reay, "Protection or Peril: An Analysis of Firearm-Related Deaths in the Home," *New England Journal of Medicine* 314, no. 24 (June 12, 1986): 1557–60; and Garen Wintemute, Stephen Teret, and Jess Kraus, "The Epidemiology of Firearms Deaths Among Residents of California," *Western Journal of Medicine* 146, no. 3 (March 1987): 374–77.

33. Kates has examined combined suicide and homicide rates for a variety of nations and demonstrated that the combined rates are higher in a number of nations than in the United States due to higher suicide rates; see *Guns, Murder, and the Constitution: A Realistic Assessment of Gun Control* (San Francisco: Pacific Research Institute for Public Policy, 1990).

34. A number of persons interviewed during my research in 1992 and 1993 viewed this paradigm as having the potential for largely shifting the entire policy argument. Legislative staff of the California State Legislature noted that health care professionals were particularly effective in pushing for new legislation in that state in 1979. Although physicians have become a presence in the gun-control-policy community, neither their presence nor the public health paradigm has yet to reshape the issue significantly.

35. Don B. Kates et al., "Guns and Public Health: Epidemic Violence or Pandemic of Propaganda?" *Tennessee Law Review* 62 (1995): 513–96. Kleck has been very critical of the quality of research conducted by the public health community; see *Targeting Guns*, 56–60.

36. Wilbur Edel, *Gun Control: Threat to Liberty or Defense Against Anarchy?* (Westport, CT: Praeger, 1995), 108.

37. Ford's administration had a very moderate record on gun control; see chapter 8.

38. The late Frank Church (D-Idaho), a prominent liberal, wrote the foreword in Don B. Kates's, *Restricting Handguns*. Both former House Speaker Tom Foley (D-Wash.) and former House Judiciary Chairman Jack Brooks (D-Tex.) were long associated with opposition to gun control. The Gun Control Act of 1968 barely passed a Democratic Congress, in spite of strong lobbying by the Johnson administration. Even in 1994, about a third of House Democrats voted against the final version of the assault weapons ban in 1994.

39. Brad O'Leary, "Firepower," *Campaigns and Elections* 16, no. 1 (December 1994): 32–34.

40. Interview with Gregory Haydon, Counsel for the House Judiciary Committee, March 1993.

41. With its large and diverse population, California has long been a bellwether for political trends, from tax limitation to opposition to affirmative action. In the 1998 campaign, Democratic gubernatorial candidate Gray Davis and senatorial candidate Barbara Boxer both featured television advertisements on gun control, and the *Sacramento Bee* included gun control in the five "key-position" listings for candidates for Congress and the legislature; see "Election '98," October 25, 1998.

CHAPTER TWO

1. Kevin N. Wright, *The Great American Crime Myth* (Westport, CT: Greenwood Press, 1985), 3–70; Paul S. Maxim and Paul C. Whitehead, *Explaining Crime* (Boston: Butterworth-Heinemann, 1998), 53–126.

2. Ibid.; also Diana Gordon, *The Justice Juggernaut: Fighting Street Crime, Controlling Citizens* (Newark, NJ: Rutgers University Press, 1990).

3. David McDowall and Colin Loftin, "Comparing the UCR and NCS Over Time," *Criminology* 30 (February 1992): 125–32. The greatest disparity appears for crimes such as larceny, and not for crimes of violence. Also see Bureau of Justice Statistics, "Criminal Victimization, 1973–1995" (Washington, DC, 1997); and Maxim and Whitehead, chapters 4 and 5. The Uniform Crime Reports seem to lag the Crime Survey by a couple of years for general crime trends, but far less so for serious crimes. There is fairly wide consensus in the field of criminology that murder and auto theft constitute the most reliable measures in the UCR. Thefts, minor burglaries, assaults between acquaintances or those resulting in little or no injury, crimes within families, and sexual assaults by acquaintances are generally assumed to be the most underreported offenses. An examination of reported rates of murder and robbery per 100,000 population for the past 20 years closely track each other, although robbery has increased at a slightly faster rate since 1985. A comparison of both these rates with the rate of all violent crimes for the same period reflects that the general rate closely tracks the other two.

4. The most overwhelming evidence of underreporting to police is the NCVS itself. There is also evidence that crimes such as domestic and sexual assaults are seriously underreported even in the NCVS; see Colin Loftin and Ellen J. MacKenzie, "Building National Estimates of Violent Victimization" (paper presented at the National Research Council Symposium on Understanding and Control of Violent Behavior, Destin, Florida, April 1990).

5. Although operationally useful, this definition is not strictly true. Some incidents reported to NCVS were not crimes, and some crimes reported to police might be overlooked by the victim at a later date when they are surveyed, but this should be an uncommon event.

6. While all murders are not known to the police, a larger proportion are than any other crime. Bodies are difficult to dispose of and both the police and public at large take the crime very seriously. Along with murder, auto theft is often used for tracking crime rates on the assumption that most people report the theft of a car for insurance purposes.

7. Margaret A. Zahn and Patricia L. McCall, "Homicide in the Twentieth-Century United States: Trends and Patterns," in ed. M. Dwayne Smith and Margaret A. Zahn, *Studying and Preventing Homicide* (Thousand Oaks, CA: Sage Publications, 1999).

8. Ibid.

9. Keith D. Harries, *Serious Violence: Patterns of Homicide and Assault in America* (Springfield, IL: Charles C. Thomas, 1990), 3–14.

10. Federal Bureau of Investigation, *Crime in the United States—1991* (Washington, DC: 1992), 58.

11. Federal Bureau of Investigation, *Crime in the United States—1997* (Washington, DC, 1998).

12. Bureau of Justice Statistics, *Violent Crime in the United States* (Washington, DC, 1991).

13. Harries, 7–9. For a more recent commentary, see Frank E. Zimring and Gordon Hawkins, *Crime Is Not the Problem* (New York: Oxford University Press, 1997), chapter 3.

14. British Home Office, *Offenses Reported to the Police* (London, 1997), chapter 4.

15. Rates are calculated using the UCR and the Home Office figures.

16. British Home Office.

17. Harries, 8. Updated rates provided by the Canadian Center for Justice Statistics. In 1996 the U.S. rate was down to 3.52 times the Canadian rate.

18. James D. Wright, Peter H. Rossi, and Kathleen Daly, *Under the Gun: Weapons, Crime, and Violence in America* (Hawthorne, NY: Aldine de Gruyter, 1983), 2; Federal Bureau of Investigation, *Crime in the United States—1998* (Washington, DC, 1999), 17.

19. Based on a historical review of the Uniform Crime Reports.

20. Zimring and Hawkins, 1997, chapter 2.

21. Gary Kleck, "*Crime Is Not the Problem*: Lethal Violence in America," *American Journal of Sociology* 104, no. 1 (March 1999): 1543–45.

22. Discussion between Zimring and Kleck at author-meets-critic panel, American Society of Criminology Annual Conference, Washington, DC, November 13, 1998. Kleck's point on comparison of data is well taken. A review of Zimring and Hawkins's data reveals that the ratio of homicide to aggravated assaults is 1:26 in Italy but 1:488 in the United Kingdom. One can only conclude that the English are incredibly ineffective at assault or far more likely to report minor incidents in victim surveys.

23. Rushforth et al., "Accidental Firearms Death in a Metropolitan County (1958–1975)," *American Journal of Epidemiology* 100 (1975): 499–505; and Kellerman and Reay.

24. Don B. Kates, Jr., et al., "Guns and Public Health: Epidemic Violence or Pandemic of Propaganda?" *Tennessee Law Review* 62 (1995): 513–96. Kleck has also questioned the methodology of numerous public health researchers; see Kleck, 1997, 56–60.

25. Gary Kleck and Marc Gertz, "Armed Resistance to Crime: The Prevalence and Nature of Self-Defense with a Gun," *Journal of Criminal Law and Criminology* 86, no. 1 (1995): 150–87.

26. Ibid.

27. Kleck, 1997, 151–52.

28. Even Kleck, who raises serious question regarding the use of NCVS data for calculating DGU, turns to the survey in the following pages to support other aspects of his position; ibid., 160.

29. Emphasis has varied somewhat. In interviews, NIJ staff advised me that they were discouraged from conducting any research on the linkage between guns and crime during the Reagan and Bush administrations. That has obviously changed under the Clinton administration.

30 Marvin E. Wolfgang, "A Tribute to a View I Have Opposed," *Journal of Criminal Law and Criminology* 86, no. 1 (fall 1995): 188–92.

31. Kleck and Gertz, 1995.

32. Gary Kleck and Marc Gertz, "The Illegitimacy of One-Sided Speculation: Getting the Defensive Gun-Use Estimate Down," *Journal of Criminal Law and Criminology* 87, no. 4 (1997): 1446–61.

33. Phillip J. Cook and Jens Ludwig, "Guns in America: Nation Survey on Private Ownership and Use of Firearms," National Institute of Justice, 1997.

34. David Hemenway, "Survey Research and Self-Defense Gun Use: An Explanation of Extreme Overestimates," *Journal of Criminal Law and Criminology* 87, no. 4 (1997): 1430–45.

35. This is based on the 2.2 million defensive uses estimated by Kleck and Gertz. Homicides reported in the UCR for 1994.

36. The demographics of gun ownership undercut such an assumption. Gun-ownership rates are higher for whites than blacks and for rural rather than urban residents. In both cases, homicide rates run counter to gun-ownership rates. Gun-ownership probably is high among the most at-risk group: young, inner-city males actively engaged in crime. However, they likely are not well represented in any survey. It is also improbable to assume that all homicide victims are in the unarmed population. If risk levels were as

high as these figures imply, some armed targets would have to become victims, further skewing the risk figures.

37. Hemenway; Tom W. Smith, "A Call for a Truce in the DGU War," *Journal of Criminal Law and Criminology* 87, no. 4 (1997): 1462–69. These two articles and the response by Kleck and Gertz in the same journal provide a comprehensive examination of the issue from three perspectives.

38. Any reader with a serious interest in the topic should read chapter 5 in Kleck, 1997, as well as Cook's work on the subject.

39. Ibid.

40. The Cook thesis for explaining the high incidence of reported DGU in numerous surveys is entirely dependent upon this assumption. Kleck makes this assumption regarding underreporting on the NCVS (1997, chapter 5) and reporting of household gun ownership (1997, 66–67). Hemenway makes the telling point that Kleck and Gertz are willing to assume that the vast majority of respondents with DGU experiences would fail to disclose them in the NCVS interviews.

41. Even opportunities to arrest persons after crimes have occurred are rare. I do not include crimes discovered while engaged in active patrol or with some advance information.

42. These two factors would greatly increase the probability of being a crime victim. In combination, they might well assure it.

43. NRA membership does not constitute an ideal proxy for activist opposition to gun control, but it does require financial contribution to an organization primarily identified with opposition to gun control. Approximately 2 percent of the population at large belongs to the NRA. The DGU respondents, adult and disproportionately male, would have a membership significantly higher than this.

44. Samuel J. Keith et al., "Schizophrenic Disorder," in ed. Lee N. Robins and Darrel A. Regier, *Psychiatric Disorders in America* (New York: Free Press, 1991), 33–52.

45. Although Kleck and Gertz assume these responses to be whimsical and misinterpreted by Hemenway as serious, Hemenway offered the example to prove that "a small percentage of respondents may report anything."

46. Tom Smith contends that additional research and reduced advocacy could significantly resolve the widely divergent estimates of DGUs.

47. Those expert in public-opinion polling have long known that a variety of influences must be considered to accurately project from polls. Kleck acknowledges this when he assumes underreporting of defensive uses and also in his discussion of polling on gun possession, in which he concludes that women likely underreport the presence of firearms in the home. For a discussion of the difficulties of polling in a political context, see Leo Bogart, "Politics, Polls and Poltergeists: Interpreting Election Polls," *Society* (May 15, 1998): 8.

48. There is controversy over both the NCVS and UCR figures on guns used in crime; see Kleck, 1997, 8. No one, however, denies that gun crimes in the United States are high by international standards. Likewise, even the lowest NCVS estimate of DGU is 64,000 per year, and the number is most probably significantly higher than this.

49. Carolyn Weiss, "Ideology, Interest, and Information: The Basis of Policy Positions," in ed. Daniel Callahan and Bruce Jennings, *Ethics, the Social Sciences, and Policy Analysis* (New York: Plenum, 1983). One can examine such issues as needle exchange, bilingual education, sentencing policy, and drug treatment—to name but a few—and find little influence on the policy process from research findings.

50. Kates, 1992.

51. Spitzer, 187–92.

52. Kates, 1992.

53. Jeffrey R. Snyder, "A Nation of Cowards," *Public Interest* 113 (fall 1993): 40–55.

54. Although the gun magazines feature articles ad nauseam regarding the most suitable firearms for self- and home defense, a pump shotgun provides a homeowner with both deterrence and the ability to match most, if not all, likely opponents. Argument can be made that handguns are more advantageous in a limited number of situations where mobility is necessary.

55. John R. Lott, Jr., *More Guns, Less Crime* (Chicago: University of Chicago Press, 1998); John R. Lott, Jr., "The Concealed Handgun Debate," *Journal of Legal Studies* 27, no. 1 (January 1998): 221–43; John R. Lott, Jr. and David Mustard, "Crime Deterrence and Right-to-Carry Concealed Handguns," *Journal of Legal Studies* 26, no. 1 (January 1997): 1–68; Stephen G. Bronars and John R. Lott, Jr., "Criminal Deterrence, Geographic Spillovers and the Right to Carry Concealed Handguns," *American Economic Review* 88, no. 2 (May 1998): 475–79.

56. Denise Griffin, "Up in Arms Over Guns," *State Legislatures* 21, no. 9 (October/November 1995): 32.

57. Kleck, 1997, 196–98.

58. I once discussed the concept of researching the pattern and nature of carrying among licensees with NRA lobbyist and retired narcotics agent Steve Helsley. His response was: "You and I both know the answer," meaning that our experience in law enforcement had demonstrated that gun carrying decreases rapidly after the first year or two on the job.

59. See George D. Newton and Franklin E. Zimring, *Firearms and Violence in American Life* (Washington, DC: National Commission on the Causes and Prevention of Violence, 1969); Zimring, 1975; Wright, Rossi, and Daly; Vizzard, 1993; and Kleck, 1997.

60. Newton and Zimring.

61. I spent over two years in the Firearms Enforcement Branch of ATF and am familiar with the methodology and resources available to ATF. I extend no greater credibility to the ATF figures than those of Wright, Rossi, and Daly. I have critiqued their methodology more closely, because it is the only methodology published and available.

62. Wright, Rossi, and Daly, 25–44.

63. As an example, the authors describe a pistol used by Squeaky Fromme in her attempt to assassinate President Ford as being manufactured in 1911, when, in actuality, it was a Colt model 1911. The date is the date of patent, not of manufacture. This unfamiliarity with firearms results in overestimates of the number removed from the market as well as some mistaken interpretations of market demand. These details are dealt with more specifically later in the text.

64. Newton and Zimring developed the so-called "fear-and-loathing" argument in their 1969 report, arguing that the increase in firearm sales was a response to fear generated by riots and perceptions of increased crime. Wright et al. argue that the increased firearm sales can be explained by collectors, normal growth in demand from increased households, increased demand from hunters, and other more benign factors.

65. Wright, Rossi, and Daly, 43. The authors stated that this estimate was more conservative than most others, including both opponents and proponents of gun control.

66. Based on ATF data collected from manufacturers and importers.

67. During almost three decades in ATF, including an extended period in headquarters monitoring firearm cases from throughout the country, I never was aware of a case involving significant smuggling of guns into the United States. Import violations invariably involved falsification of information on documents but not undeclared guns.

68. I personally supervised numerous investigations in which individuals were transporting firearms out of the United States. In several of these cases the suspects purchased guns in lots of as many as a hundred at a time. Other investigations have revealed narcotics smugglers exporting firearms in the same vehicles they used to import drugs, and licensed firearm dealers who delivered the firearms with no records, knowing they would be exported. It is generally known within ATF that the United States is the primary-source country for illicit civilian firearms. This trade is dwarfed by the trade in surplus military arms carried on by national governments and their proxies.

69. An experienced gunsmith estimated the average lifespan of a Colt Government Model .45 caliber pistol as half-a-million rounds, at which point it would require complete rebuilding. This particular firearm was adopted by the U.S. Army in 1911 and last purchased during World War II. Yet, my son was issued an M1911 during the 1991 Gulf War. Although the last of these pistols were taken out of active use shortly after that, they were still quite serviceable.

70. In over 40 years of engaging in shooting sports and nearly 30 years of law enforcement, I can recall very few instances of seeing or hearing of firearms that wore out to the point of being discarded. Until the recent wave of replacement of revolvers with pistols in law enforcement, revolvers that were 20 or more years old were common among law-enforcement personnel. ATF and the Secret Service, for instance, went 20 years without purchasing new handguns for their agents. The revolvers taken out of service when new 9mm pistols were issued were quite serviceable.

71. Kleck used an estimated figure of 235 million guns as of 1994; see Kleck, 1997, 64. The Bureau of Alcohol, Tobacco, and Firearms continued to use the figure of 200 million as recently as November 1998. The most recent figures available from ATF are for 1997, when about 4.5 million guns were added to existing stocks.

72. Wright, Rossi, and Daly, 34–35. The number of households reporting guns present remained at about 50 percent in most polls for many years. The Gallup Organization reported that 30 years of polling consistently reflected numbers that clustered around this percentage; see *Gallup Poll News Service* 55, no. 2 (September, 26, 1990). Recent research reflects a downward trend in the number of households reporting gun ownership; see Cook and Ludwig; Robert J. Blendon, John T. Young, and David Hemenway, "The American Public and the Gun Control Debate," *Journal of the American Medical Association* 275, no. 22 (June 12, 1996): 1719–23; and John T. Young, David Hemenway, Robert J. Blendon, and John M. Benson, "The Polls—Trends: Guns," *Public Opinion Quarterly* 60, no. 4 (winter 1996): 634–50.

73. The model counts hunters, collectors, and recreational shooters as three separate categories. My experience is that the overlap among these groups is extensive. In addition, the number of hunters was calculated by adding total licensed hunters to the purchasers of duck stamps. All states require a license to hunt migratory fowl, in addition to a federal duck stamp—thus this resulted in double counting. The collector estimates are based on survey data. In my experience, serious collectors are rare and account for very few new guns, since the essence of collecting is pursuit of the rare and unusual. The term "collector" is commonly used by some who simply like to buy guns, and also in some cases by unlicensed dealers. Likewise, serious target shooters are few. In the mid-1960s, NRA membership was in the range of a million. Virtually all serious competition shooters are members of the NRA, but only a minority of NRA members are serious competitive shooters. Most important, if one allows for the household-growth considerations made by Wright et al., there was still an additional increase of 10 million handguns during the period 1968 to 1978. The excess was probably higher, as this was a period of high divorce rates, resulting in numerous female-headed households,

and the rate of gun ownership is considerably lower among women. Anyone familiar with the type of firearms and shooting sports was keenly aware that the majority of handgun sales was not for competition. Sales to police agencies normally should not be used to reduce the number of additional guns in circulation, because they normally resulted in the current police inventory being sold to the public, thus offsetting the arms purchased by police.

74. Researchers on both sides of the gun-control issue apparently agree that fear of crime generates increased demand for guns, particularly handguns. See Zimring and Hawkins, 83–92, and Kleck, 1991, 27. In addition, the California Department of Justice figures for handgun sales in Los Angeles County following the 1992 riots and preceding the 1993 civil-rights trial support this same thesis.

75. Semi- and full-automatic designs have been available since the turn of the century and the double-action semi-automatic was introduced before World War II. Although there have been some refinements in materials, basic design in personal weapons has remained amazingly static in an era of product innovation and change.

76. Newton and Zimring, 19.

77. *Gun Digest*, 14th ed., 1960.

78. *Gun Digest*, 47th ed., 1993.

79. Some forms of rifle competition require military-type arms to compete; only a small minority of such firearms are used in these events.

80. The original M1 carbine design lacked the capacity for full-automatic fire, which was added to the later M2 version, but the principals of low-intensity cartridge, high magazine capacity, and ease of mobility were all incorporated into the U.S. carbine.

81. This is not to be confused with visual appeal, which is their primary apparent asset. As with all military weapons, most firearms in this class lack the fit and finish of quality sporting firearms.

82. These firearms could not be offered with shoulder stocks because they would be classified as short-barreled rifles and subject to the National Firearms Act. Although they made very poor pistols—awkward and hard to shoot—customers purchased them.

83. Lyman H. Shaffer and William J. Vizzard, "Increased Automatic Weapons Use," *Police Chief* 48, no. 5 (May 1981): 58–60. Before the Stockton shooting, a bill had been introduced into the California legislature at the behest of police from Los Angeles and Oakland, but the bill received little attention.

84. Vizzard, "Crafting for Compromise." Unpublished paper, delivered at the Academy of Criminal Justice Sciences, Boston, March 1995.

85. Ibid.

86. 18 USC 922(v)(1).

87. The sudden increase in demand for any firearm that appears threatened by law seems to be a consistent phenomenon. During the period from 1992 through 1994 the general downward trend in gun-manufacturing figures reversed, apparently in response to fears that a Democratic administration would support restrictions. By 1995 the downward trend had resumed. Gun dealers routinely report a surge in gun sales during any discussion of controls.

88. Peculiarly, combat-type firearms seem to be most commonly purchased in this category and not unique collectors items or high-quality sporting firearms. Apparently, many buyers of assault weapons and combat handguns purchase these items simply to have them. Few people would have need for more than one handgun for self-defense, yet it is not uncommon to find persons who possess many handguns. Although these purchasers are often described as collectors, they have more in common with gadget pur-

chasers or compulsive clothes buyers than serious collectors. These impulse buyers sustain gunshows and many gun dealers and are probably one of the reasons that waiting periods are not popular with many dealers. Some of the growth in gun sales during the middle 1960s resulted from the demographics of the baby-boom generation reaching majority. Until 1969, most jurisdictions did not require handgun purchasers to be 21 years of age. In 1964, the first of the baby-boom wave would have been turning 18 years old and entering the labor market.

89. Zimring and Hawkins, 86–87. California Department of Justice records reflect a sharp increase in handgun sales following the 1965 and 1992 Los Angeles riots. Gun dealers report that numerous handgun buyers are first-timers, who do not have an interest in guns but express fear about crime.

90. The decline in demand might seem to contradict the thesis that fear of crime is the motivator behind much of the current demand for guns. If, however, one examines the durability of firearms, there is no apparent contradiction.

91. Calculated by adding import and manufacturing figures provided by ATF and subtracting exports.

92. Interview with John Acquilino, former NRA employee, Washington, DC, March 23, 1993.

93. Marianne W. Zawitz, "Guns Used in Crimes" (Washington, DC: Bureau of Justice Statistics, 1995). This figure probably represents the minimum estimate. The potential underreporting problems of the NCVS were discusses earlier in relation to the work of Kleck and Gertz. The same potential exists here, particularly for crimes committed by domestic partners and others close to the subjects. Concurrently, the actual figure is probably in decline as the violent crime rate declines.

94. This estimate assumes that gun owners constitute about 25 percent of the adult population; see Cook and Ludwig.

95. I was closely associated with several ATF trace studies and have read numerous others. Also see Paul H. Blackman, "The Uses and Limitations on BATF Firearms Tracing Data for Law Enforcement, Policymaking, and Criminological Research." Paper presented at the American Society of Criminology, San Diego, November 1997. With the assistance of the NIJ, ATF is attempting to improve upon this source of information.

96. Mark Moore, "The Supply of Handguns: An Analysis of the Potential and Current Importance of Alternative Sources of Handguns to Criminal Offenders." Unpublished paper, 1979); Mark Moore "Keeping Handguns from Criminal Offenders," *Annals of the American Academy of Political and Social Science* 455 (1981): 107–9; Mark Moore "The Bird in Hand: A Feasible Strategy for Gun Control," *Journal of Policy Analysis and Management* 2 (1983): 188–93.

97. Ibid.

98. Phillip J. Cook, Stephanie Molliconi, and Thomas B. Cole, "Regulating Gun Markets," *Journal of Criminal Law and Criminology* 86, no. 1 (fall 1995): 59–92. I examined all the studies conducted by ATF prior to 1994 and personally oversaw an extensive trace study that examined all firearms seized by police in the City of San Francisco for three years. Wright and Rossi's interviews found that most incarcerated felons indicated that private transactions and theft were the primary means of obtaining firearms. The nature of their population may have reduced the importance of dealers for two reasons: First, individuals incarcerated are probably the most impulsive and least methodical of criminal violators, thus are more likely to take what they come across. Second, dealers are usually the source for traffickers, who in turn resell, thus producing a private trans-

fer. Incarcerated persons would have little reason to distinguish between the occasional trafficker and an individual making a single, private transfer.

99. Prior to 1969, there was no federal prohibition to prevent persons from purchasing a handgun outside their state of residence. Therefore prohibited persons in states that required permits or checked buyers' criminal records could bypass that process by driving across a state line. The upper New England states thus became gun sources for Boston, Virginia for the District of Columbia, Nevada for California, Ohio for Michigan, etc. See U.S. Congress, Senate. Committee on the Judiciary, Subcommittee to Investigate Juvenile Delinquency, *Federal Firearms Act, Hearings.* 89th Congress, 1st Session, 1965, 3–5, 343–74, and 602–14.

100. D. E. S. Burr, *Handgun Regulation* (Orlando: Florida Bureau of Criminal Justice, 1977).

101. The most extensive survey of adults is reported in James D. Wright and Peter H. Rossi, *Armed and Considered Dangerous: A Survey of Felons and Their Firearms* (Hawthorne, NY: Aldine de Gruyter, 1986). Additional studies included Allen Beck et al., "Survey of State Prison Inmates" (Bureau of Justice Statistics, 1991); National Institute of Justice, "Arrestees and Guns: Monitoring the Illegal Firearms Market," 1995; and Sheley and Wright, 1995.

102. Wright and Rossi, 1986.

103. Ibid., chapter 3.

104. Ibid., table 4.73.

105. Julius Wachtel, "Sources of Crime Guns in Los Angeles, California," *Policing: An International Journal of Police Strategies and Management* 21, no. 2 (1998): 220–39.

106. Daniel D. Polsby, "The False Promise of Gun Control," *Atlantic Monthly* 273, no. 3 (March 1993).

107. Ibid.

108. Cook, Molliconi, and Cole, 1995.

109. James D. Wright, Peter H. Rossi, and Kathleen Daly. "The Great American Gun War," in ed. Lee Nesbet, *The Gun Control Debate* (Buffalo, NY: Prometheus Books, 1990). The need for self-defense is virtually a universal response; also see Sheley and Wright; and Scott H. Decker, Susan Pennell, and Ami Caldwell, "Arrestees and Their Guns: Monitoring the Illegal Firearms Market," Final Report (Washington, DC: National Institute of Justice, 1996).

110. Kleck, 1991, 27 and 38–39.

111. The criminal population is concentrated among young males, for whom such weapons apparently have the greatest appeal. In addition, the criminal population is skewed toward violence and aggressive behavior.

112. Sheley and Wright; Cook, Molliconi, and Cole, 1995; David Kennedy et al., "Youth Violence in Boston: Gun Markets, Serious Youth Offenders and a Use-Reduction Strategy," *Law and Contemporary Problems* 59, no. 1 (winter 1996): 147–96.

113. Wright, Rossi, and Daly; Kleck; Moore; Cook; and even Zimring have all recognized this as the most significant pragmatic impediment to successful implementation of any policy to deny access effectively to the crime-prone.

114. Decker, Pennell, and Caldwell, table 3.4.

115. Ibid., table 4.131.

116. Kleck, 1997, 386.

117. For an example of early ATF efforts, see the Bureau of Alcohol, Tobacco, and Firearms, *Project Identification* (Washington, DC: ATF, 1976); for the most recent ATF efforts, see the Bureau of Alcohol, Tobacco, and Firearms, *Commerce in Firearms* (Washington, DC: ATF, 2000).

118. Ibid.
119. Fox Butterfield, "Firearms Agency Intensifies Scrutiny of Suspect Dealers," *New York Times*, February 4, 2000; *Sacramento Bee*, "Clinton Plans Gun-Law Enforcement Push" (January 18, 2000): B8.
120. Only 70 percent of licensees are retail dealers. A random survey of retail dealers by ATF in 1998 revealed only 11 percent to be located in a business premises such as a gunshop or sporting-goods store. Many sporting-goods stores and gunsmiths sell few guns. Thus the 1.2 percent figure constitutes 20 percent or more of the active volume dealers; see Alcohol, Tobacco, and Firearms, 2000.
121. Vizzard, 1997, chapters 5 and 6.

CHAPTER 3

1. Jeffrey R. Snyder, "Fighting Back: Crime, Self-Defense, and the Right to Carry a Handgun" (Washington, DC: Cato Institute, 1997).
2. Ibid.
3. Ibid. A few states, such as Alaska and Arizona, allowed carrying of firearms openly but did not provide for permits to carry concealed ones.
4. National Rifle Association, "Right-to-Carry," available on NRA website.
5. Snyder, 1997. Clayton E. Cramer and David B. Kopel, "'Shall Issue': The New Wave of Concealed Handgun Permit Laws," *Tennessee Law Review* 62, no. 3 (spring 1995): 679–757.
6. Ibid.
7. Ibid. Also, a review of California Department of Justice data.
8. Washington State's law required the issuance of a concealed-weapons permit to anyone allowed to lawfully possess a firearm under the Revised Code of Washington. This included felons not convicted of a "crime of violence." Curiously, second-degree assault, a felony, was not defined as a crime of violence, but burglary was so defined. I was an ATF agent in Seattle in 1968. With the passage of the GCA, which prohibited all felons from possessing guns, police officials began to refuse to issue to any felon. The Washington law made no provision for testing or competency.
9. W. E. Lyons and David Lowery, "Government Fragmentation versus Consolidation: Five Public-Choice Myths About How to Create Informed, Involved, Happy Citizens," *Public Administration Review* 49, no. 6 (November/December 1989): 533–43.
10. Robert J. Cottrol and Raymond T. Diamond, "The Fifth Auxiliary Right," *Yale Law Review* 104 (1995): 995.
11. Kleck, 1991, 12.
12. Federal statutes will be cited as follows: Title 18, U.S. Code, Sec. 1715 will be cited in the usual legal shorthand, 18 USC 1715. This section prohibited the mailing of handguns to private individuals, but exempted shipments to dealers and government agencies. In an era of private parcel services, this statute has little importance.
13. Carol S. Leff and Mark H. Leff. "The Politics of Ineffectiveness: Federal Gun Legislation 1919–38," *Annals of the American Academy of Political and Social Science* 455 (May 1981): 48–62.
14. See Chapter 53, Title 26 USC and 17 Code of Federal Regulations 179 (hereafter cited as "CFR").
15. Leff and Leff.
16. *Haynes v. United States*, 390 US 85, 1968
17. *Marchetti v. United States*, 390 US 39, 1968, and *Grosso v. United States*, 390 US 62, 1968.

18. Vizzard, 1997, 6–10.
19. For some time the exact meaning of the prohibition in Title VII remained in question. The law prohibited the receipt, possession, and transportation in commerce of firearms by the designated categories of persons. The meaning was originally interpreted as prohibiting receipt and transportation in commerce. The court subsequently ruled that the commerce requirement applied to possession as well. For a time this rendered the law ineffectual at prohibiting the possession by felons, in *Bass v. United States* the supreme court suggested in a footnote to the decision that previous movement in commerce would suffice to meet the elements of the violation. As a result, the government has included proof of prior interstate movement in all charges of possession under this statute and its replacement in the GCA, 18 USC 922(g). Practically this means that the possession of a firearm by a felon is lawful, so long as the firearm has never moved in interstate commerce. The same law applies to ammunition. Although this limits very few prosecutions, it does reflect the implementation problems created by a strict interstate-nexus requirement. The compromise makes little rational sense, since firearms that have once moved in commerce have no more impact on commerce than those that have not. It appears to be a face-saving technical solution by the court. This problem could be overcome as it was in the narcotics laws in 1968 by a Congressional finding that narcotics affect interstate commerce. The treatment of the two commodities has long differed, however.
20. Because the U.S. Codes are divided into titles, the use of the same term within the GCA creates unnecessary confusion.
21. The definition excluded fireworks, shotguns, muzzle loaders, and other items not likely to be used as weapons. Little noticed for the first few months by ATF, the destructive-device provision provided the only general federal jurisdiction for bombings and some arsons in a period of violent social unrest. This gave ATF an early jurisdictional lead on the FBI in many bombings and resulted in a major expansion of ATF jurisdiction. The subsequent Explosives Control Act of 1970 was assigned jointly to the Attorney General and Secretary of the Treasury for enforcement. ATF was able to maintain a significant portion of jurisdiction due to its ability to administer the regulatory and licensing portions of the Act. The FBI and ATF entered into a memorandum of understanding that granted most political bombings to the FBI and most other bombings to ATF. Subsequent amendments to the Explosives Control Act have provided ATF with jurisdiction in all commercial arsons as well as bombings.
22. 26 USC 5848.
23. The law exempted antiques, defined as firearms manufactured before 1898.
24. All acts cited within 18 USC 922.
25. See Section 101, titled "Purpose of Public Law 90–618."
26. 18 USC 923.
27. 18 USC 924.
28. 27 CFR 178 and 27 CFR 179.
29. I was employed as a special investigator, later changed to special agent, for ATF during this period and worked in several offices on permanent assignment and temporary detail. I have since interviewed numerous other persons who were so employed and conducted numerous examinations of the records of ATF. All sources are consistent with the use of resources reported here.
30. In general, federal interest was interpreted to mean those areas in which the states could or would not act due to lack of authority, resources, or political will. The concept has always been somewhat inconsistently applied. For instance, bank robberies have seldom

been questioned, although they are a crime for which the states have both resources and expertise. In general, federal interest has been viewed as a somewhat imprecise method of separating out the mundane from the significant. As such, its interpretation has depended on time, place, resources, and public opinion. For instance, what might not be considered a federal-interest drug case in New York might meet the standard in Kansas. *Federal interest* is not to be confused with *federal jurisdiction*, which now extends in some way to many crimes. The ultimate arbiter of federal interest is always the U.S. Attorney for the federal judicial district of the offense.

31. 18 USC 926.
32. 18 USC 923; the law allowed additional inspection of records in the course of a criminal investigation or gun trace.
33. *Plyman v. United States*, 551 F 2nd 965.
34. In one case I supervised, the informant was arrested for an unrelated crime several months after the culmination of an investigation that lasted six months. He refused to testify on the grounds that he would be branded a "snitch" in jail and his life endangered. The case had to be dropped.
35. 18 USC 921.
36. Ibid.
37. In the eight years between the change in the law and my retirement from ATF, unlicensed-dealing cases virtually ceased nationwide. Although ATF did not maintain statistics in a form allowing for exact calculation, the Office of Law Enforcement produced a weekly report of the most significant arrests, seizures, and prosecutive actions. Less than half-a-dozen cases of unlicensed dealing were reported in these documents between 1986 and 1994. Numerous interviews with agents and supervisors supported the same conclusion, although prosecutors were displaying some willingness to accept cases involving very large quantities of firearms at my retirement.
38. This change was patterned after a section in the 1968 law that included machine-gun-conversion parts in the NFA.
39. For all sentencing guidelines, see U.S. Sentencing Commission, *Federal Sentencing Guidelines Manual* (Washington, DC: 1998).
40. Severely wounded in an attempt on President Reagan's life, Brady and his wife Sarah became tireless campaigners for handgun control.
41. 18 USC 922(s)(1).
42. 18 USC 922(s)(1) and (2).
43. A variety of exceptions are provided for under 18 USC 922(s). Approximately half of the states had some provision for checking handgun-purchaser records already in place in 1993.
44. 18 USC 922(s)(3) and (6).
45. 18 USC 922(t)(1).
46. Ibid.
47. *Printz v. United States*, 521 U.S. 898, December 3, 1996.
48. *National Rifle Association of America v. Janet Reno*, filed in the U.S. District Court for the District of Columbia.
49. A primary objective of the McClure-Volkmer Bill was a prohibition against future federal regulations requiring submission of records to be retained by the federal government or any state. During my tenure overseeing ATF law-enforcement data systems, I was repeatedly reminded that retention of any information regarding firearm purchasers or owners was highly sensitive and would result in immediate reaction by the NRA and other firearm-interest groups.

50. Interview with Senate Judiciary Staff member Brian Lee.
51. 18 USC 922(v) and (w).
52. As critics are quick to point out, "assault weapon" is not a well-defined term; see chapter 10. The specific features can be found under section 921, definitions.
53. Reported to me after the passage of the law and before its implementation date by another dealer who believed this action to be unscrupulous.
54. 18 USC 925.
55. Public Law 102–393, 1992.
56. 18 USC 922(g)(8) and (9).
57. 18 USC 922(q)(2)(A) and 922(x)(1) and (2).
58. Roberto Suro and Philip P. Pan. "Law's Omission Disarms Some Police," *Washington Post* (December 27, 1996): A16.
59. 18 USC 923(d)(1)(F), passed in the 1994 Crime Bill, expanded the requirements for applicant compliance and made clear that noncompliance with local or state law was grounds for denial or revocation.
60. Bureau of Alcohol, Tobacco, and Firearms.
61. The most widely publicized of these involved Charles P. MacDonald, who lived in a Los Angeles skid-row hotel and apparently sold guns to virtually anyone without records or without complying with state reporting or waiting periods (see "Sales Put L.A. Under the Gun," *Los Angeles Times*, May 19, 1992). This case was featured on the television series *20–20*. Subsequently, ATF offices experienced a sharp upturn in inquires about licenses and requests for application forms.
62. In 1993 the Office of Compliance Operations announced a program to at least contact all new applicants by telephone and increase the number of inspections. Given the number of licensees, the task was daunting. Assuming half of all inspector time was devoted to inspecting dealers, each inspector would have to conduct 600 inspections per year in order to visit each dealer once annually.
63. Interview with Inspector Diana Gatti, September 18, 1998.
64. Although the exact number of firearm transactions by unlicensed individuals is not documented, all writers on this issue have alluded to the existence and importance of such a private market; see work by Wright, Rossi, and Daly; Moore; Kates; Kleck; Cook; and Zimring. My own experience confirms this, as do numerous interviews with other ATF enforcement personnel and a number of ATF trace studies of firearms seized by police.
65. Wright, Rossi, and Daly reviewed the existing literature thoroughly and estimated about 20,000 (page 244). As an example, California's Dangerous Weapons Control Law takes 85 pages to print. This does not include any local ordinances.
66. The District of Columbia is treated here as a state.
67. The NRA website provides the most convenient source of current information on state laws, although it lacks the full text. ATF publishes a complete compendium of state laws and local ordinances with the full text. Although the latter is a more authoritative source, the publication always lags behind changes in the law due to the inevitable delays between data collection and publication.
68. National Rifle Association, "Right to Carry," available at <www.nra.org>.
69. As an example, rural counties in California issue far more permits than do urban counties in both absolute numbers and relative to population; California Department of Justice, 1999.
70. Bureau of Alcohol, Tobacco, and Firearms, *State Laws and Published Ordinances: Firearms*, 19th ed. (Washington, DC: ATF, 1998). All statutes are listed by jurisdiction. This doc-

ument is produced by ATF through a national survey. Although it is probably not an exhaustive list, it is the most complete one available.

71. 18 USC 921, definitions.

72. Although New York State law requires a permit to possess a handgun, permits issued elsewhere in the state are not valid in New York City. Persons familiar with New York report that jurisdictions outside New York City often issue permits quite liberally, but the New York City Police follow a very restrictive policy. New York City also imposes permissive licensing on long guns that does not apply throughout the rest of the state.

73. Sanford Levinson has referred to it as "perhaps the worst drafted of all provision" in "The Embarrassing Second Amendment," *Yale Law Journal* 99 (1989): 637–59. For an opposing view on the clarity of the text, see Nelson Lund, "The Past and Future of the Individual's Right to Arms," *Georgia Law Review* 31, no. 1 (1996): 1–75.

74. Stephen P. Halbrook, *That Every Man Be Armed* (Albuquerque: University of New Mexico Press, 1984), 76.

75. Garry Wills, "To Keep and Bear Arms," *New York Review of Books* (September 21, 1995): 62.

76. For an exhaustive bibliography of articles on the topic, see David B. Kopel, "Comprehensive Bibliography of the Second Amendment in Law Reviews," *Journal on Firearms and Public Policy* 11 (fall 1999): 5–45.

77. The Supreme Court has heard only three Second Amendment cases in its history and only one during the twentieth century, although lower courts have addressed the issue more often.

78. 307 U.S. 174 (1939).

79. *Cruikshank v. United States*, 92 U.S. 542 (1876); *Presser v. Illinois*, 116 U.S. 252 (1886); *Miller v. Texas*, 153 U.S. 535 (1894). The court has since refused to review the issue of incorporation; see Michael J. Quinlan, "Is There a Neutral Justification for Refusing to Implement the Second Amendment or Is the Supreme Court Just 'Gun Shy'?" *Capital University Law Review* 22 (1993): 641–92.

80. A simple survey of the literature supports the argument that individual-rights arguments are more frequently made in academic literature. For the argument on contemporary scholarly consensus, see Randy E. Barnett and Don B. Kates, "Under Fire: The New Consensus on the Second Amendment," *Emory Law Journal* 45, no. 4 (fall 1996): 1140–1259. The proliferation of articles supportive of the individual-rights interpretation should probably be viewed with some healthy skepticism. Articles questioning conventional wisdom are likely more interesting to write and publish than those rehashing the status quo. In addition, Academics of the Second Amendment has actively encouraged scholars to pursue such writing with seminars and source materials. Finally, control advocates are probably less motivated to pursue an argument in journals that they are winning in the courts.

81. Conversation with Henigan. Also see Wills, and Andrew D. Herz, "Gun Crazy: Constitutional False Consciousness and Dereliction of Dialogic Responsibility," *Boston University Law Review* 75 (1995): 57–148. Although Herz names a slightly different cast of conspirators than that cited here, his argument is in the same vein.

82. I have waded through virtually every article written on the subject on several occasions. While I find these writers to be advocates for a position, I cannot dismiss their work a priori on those grounds. Most of the writers on this topic are advocates of some sort. In fact, one would expect that most writers on constitutional issues are not agnostic on issues of state authority and individual rights. For a discussion of the relationship between a number of individual-rights authors and the gun lobby, see Barnett and Kates.

83. Academics for the Second Amendment, an organization directed by law professor Joseph Olsen and attorney Don Kates, unashamedly states that it exists to foster an individual-rights interpretation of the Second Amendment, open letter to scholars from Joseph Olsen under the letterhead of Academics for the Second Amendment (not dated) provided to author by Professor Olsen.

84. Don Higginbotham, "The Federalized Militia Debate: A Neglected Aspect of Second Amendment Scholarship," *William and Mary Quarterly* 55, no. 1 (January 1998): 39–58.

85. Even some of the most ardent advocates of an individual-rights interpretation concede that a variety of gun laws are still constitutional, including permissive registration and licensing; see Don B. Kates, Jr., "Handgun Prohibition and the Original Meaning of the Second Amendment," *Michigan Law Review* 82 (November 1983): 203–73.

86. Levinson postulates that such an interpretation is reasonable.

87. Conversation with Dennis Henigan. The assumption is that most conservative judges lean far more toward being statist than libertarian.

88. Nelson Lund argues for the general militia or collective-populace view in his strongly individual-rights-oriented article. Interestingly, he cites the language of the Articles of Confederation, note 50, as support for the view that the use of the term "militia" in a legal context referred to the general militia, or all free men. Ironically, Article 4 of the Articles of Confederation also discusses public stores of fieldpieces, arms, and ammunition. This raises two difficult issues: The first is the collective nature of arms bearing as a part of a "well-regulated and -disciplined militia" with arms held in common and under collective control. The second is the recognition of fieldpieces and tents as the arms and stores of the militia. Such language is either supportive of a collective view of the general militia or an interpretation that "militia" referred to the select or organized militia. Most individual-rights advocates, typified by Lund and Halbrook, concentrate on a tradition of the general militia providing their own personal weapons, and contend that the militia was an armed citizenry, both in fact and law. However, some scholars who accept the general-militia definition do not subscribe to the individual-rights implications; see David C. Williams, "Civic Republicanism and the Citizen Militia: The Terrifying Second Amendment," *Yale Law Review* 101, no. 3 (1991): 551–615.

89. Lund goes so far as to argue that "well regulated" meant not excessively regulated, essentially standing the term on its head.

90. Herz; Bogus; and Keith A. Ehrman and Dennis A. Henigan, "The Second Amendment in the Twentieth Century: Have You Seen Your Militia Lately?" *University of Dayton Law Review* 5 (1989): 18–34.

91. Lund, 1996.

92. Some gun-control advocates have contended that sawed-off shotguns were used in World War I and thus the issue of utility for militia service is irrelevant. In fact, model 97 Winchester trench guns with 20-inch barrels were used on occasion. These differ significantly from the common sawed-off shotgun with a very short barrel and no stock. In addition, the justices may have mistakenly taken judicial notice that shotguns could not be used in militia service without any knowledge of their military use.

93. See Michael J. Quinlan, "Is There a Neutral Justification for Refusing to Implement the Second Amendment or Is the Supreme Court Just 'Gun Shy'?" *Capital University Law Review* 22 (1993): 641–92; also see Spitzer, 55.

94. 81 F 3rd 1998 (9th Cir.).

95. Halbrook, 84–87; Kates, 1983; Lund, 1996; David T. Hardy, "The Second Amendment and Historiography of the Bill of Rights," *Journal of Law and Politics* 4 (1987): 1–62; and Daniel Polsby, "Second Reading: Treating the Second Amendment as Normal Constitutional Law," *Reason* 27, no. 10 (March 1996): 32–36.

96. Ehrman and Henigan.
97. Halbrook, 193–97; Lund, 1996; Hardy, 1987; Polsby, 1996.
98. Ehrman and Henigan.
99. Hardy, 1987; Lund, 1996.
100. Dennis A. Henigan, "Arms Anarchy and the Second Amendment" (Washington, DC: Center to Prevent Handgun Violence, 1991).
101. Akhill Reed Amar, "The Bill of Rights as a Constitution," *Yale Law Journal* 100 (1991): 1132–1210.
102. Williams provides one of the most compelling conceptual arguments regarding the origins and purpose of the Amendment, which he sees as a direct outgrowth of republican theory.
103. Hardy, 1987.
104. Henigan, 1991; Wills; Bogus; and Higginbotham.
105. Bogus; Higginbotham.
106. Richard Stillman, "The Peculiar 'Stateless' Origins of American Public Administration and Consequences for Government Today," *Public Administration Review* 50, no. 2 (March/April 1990): 156–67. Although they do not make this argument about the meaning of the Amendment, Hardy, 1987; Wills; and Bogus (1998) also discusses this diversity in positions and conflict over ratification. Higginbotham extends this argument from the Constitution to the amendments.
107. Higginbotham.
108. Reconstructed logic is characterized by linear thinking, clarity, and simplicity. Logic in use is normally evolutionary, muddled, and complex.
109. Lawrence H. Tribe and Akhill Reed Amar, "Well-Regulated Militias, and More," *New York Times* (October 28, 1999): A31.
110. Established in Justice Marshall's 1833 opinion in the case of *Barron v. Baltimore*, 32 U.S. (7 Pet.) 243. The proposition that the Bill of Rights served only as a constraint on Congress has been widely accepted by most legal scholars. However, there has always been a minority who contend that Marshall erred and that some or all of the enumerated rights also constrained the actions of the states; see Richard L. Aynes, "On Misreading John Bingham and the Fourteenth Amendment," *Yale Law Journal* 103, no. 57 (1993): 57–104, and Halbrook, 84–85. Although the privileges and immunities clause of the Fourteenth Amendment might have served to incorporate the first ten amendments, in toto, the Supreme Court effectively negated the importance of that clause in the *Slaughterhouse* cases, 83 U.S. 36 (1873). The court did not begin the incorporation process until 1897, with the *Chicago, B. & O. Railroad Co. v. Chicago*, 166 U.S. 226.
111. *Cruikshank v. United States*, 92 U.S. 542, 553 (1875), and *Presser v. Illinois*, 116 U.S. 252, 267 (1886). Not surprisingly, even the meaning of these cases is in controversy. For an example, compare Halbrook (159–61) with Levinson (652–53).
112. Lund, 1996.
113. *Quilici v. Village of Morton Grove*, 695 F.2d 261(7th Cir., 1982), cert. denied, 464 U.S. 863 (1983), and *Fresno Rifle and Pistol Club, Inc. v. Van De Kamp*, 965 F.2d 723 (9th Cir., 1992).
114. Lund, 1996; Halbrook, 1984, 170; Quinlan.
115. Edel, 145; Blendon, Young, and Hemenway; Levinson.
116. Edel, 145. Also see Subcommittee on the Constitution of the Committee on the Judiciary, *The Right to Keep and Bear Arms, Hearings*. 97th Congress, 2d Session (1982).
117. 81 F. 3d. 98 (9th Cir., 1996)
118. Kates, 1983; Glenn Harlan Reynolds, "A Critical Guide to the Second Amendment," *Tennessee Law Review* 62 (1995): 461–503; Nelson Lund, "The Second Amendment,

Political Liberty, and the Right of Self-Preservation," *Alabama Law Review* 39, no. 1 (1987): 103–30.

119. Hardy openly makes the argument for limitation on pragmatic political grounds; see David Hardy, "Armed Citizens, Citizen Armies: Toward a Jurisprudence of the Second Amendment," *Harvard Journal of Law and Public Policy* 9 (1986): 559–638.

120. Kates, 1983; Reynolds; Polsby, 1996.

121. Reynolds; Polsby, 1996.

122. Halbrook, 1984, 191; Kates, 1983 and 1992.

123. Halbrook, 1984, 191; Kates, 1983; Reynolds.

124. For excellent examples of both, see Levinson, and Williams.

CHAPTER 4

1. Trudi Miller, "The Operation of Democratic Institutions," *Public Administration Review* 49, no. 6 (November/December 1989): 511–21, is typical of the first criticism, while the latter argument—that some policies reflect collective and not narrow concerns—is discussed in detail by Robert Reich in the introduction to *The Power of Public Ideas*. Reich makes clear, however, that he views these "public ideas" that move people away from narrow special interest as the exception and not the rule.

2. Josh Sugarmann, *The National Rifle Association: Money, Firepower, and Fear* (Washington, DC: National Press Books, 1992), 27.

3. Leff and Leff; also see the testimony of General Milton Reckford, NRA executive vice president, before Congress: The House Subcommittee on Interstate and Foreign Commerce, *Hearings on S3*, June 22, 1937. Gen. Reckford stated: "We withdrew our objections when they met our position and deleted pistols and revolvers."

4. Leff and Leff; Sherrill, 65.

5. Sugarmann, 37.

6. Neal Knox interview, March 1993; John Acquilino interview, March 1993; also see Davidson, 31.

7. Vizzard, 1997, 10–11.

8. Interviews with former NRA employees.

9. Acquilino attributes the attention in *The American Rifleman* almost entirely to John Snyder, who has gained great subsequent notoriety as the representative of the Citizens' Committee to Keep and Bear Arms but at that time a writer for *The American Rifleman*, rather than any intentional campaign by the NRA leadership.

10. Knox interview.

11. Sugarmann, 45–52; Davidson, 34–35.

12. Ibid. (both).

13. Knox interview.

14. David Brock, "Wayne's World," *American Spectator* (May 1997): 36–45, 81–83.

15. Ibid.

16. Sugarmann, 61.

17. Id, 61–84.

18. Davidson, 241; Brock.

19. As one insider noted: "Neal's more my kind of guy. He really knows guns, but the rank-and-file membership love Wayne."

20. As with many books "authored" by organizational leaders with large staffs, questions of authorship have arisen regarding this book.

21. Jill Smolowe, "The NRA: Go Ahead, Make Our Day," *Time* (May 20, 1995): 18–21.

22. Brock.

23. Ibid.
24. Ibid. Baker, a smooth and accomplished lobbyist and Washington insider, left for a better-paying position and did not publicly attribute his departure to Knox.
25. Ibid.
26. Ibid.
27. Ibid.
28. *Sacramento Bee*, "Heston to Target Image Control as NRA President" (June 9, 1998): A5.
29. Anne Gearan, "NRA's Tough-Talking Lobbyist Quits," *Washington Post* (October 8, 1998), available at <www.washingtonpost.com>.
30. See Les AuCoin, "Confessions of a Former NRA Supporter," *Washington Post*, March 18, 1991. See Davidson, 211–28 and 243–47 for a discussion of these defections.
31. O'Leary.
32. *Time*, May 29, 1995.
33. See *Sacramento Bee*, June 9, 1998. Also see "Black Helicopters and Flights of Fantasy," an undated pamphlet produced by the NRA.
34. Interview with James Baker, November 10, 1998.
35. O'Leary.
36. Sugarmann, 129–36.
37. Personal conversations with Kates and Olson.
38. See both Herz, who alleges a systematic effort by Scholars for the Second Amendment, and Barnett and Kates, who respond.
39. Based on interviews with present and former congressional and legislative staffs.
40. No doubt, the unwillingness to take a public position resulted from both a personal distaste for all firearms regulation and fear of alienating friends and customers.
41. Irwin Nowick, staff, California State Senate, interviewed August 1998.
42. Diana Lambert, "Trying to Stop the Craziness of This Business: Gun Control," in Bruce and Wilcox, 1998; and Gregg Lee Carter, ed., *The Gun Control Movement* (New York: Twayne Publishers, 1997), 72–78. Unlike the NRA, which has fixed yearly dues, HCI maintains more of a mailing list. Supporters regularly are sent requests for funds, but there is little sense of membership or participation.
43. A series of bills mandating registration, licensing, or selective prohibition of handguns had failed in Congress between 1968 and 1978. In 1982, California voters rejected by a large margin a proposal to freeze the number of handguns in the state. The gun-control movement needed a political victory to keep the issue alive.
44. This conclusion was based on regular reading of the HCI literature and several discussions with Pete Shields and members of the HCI Board of Directors; and Sugarmann, 253–63.
45. Although HCI published a number of documents that refer to a comprehensive national legislative agenda, a review of its current literature reveals no discussion of this agenda. HCI staff could not produce a current document that outlined this agenda when I made a request in November 1998. The closest it could come up with was a reprint of an article by HCI Research Director Douglas Weil titled "Gun Control Laws Can Reduce Crime," *The World and I* (February 1997): 301–10. This article calls for universal registration of handguns and permits in order to purchase for guns. Past HCI publications are not inconsistent with these aims, but they hardly outline a detailed agenda.
46. Carter, 75; Lambert.
47. This conclusion is based on discussions with Michael Beard and HCI staff. Interestingly, the personal agendas of the leadership of the two groups appear similar. If anything, the

Coalition leadership might be more sympathetic to ownership of long guns. Although HCI assiduously avoids advocating prohibition of handguns, conversations with some supporters and former employees reveal that it contains a core of supporters who may advocate this policy.

48. Interview with Eric Gorovitz, January 2000.
49. Interview with Bob Walker and Dennis Henigan, Washington, DC, November 10, 1998.
50. Davidson, 85–115.
51. As an example, see Edel, chapters 8 and 9.
52. The General Social Survey has reflected support for requiring a permit to purchase firearms to be above the 70-percent level for almost 25 years, with strong support evident in every available demographic category; see David R.Harding Jr., "Public Opinion and Gun Control: Appearance and Transparence in Support and Opposition," in Bruce and Wilcox.
53. See Kleck, 1991 and 1997; Harding; and Spitzer.
54. Kleck, 1991, 365.
55. Ibid., 370–71.
56. Howard Schuman and Stanley Presser, "The Attitude–Action Connection and the Issue of Gun Control," *Annals of the American Academy of Political and Social Science* 455 (May 1981): 40–47.
57. Ibid.
58. Kleck, 1991, 374.
59. My own observations reveal an ever-increasing number of gun enthusiasts with a primary interest in combat weapons, particularly in more urban areas.
60. Only once between December 1997 and January 1999 did 1 percent of those surveyed list gun control as the most important problem facing the country in the Gallup poll, and in the Harris poll, gun control attained the 3 percent level only once between 1993 and early 1999.
61. Harris poll 57, 1999.
62. *Gallop Poll News Service* 55, no. 20 (September 26, 1990), and Harding.
63. *Gallup Poll News Service*, available at "Guns" <www.gallop.com>.
64. Ibid.
65. Spitzer, 71.
66. Wright, Rossi, and Daly, 215–17.
67. Ibid., 222–31.
68. See Blendon, Young, and Hemenway for comparison of gun owners and nonowners.
69. Ibid. My own observations and experience have convinced me that a majority of gun owners would willingly support owner licensing and competency testing, if they did not see it as an incremental step toward prohibition. Support for registration seems to be more problematic, although *Newsweek* reported that 66 percent of gun owners surveyed in their most recent poll favored registration; see Howard Fineman, "The Gun War Comes Home" *Newsweek* (August 23, 1999): 26–32.
70. In my personal experience, many people who do not own guns believe that current law requires registration and often licensing of at least handguns. If this is the case, it could explain the failure of many proponents to pursue stronger laws through organization or other means. Such beliefs might also explain the acceptance of the assumption that control advocacy groups are focused on prohibition, since this would be the next escalation up from licensing. This might also explain some of the apparent lack of faith in the efficacy of gun control.

71. Young et al.; Harding; Kleck, 1991, 369.

72. Ibid. (all); Blendon, Young, and Hemenway. The percentage of respondents support-ing handgun prohibition has varied between about 20 and 40 percent, depending on how the question is asked.

73. Blendon, Young, and Hemenway.

74. Wright, Rossi, and Daly, 221–40.

75. Vizzard, 1993; Kleck, 1991, 363; Ron Faucheux, "Gun Play: How the NRA Defeated Initiative 676 in Washington," *Campaigns and Elections* 19 (February 1998): 34–40.

76. Wright, Rossi, and Daly, 122; Blendon, Young, and Hemenway.

77. Wright, Rossi, and Daly, 104.

78. Kleck, 1997, 74; Blendon, Young, and Hemenway; Vizzard, 1993.

79. Kleck, 1997, 117.

80. The General Social Survey reflects a decline in respondents who say that they or their spouses hunt, from about 37 to less than 19 percent between 1959 and 1994 (an almost linear 0.5 percent rate of decline per year).

81. As an example, African Americans consistently have reported considerably lower levels of gun ownership than whites. Although these rates may be accurate, two phenomena might explain possible underreporting: First, a disproportionate number of black males are convicted felons, on probation and parole. They or their cohabitants might well fear reporting gun ownership that would constitute a violation of law and grounds for a search. In addition, a large body of literature exists documenting minority suspicion and fear of government.

82. Examples can be seen in Wayne LaPierre, Charlton Heston, Tanya Metaska, and Don Kates.

CHAPTER 5

1. *Congressional Quarterly Weekly Report*, "Marathon Talks Produce New Anti-Crime Bill" (August 20, 1994). 2449–54.

2. Christopher Caldwell, "The Southern Captivity of the GOP," *Atlantic Monthly* (June 1998): 55–72.

3. The crime issue appears to have worked well for Republicans in 1968, 1972, 1980, 1984, and 1988.

4. *Congressional Quarterly Weekly Report*, "Gun Ban 'Energizes' NRA Members" (August 20, 1994): 2454.

5. O'Leary, 1994; and Jim VandeHei, "On the Hill: Guns 'n' Poses," *New Republic* (June 28, 1999): 15–18.

6. Ted Gest, "Popgun Politics," *U.S. News & World Report* (September 30, 1996): 30–37; Richard Lacayo, "Jabs, No Knockout," *Time* (October 6, 1996): 40–41; Adam Cohen, "Where They Stand," *Time* (November 11, 1996): 44–46.

7. In numerous interviews with present and former congressional and legislative staffs, I have found very little policy expertise in gun issues.

8. Laura B. Weiss, "House Blocks Proposed Gun Regulations" *Congressional Quarterly* 36, no. 24 (June 17, 1978): 1557–58.

9. For an in-depth discussion of the planning, execution, and aftermath of the ATF raid at Waco, see Vizzard, 1997, chapters 9, 12, and 13.

10. For a detailed examination of the Weaver case, see Jess Walter, *Every Knee Shall Bow* (New York: HarperCollins, 1995). For a discussion of the relationship between the Weaver and Waco events, see Vizzard, 1997, chapter 9, and Tom Morganthau, Michael Isikoff, and Bob Cohn, "The Echoes of Ruby Ridge" *Newsweek* (August 28, 1995): 26–33.

11. See Michael Barkum, *Religion and the Racist Right: The Origins of the Christian Identity Movement* (Chapel Hill: University of North Carolina Press, 1994).
12. See Walter for a detailed chronology of events. Even Walter's detailed research, a subsequent trial, and Senate hearing have not entirely clarified all events, however.
13. Alan Bock, "Ties That Bind," *National Review* (May 15, 1995): 25–35; and Joseph P. Shapiro, "An Epidemic of Fear and Loathing," *U.S. News & World Report* (May 8, 1995): 37–42.
14. Peter Annin and Evan Thomas, "Judgement Day," *Newsweek* (March 24, 1997): 42–45.
15. Jeffrey Toobin, "The Plot Thins: The Oklahoma City Conspiracy That Wasn't," *New Yorker*, January 12, 1998.
16. Vizzard, 1997, 205.
17. Kopel and Blackman, 1998, 251.
18. Vizzard, 1997, 205.
19. Ibid.
20. Ibid., 205–6.
21. Fred Bruning, "Decency, Honor and the Gun Lobby," *McCleans* 108, no. 24 (June 19, 1995): 9.
22. Both California senators, gubernatorial candidate Grey Davis, and attorney general candidate Bill Lockyer successfully used the gun issue to paint their opponents as being too conservative and agents of the NRA; see *Sacramento Bee*, "Election Year Gun Duel Looms" (October 1, 1997): A3; "Boxer, Feinstein Take Aim at Guns" (October 10, 1997): A1; "Crime, Gun Control Offer Ammunition for '98 Races" (March 1, 1998): A1; "Attorney General's Race Candidates Face to Face" (October 10, 1998): A3; "Voters Support Boxer on Education, Health, Favor Fong on Taxes" (October 10, 1998): A3; and "Boxer, Fong Tangle Over Abortion Rights, Gun Control," October 13, 1998.
23. See, *Sacramento Bee*, "Crime, Gun Control Offer Ammunition for '98 Races" (March 1, 1998): A1; and "Boxer, Feinstein Take Aim at Guns" (October 10, 1997): A1, for two examples of the coverage of Democratic adoption of gun control as a core identity issue.
24. Interviews with Assemblyman Jack Scott and Senator Leroy Green; legislative staff members Erin Niemela, Erwin Nowick, and Simon Haines; and political consultant Phil Giarrizzo. In addition, I contacted a number of other staff members seeking interviews with members advancing gun-control legislation. These conversations revealed that the staff members possessed very little knowledge of gun laws and did not want to expose themselves or their employers to any detailed discussion of policy.
25. With the exception of two key staff members, the entire legislature appears to be ignorant of the law and the lack of enforcement.
26. California Penal Code, Section 12082.
27. Long-gun purchasers are checked for criminal records but then no record is retained. This falls short of registration, because no penalty extends to possession of unregistered firearms.
28. Stephen Green, "Lockyer Seeks Funds to Police Gun-Show Sales," *Sacramento Bee* (May 12, 1999): A4.
29. Based on my own informal surveys of gun owners.
30. Birkland, chapters 1 and 2.
31. *Congressional Quarterly Weekly Report*, "House Members Duel on Crime: Assault Gun Ban Is Rejected" (October 19, 1991): 3038–39.
32. Birkland, 39.

33. Ibid., 144–45.

34. Daniel Glick et al., "Anatomy of a Massacre" *Newsweek*, May 3, 1999.

35. Daniel Glick et al., "Why the Young Kill," *Newsweek*, May 3, 1999.

36. The reasons for the public response are not clear. The level of sophistication of the planning and level of ruthlessness did exceed earlier events, but one earlier shooting had involved two participants and the use of a fire alarm to lure students into the open as targets. Perhaps columnist Mark Shields captured the reason in a discussion on *The News Hour* when he attributed it to the fact that Littleton "is the town where most America want to live."

37. Frank Bruni, "Driving Gun Control: It's About Elections, Stupid," *New York Times*, May 30, 1999 <nytimes.com>.

38. Representative Robert Matsui (D–Cal.) stated that the "Littleton shooting affected the members of Congress like nothing else has" (*California Capital Week*, produced by Capital Public Radio, June 14, 1999). Public interest is reflected in The Pew Research Center for The People and the Press, "Record News Interest in Littleton Shooting," April 24, 1999.

39. Frank Bruni, "Senate Democrats Unveil Gun Control Package," *New York Times*, May 7, 1999, <nytimes.com>.

40. *Sacramento Bee*, "Switch by GOP on Gun Control" (May 14, 1999): A1; and "Senate Oks GOP Gun Bill: President Calls it Phony" (May 15, 1999): A6.

41. Alison Mitchell, "Democrats Gain Ground, an Inch, on Gun Control," *New York Times*, May 21, 1999, <nytimes.com>.

42. Frank Bruni, "House Speaker Expects a Gun Bill to Pass," *New York Times*, May 26, 1999, <nytimes.com>.

43. Frank Bruni: "Speaker Shifts His Position on Pressing for Gun Control," *New York Times*, June 11, 1999; "GOP to Separate Gun-Control Measures From Juvenile-Crime Bill," *New York Times*, June 15, 1999; "Two Sides Locked in Fierce Fight for Swing Votes on Gun Control," *New York Times*, June 16, 1999 <nytimes.com>.

44. James Dao, "Michigan Lawmaker's Agenda Highlights a Split," *New York Times*, June 18, 1999 <nytimes.com>.

45. Frank Bruni and James Dao, "Gun-Control Bill Is Rejected in House in Bipartisan Vote," *New York Times*, June 19, 1999 <nytimes.com>.

46. Frank Bruni, "3 Democratic Women Lead on Gun Control," *New York Times*, June 14, 1999; and Alison Mitchell, "Politics Among Culprits in Death of Gun Control," *New York Times*, June 19, 1999 <nytimes.com>.

47. Elizabeth Angell, "Guns and Their Deadly Toll," *Newsweek* (August 23, 1999): 21.

48. Fox Butterfield, "Results in Tobacco Litigation Spur Cities to File Gun Suits," *New York Times*, December 24, 1998 <nytimes.com>; and Roberto Suro, "Targeting Gun Makers With a Cigarette Strategy," *Washington Post National Weekly Edition* (January 4, 1999): 30.

49. Tony Bizjak, "Cities' Lawsuits Similar to Attacks on Tobacco," *Sacramento Bee* (May 30, 1999): A1.

50. Vanessa O'Connell and Paul M. Barrett, "How a Jury Placed the Firearms Industry on the Legal Defensive," *Sacramento Bee* (February 21, 1999): H1.

51. Ibid. Interview with jurors indicate that the jury's action reflected emotion and a desire to compromise but little attention to evidence.

52. Herbert A. Sample, "Gun Backers, Boxer Push Dueling Bills on Local Suits," *Sacramento Bee* (March 24, 1999): A6; and Sharon Walsh, "The NRA Fires Back," *Washington Post National Weekly Edition* (March 8, 1999): 30.

53. Suro. The best available analysis of existing theories can be found in Michael J. McCrystle, "The Smoking Gun: Municipal Lawsuits Against Gun Manufacturers," paper presented to the American Society of Criminology, Toronto, November 17, 1999.

54. ABC News, "Building Safer Guns," June 10, 1999 <abcnews.go.com>.

55. Few gun deaths result from accidents caused by faulty design. The safety devices normally discussed would prevent anyone but the owner from using the firearm—such as integral locks or a computer chip that recognized the owner. The need for compact size and absolute reliability makes the addition of any device to a handgun problematic. None of these devices would offer more safety than locking the gun in a secure container.

56. Bob Walker and Dennis Henigan of HCI expressed enthusiasm for this approach during my conversations with them, and M. Kristen Rand of the Violence Policy Center made that organization's position clear in "Cities Should Sue Gun-Makers," *Sacramento Bee* (March 26, 1999): B7.

57. The NRA's James Baker identified the litigation strategy as the primary efforts of "the other side" during our most recent interview.

58. James Dao, "After Littleton, Gun Industry Sees Gap Widen with NRA," *New York Times*, May 25, 1999 <nytimes.com>. James Baker's June 23, 1999 address to the Outdoor Writers Association, available at <nraila.com>, reflects the NRA concern with holding the disparate gun interests together.

59. All would channel more commerce through dealers.

60. Matt Bai, "Caught in the Cross-Fire," *Newsweek* (June 28, 1999): 31.

61. Gallup Organization, "Social and Economic Indicators—Guns" (May 28, 1999) and "U.S. Gun Ownership Continues Broad Decline" (April 6, 1999), available at <gallup.com>. Gary Kleck theorizes that demonization of gun ownership and paranoia among gun owners may have increased false negatives, a position embraced by Paul Blackman of the NRA. Although this may be occurring, paranoia about gun ownership is not new and the trend line appears to be consistent. The continued urbanization of the country and the decline in hunting licenses tend to support the decline theory.

62. Ibid.

63. The most recent Gallop poll reports support for gun registration among women at 19 percentage points higher than support among men; see Gallop Organization, "Americans Support Wide Variety of Gun-Control Measures," June 16, 1999 <gallup.com>. The spread for reporting a gun in the home was 20 percentage points; see Gallop Organization, April 6, 1999 <gallup.com>.

64. Erik Eckholm, "Thorny Issue in Gun Control: Curbing Responsible Owners," *New York Times*, April 3, 1999 <nytimes.com>.

CHAPTER 6

1. Cottrol and Diamond, 1991.

2. Ibid.; Kates, 1979.

3. Ibid. (both).

4. New York's licensing system allows local authorities discretion regarding the issuances of permits to possess concealable firearms. Permits issued elsewhere in the state do not apply in New York City. Other states do have permissive permit systems, which require police to issue permits to all eligible persons; the District of Columbia has a system similar to New York's.

5. Kennett and Anderson, 171–79.

6. Ibid., 178.

7. Ibid., 193–96.
8. As an example, the California Penal Code defined machine guns to include semi-automatic firearms with magazines of more than 10-round capacity. Prior to the revocation of this law, several firearms—including the Browning HiPower pistol, M1 carbine, and AR-15 rifle—were commercially available. The law was changed in 1964 to conform with the federal definition of machine guns. Another example can be found in South Carolina, which had a very restrictive handgun-licensing law for many years that it did not enforce.
9. Kates, 1979.
10. See the statement of Mark K. Benenson, July 20, 1967, before U.S. Congress, Senate Subcommittee to Investigate Juvenile Delinquency of the Committee on the Judiciary, *Federal Firearms Act, Hearings*. 90th Congress, 1st Session, 1967.
11. For examples, see the statements of Harold Glassen, NRA President, on June 26, 1968, and Representative John Dingell, NRA Board Member, June 28, 1968, before U.S. Congress, Senate Subcommittee to Investigate Juvenile Delinquency of the Committee on the Judiciary, *Federal Firearms Legislation*, 90th Congress, 2nd Session, 1968.
12. Kennett and Anderson, 199–200.
13. Leff and Leff.
14. Ibid.
15. Kennett and Anderson, 204.
16. Leff and Leff.
17. Kennett and Anderson, 207–8.
18. U.S. Congress, Senate Subcommittee on S.885, S.2258, and S.3680. *To Regulate Commerce in Firearms, Hearings*, 73rd Congress, 2nd Session, 1934; also see House Subcommittee of the Committee on Interstate and Foreign Commerce. *To Regulate Commerce in Firearms, Hearings*. 75th Congress, 1st Session, 1937, testimony of Gen. Milton Reckford, executive vice president of the NRA, 11.
19. Kennett and Anderson, 205–6, Sugarmann, 30.
20. Kennett and Anderson, 210; Leff and Leff.
21. Sugarmann, 33.
22. Senate Hearings, 1934.
23. House Hearings, 1934, 124–25.
24. Sugarmann, 33.
25. Sugarmann, 34; Kennett and Anderson, 211. Also see, U.S. Congress, House, 1937, testimony of NRA executive vice president Reckford. Reckford explained the proposed legislation to the subcommittee members more as an author than an interested advocate.
26. For an in-depth evaluation of the failings of the FFA, see U.S. Congress, Senate Hearings, 1965, 65–185, 274–90, 343–73, and 421–59.
27. U.S. Congress, House, 1937.
28. Kennett and Anderson, 192–93; Sugarmann, 30.
29. Sugarmann, 30.
30. Bureau of Justice Statistics, *Violent Crime in the United States* (Washington, DC, 1991).
31. Kennett and Anderson, 187–216; Leff and Leff.
32. Kennett and Anderson, 205, 209.
33. Although no precise records exist to document the attitudes and assumptions, some assumptions can be drawn from the statements, testimony, and questions of senators and representatives. For an excellent example, see the speech of Thomas Blanton of Texas in opposition to H.R. 9093 on December 17, 1924 (*Congressional Record*, 66:730).
34. See the testimony of Reckford to U.S. Congress, Senate, 1934.

212   SHOTS IN THE DARK

35. Sugarmann, 34.
36. Zimring, 1975. The author's personal experience and observations in 1967 also confirm this information.
37. Zimring, 1975.

CHAPTER 7

1. Vizzard, 1993; and Franklin Zimring, "Firearms and Federal Law: The Gun Control Act of 1968," *Journal of Legal Studies* 4, no. 1 (1975): 133–98.
2. 26 USC 5842 also defined short-barreled shotguns and rifles, weapons made from rifles and shotguns, shotgun pistols, and all concealable firearms other than pistols or revolvers as controlled firearms.
3. Zimring, 1975. I investigated violations of the FFA as a special investigator with the Alcohol, Tobacco Tax Division in 1967 and 1968. Based on my own experience and that of numerous senior investigators with whom I worked, even Zimring's argument for the Law's limited potential utility underestimates the difficulties of actual investigations and takes no account of the attitudes of U.S. Attorneys and the minimal sentencing potential of the FFA.
4. Ibid.
5. S.3714, 85th Congress, 2d Session (1958).
6. Between 1955 and 1958 imports increased from less than 3 percent of the domestic rifle market to approximately one-third; although the increase in handguns lagged somewhat behind that of rifles in the early years, a similar pattern existed. See Zimring, 1975.
7. 22 USC 1934(b).
8. Zimring, 1975.
9. Ibid.
10. Ibid. Also Neal Knox, "The 30-Year War for Gun Ownership," *Guns and Ammo* (August 1988). Shipping handguns to private individuals by mail was already prohibited. Although the term "mail-order sale" is normally used to describe the Dodd Bill, it actually covered remote orders of any type. Shipment normally occurred by commercial shipping company.
11. Zimring, 1975.
12. Ibid.
13. U.S. Congress, 1965, 1.
14. U.S. Congress, Senate, Committee on the Judiciary, Subcommittee to Investigate Juvenile Delinquency, *Federal Firearms Act, Hearings*. 90th Congress, 1st Session, 1967, 3.
15. Testimony of NRA Executive Vice President Franklin Orth and NRA President Harlon Carter, U.S. Congress, 1965, 195–218, and testimony of NRA President Harold Glassen, U.S. Congress, 1967, 495.
16. Knox, 1988. Also see testimony of NRA Executive Vice President Franklin Orth and NRA President Harlon Carter, U.S. Congress, 1965, 195–218.
17. Knox; U.S. Congress, 1967, 495.
18. U.S. Congress, 1965, 212.
19. See the testimony of Thomas J. Siatos, publisher and editorial director of *Guns and Ammo*, U.S. Congress, 1965, 615–28. Neal Knox also supported this position in March 1993 interviews with me. Being then a reporter for *Gun Week*, Knox has been a key figure in both the gun press and the NRA for almost 40 years.
20. Testimony of Franklin Orth and Harlon Carter, U.S. Congress, 1965, 212 and 215; interviews with Knox.
21. Sugarmann 45–52; Davidson, 34–35; Knox interviews.

22. Interview with Peter W. Velde, Alexandria, Virginia, March 1993. Velde was hired by Hruska as minority counsel for the subcommittee and retained close ties to the senator. The acrimony between Hruska and Dodd is often apparent on both personal and philosophical levels during the Hearings; see U.S. Congress, 1968, 592 and 593 for examples. Also see Robert Sherrill, *The Saturday Night Special and Other Guns with which Americans Won the West, Protected Bootleg Franchises, Slew Wildlife, Robbed Countless Banks, Shot Husbands Purposely and by Mistake and Killed Presidents—Together with the Debate Over Continuing Same* (New York: Charterhouse, 1973), 68–69.

23. Velde; my review of Hruska's statements in committee support Velde's view, and my research revealed no documentation linking Hruska to the NRA.

24. Velde contended that Hruska's opposition to much of Dodd's legislation resulted largely from his dislike of Dodd and his belief that Dodd was attempting to steamroll minority objections. A review of Hruska's questioning during several years of hearings also reveals a very strong emphasis on the rural perspective and concern for the impact of the law on individuals.

25. U.S. Congress, 1965, 12–15; and 1967, 20–23 and 31.

26. U.S. Congress, 1965, 6–12.

27. U.S. Congress, 1967, 124–27.

28. Ibid., 24.

29. Velde stated that the committee was engaged in marking up Hruska's bill as T-IV of the Omnibus Crime Bill, and that the full committee was evenly divided between supporters of the Hruska bill or the Dodd bill, with Chairman Eastland favoring the former. After the assassination of Robert Kennedy, two proxy votes shifted the balance in favor of Dodd's bill, which the committee passed after deleting restrictions on interstate long-gun sales.

30. S.Rep. No. 1097, 90th Congress, 2d Sess. (1968).

31. 114 *Congressional Record* 14,775 (May 23, 1968).

32. Ibid., at 14,798.

33. Ibid., at 16,300.

34. Public Law 90-618, 90th Congress, H.R. 17735, October 22, 1968.

35. Ibid.

36. Ibid.

37. 114 *Congressional Record* 14,775 (May 23, 1968).

38. See *Bass v. United States*, 404 U.S. 336 (1971). The court contributed the following observations: "[T]he statute does not read well under either view," 2; "the legislative history hardly speaks with that clarity of purpose which Congress supposedly furnishes courts," 4; and "the Government concedes that 'the statute is not a model of logic or clarity,'" 4.

39. See *Bass v. United States*, dissenting opinion of Justice Blackmun, 8–9.

40. See response of Senator Long to Senator McClellan, May 23, 1968, 114 *Congressional Record* 14,773-75 (May 23, 1968).

41. Velde stated that Senator Long made a personal appeal to his colleagues for last-minute inclusion of T-VII into the Omnibus bill without a hearing based on his perception of needs for the next election. According to Velde, subsequent changes were to be made in committee, but the law was passed on a voice vote and no changes could be made. Some senators and staff members considered the section of the law that made possession of a firearm by the employee of a felon to be unconstitutional. Also see the testimony of Attorney General Ramsey Clark, U.S. Congress, 1968, 69. For a thorough review of the legislative history, see *Stevens v. United States*, 440 F 2nd 144 (1971).

42. See Senator Tydings's statements, U.S. Congress, 1965, 422, and Senator McGovern's statements, U.S. Congress, 1967, 1099.
43. The Gallup Organization, *Public Opinion News Service*, "Eight in Ten Persons Favor Law Requiring Police Permit for Gun," January 12, 1964.
44. U.S. Congress, 1968, 579–82. Even some manufactures of firearms were publicly supporting much stronger action.
45. *Congressional Quarterly Annual Almanac 1968*, "Gun Controls Extended to Long Guns, Ammunition" (Washington, DC: CQ, 1969), 225.
46. Tydings was defeated in 1970 with considerable opposition from gun interests. Although the impact of his support for gun control on the election remains unclear, his defeat came to symbolize the risk of supporting gun control for the next 20 years.
47. See the testimony of Attorney General Ramsey Clark, U.S. Congress, 1968, 57–59, and S.3634 and S.3691, 90th Congress, 2nd Session.
48. Ibid.
49. Ibid.
50. U.S. Congress, 1968 covers the entire hearings.
51. Spitzer, 144–45.
52. Vizzard, 1995.
53. Ibid.
54. The use of "title" is somewhat confusing in this use. Normally used to refer to separate federal codes, it concurrently defines subdivisions in the Act.
55. Ultimately incorporated into a single Act, the GCA and T-VII were routinely viewed as one piece of legislation by those implementing the law.
56. The NFA did not prohibit machine guns and other regulated firearms, but imposed a $200 tax on the making or transfer of such weapons.
57. The firearms originally covered by 26 USC 5845 included machine guns, silencers, short-barreled rifles and shotguns, and certain other unique firearms.
58. 26.USC 5845(f).
59. Vizzard, 1997, 40–41.
60. Ibid., 64.
61. My personal experience as special investigator with the Alcohol, Tobacco Tax Division in 1967 and 1968.
62. Section 207(b), Public Law 90-618 (October 22, 1968).
63. 26 USC 5848.
64. 390 U.S. 85 (1967). Possessors could no longer claim that the act of registration would subject them to risk of prosecution, thus requiring self-incrimination.
65. The justification for any national firearms registration and licensing system depends largely upon the utility of the registration information for general law enforcement; see Vizzard, fall 1999. This precedent if extended to a general registration scheme would preclude use of that information.
66. 18 USC 922(a)(1).
67. 18 USC 922(b)(1–3) and 922(d).
68. 18 USC 922(b)(5).
69. 18 USC 922(a)(2) and 922(c).
70. 18 USC 923(i).
71. 18 USC 925(d)(3).
72. 18 USC 922(d) and (h). The exceptions being persons under 18 years of age for long guns and under 21 years of age for handguns. No restriction on receipt existed for these classes.

73. 18 USC 922(a)(5).
74. 18 USC 1202(a) applied to persons who had been: convicted of a felony, dishonorably discharged from the armed forces, adjudicated mentally incompetent, had renounced their citizenship, or who were aliens unlawfully in the country. 18 USC 922(h) applied to persons who were under indictment for or convicted of a crime that was punishable by more than 1-year imprisonment, fugitives from justice, unlawful users of prohibited drugs, or had been adjudicated mentally defective or committed to a mental institution.
75. 404 U.S. 336 (1971). Although the Court adopted a restrictive view of the statutory wording that required the government to prove "possession in commerce," a footnote in the decision suggested that prior movement of the firearm in interstate commerce would fulfill that element. This provided the government with a practical means of charging possession in most cases.
76. Based on my experience as a special agent with ATF during these years.
77. *Scarborough v. United States*, 431 U.S. 563.
78. 18 USC 922(g).
79. On some occasions, manufacturers ship to wholesalers in another state, who ship the firearm back to the state of origin. In these cases, prior interstate movement can be documented through dealer records.
80. The improvisation of investigators and prosecutors has reduced pressure to address the problems of drafting. Most firearms have traveled in interstate commerce and thus meet the current standard for federal nexus.
81. 18 USC 923(g)(1)(A) requires maintenance of records as prescribed by the Secretary. Part 178 CRF section H specifies the required records.
82. Interviews with former ATF Director Rex Davis by author in March 1993.
83. 18 USC 923(g)(1)(A).
84. 18 USC 922(s).
85. Section 101 titled "Purpose of Public Law 90-618."
86. 18 USC 923(b). Curios and relics are defined in 178.11 CRF.
87. 18 USC 922(a)(1).
88. Vizzard, 1997, 67–68.
89. Ibid.; also see, Cook, Molliconi, and Cole, 1995.
90. 18 USC 923(d)(2).
91. Possession of a license allows an individual to order firearms directly from a variety of wholesalers, often at substantial savings.
92. Vizzard, 1997, 67. ATF never pursued a policy of revocation, but routinely refused to renew licenses. More often, inspectors convinced the licensee to voluntarily surrender his license.
93. Ibid.
94. Vizzard, 1997, 66–68.
95. The purpose of regulatory law and licensing is to ensure compliance with procedures or competency. The desire or lack thereof to make sales is an irrational criterion for qualification. A fee adequate to cover issuing and inspection costs would have limited the number of licenses without placing the government in this irrational position.
96. 18 USC 926. Regulations are contained in 27 CFR Parts 178 and 179.
97. Vizzard, 1997, 55–56.
98. 18 USC 921(a).
99. The combination of excluding firearms manufactured before 1898 and creating a collector license for firearms over 50 years old allowed substantial interstate shipment of

collector arms. Individuals could also obtain firearms from out of state by having them shipped through a dealer in the state of acquisition.

100. See the testimony of Leonard S. Blondes, Vice President of the National Council for Responsible Firearms Policy, U.S. Congress, 1967, 841.

101. Representatives of both groups appeared on several occasions before congressional committees in support of the Dodd bills, and the IACP supported both licensing and registration; see testimony of Quinn Tamm, President of IACP, U.S. Congress, 1968, 526.

102. A reading of testimony by Justice and Treasury representatives reflects that Justice was clearly in the lead on policy-making, while Treasury was more focused on details of implementation. At congressional hearings, Justice was extensively represented by the attorney general, while Treasury was usually represented either by an assistant secretary or the Commissioner of Internal Revenue. Justice's dominate policy role became most clear in 1968 with the introduction of licensing and registration proposals.

103. See the following for examples: *Saturday Evening Post*, "Speaking Out—Too Many People Have Guns" (February 1, 1964): 12; *Washington Post*, "Fire at Will," June 26 1968; *Advertising Age*, "Guns Must Go" (June 17, 1968): 1; and the *New York Times Magazine*, "The Gun and How to Control It" (September 25, 1966): 34–35, 133–40.

104. U.S. Congress, 1965, 212; and 1968, 399.

105. In the author's experience virtually all competitive shooters and arms collectors are NRA members. Although many hunters are not, those who are members of outdoor associations most likely are. In some cases those who testified for these groups also held key positions in the NRA; see testimony of C. R. Gutermuth, Vice President of Wildlife Management Institute, U.S. Congress, 1965, 296.

106. The Dodd Bill restricted imports of firearms—a benefit for domestic manufactures— yet the NRA consistently opposed the Bill. The Dodd Bill also potentially benefited retailers of firearms and ammunition by controlling mail-order sales, thus reducing competition for most retailers. On the first day of the 1968 hearings, Senator Dodd announced the support of several manufactures of firearms (see U.S. Congress, 1968, 2). This constituted a major break with the NRA position.

107. E. E. Schattschneider, *The Semisovereign People* (Hindale, IL: Dryden Press, 1960), 2.

108. See *NRA Bulletin* dated April 9, 1965, not titled but in reference to S.1592.

109. See testimony of: Carl Miller, 274–81; Richard Caples, 343–73; Arthur J. Sills, 394–407; and James Bennett, 495–503 (U.S. Congress, 1965).

110. See testimony of: Ramsey Clark, 615–57; John Lindsay, 88–103; and John Glenn, 113–18 (U.S. Congress, 1968).

111. U.S. Congress, 1967, 997–99.

112. See testimony of Merton Howe (133–60) and Jess Gonzalez (160–85) in U.S. Congress, 1965.

113. See testimony of New Jersey Governor Richard Hughes (997–1030) and Quinn Tamm (1052–62) in U.S. Congress, 1967.

114. U.S. Congress, 1968, 566.

115. See the testimony of John Dingell (468–526) in U.S. Congress, 1968.

116. See the testimony of: Harry Woodward, 185–94; Franklin Orth, 195–215; Senator Paul Fannin, 241–43; Representative Gordon Allott, 247–54; Thomas Kimball, 254–58; and Harmon C. Leonard, 269–71 (U.S. Congress, 1965). Also see the testimony of John Saylor, 156–58; John Dingell, 152–56; Harold Glassen, 438–44; Robert Dennis, 584–91; and James Jungroth, 598–604 (U.S. Congress, 1967).

117. See the testimony of Neal Knox in U.S. Congress, 1967, 662; also see the testimony of Franklin Orth and John Dingell in U.S. Congress, 1968, 395 and 152–56, respectively.

118. See the testimony of Leon C. Jackson in U.S. Congress, 1967, 634.

119. U.S. Congress, 1967, 418, 504, 507, 646, and U.S. Congress, 1968, 202, 473, 542.

120. U.S. Congress, 1968, 190 and 201.

121. See the testimony of Under-Secretary of the Treasury Joseph Barr in U.S. Congress, 1967, 40.

122. Cook, Molliconi, and Cole, 1995. The numbers of licensees are documented by ATF licensing figures and the relative proportion of "legitimate" dealers is confirmed by my experience as a supervisory special agent with ATF until 1994.

123. Kleck, 1991, table 2.1, 49–51.

124. Cook, Molliconi, and Cole, 1995; Vizzard, 1999.

125. Velde interview.

126. Ibid.

127. As examples, see the testimony of Senators Bourke Hickenlooper (163), Frank Church (415), and Peter Dominick (882) in U.S. Congress, 1967.

128. Both served on the NRA board of directors.

129. See the questioning of Attorney General Ramsey Clark by Senator Thurmond, U.S. Congress, 1968, 635–50, and the questioning of Governor Richard Hughes by Senator Hruska, U.S. Congress, 1967, 1018.

130. Interviews with both current and former staff members of congress cited the inability to invoke party discipline as a key factor in the inability to pass firearms legislation prior to the Brady Law.

131. Nelson Polsby, *Political Innovation in America* (New Haven, CT: Yale University Press, 1984), 170.

132. Vizzard, 1997, 52–56.

CHAPTER 8

1. Within ATF the two operational functions have had a series of official names or designations: The regulatory function has been designated as permissive, regulatory enforcement, and compliance operations; while the law-enforcement function has been designated as enforcement, criminal enforcement and law enforcement.

2. Vizzard, 1997, 7–8.

3. Ibid.

4. Vizzard, 1997, chapter 3.

5. I spent months contacting as many as 15 dealers per day in Alaska and Washington during the final months of 1968 and the early months of 1969, and continued to perform this function intermittently for several years thereafter in Washington and California.

6. Ibid.

7. As with much of the general description of ATTD–ATF operations, this is based on personal observation, innumerable discussions with others in the organization over many years, and interviews with key former personnel, including directors and assistant directors.

8. Vizzard, 1997, 11–13.

9. Ibid.

10. Ibid.

11. Ibid., 66.

12. U.S. Congress, House, Subcommittee on Crime of the Judiciary Committee, *Handguns and Crime*. 94th Congress, 1st Session, March 20, 1975, testimony of Rex Davis, Director, ATF. My own experience and observations and those of many others in ATF support this view.

13. U.S. Congress, Senate, Subcommittee to Investigate Juvenile Delinquency of the Committee on the Judiciary, *Handgun Crime Control—1975–1976*. 94th Congress, 1st Session, 528, 1976.

14. This assumption was largely confirmed in an interview with former ATF Director Rex Davis, who referred to the Ford and Nixon administrations as mildly supportive but not very publicly so until the appointment of Levi. Former ILA Director Neal Knox also confirmed that the Nixon administration courted the gun lobby but failed to deliver active support.

15. Five commissions had recommended stricter gun control: In 1967 the President's Commission on Law Enforcement and Administration of Justice (the Katzenbach Commission) recommended registration and licensing of handguns; in 1968 the National Advisory Commission on Civil Disorders (the Kerner Commission) made similar recommendations; in 1969 the National Commission on the Causes and Prevention of Violence (the Eisenhower Commission) recommended very restrictive licensing of handguns and prohibition of Saturday night specials; in 1971 the National Commission on Reform of Federal Criminal Laws (the Brown Commission) recommended the prohibition of private ownership of handguns; and in 1973 the National Advisory Commission on Criminal Justice Standards and Goals recommended prohibition of private ownership of handguns.

16. Senate Hearings, 1975, 45.

17. See the testimony of Franklin Orth, executive vice president of the NRA, before the Senate Hearings, May 21, 1965.

18. Interviews with Acquilino and Knox.

19. See the statement of Representative Conyers, *Congressional Record*, Vol. 121, December 17, 1975, H12,896.

20. See Senator Kennedy's statement before Senate Hearings, April 23, 1975. The proposal would have restricted handguns to those with barrels over 6 inches in length.

21. Speech delivered by Attorney General Edward Levi before the Law Enforcement Executives Narcotics Conference on April 6, 1975, in Washington, DC.

22. Ibid. In this address, Levi specifically cites the demand of such groups as the International Association of Chiefs of Police and the U.S. Conference of Mayors for stricter federal controls. He also cites the concerns of those opposed, who reside in areas in which crime rates are of far less concern.

23. See Levi's testimony before the Senate Hearings, July 22, 1975. Levi acknowledged that the Department of Justice had concluded that the earlier proposal was not practical. He did not acknowledge any political considerations in its abandonment.

24. Ibid.

25. U.S. Congress, Senate, S.750, *A Bill to Prohibit the Importation, Manufacture, Sale, Purchase, or Transportation of Handguns, Except for or by Members of the Armed Forces, Law Enforcement Officials and, as Authorized by the Secretary of the Treasury, Licensed Importers, Manufacturers, Dealers, Antique Collectors and Pistol Clubs*, 94th Congress, 1st Session, February 10, 1975.

26. U.S. Congress, Senate, S.141, *A Bill to Repeal the Gun Control Act of 1968*, 91st Congress, 1st Session, January 15, 1975.

27. In S.750, the preamble clearly establishes the logic of the bill and its intended purpose.

28. U.S. Congress, *Congressional Record*, January 15, 1975; Senator McClure delineated the rationale of his bill, focusing primarily on individual sovereignty and constitutional rights and secondarily on the utility of gun control as a crime control mechanism.

29. One former Democratic congressional-staff member who was very heavily involved in this issue cited the poor-quality staffwork of Conyers's subcommittee as a key to the

failure to pass a Saturday-night-special bill. From the opposing ranks, Neal Knox stated that "a Saturday-night-special bill would have passed except that Conyers was more interested in holding hearings than passing legislation."

30. Former ATF Director Davis remembered inquires as to ATF's potential contribution, but no participation in the planning process prior to the announcement. I participated in ATF planning at the regional level, and that planning did not begin until after the president made his proposal public.

31. This conclusion is drawn from the timing of the event, Levi's proposals, and a reading of Zimring's 1975 article "Firearms and Federal Law."

32. See the Comptroller General of the United States, *Handgun Control: Effectiveness and Costs* (Washington, DC: General Accounting Office, February 6, 1978), 43; Tanna Pesso, "Gun Control (B): The Bureau of Alcohol, Tobacco and Firearms," an unpublished case study (Kennedy School of Government, Harvard University, 1981).

33. Vizzard, 1997, 50–51.

34. Ibid.

35. Comptroller General; Pesso; also based on my personal conversations with numerous agents and supervisors who participated in this operation, and my observations in ATF headquarters during the internal analysis of this operation.

36. Even after the passage of the GCA, the Southeast region of ATF had retained more personnel than any of the other six, with Georgia still having more special agents than California. Each state in the Southeast region remained a separate district until 1981, although districts in other regions such as Seattle contained as many as six states. Although CUE ended the concentration of personnel in the Southeast, managers from that region dominated the law-enforcement operation in ATF for 10 more years.

37. Senate Hearings, 1975, 524, 543.

38. Beard and Knox interviews.

39. After the passage of the GCA, the membership expanded to over a million members; see Kennett and Anderson, 238.

40. Acquilino and Knox interviews.

41. Ibid.

42. Knox interview.

43. Vizzard, 1997, 52.

44. Acquilino interview.

45. Senate Hearings, April 23, 1975; see the exchange between Senators Hart and Kennedy, 30–31.

46. Knox told me that the election of the 1974 "Watergate" class in Congress significantly affected many in the NRA and generated fear that legislation would now be passed. On the opposing side, Michael Beard remembers this as a time of optimism that legislation would pass Congress to significantly restrict the uncontrolled possession and transfer of handguns.

47. Roger Davidson, *The Postreform Congress* (College Park: University of Maryland Press, 1992), 14.

48. Acquilino cited ATF action at gun shows and against unlicensed dealers in conjunction with press releases from ATF on these actions as being the key elements in developing the consensus in the NRA that there was a well-organized conspiracy to "take our guns." Neal Knox continues to contend that ATF and Treasury had a plan to pursue registration and eventually the licensing of firearms if not prohibition, most recently stated in his review of my last book. See Neal Knox, "BATF View of NRA," *Shotgun News* 52, no. 2 (February 1998).

49. Rex Davis and G. R. Dickerson interviews, March 1993. I personally attempted to

explain that the gun lobby differed from other lobbies and thrived on conflict in 1979. Although he rejected the analysis at the time, Dickerson has since come to the same conclusion.

50. Vizzard, 1997, 54.

51. In his 1965 testimony before the Senate Hearings, NRA Executive Vice President Franklin Orth spoke in glowing terms of the NRA's "many friends in ATTD" and the "admirable job" done by the agency (see page 200).

52. A comparison of the testimony by the two departments reveals that Treasury officials regularly made more modest proposals than did those from the Department of Justice. During the 1970s Treasury focused on mild "clean-up" legislation that would not alter policy in any significant way. Justice officials advocated prohibiting a substantial number of handguns with a bill similar to Senator Kennedy's. More importantly, the attorney general openly stated that the Second Amendment did not apply to individual possession of firearms and that guns in the home were more of a danger to the owner than to criminals. The symbolism of these statements was very likely more important than any proposal for legislation, because they attack the critical underpinning for the sovereignty and worldview paradigms.

53. Based on my interviews with former Assistant Secretary Richard Davis, April 5, 1993.

54. Rex Davis and Richard Davis.

55. Weiss, 1978.

56. Weiss, 1978; Richard Davis.

57. Richard Davis and Rex Davis.

58. *American Rifleman*, "Congress Moves Against BATF Regs" (June 1978): 28–29; see also Weiss, 1978.

59. *American Rifleman*, "Carter White House Gets Taste of Gun Lobby Might" (June 1978): 78–80.

60. Bureau of Alcohol, Tobacco, and Firearms.

61. Based on conversations with personnel who reviewed the letters.

62. *American Rifleman*, "Carter White House Gets Taste of Gun Lobby Might."

63. 18 USC, Sec. 223(g), October 22, 1968.

64. Neither in my experience or my research have I ever encountered even a discussion of the topic. Although some in ATF were aware of the theoretical option, no one advanced it. Such an initiative would have had to come from outside ATF.

65. Testimony of Franklin Orth, executive vice president of the NRA, before Senate Hearings, July 19, 1967.

66. Dealers had been required to submit their records to ATF upon going out of business since 1968, but not all comply. No effective mechanism existed to ensure compliance.

67. Because ATF does not know what guns a dealer has sold, there is no effective way of auditing the dealer's books. An unscrupulous dealer can fail to record a portion of his inventory in either his acquisition or disposition records, a fairly common means of circumventing the law. The only means of auditing a dealer suspected of such actions requires ATF to contact identifiable wholesalers and obtain records of all guns shipped to the dealer; this is known as a "forward trace."

68. *American Rifleman*, "Carter White House Gets Taste of Gun Lobby Might."

69. Knox interview; and Knox, 1998.

70. Rex Davis interview.

71. Knox interview.

72. Weiss, 1978; Rex Davis interview.

73. I was detailed to ATF headquarters in 1978 and assigned there from 1980 to 1985. For

three of those years I was assigned to the Firearms Enforcement Branch, and for more than two I managed all law-enforcement computer operations. ATF did not obtain its first mainframe computer until 1985, when I obtained a cast-off IBM from the Customs Service. ATF management feared asking for any funds for a mainframe computer and farmed out all computing to other agencies.

74. Dickerson interview and prior conversations.
75. Both Richard Davis and Rex Davis told me that the White House lost all interest in the topic of gun control after the furor over new regulations. Rex Davis said he also felt abandoned by officials at Treasury. Rex Davis did not choose the timing of his departure, and it is likely that the administration hoped to reduce conflict by making a new appointment.
76. Vizzard, 1997, 78.
77. Here I use "conservative" in the American context, meaning deference to local over central authority and favoring limited government.
78. See chapter 8.

CHAPTER 9

1. For a more extensive examination of ATF's organizational culture, see Vizzard, 1997.
2. As an example, the San Francisco Field Division concentrated almost exclusively on bombings, arsons, illegal-firearms trafficking, outlaw motorcycle groups, and prison gangs.
3. The testimony before the various oversight committees in 1979 and 1980 is replete with these two issues, as are numerous articles in every firearm journal. For an in-depth presentation of the argument, see David T. Hardy, *The BATF's War on Civil Liberties: The Assault on Gun Owners* (Bellevue, WA: Second Amendment Foundation, 1979).
4. I personally traced numerous guns to these shows, where the sellers could not identify the buyers. Sellers often sold guns within hours of purchasing them, while claiming to be collectors. For recommendations on how to buy at gun shows, see the pamphlet by Will B. Outlaw, "Guns and Politics" (East Palo Alto, CA: Venceremos Publications, 1969).
5. Occasionally unlicensed dealers would sell new guns, invariably obtained from a cooperative licensed dealer.
6. I supervised numerous investigations of unlicensed dealers and reviewed many more while assigned to the Firearms Enforcement Branch of ATF Headquarters.
7. The law has since been changed to prohibit private transfers to a prohibited person.
8. U.S. Congress, Senate, Committee on the Judiciary, Subcommittee to Investigate Juvenile Delinquency, *Handgun Crime Control—1975–1976*. 94th Congress, 1st Session, Vols. I and II, 1976, 118–19.
9. Several dealers—who advised me that undercover agents posing as prohibited persons had attempted to purchase firearms from them—had never been the subject of ATF investigations.
10. I base my conclusions here on personal discussions with Dickerson—his testimony and my own observation of events.
11. DeConcini later became a regular defender of ATF's budget and came to ATF's support in the aftermath of the Branch Davidian case in Waco, Texas, by holding the first and most sympathetic hearings. In 1990 DeConcini became the object of NRA wrath when he sponsored an assault-weapon bill.
12. U.S. Congress, Senate, Committee on Appropriations, *Oversight Hearings on Bureau of Alcohol, Tobacco, and Firearms*, 96th Congress, 1st Session, July 11, 1979, 16–20.

13. U.S. Congress, Senate, Committee on the Judiciary, Subcommittee on the Constitution, *Gun Control and Constitutional Rights, Hearings*, 96th Congress, 2nd Session, September 15, 1980, 331.
14. Vizzard, 1997, 70–71.
15. See Hardy, 1979; also see the testimony of Neal Knox, September 15, 1980, U.S. Congress, 1980.
16. Ibid.
17. John Mintz, "Who Are the Bad Guys? The NRA and the ATF Duel Over the Truth
in Accounts of Raids on Gun Owners," *Washington Post National Weekly Edition* (May
22, 1995): 31; also see David B. Kopel and Paul H. Blackman, *No More Wacos: What's
Wrong with Federal Law Enforcement and How to Fix It* (Buffalo, NY: Prometheus Books,
1997), and William J. Vizzard, "No More Wacos" (book review), *Police Quarterly* 1, no.
2 (1998): 111–19.
18. Hardy, 1979; also see the conclusions and testimony of Neal Knox before the Senate
Hearings, September 15, 1980. For a recent example of this pattern, see Kopel and
Blackman, 1997.
19. Vizzard, 1997, 71.
20. U.S. Congress, 1980, 335.
21. Senator Orrin Hatch, as an example, has repeatedly referred to the record of abuse of
rights as established in these oversight hearings as an undisputed fact; see "Should Semi-
automatic Assault-Style Weapons be Banned by Congress?" *Congressional Digest* 69, no.
11 (November 1990): 266–76. The NRA and associated organizations have likewise
repeatedly used this "official record" as evidence of the mischief that gun laws can do.
22. Undated press release entitled "Gun Control" from the Reagan–Bush Committee.
23. Osha Gray Davidson, *Under Fire: The NRA and the Battle for Gun Control* (Washington,
DC: National Press Books, 1992), 51. Assigned to ATF Headquarters at the time and
keenly attuned to the issue, I made the same observations.
24. Interview with Robert Powis, former Deputy Assistant Secretary of Treasury in the
Reagan administration, April 1993. and Richard Davis.
25. The administration advised Dickerson that he would be reassigned to the Customs Service. ATF's management was largely in disarray. Many law-enforcement managers
favored the merger, and many regulatory managers displayed ambivalence. For a more
in-depth discussion of reaction to the merger, see Vizzard, 1997, chapter 6.
26. The secretary could eliminate or merge bureaus created by executive order without
specific statutory authorization.
27. The majority of ATF employees, particularly the special agents, had become so dis-
heartened with the agency's weakness that they welcomed the merger.
28. Vizzard, 1997, 80–81.
29. Although numerous managers in ATF and Treasury recognized Senator Abnor's role-
reversal, none have offered an explanation.
30. By 1992, ATF had 2,000 special agents and ATF prosecutions were receiving the highest prosecutive priority in its history. Although the majority of the firearms cases were
directed at violent felons and armed drug traffickers, the number of cases involving
licensed dealers rebounded somewhat with no complaint from Congress or even the
pro-gun lobby.
31. According to Michael Beard, NCBHG opposed the idea of the initiative while HCI
supported it. John Phillips advised me that neither group provided significant financial
or organizational support to the qualification of the initiative or the campaign.
32. A key theme of the opponents was the inability of "law-abiding" citizens to acquire a

handgun if the initiative passed. This probably generated fear in many citizens, who associate handguns with self-defense. A second aspect of the issue that does not appear to be as much recognized by the gun-control advocates is the equity issue: The law would have treated citizens differently by allowing some to retain guns, while others were denied the right to obtain them. Such "grandfather" schemes are a common means of defusing the resistance of stakeholders and often are successful. In this case, the organization and ideological nature of the stakeholders, combined with their interest in future gun transactions, negated the value. At the same time, the initiative was open to attack for unequal treatment of citizens, thus violating a key tenant of American political values—equity.

33. In March 1993 interviews Eric Sterling (staff member of the House Judiciary from 1981 to 1989), Josh Sugarmann (executive director of the Violence Policy Center and a long-time gun-control activist), Michael Handcock (former counsel to the Coalition to Ban the Handgun), and Michael Beard all expressed this opinion. John Phillips took an opposing view—that Proposition 15 raised awareness and benefited HCI in the long run.

34. The polls had indicated that the proposition would be favored in California, but the support did not hold as the campaign evolved.

35. With the exception of Phillips, pro-gun-control advocates that were interviewed cited several significant results of the Proposition 15 loss. The press lost interest in gun control and the news media ceased to advocate as intensely. Morale in NCBHG and HCI dropped and some supporters drifted away. Legislators clearly took this as a sign that gun control was not a political "winner" and was an issue to avoid. Gary Kleck, who has examined the issue extensively, has contended for some time that gun control is not a winning political issue.

36. Interviews with Nelson "Pete" Shields and Michael Beard.

37. Both Proposition 15-backer John Phillips and ILA Director James Baker concurred in the conclusion that Proposition 15's defeat motivated the future efforts by HCI to cultivate police support.

38. Interview with political-consultant Phil Giarrizo, 1998. The NRA suffered a similar defeat in the 1999 concealed-weapons initiative in Missouri, in spite of superior organization and funding; see *Kansas City Star*, "Firearms Proposition Narrowly Defeated, St. Louis Opposition Decisive" (April 7, 1999): A1.

39. Barbara A. Serrano, "Handgun Proposal Is Trounced," *Seattle Times*, November 5, 1997, available at <seattletimes.com>.

40. Sugarmann, Beard, Sterling, and Handcock interviews, as well as my own observations.

41. This conclusion is based on several extensive discussions with Pete Shields and interviews with Michael Beard and others associated with NCBHG.

42. Gun-control activists from the early 1980s universally acknowledged the need for widespread law-enforcement support and the need to drive a wedge between the NRA and the police. James Baker concurred that Proposition 15 demonstrated the importance of this strategy. Baker acknowledged the "cop-killer bullet" issue as a strategic success for the pro-control interests in their effort to define the NRA as opposed to law-enforcement interests.

43. Contrary to popular belief, pistol bullets seldom cause instant disability, and prior to the 1970s, most pistol ammunition used solid bullets that caused minimal initial trauma upon striking a subject.

44. The same problem arose with penetration of armor in the Middle Ages, the bombardment of fortified walls by cannon, and the use of antitank weapons against armored vehicles.

45. Davidson, 1992, 87.
46. Michael Beard stated that Sam Fields, formerly of NCBHG, was the originator of the term and first understood the potential of the issue. Mary Louise Cohen credits Charles Orison of HCI.
47. Although they are not willing to be quoted, virtually every advocate acknowledges this fact. There was no documentation of any significant impact of such ammunition; see Kleck, 1991, 82. The technical staff at ATF consistently advised that no workable definition could be developed.
48. Although the control of such ammunition had little utility, it likewise had little or no impact on shooters, gun owners, or collectors. A compromise by the NRA would have had no practical effect on its constituency.
49. For an in–depth review of the issue, see Davidson, 1992, 85–95.
50. Ibid., 98–99. The controversy was over plastic guns, which are not detectable by airport magnetometers. The guns were not plastic and were detectable.
51. Every person involved with advocacy of the McClure-Volkmer bill that was interviewed expressed the opinion that the oversight hearings were the first step in advancing the bill and had been critical in the strategy.
52. Sugarmann, 61–64; Davidson, 1992, 182–83.
53. Knox remains unrepentant in his invocation of a sovereignty paradigm. For Knox, the right to bear arms is absolute and inalienable. Unlike many others who oppose firearm control, he does not turn easily to implementation arguments.
54. Sugarmann, 61–64; Davidson, 1992, 182–83.
55. Powis interview; also numerous conversations and interviews with ATF staff by the author.
56. President Reagan addressed the 1983 NRA convention. Both the Treasury and Justice Departments avoided any association with the issue. Lois Mock (interviewed by the author, Washington, DC, March 25, 1993) stated that National Institute of Justice personnel were instructed to avoid funding any studies involving gun control. ATF Director Steven Higgins (interviewed by the author, Washington, DC, March 19, 1993) confirmed what was known by most employees, that no initiative that could be viewed as advocating control was allowed. Senator Dole, who had never shown any interest in the issue, became a key to pushing the McClure-Volkmer bill through the Senate.
57. This was generally agreed upon by former and current staffers that were familiar with the House during the mid-1980s.
58. Interview of Ken Schloman, former House Republican staff member, March 1993.
59. For a detailed description of the political events leading up the bill's passage, see Davidson, 1992, 60–81.
60. Cohen interview. Although 18 USC 922(o) prohibits possession of machine guns, it exempts those machine guns that are lawfully possessed under the NFA at the Bill's passage. Thus it effectively became a ban on the future manufacture of machine guns.
61. The term "engaging in the business" was not actually defined. The law provided several affirmative defenses that largely precluded future prosecutions of unlicensed dealers. Reducing all record-keeping violations to misdemeanors likewise reduced the probability of prosecution of licensed dealers. The result was to encourage a substantial increase in trafficking to prohibited persons and across state lines. An actual definition of "engaging in the business," for instance by setting a maximum number of sales per year, would have alleviated much of the problem without such a result.

    By creating a misdemeanor section for knowing but not willful violations of record-keeping requirements, serious violators could have been prosecuted and lesser ones ignored or allowed to plea to misdemeanors. Such results would have been less satisfying to the hard core opponents of gun control, but would have generated less demand for future action.

62. Schloman interview.

CHAPTER 10

1. Snyder, 1997, 7–8.
2. True registration, such as the NFA, requires the reporting of all transfers. The reporting systems in most states only required the reporting of the initial retail sale. All subsequent transactions between individuals were exempt from the requirement.
3. Opponents successfully challenged this mandate as a violation of the Tenth Amendment in *Printz v. United States*.
4. I have had extensive experience with both systems. California's system can provide the name of the last retail purchaser of a firearm in less time than one can submit a trace to ATF. Traces, when successful, can take weeks to complete.
5. Few in ATF showed much interest in what they viewed as a largely symbolic bill.
6. *Congressional Quarterly Weekly Report*, "NRA Shows It Still Has What It Takes to Overcome Gun Control Advocates" (September 17, 1988): 2564–65.
7. *Congressional Quarterly Weekly Report*, "Brady's Solid House Victory Is a Gun Control Milestone" (May 11, 1991): 1196–1202.
8. *Congressional Quarterly Weekly Report*, "Crime Measure Is a Casualty of Partisan Skirmishing" (November 30, 1991): 3528.
9. Vizzard, 1997, chapter 7.
10. Ibid.
11. Ibid.
12. Ibid.
13. George Bush had proven neither hostile nor supportive of gun control. Bush voted for the original GCA and apparently remained a moderate on the topic thereafter. Although Ronald Reagan spoke against gun control, neither Bush nor Reagan expended political capital in opposition. During his last two years in office, Bush equivocated on Brady by saying he would sign it only as part of a larger crime bill. Alternatively, Bill Clinton has used gun control to counter the Republican strategy of characterizing Democrats as being soft on crime, but has risked little political capital in pursuit of legislation.
14. *Congressional Quarterly Weekly Report*, "Congress Responds to Violence; Tackles Guns and Criminals" (November 13, 1993): 3127–30.
15. *Congressional Quarterly Weekly Report*, "Long Time Second Party Scores a Long List of GOP Firsts" (November 12, 1994): 3232–39. Although the NRA remained neutral, other groups in opposition to gun control targeted Brooks.
16. *Congressional Quarterly Weekly Report*, "Handgun Control" (December 18, 1993): 3459.
17. Spitzer, 161.
18. Shaffer and Vizzard.
19. Large manufacturers such as Colt as a precaution often submit new designs to ATF for advance examination.
20. The resulting firearms lacked the compactness of a pistol and the accuracy of a carbine. Their only saving grace was their ability to stir customer interest through their menacing appearance.
21. In my experience this description was ubiquitous. Also see Steve Berry and Jeff Brazil, "Owners' Numbers Are Small But Impact Is Powerful," *Los Angeles Times* (August 26, 1997): A1.

22. Numerous designations have been used for versions of the AK-47 design, which has become the most commonly used military arm in the world. I will not attempt to differentiate specific designs other than to designate whether the firearm is a full- or semi-automatic version.

23. In 1984 James Huberty killed 21 people in a San Ysidro, California, MacDonald's restaurant with a semi-automatic "assault pistol."

24. Interviews with Brian Tauger, Allan Sumner, and Steven Helsley. All three served in high-level positions in the California Department of Justice during this period.

25. Ibid. Interview with former California State Senate Judiciary Committee staff-member Greg Schmidt. Also see California State Assembly, *Assault Weapons: Proceedings in the Committee of the Whole* (February 13, 1989).

26. All the interviewed staff of the Department of Justice and the legislature agreed that the NRA assumed a position of opposition and refused to participate and that this strategy served to exclude perspective and expertise from the drafting process.

27. Again, interviews universally supported this conclusion. I have also reviewed Helsley's personal papers.

28. Helsley's recruitment by the NRA came after his retirement in an apparent effort to restore NRA credibility with the California legislature in the aftermath of its disastrous strategy during the passage of assault-weapon and subsequent firearm legislation.

29. California Penal Code, Section 12280.

30. All interviews support the conclusion that appearance constituted the primary reason for placing a firearm on the list. In addition, certain firearms possessed too great a constituency to ban. One staff member told me that a key legislator refused to vote any bill out of committee that included the Ruger Mini-14 rifle.

31. For an in-depth criticism of the legislation, see Eric C. Morgan and David B. Kopel, *The Assault Weapon Panic* (Golden, CO: Independence Institute, 1993).

32. Jeff Brazil and Steve Berry, "Crackdown on Assault Weapons Has Missed Mark," *Los Angeles Times* (August 24, 1997): A1.

33. On July 19, 1999, Governor Gray Davis signed a bill that encompasses many of the firearms designed to circumvent the earlier restrictions; see Dan Smith, "Davis Oks Assault-Weapons Limits, Handgun Bill," *Sacramento Bee* (July 29, 1999): A2.

34. Five other states—Connecticut, Maryland, New York, New Jersey, and Massachusetts—have passed some form of assault-weapon prohibition.

35. Gerald M. Boyd, "Bush Opposes a Ban on Assault Firearms But Backs State Role," *New York Times*, February 17, 1989.

36. Charles Mohr, "U.S. Bans Imports of Assault Rifles in Shift by Bush," *New York Times*, March 21, 1989.

37. Based on conversations with members of the Firearms Technology Branch.

38. During this period I regularly communicated with firearms dealers, who reported that customers were buying up these firearms on the belief that they would soon become unavailable.

39. *Congressional Quarterly Weekly Report*, "Foley Caught Between His Party and His Constituency on Gun Control" (May 11, 1991): 1198–99.

40. *Congressional Quarterly Weekly Report*, May 11, 1991.

41. *Congressional Quarterly Weekly Report*, "Senate-Passed Crime Bill" (July 27, 1991): 2102–5.

42. *Congressional Quarterly Weekly Report*, "House Members Duel on Crime: Assault Gun Ban Is Rejected" (October 19, 1991): 3038–39.

43. *Congressional Quarterly Weekly Report*, "Gun Rights and Restrictions: The Territory Reconfigured" (April 24, 1993): 1021–26.

44. Both Foley and Brooks were on record as opposing assault-weapon legislation and voted against it. In spite of this, both would lose their seats in elections where gun control opponents played key roles.
45. Even the author of the original assault-weapon bill, Senator Dennis DeConcini (D-Ariz.) acknowledged that the bill (S639) "did not cover enough weapons to be highly effective." See *Congressional Quarterly Weekly Report*, "Brady Bill and Beyond" (April 24, 1993): 1024.
46. *Congressional Quarterly Weekly Report*, April 24, 1993.
47. The Black Caucus and some liberal Democrats refused to support the bill because of concerns over extension of the death penalty and limits on death-penalty appeals in federal court.
48. *Congressional Quarterly Weekly Report*, "Brooks Puts Six Easier Pieces on Anti-Crime Program" (October 30, 1993): 2978–80.
49. *Congressional Quarterly Weekly Report*, November 13, 1993.
50. *Congressional Quarterly Weekly Report*, "Crime Bill/Assault Weapons" (December 18, 1993): 3458.
51. *Congressional Quarterly Weekly Report*, "House Nearing Showdown on Assault Weapons Ban" (April 30, 1994): 1069.
52. *Congressional Quarterly Weekly Report*, "Democrats Disagreement Delay, Imperil Crime Bill" (July 23, 1994): 2048–49.
53. *Congressional Quarterly Weekly Report*: "Assault Weapon Ban, Death Penalty Stall House Action on Crime Bill" (August 6, 1994): 2255; "Clinton, Democrats Scramble to Save Anti-Crime Bill" (August 13, 1994): 2340, "Marathon Talks Produce New Anti-Crime Bill" (August 20, 1994): 2449–54; "$30 Billion Anti-Crime Bill Heads to Clinton's Desk" (August 27, 1994): 2488–93.
54. 18 USC 922(v)(1). For the definition of assault weapon, see 18 USC 921. To qualify, rifles must accept detachable magazines and have two or more of the following: folding or telescoping stock, pistol grip, bayonet mount, flash suppressor, or threaded barrel or grenade launcher. Pistols must accept a detachable magazine and possess two or more of the following: magazine that attaches outside the pistol grip, threaded barrel, barrel shroud, weight over 50 ounces, or a design derived from an automatic firearm. Shotguns must possess two or more of the following: folding or telescoping stock, pistol grip, magazine capacity over five rounds, or the ability to accept a detachable magazine.
55. *Congressional Quarterly Weekly Report*, August 20, 1994.
56. 18 USC 922(w)(2).
57. One reviewer of this book took umbrage that this was not noted.
58. The only important exemptions were the Ruger Mini-14 and the M-1 carbine.
59. Dan Smith, July 20, 1999.
60. The popular Ruger Mini-14, as an example, remained unaffected. The law remains largely symbolic, at least in the short run; see Todd S. Purdum, "California Governor 'Fights Back,' Signs Ban on Assault Weapons," *New York Times*, July 20, 1999 <nytimes.com>.
61. Morgan and Kopel.
62. No means exists for calculating the number of magazines in circulation; however, the low price of magazines implies a large existing inventory and knowledgeable sources advise me that brokers currently hold warehouse-size inventories of AK-type magazines. California has prohibited the transfer of magazines.
63. Numerous writers have made these points, but Morgan and Kopel synthesize them as well as any.
64. Morgen and Kopel. Kleck, 1997, 112–13. Kleck's review of the issue is particularly thorough and should be reviewed before accepting claims of high incidence. Although

my own experience has convinced me that a significant number of active offenders show an affinity for such firearms, available data does not support their being often used in documented crimes.

65. Even the capacity to inflict fatal injuries on tightly packed persons is more constrained than most believe. If the shooter is too close, the shot fails to disperse; if too distant, the shot fails to produce lethal wounds.

66. Although common in rural environments, rifles have not been common in the high-crime-rate urban areas where hunting and competition shooting are not popular activities.

67. Although many assault rifles have only modest accuracy by rifle standards, their accuracy and range far exceeds that of police handguns. Unlike citizens engaged in self-defense, police have an obligation to engage and apprehend armed offenders.

68. James A. Fox and Marianne W. Zawitz, "Homicide Trends in the United States" (Washington, DC: Bureau of Justice Statistics, January 1999).

69. Interestingly, one of the most intense criticisms of this militarization trend appears in David B. Kopel and Paul H. Blackman, *No More Wacos: What's Wrong with Federal Law Enforcement and How to Fix It* (Buffalo, NY: Prometheus Books, 1997); also see Peter Kraska and Victor Kappler, "Militarizing American Police: The Rise and Normalization of Paramilitary Units," in ed. Larry Gains and Gary Cordner, *Policing Perspectives: An Anthology* (Los Angeles: Roxbury, 1999).

70. *Sacramento Bee*, "Clinton to Widen Gun Ban" (April 6, 1998): A1. The permanent ban came after an ATF inquiry into the sporting use of the firearms and applied primarily to modified versions of previously excluded arms.

71. William Glaberson, "Right to Bear Arms: A Second Look," *New York Times*, May 30, 1999 <nytimes.com>. Also see the decision of Judge Sam R. Cummings, U.S. District Court, Northern District of Texas, in the matter of *United States of America v. Timothy Joe Emerson*, No. 6:98-CR-103-C, February 26, 1999.

72. Interview with Randy Rossi, Director, Firearms Division, California Department of Justice, Sacramento, November 1999.

73. Maryland passed a "Saturday-night-special" law that has proven largely irrelevant, and Virginia enacted a restriction of one handgun purchase per person per month.

74. Cramer and Kopel.

75. Available from the NRA at <nraila.com>.

76. Lott, 1998; Lott and Mustard; Bronars and Lott.

77. Ibid. (all).

78. William Bartley, Mark Cohen, and Froeb Luke, "The Effect of Concealed Weapon Laws: An Extreme Bounds Analysis," *Economic Inquire* 36, no. 2 (April 1998): 258–66; Dan Black and Daniel Nagin, "Do 'Right to Carry' Laws Deter Violent Crime?" *Journal of Legal Studies* 27, no. 1 (January 1998): 209–19; Hashem Dezhbakhsh and Paul Rubin, "Lives Saved or Lives Lost? The Effects of Concealed-Handgun Laws on Crime," *American Economic Review* 88, no. 2 (May 1998): 468–74.

79. Kleck, 1997, 372.

80. This analysis is based on the FBI crime figures and is not offered as a sophisticated methodological refutation of Lott's work. As a methodologist, I am not in John Lott's league. I offer these observations as a means of putting the complex econometric models in perspective for ordinary readers.

81. Michael K. Beard, "An 'Anti' Perspective," *Campaigns and Elections* (August 1996): 55–56.

82. For arguments on both sides of this issue, see the Fall 1995 issue of the *Journal of Criminal Law and Criminology*, which includes the report on the original study, critique, and response to the critique.

83. Griffin, 1995.
84. *Kansas City Star*, "Firearms Proposition Narrowly Defeated, St. Louis Opposition Decisive" (April 7, 1999): A1.
85. *Denver Post*, "NRA Nears Its Agenda" (April 18, 1999), and "Concealed Weapons Bill Tabled" (April 22, 1999) <denverpost.com>.
86. Gary Kleck and Marc Gertz, "Carrying Guns for Protection: Results from the National Self-Defense Survey," *Journal of Research in Crime and Delinquency* 35, no. 2 (May 1998): 193–224.
87. Ibid.
88. Ibid.
89. See Cramer and Kopel; also see Griffin. Although these sources are somewhat dated, a sampling of states in 1999 revealed no changes. Washington State continues to have the highest percentage of permit holders, at about 4 percent of the population; Florida reports only about 1$^1/_2$ percent; and Texas less than 1 percent.
90. Florida Department of State.
91. This does not constitute as unlikely an assumption as it might appear. In my personal experience, some persons with permits obtain them only to be able to carry a firearm, but do not do so. More commonly, permitees only carry a gun in their vehicles.
92. Most police officers soon tire of carrying firearms when not on duty, and they are largely buffered from social embarrassment by their position. Most people simply do not feel comfortable around others carrying guns; this becomes far more true if the carrying is not legitimated by their occupation.
93. Joyce Lee Malcolm, "The Disappearance of a Meaningful Right of Self-Defense in England." Paper presented at the American Society of Criminology, San Diego, November 1998.
94. Gun Owners of America, "Why Adopt a Vermont-Style CCW Law?" 1999, available at <gunowners.org>.
95. See Kleck, 1997, chapter 9 for a detailed discussion.
96. Ibid.

CHAPTER 11

1. Gallup Organization, "Most Important Problem," undated, available at <gallup.com>.
2. Jeffrey L. Pressman and Aaron Wildavsky, *Implementation* (Berkeley: University of California Press, 1973), 143.
3. Eckholm, 1999.
4. Opposition to comprehensive policy at the federal level has encouraged the proliferation of local and state initiatives, and gun-lobby pressure has often undercut enforcement efforts; see Vizzard, 1997, 70–71.
5. See the explanation in chapter 3.
6. Although few polls provide adequate information to determine definitively the level of support for specific options by defined populations, evidence supports that a majority of gun owners may accept registration or licensing in principle; see Blendon, Young, and Hemenway, and Howard Fineman, "The Gun War Comes Home," *Newsweek* (August 23, 1999): 26–32.
7. The NRA has supported the prohibition against possession of firearms by felons since the 1938 FFA hearings.
8. William J. Vizzard, "A Systematic Approach to Controlling Firearm Markets," *Journal of Firearms and Public Policy* 11 (fall 1999): 177–220.
9. ATF has periodically examined markets by using trace studies and other mechanisms. The examination became most intensified from 1978 to 1980 and from 1996 to 2000.

Although the agency more often has ignored markets than studied them, some individuals within the agency have consistently monitored and studied market patterns and trends. Marc Moore, Phil Cook, James Jacobs, Julius Wachtel, and David Kennedy have published gun-market studies.

10. Cook, Molliconi, and Cole, 1995.

11. Ibid.

12. Familiarity seems to constitute the primary variable. For many years individuals from poor urban environments seemed to be little interested in which particular firearms they acquired. This pattern seems to have largely disappeared with population dispersal, increased mobility, and the flow of drug money to young offenders in the inner-cities.

13. Cook, Molliconi, and Cole, 1995.

14. Bureau of Alcohol, Tobacco, and Firearms, *Crime Gun-Trace Analysis Reports: The Illegal Youth Firearms Market in 27 Communities* (Washington, DC: ATF, 1998), 14.

15. The exact fee required to support adequate regulatory oversight would require calculation; however, the cost of two inspectors (including administrative support) for half of one day each year would raise the fee to about $500 per year.

16. James B. Jacobs and Kimberly Potter, "Keeping Guns Out of the 'Wrong' Hands: The Brady Law and the Limits of Regulation," *Journal of Criminal Law and Criminology* 86, no. 1 (fall 1995): 93–120.

17. Current technology allows investigators to identify most persons with a criminal record from a single fingerprint.

18. Snyder, 15–16.

19. Many ex-service men hid away machine guns after World War II and Korea. Over time, most of these firearms were voluntarily surrendered by the owner or others, who discovered the guns when the owner became ill or died.

20. Daniel D. Polsby, 1993.

21. Cook, Molliconi, and Cole, 1995.

22. Between 1993 and 1995, 24 states passed "three-strikes laws"; see Donna Lyons, "Three Strikes: Legislation Update" (Washington, DC: National Conference of State Legislatures, December, 1995).

23. Wright and Rossi, 13 and 75.

24. Ibid., 100–101.

25. Richard T. Wright and Scott H. Decker, *Armed Robbers in Action* (Boston: Northeastern University Press, 1997), 13 and 17.

26. The NRA has recently expressed support for projects targeting felons with guns in Philadelphia and Richmond.

27. Wright and Decker, chapter 2. My own experience and those of numerous investigators, police officers, and parole agents with whom I have discussed the issue support a similar conclusion.

28. John Clark, James Austin, and D. Alan Henry, "Three Strikes and You're Out: A Review of State Legislation" (Washington, DC: National Institute of Justice, 1997).

29. California Penal Code, Section 1170.12(c)(2).

30. 18 USC 924(e).

31. William J. Vizzard, "Reexamining the Importance of Firearms Investigations," *FBI Law Enforcement Bulletin* 68, no. 5 (May 1999): 1–9; and Vizzard, 1999.

32. *Terry v. Ohio*, 392 U.S. 1(1968).

33. Vizzard, May 1999.

34. *United States v. Leon*, 468 U.S. 897 (1984), established the good-faith rule, which vir-

tually assures the admission of any evidence seized under authority of a search warrant, unless police falsified the probable cause.

35. Kennedy et al.
36. Tom Hamburger, "Federal 'Exile' Helps Town Stop Gun Crimes," *Sacramento Bee* (May 22, 1999): A1, and *Morning Edition*, National Public Radio, July 19, 1999.
37. Kennedy et al.; Hamburger; and *Morning Edition*.
38. Interview with District Court Judge Richard Williams, *Morning Edition*. This hostility to "police cases" is common among federal judges.
39. I managed the ATF–LEAA firearm-investigation classes delivered throughout the country (instructed in organized-crime- and bombing-investigation schools throughout the country) and the state and local training program at the Federal Law Enforcement Training Center, in addition to working as a deputy sheriff and ATF agent. Whenever possible, I made it a point to inquire about firearm-investigation policies and procedures with agents and officers I encountered.
40. Ninety-three percent of defendants convicted of weapons offenses pleaded guilty; see Lawrence A. Greenfeld and Marianne W. Zawitz, "Weapons Offenses and Offenders" (Washington, DC: Bureau of Justice Statistics, 1995).
41. Although the maximum sentence was two years, with good behavior inmates only served one-third of their sentences. The armed career-criminal provisions, first enacted in 1986, set a minimum incarceration of 15 years and no maximum. Current sentencing guidelines require federal inmates to serve at least 85 percent of their sentences in custody.
42. Some individual officers did not exhibit these patterns, not so much because they differed in their attitude toward gun cases, but because they took pride in their investigative skills in any case. Others, such as homicide investigators, routinely did a better job of handling gun evidence, because they assumed a probability that the evidence related to a "real" crime.
43. Kleck, 1991, 432, and Wright and Rossi, 220.
44. Sheley and Wright, 1993.

CHAPTER 12

1. Vizzard, 1995.
2. Spitzer, 4; Lowi.
3. In a March 1993 interview, ILA Director James Baker acknowledged to me that the Brady bill constituted innocuous legislation and that it would pass.
4. Cobb and Elder, 10–22, 28.
5. Ibid., 85–87.
6. John W. Kingdon, *Agendas, Alternatives, and Public Policy* (New York: HarperCollins, 1984), 188–200; Baumgartner and Jones, part I; and Birkland.
7. Birkland.
8. Spitzer, 192–93. See Kennedy et al. for an analysis of the escalation pattern.
9. Weiss, 1983.
10. One former congressional staffer, Mary Louis Cohen, stated that no more than ten members of the Senate understood the contents of the McClure-Volkmer bill or the GCA when they voted in 1986. Numerous other staffers report similar levels of knowledge and interest.
11. When asked if the NRA might not benefit from helping to shape gun legislation, ILA Director Baker stated that one rule of lobbying is: "Never make a bad law better."
12. No present or former congressional staff member that I have interviewed described ATF as a primary source of information.

13. See the comments of ATF Director John Magaw in Fox Butterfield, "Limits on Power and Zeal Hamper Firearms Agency," *New York Times* (July 22, 1999): A1.
14. Judiciary staff members in both the House and Senate advised me that such bills were common from other law-enforcement agencies, but not from ATF.
15. Barber, 107.
16. Charles E. Lindblom, *Politics and Markets* (New York: Basic Books, 1977), 257.
17. Ibid., 346.
18. Barber, 124.
19. Marcus Stern, "A Semi-Tough Policy on Illegal Workers," *Washington Post National Weekly Edition* (July 13, 1998): 22.
20. Interview with Baker.
21. Joseph A. Califano, Jr., "LBJ's Tough Stance on Gun Control," *Washington Post National Weekly Edition* (July 5, 1999): 26.

AFTERWORD

1. Many advocates seem to pride themselves on never having had any association with firearms. Legislative staff members report that this is one of the principal difficulties in drafting control legislation. Control advocates know little about firearms and those that do are seldom supportive.
2. Hofstadter.
3. Kennett and Anderson.
4. Bruce-Briggs.
5. William R. Tonso: *Gun and Society: The Social and Existential Roots of the American Attachment to Firearms* (Washington, DC: The University Press, 1982); *The Gun Culture and Its Enemies* (Bellevue, WA: Second Amendment Foundation, 1990); and "Guns and the Ruling Elite," *Liberty* 10, no. 1 (September 1996): 40–44.
6. Sugarmann and Davidson.
7. Sherrill.
8. Ibid., 322–24.
9. David B. Kopel, *The Samurai, the Mountie, and the Cowboy: Should America Adopt the Gun Controls of Other Democracies?* (Buffalo, NY: Prometheus Books, 1992). Kopel has written on a variety of gun topics, including constitutional issues, assault-weapon legislation, and concealed-carry laws.
10. Spitzer and Edel.
11. Leff and Leff.
12. Although unpublished, my doctoral dissertation does deal extensively with the details of the development and passage of the Law. A published source that addresses the topic in considerably less detail can be found in Edel's *Gun Control*.
13. Kennett and Anderson, *The Gun in America*; and Zimring, 1975.
14. Vizzard, 1993 and 1997, 37–62.
15. See Wright, Rossi and Daly; and James D. Wright and Peter H. Rossi, "Weapons, Crime, and Violence in America: Executive Summary" (Washington, DC: National Institute of Justice, 1981).
16. James D. Wright, "Second Thoughts About Gun Control," *Public Interest* 91 (spring 1988): 23–39.
17. Wright and Rossi, 1986, 23.
18. Sheley and Wright, 1995.
19. Zimring and Hawkins, 1987.

20. Franklin E. Zimring, "Is Gun Control Likely to Reduce Violent Killings?" *University of Chicago Law Review* 35 (1968): 721–37.
21. Zimring and Hawkins, 1997.
22. Ibid., chapter 7.
23. See Gary Kleck, "The Relationship Between Gun Ownership Levels and Rates of Violence in the United States" and "Policy Lessons from Recent Gun Control Research" in *The Gun Control Debate*, ed. Lee Nisbet (Buffalo, NY: Prometheus Books, 1990).
24. Kleck, 1997, chapter 11.
25. Kleck, 1991, 432, and personal conversations with the author.
26. Ibid., 359–66.
27. Ibid., 370–72.
28. See Kates, 1979; and Kates, *Firearms and Violence: Issues of Public Policy* (Cambridge, MA: Ballinger, 1984).
29. Barnett and Kates.
30. Ibid.; and Kates 1992.
31. Phillip J. Cook, "The Effect of Gun Availability on Violent Crime Patterns," *Annals of the American Academy of Political and Social Science* 455 (May 1981): 63–79.
32. Cook and Ludwig.
33. Phillip J. Cook and James A. Leitzel, "'Perversity, Futility, Jeopardy': An Economic Analysis of the Attack on Gun Control," *Law and Contemporary Problems* 59, no. 1 (winter 1996): 91–118.
34. Cook, Molliconi, and Cole, 1995.
35. Lott, 1998; Lott and Mustard; Bronars and Lott.
36. Bartley, Cohen, and Luke; Black and Nagin; Dezhbakhsh and Rubin.

BIBLIOGRAPHY

ABC News. "Building Safer Guns" (June 10, 1999) <abcnews.go.com>.

Advertising Age. "Guns Must Go" (June 17, 1968): 1.

Aho, James A. *The Politics of Righteousness: Idaho Christian Patriotism.* Seattle: University of Washington Press, 1990.

Amar, Akhill Reed. "The Bill of Rights as a Constitution," *Yale Law Journal* 100 (1991): 1132–1210.

American Rifleman. "Congress Moves Against BATF Regs" (June 1978): 28–29.

——. "Carter White House Gets Taste of Gun Lobby Might" (June 1978): 78–80.

Angell, Elizabeth. "Guns and Their Deadly Toll," *Newsweek* (August 23, 1999): 21.

Annin, Peter, and Evan Thomas. "Judgement Day," *Newsweek* (March 24, 1997): 42–45.

AuCoin, Les. "Confessions of a Former NRA Supporter," *Washington Post,* March 18, 1991.

Aynes, Richard L. "On Misreading John Bingham and the Fourteenth Amendment," *Yale Law Journal* 103, no. 57 (1993): 57–104.

Bai, Matt. "Caught in the Cross-Fire," *Newsweek* (June 23, 1999): 31–32.

Barber, Benjamin. *Strong Democracy.* Berkeley: University of California Press, 1984.

Barkum, Michael. *Religion and the Racist Right: The Origins of the Christian Identity Movement.* Chapel Hill: University of North Carolina Press, 1994.

Barnett, Randy E., and Don B. Kates. "Under Fire: The New Consensus on the Second Amendment," *Emory Law Journal* 45, no. 4 (fall 1996): 1140–1259.

Bartley, William, Mark Cohen, and Froeb Luke. "The Effect of Concealed Weapon Laws: An Extreme Bounds Analysis," *Economic Inquire* 36, no. 2 (April 1998): 258–66.

Baumgartner, Frank R., and Bryan D. Jones. *Agendas and Instability in American Politics.* Chicago: University of Chicago Press, 1993.

Beard, Michael K. "An 'Anti' Perspective," *Campaigns and Elections* (August 1996): 55–56.

Beck, Allen, et al. "Survey of State Prison Inmates." Washington, DC: Bureau of Justice Statistics, 1991.

Berry, Steve, and Jeff Brazil. "Owners' Numbers Are Small But Impact Is Powerful," *Los Angeles Times* (August 26, 1997): A1.

Birkland, Thomas A. *After Disaster: Agenda Setting, Public Policy, and Focusing Events.* Washington, DC: Georgetown University Press, 1997.

Bizjak, Tony. "Cities' Lawsuits Similar to Attacks on Tobacco," *Sacramento Bee* (May 30, 1999): A1.

Black, Dan, and Daniel Nagin. "Do 'Right to Carry' Laws Deter Violent Crime?" *Journal of Legal Studies* 27, no. 1 (January 1998): 209–19.

Blackman, Paul H. "The Uses and Limitations on BATF Firearms Tracing Data for Law

Enforcement, Policymaking, and Criminological Research." Paper presented at the American Society of Criminology, San Diego, 1997.

Blendon, Robert J., John T. Young, and David Hemenway. "The American Public and the Gun Control Debate," *Journal of the American Medical Association* 275, no. 22 (June 12, 1996): 1719–23.

Bock, Alan. "Ties That Bind," *National Review* (May 15, 1995): 25–35.

Bogart, Leo. "Politics, Polls and Poltergeists: Interpreting Election Polls," *Society* (May 15, 1998): 8.

Bogus, Carl. "The Hidden History of the Second Amendment," *University of California Davis Law Review* 31, no. 2 (winter 1998): 309–408.

Boyd, Gerald M. "Bush Opposes a Ban on Assault Firearms But Backs State Role," *New York Times*, February 17, 1989.

Brazil, Jeff, and Steve Berry. "Crackdown on Assault Weapons Has Missed Mark," *Los Angeles Times* (August 24, 1997): A1.

British Home Office. *Offenses Reported to the Police.* London: BHO, 1997.

Brock, David. "Wayne's World," *American Spectator* (May 1997): 36–45, 81–83.

Bronars, Stephen G., and John R. Lott, Jr. "Criminal Deterrence, Geographic Spillovers and the Right to Carry Concealed Handguns," *American Economic Review* 88, no. 2 (May 1998): 475–79.

Bruce, John M., and Clyde Wilcox, ed. *The Changing Politics of Gun Control.* Lanham, MD: Rowman & Littlefield, 1998.

Bruce-Briggs, Barry. "The Great American Gun War," *Public Interest*, no. 45 (fall 1976): 37–62.

Bruni, Frank. "Senate Democrats Unveil Gun Control Package," *New York Times*, May 7, 1999.

———. "House Speaker Expects a Gun Bill to Pass," *New York Times*, May 26, 1999.

———. "Driving Gun Control: It's About Elections, Stupid," *New York Times*, May 30, 1999.

———. "Speaker Shifts His Position on Pressing for Gun Control," *New York Times*, June 11, 1999.

———. "3 Democratic Women Lead on Gun Control," *New York Times*, June 14, 1999.

———. "GOP to Separate Gun-Control Measures From Juvenile-Crime Bill," *New York Times*, June 15, 1999.

———. "Two Sides Locked in Fierce Fight for Swing Votes on Gun Control," *New York Times*, June 16, 1999.

Bruni, Frank, and James Dao. "Gun-Control Bill Is Rejected in House in Bipartisan Vote," *New York Times*, June 19, 1999.

Bruning, Fred. "Decency, Honor and the Gun Lobby," *McCleans* 108, no. 24 (June 19, 1995): 9.

Bureau of Alcohol, Tobacco, and Firearms. *Project Identification.* Washington, DC: ATF, 1976.

———. *State Laws and Published Ordinances: Firearms*, 19th ed. Washington, DC: ATF, 1998.

———. *Crime Gun-Trace Analysis Reports: The Illegal Youth Firearms Market in 27 Communities.* Washington, DC: ATF, 1998.

———. *Commerce in Firearms.* Washington, DC: ATF, 2000.

Bureau of Justice Statistics. *Violent Crime in the United States.* Washington, DC: Department of Justice, 1991.

———. "Weapons Offenses and Offenders," Washington, DC: Department of Justice, 1995.

———. "Criminal Victimization, 1973–1995." Washington, DC: Department of Justice, 1997.

Burr, D. E. S. *Handgun Regulation.* Orlando: Florida Bureau of Criminal Justice, 1977.

Butterfield, Fox. "Waco Inquiry Is Said to use NRA Support," *New York Times,* July 13, 1995.

———. "New Chapter in Whitewater and Waco," *New York Times,* July 17, 1995.

———. "Waco Witness Says NRA Consultant Posed as a House Aid," *New York Times,* July 17, 1995.

———. "Us of NRA is Criticized in Raid Case," *New York Times,* July 19, 1995.

———. "Examination of Waco Raid Goes Partisan," *New York Times,* July 20, 1995.

———. "Diametric Views of Waco: Federal Agents as Aggressors—and as Victims of Outlaws," *New York Times,* July 21, 1995.

———. "Federal Program Will Track Sales of Guns to Youth," *New York Times,* July 8, 1996.

———. "Clinton Challenges Dole on Assault Weapons Stance," *New York Times,* July 11, 1996.

———. "GOP Report Faults Reno in Waco Raid," *New York Times,* July 12, 1996.

———. "NRA Unlikely to Endorse Dole Official Says," *New York Times,* July 18, 1996.

———. "Dole Sends Message of Inclusion to Abortion-Rights Republicans" *New York Times,* July 22, 1996.

———. "Results in Tobacco Litigation Spur Cities to File Gun Suits," *New York Times,* December 24, 1998.

———. "Limits on Power and Zeal Hamper Firearms Agency," *New York Times* (July 22, 1999): A1.

———. "Firearms Agency Intensifies Scrutiny of Suspect Dealers," *New York Times,* February 4, 2000.

Caldwell, Christopher. "The Southern Captivity of the GOP," *Atlantic Monthly* (June 1998): 55–72.

Califano, Joseph A. Jr. "LBJ's Tough Stance on Gun Control," *Washington Post National Weekly Edition* (July 5, 1999): 26.

California State Assembly. *Assault Weapons: Proceedings in the Committee of the Whole.* Sacramento: California State Assembly, February 13, 1989.

Carter, Gregg Lee, ed. *The Gun Control Movement.* New York: Twayne Publishers, 1997.

Clark, John, James Austin, and D. Alan Henry, "Three Strikes and You're Out: A Review of State Legislation." Washington, DC: National Institute of Justice, 1997.

Cobb, Roger W., and Charles D. Elder. *Participation in American Politics: The Dynamics of Agenda-Building.* Baltimore: Johns Hopkins University Press, 1972.

Cobb, Roger W., and Marc H. Ross. *Cultural Strategies of Agenda Denial.* Lawrence: University of Kansas Press, 1997.

Cohen, Adam. "Where They Stand," *Time* (November 11, 1996): 44–46.

Committee to Elect Reagan–Bush. "Gun Control," Undated press release from the 1980 campaign furnished by the Ronald Reagan Library.

Comptroller General of the United States. *Handgun Control: Effectiveness and Costs.* Washington, DC: General Accounting Office, February 6, 1978.

Congressional Digest. "Should Semiautomatic Assault-Style Weapons be Banned by Congress?" 69, no. 11 (November 1990): 266–76.

Congressional Quarterly Annual Almanac 1968. "Gun Controls Extended to Long Guns, Ammunition." Washington, DC: CQ, 1969, 225.

Congressional Quarterly Weekly Report. "House Blocks Proposed Gun Regulations" (June 17, 1978): 1557–58.

———. "NRA Shows It Still Has What It Takes to Overcome Gun Control Advocates" (September 17, 1988): 2564–65.

————. "Brady's Solid House Victory Is a Gun Control Milestone" (May 11, 1991): 1196–1202.

————. "Foley Caught Between His Party and His Constituency on Gun Control" (May 11, 1991): 1198–99.

————. "Senate-Passed Crime Bill" (July 27, 1991): 2102–5.

————. "House Members Duel on Crime: Assault Gun Ban Is Rejected" (October 19, 1991): 3038–39.

————. "Crime Measure Is a Casualty of Partisan Skirmishing" (November 30, 1991): 3528.

————. "Gun Rights and Restrictions: The Territory Reconfigured" (April 24, 1993): 1021–26.

————. "Brady Bill and Beyond" (April 24, 1993): 1024.

————. "Brooks Puts Six Easier Pieces on Anti-Crime Program" (October 30, 1993): 2978–80.

————. "Congress Responds to Violence; Tackles Guns and Criminals" (November 13, 1993): 3127–30.

————. "Handgun Control" (December 18, 1993): 3459.

————. "Crime Bill/Assault Weapons" (December 18, 1993): 3458.

————. "House Nearing Showdown on Assault Weapons Ban" (April 30, 1994): 1069.

————. "Democrats Disagreement Delay, Imperil Crime Bill" (July 23, 1994): 2048–49.

————. "Assault Weapon Ban, Death Penalty Stall House Action on Crime Bill" (August 6, 1994): 2255.

————. "Clinton, Democrats Scramble to Save Anti-Crime Bill" (August 13, 1994): 2340.

————. "Marathon Talks Produce New Anti-Crime Bill" (August 20, 1994): 2449–54.

————. "Gun Ban 'Energizes' NRA Members" (August 20, 1994): 2454.

————. "$30 Billion Anti-Crime Bill Heads to Clinton's Desk" (August 27, 1994): 2488–93.

————. "Long Time Second Party Scores a Long List of GOP Firsts" (November 12, 1994): 3232–39.

Congressional Record. Vol. 114, May 23, 1968.

————. Vol. 121, January 15, 1975.

————. Vol. 121, December 17, 1975.

————. Vol. 132, May 6, 1986.

Cook, Phillip J. "The Effect of Gun Availability on Violent Crime Patterns," *Annals of the American Academy of Political and Social Science* 455 (May 1981): 63–79.

Cook, Phillip J., and James A. Leitzel. "'Perversity, Futility, Jeopardy': An Economic Analysis of the Attack on Gun Control," *Law and Contemporary Problems* 59, no. 1 (winter 1996): 91–118.

Cook, Phillip J., and Jens Ludwig. "Guns in America: National Survey on Private Ownership and Use of Firearms" (government report). Washington, DC: National Institute of Justice, 1997.

Cook, Phillip J., Stephanie Molliconi, and Thomas B. Cole. "Regulating Gun Markets," *Journal of Criminal Law and Criminology* 86, no. 1 (fall 1995): 59–92.

Cottrol, Robert J., and Raymond T. Diamond. "The Second Amendment: Toward an Afro–Americanist Reconsideration," *Georgetown Law Review* 80 (1991): 309–61.

————. "The Fifth Auxiliary Right," *Yale Law Review* 104 (1995): 995.

Cramer, Clayton E., and David B. Kopel. "'Shall Issue': The New Wave of Concealed Handgun Permit Laws," *Tennessee Law Review* 62, no. 3 (spring 1995): 679–757.

Dahl, Robert. *Dilemmas of Pluralist Democracy.* New Haven, CT: Yale University Press, 1982.

Dao, James. "After Littleton, Gun Industry Sees Gap Widen with NRA," *New York Times,* May 25, 1999.

————. "Michigan Lawmaker's Agenda Highlights a Split," *New York Times,* June 8, 1999.

Davidson, Osha Gray. *Under Fire: The NRA and the Battle for Gun Control.* Washington, DC: National Press Books, 1992.

Davidson, Roger. *The Postreform Congress.* College Park: University of Maryland Press, 1992.

Decker, Scott H., Susan Pennell, and Ami Caldwell. "Arrestees and Their Guns: Monitoring the Illegal Firearms Market. Final Report." Washington, DC: National Institute of Justice, 1996.

De La Cruz, Donna. "Murder Tolls Keep Falling in Most Major U.S. Cities," *Sacramento Bee* (December 31, 1998): A8.

Denver Post. "NRA Nears Its Agenda," April 18, 1999, <denverpost.com>.

————. "Concealed Weapons Bill Tabled," April 22, 1999, <denverpost.com>.

Dezhbakhsh, Hashem, and Paul Rubin. "Lives Saved or Lives Lost? The Effects of Concealed-Handgun Laws on Crime," *American Economic Review* 88, no. 2 (May 1998): 468–74.

Eckholm, Erik. "Thorny Issue in Gun Control: Curbing Responsible Owners," *New York Times,* April 3, 1999.

Edel, Wilbur. *Gun Control: Threat to Liberty or Defense Against Anarchy?* Westport, CT: Praeger, 1995.

Ehrman, Keith A., and Dennis A Henigan. "The Second Amendment in the Twentieth Century: Have You Seen Your Militia Lately?" *University of Dayton Law Review* 5 (1989): 18–34.

Faucheux, Ron. "Gun Play: How the NRA Defeated Initiative 676 in Washington," *Campaigns and Elections* 19 (February 1998): 34–40.

Federal Bureau of Investigation. *Crime in the United States—1991.* Washington, DC: FBI, 1992.

————. *Crime in the United States—1997.* Washington, DC: FBI, 1998.

————. *Crime in the United States—1998.* Washington, DC: FBI, 1999.

Fineman, Howard. "The Gun War Comes Home," *Newsweek* (August 23, 1999): 26–32.

Fox, James A., and Marianne W. Zawitz. "Homicide Trends in the United States" (government report). Washington, DC: Bureau of Justice Statistics, 1999.

Gallop Organization. *Public Opinion News Service,* "Eight in Ten Persons Favor Law Requiring Police Permit for Gun," January 12, 1964.

————. "Gun Control," *Gallup Poll News Service* 55, no. 2, September 26, 1990.

————. "U.S. Gun Ownership Continues Broad Decline," *Gallup Poll News Service,* April 6, 1999 <gallup.com>.

————. "Social and Economic Indicators—Guns," *Gallup Poll News Service,* May 28, 1999 <gallup. com>.

————. "Americans Support Wide Variety of Gun-Control Measures," *Gallup Poll News Service,* June 16, 1999 <www.gallup.com>.

————. "Most Important Problem" (n.d.) <gallup.com>.

Gearan, Anne. "NRA's Tough-Talking Lobbyist Quits," *Washington Post,* October 8, 1998 <www.washingtonpost.com>.

Gentry, Curt. *J. Edgar Hoover: The Man and the Secrets.* New York: W.W. Norton, 1991.

Gest, Ted. "Popgun Politics," *U.S. News & World Report* (September 30, 1996): 30–37.

Glaberson, William. "Right to Bear Arms: A Second Look," *New York Times,* May 30, 1999.

Glick, Daniel, et al. "Anatomy of a Massacre," *Newsweek,* May 3, 1999.

————. "Why the Young Kill," *Newsweek,* May 3, 1999.

Gordon, Diana. *The Justice Juggernaut: Fighting Street Crime, Controlling Citizens.* Newark, NJ: Rutgers University Press, 1990.

Green, Stephen. "Lockyer Seeks Funds to Police Gun-Show Sales," *Sacramento Bee* (May 12, 1999): A4.

Greenfeld, Lawrence A., and Marianne W. Zawitz, "Weapons Offenses and Offenders." Washington, DC: Bureau of Justice Statistics, 1995.

Griffin, Denise. "Up in Arms Over Guns," *State Legislatures* 21, no. 9 (October/November 1995): 32.

Gun Digest. Vol. 14, 1960.

————. Vol. 47, 1993.

Gun Owners of America. "Why Adopt a Vermont-Style CCW Law?" 1999 <gunowners.org>.

Halbrook, Stephen P. *That Every Man Be Armed*. Albuquerque: University of New Mexico Press, 1984.

Hamburger, Tom. "Federal 'Exile' Helps Town Stop Gun Crimes," *Sacramento Bee* (May 22, 1999): A1.

Hamilton, Alexander, James Madison, and John Jay. *The Federalist Papers*, ed. Clinton Rossiter. New York: New American Library, 1961.

Harding, David R. Jr. "Public Opinion and Gun Control: Appearance and Transparence in Support and Opposition" in ed. John M. Bruce and Clyde Wilcox, *The Changing Politics of Gun Control*. Lanham, MD. Rowman & Littlefield, 1998.

Hardy, David T. *The BATF War on Civil Liberties: The Assault on Gun Owners*. Bellevue, WA: Second Amendment Foundation, 1979.

————. "Armed Citizens, Citizen Armies: Toward a Jurisprudence of the Second Amendment," *Harvard Journal of Law and Public Policy* 9 (1986): 559–638.

————. "The Second Amendment and Historiography of the Bill of Rights," *Journal of Law and Politics* 4 (1987): 1–62.

Harries, Keith D. *Serious Violence: Patterns of Homicide and Assault in America*. Springfield, IL: Charles C. Thomas, 1990.

Haughton, James G. "Doctors Should be Fighting to Ban Guns," *Medical Economics* 66, no. 16 (August 21, 1989): 24–27.

Hemenway, David. "Survey Research and Self–Defense Gun Use: An Explanation of Extreme Overestimates," *Journal of Criminology and Criminal Law* 87, no. 4 (1997): 1430–45.

Henigan, Dennis A. "Arms Anarchy and the Second Amendment." Washington, DC: Center to Prevent Handgun Violence, 1991.

Herz, Andrew D. "Gun Crazy: Constitutional False Consciousness and Dereliction of Dialogic Responsibility," *Boston University Law Review* 75 (1995): 57–148.

Higginbotham, Don. "The Federalized Militia Debate: A Neglected Aspect of Second Amendment Scholarship," *William and Mary Quarterly* 55, no. 1 (January, 1998): 39–58.

Hofstadter, Richard. "America as a Gun Culture," in ed. Richard Hofstadter and Michael Wallace, *American Violence: A Documentary History*. New York: Knopf, 1970.

Idelson, Holly. "House GOP Crime Bills Win Easy Passage," *Congressional Quarterly Weekly*, February 11, 1995.

Jacobs, James B., and Kimberly Potter. "Keeping Guns Out of the 'Wrong' Hands: The Brady Law and the Limits of Regulation," *Journal of Criminal Law and Criminology* 86, no. 1 (fall 1995): 93–120.

Jones, Jaurie. "MD Groups Support Semiautomatic Gun Ban," *American Medical News* 33, no. 8 (February 23, 1990): 11.

Kansas City Star. "Firearms Proposition Narrowly Defeated, St. Louis Opposition Decisive" (April 7, 1999): A1.

Kaplan, John. "The Wisdom of Gun Prohibition," *Annals of the American Academy of Political and Social Science* 455, May 1981.

Kates, Don B. Jr. *Restricting Handguns: The Liberal Skeptics Speak Out*. Croton-on-Hudson, NY: North River Press, 1979.

———. "Toward a History of Handgun Prohibition in the United States," in ed. Don B. Kates, Jr., *Restricting Handguns: The Liberal Skeptics Speak Out*. Croton-on-Hudson, NY: North River Press, 1979.

———. "Handgun Prohibition and the Original Meaning of the Second Amendment," *Michigan Law Review* 82 (November 1983): 203–73.

———. *Firearms and Violence: Issues of Public Policy*. Cambridge, MA: Ballinger, 1984.

———. *Guns, Murder, and the Constitution: A Realistic Assessment of Gun Control*. San Francisco: Pacific Research Institute for Public Policy, 1990.

———. "Comparisons Among Nations and Over Time," in ed. Lee Nisbet, *The Gun Control Debate*. Buffalo, NY: Prometheus Books, 1990.

———. "Bigotry, Symbolism, and Ideology in the Battle over Gun Control," *Public Interest Law Review* (1992): 31–46.

Kates, Don B. Jr., Henry E. Schaffer, John K. Lattimer, George B. Murray, and Edwin H. Cassem. "Guns and Public Health: Epidemic Violence or Pandemic of Propaganda?" *Tennessee Law Review* 62 (1995): 513–96.

Keith, Samuel J., Darrel A. Regier, and Donald S. Rae. "Schizophrenic Disorder," in ed. Lee N. Robins and Darrel A. Regier. *Psychiatric Disorders in America*. New York: Free Press, 1991.

Kellermann, Arthur, and Donald Reay. "Protection or Peril: An Analysis of Firearm-Related Deaths in the Home," *New England Journal of Medicine* 314, no. 24 (June 12, 1986): 1557–60.

Kennedy, David, Deborah Prothrow-Stith, Jack M Bergstein, Soscanna Ander, and Bruce P. Kennedy. "Youth Violence in Boston: Gun Markets, Serious Youth Offenders and a Use-Reduction Strategy," *Law and Contemporary Problems* 59, no. 1 (winter 1996): 147–96.

Kennett, Lee, and James Anderson. *The Gun in America: The Origins of an American Dilemma*. Westport, CT: Greenwood Press, 1975.

King, Patricia. "Vipers in the Burbs," *Newsweek* (July 15, 1996): 20–23.

Kingdon, John W. *Agendas, Alternatives, and Public Policy*. New York: HarperCollins, 1984.

Kleck, Gary. "The Relationship Between Gun Ownership Levels and Rates of Violence in the United States," in ed. Lee Nisbet, *The Gun Control Debate*. Buffalo, NY: Prometheus Books, 1990.

———. "Policy Lessons from Recent Gun Control Research," in ed. Lee Nisbet, *The Gun Control Debate*. Buffalo, NY: Prometheus Books, 1990.

———. *Point Blank: Guns and Violence in America*. Hawthorne, NY: Aldine de Gruyter, 1991.

———. *Targeting Guns: Firearms and Their Control*. Hawthorne, NY: Aldine de Gruyter, 1997.

———. "*Crime is Not the Problem*: Lethal Violence in America" (book review) *American Journal of Sociology* 104, no. 1 (March 1999): 1543–45.

Kleck, Gary, and Marc Gertz. "Armed Resistance to Crime: The Prevalence and Nature of Self-Defense with a Gun," *Journal of Criminal Law and Criminology* 86, no. 1 (1995): 150–87.

———. "The Illegitimacy of One-Sided Speculation: Getting the Defensive Gun-Use Estimate Down," *Journal of Criminal Law and Criminology* 87, no. 4 (1997): 1446–61.

———. "Carrying Guns for Protection: Results from the National Self-Defense Survey," *Journal of Research in Crime and Delinquency* 35, no. 2 (May 1998): 193–224.

Knox, Neal. "The 30-Year War for Gun Ownership," *Guns and Ammo*, August 1988.

———. "BATF View of NRA," *Shotgun News* 52, no. 2 (February 1998).

Kopel, David B. *The Samurai, the Mountie, and the Cowboy: Should America Adopt the Gun Controls of Other Democracies?* Buffalo, NY: Prometheus Books, 1992.

———. "Comprehensive Bibliography of the Second Amendment in Law Reviews," *Journal on Firearms and Public Policy* 11 (fall 1999): 5–45.

Kopel, David B., and Paul H. Blackman. "The God Who Answers by Fire: The Waco Disaster and the Necessity of Federal Criminal Justice Reform." Paper presented to the American Society of Criminology, 1983, revised July 19, 1995.

———. *No More Wacos: What's Wrong with Federal Law Enforcement and How to Fix It*. Buffalo, NY: Prometheus Books, 1997.

Kraska, Peter, and Victor Kappler. "Militarizing American Police: The Rise and Normalization of Paramilitary Units," in ed. Larry Gains and Gary Cordner, *Policing Perspectives: An Anthology*. Los Angeles: Roxbury, 1999.

Lacayo, Richard. "Jabs, No Knockout," *Time* (October 6, 1996): 40–41.

Lambert, Diana. "Trying to Stop the Craziness of This Business: Gun Control Groups" in ed. John M. Bruce and Clyde Wilcox, *The Changing Politics of Gun Control*. Lanham, MD: Rowman & Littlefield, 1998.

LaPierre, Wayne R. *Guns, Crime, and Freedom*. Washington, DC: Regnery Publishing, 1994.

Larson, Erik. "ATF Under Siege," *Time* (July 24, 1995): 20–29.

Leff, Carol S., and Mark H. Leff. "The Politics of Ineffectiveness: Federal Gun Legislation 1919–38," *Annals of the American Academy of Political and Social Science* 455 (May 1981): 48–62.

Levinson, Sanford. "The Embarrassing Second Amendment," *Yale Law Journal* 99 (1989): 637–59.

Lindblom, Charles E. *Politics and Markets*. New York: Basic Books, 1977.

Loftin, Colin, and Ellen J. MacKenzie. "Building National Estimates of Violent Victimization." Paper presented at the National Research Council Symposium on the Understanding and Control of Violent Behavior, Destin, Florida, April 1990.

Loftin, Colin, et al. "Effects of Restrictive Licensing of Handguns on Homicide and Suicide in the District of Columbia," *New England Journal of Medicine* 325, no. 23 (December 5, 1991): 1615–21.

Los Angeles Times. "Sales Put L.A. Under the Gun," May 19, 1992.

Lott, John R. Jr. "The Concealed Handgun Debate," *Journal of Legal Studies* 27, no. 1 (January 1998): 221–43.

———. *More Guns, Less Crime*. Chicago: University of Chicago Press, 1998.

Lott, John R. Jr., and David Mustard. "Crime Deterrence and Right-to-Carry Concealed Handguns," *Journal of Legal Studies* 26, no. 1 (January 1997): 1–68.

Lowi, Theodore. "Four Systems of Policy, Politics, and Choice," *Public Administration Review* 32 (July/August 1972): 298–310.

Lund, Nelson. "The Second Amendment, Political Liberty, and the Right of Self-Preservation," *Alabama Law Review* 39, no. 1 (1987): 103–30.

———. "The Past and Future of the Individual's Right to Arms," *Georgia Law Review* 31, no. 1 (1996): 1–75.

Lyons, Donna. "Three Strikes: Legislation Update." Washington, DC: National Conference of State Legislatures, December, 1995.

Lyons, W. E., and David Lowery, "Government Fragmentation versus Consolidation: Five Public-Choice Myths About How to Create Informed, Involved, Happy Citizens," *Public Administration Review* 49, no. 6 (November/December 1989): 533–43.

Malcolm, Joyce Lee. "The Disappearance of a Meaningful Right of Self-Defense in England." Paper presented at the American Society of Criminology, San Diego, November 1998.

Masters, Kim. "Gunfight at the NRA Corral," *Washington Post National Weekly Edition* (May 8, 1995): 12.

Maxim, Paul S., and Paul C. Whitehead. *Explaining Crime*. Boston: Butterworth-Heinemann, 1998.

McCrystle, Michael J. "The Smoking Gun: Municipal Lawsuits Against Gun Manufacturers." Paper presented to the American Society of Criminology, Toronto, November 17, 1999.

McDowall, David, and Colin Loftin. "Comparing the UCR and NCS Over Time," *Criminology* 30 (February 1992): 125–32.

McWilliams, John C. *The Protectors: Harry J. Anslinger and the Federal Bureau of Narcotics, 1930– 1962*. Newark: University of Delaware Press, 1990.

Miller, Trudi. "The Operation of Democratic Institutions," *Public Administration Review* 49, no. 6 (November/December 1989): 511–21.

Mintz, John. "Who Are the Bad Guys? The NRA and the ATF Duel Over the Truth in Accounts of Raids on Gun Owners," *Washington Post National Weekly Edition*, May 22, 1995.

Mitchell, Alison. "Democrats Gain Ground, an Inch, on Gun Control," *New York Times*, May 21, 1999.

———. "Politics Among Culprits in Death of Gun Control," *New York Times*, June 19, 1999.

Mohr, Charles. "U.S. Bans Imports of Assault Rifles in Shift by Bush," *New York Times*, March 21, 1989.

Moore, Mark H. "The Supply of Handguns: An Analysis of the Potential and Current Importance of Alternative Sources of Handguns to Criminal Offenders." Unpublished paper, 1979.

———. "Keeping Handguns from Criminal Offenders," *Annals of the American Academy of Political and Social Science* 455 (1981): 107–9.

———. "The Bird in Hand: A Feasible Strategy for Gun Control," *Journal of Policy Analysis and Management* 2 (1983): 188–93.

Morgan, Eric C., and David Kopel. *The Assault Weapon Panic*. Golden, CO: Independence Institute, 1993.

Morganthau, Tom, Michael Isikoff, and Bob Cohn, "The Echoes of Ruby Ridge," *Newsweek* (August 28, 1995): 26–33.

Naifeh, Steven, and Gregory White Smith. *The Mormon Murders*. New York: Penguin, 1989.

National Public Radio. *Morning Edition*, July 19, 1999.

National Rifle Association. "Right to Carry" <www.nra.org>.

National Institute of Justice, "Arrestees and Guns: Monitoring the Illegal Firearms Market." Washington, DC: National Institute of Justice, 1995.

Newton, George D., and Franklin E. Zimring. *Firearms and Violence in American Life: A Staff Report Submitted to the National Commission on the Causes and Prevention of Violence*. Washington, DC: National Commission on the Causes and Prevention of Violence, 1969.

New York Times. "Bob Dole vs the NRA," editorial, July 21, 1996.

New York Times Magazine. "The Gun and How to Control It" (September 25, 1966): 34–35, 133–40.

O'Connell, Vanessa, and Paul M. Barrett. "How a Jury Placed the Firearms Industry on the Legal Defensive," *Sacramento Bee* (February 21, 1999): H1.

O'Leary, Brad. "Firepower," *Campaigns and Elections* 16, no. 1 (December 1994): 32–34.

Outlaw, Will B. "Guns and Politics." East Palo Alto, CA: Venceremos Publications, 1969.

Pesso, Tanna. "Gun Control (B): The Bureau of Alcohol, Tobacco and Firearms." Unpublished case study prepared for the John F. Kennedy School of Government, Harvard University, 1981.

Polsby, Daniel D. "The False Promise of Gun Control," *Atlantic Monthly* 273, no. 3 (March 1993): 57–67.

———. "Second Reading: Treating the Second Amendment as Normal Constitutional Law," *Reason* 27, no. 10 (March 1996): 32–36.

Polsby, Nelson. *Political Innovation in America.* New Haven, CT: Yale University Press, 1984, 170.

Pressman, Jeffrey L., and Aaron Wildavsky. *Implementation.* Berkeley: University of California Press, 1973.

Price, James, Sharon Desmond, and Daisy Smith. "A Preliminary Investigation of Inner-City Adolescents' Perceptions of Guns," *Journal of School Health* 61, no. 6 (August 1991): 255–60.

Purdum, Todd S. "California Governor 'Fights Back,' Signs Ban on Assault Weapons," *New York Times,* July 20, 1999, <nytimes.com>.

Quinlan, Michael J. "Is There a Neutral Justification for Refusing to Implement the Second Amendment or Is the Supreme Court Just 'Gun Shy'?" *Capital University Law Review* 22 (1993): 641–92.

Rand, M. Kristen. "Cities Should Sue Gun-Makers," *Sacramento Bee* (March 26, 1999): B7.

Reich, Robert, ed. *The Power of Public Ideas.* Cambridge, MA: Ballinger, 1988.

Reynolds, Glenn Harlan. "A Critical Guide to the Second Amendment," *Tennessee Law Review* 62 (1995): 461–503.

Rohr, John A. "Ethical Issues in French Public Administration: A Comparative Study," *Public Administration Review* 51, no. 4 (July/August 1991): 283–98.

Rushforth, Norman, Charles S. Hirsh, Amasda B. Ford, and Lester Adelson. "Accidental Firearms Death in a Metropolitan County (1958–1975)," *American Journal of Epidemiology* 100 (1975): 499–505.

Sacramento Bee. "Election Year Gun Duel Looms" (October 1, 1997): A3.

———. "Boxer, Feinstein Take Aim at Guns" (October 10, 1997): A1.

———. "Crime, Gun Control Offer Ammunition for '98 Races" (March 1, 1998): A1.

———. "Clinton to Widen Gun Ban" (April 6, 1998): A1.

———. "Heston to Target Image Control as NRA President" (June 9, 1998): A5.

———. "Attorney General's Race Candidates Face to Face" (October 10, 1998): A3.

———. "Voters Support Boxer on Education, Health, Favor Fong on Taxes" (October 10, 1998): A3.

———. "Boxer, Fong Tangle Over Abortion Rights, Gun Control" (October 13, 1998).

———. "Election '98" (October 25, 1998).

———. "Switch by GOP on Gun Control" (May 14, 1999): A1.

———. "Senate Oks GOP Gun Bill: President Calls it Phony" (May 15, 1999): A6.

———. "Family Targeted by Invaders in Deadly Attack" (January 6, 2000): A4.

———. "Clinton Plans Gun-Law Enforcement Push" (January 18, 2000): B8.

Sample, Herbert A. "Gun Backers, Boxer Push Dueling Bills on Local Suits," *Sacramento Bee* (March 24, 1999): A6.

Saturday Evening Post. "Speaking Out—Too Many People Have Guns" (February 1, 1964): 12.

Schattschneider, E. E. *The Semisovereign People.* Hindale, IL: Dryden Press, 1960, 2.

Schuman, Howard, and Stanley Presser, "The Attitude–Action Connection and the Issue of Gun Control," *Annals of the American Academy of Political and Social Science* 455 (May, 1981): 40–49.

Serrano, Barbara A. "Handgun Proposal Is Trounced," *Seattle Times*, November 5, 1997 <seattletimes.com>.

Shaffer, Lyman H., and William J. Vizzard. "Increased Automatic Weapons Use," *Police Chief* 48, no. 5 (May 1981): 58–60.

Shapiro, Joseph P. "An Epidemic of Fear and Loathing," *U.S. News & World Report* (May 8, 1995): 37–42.

Sheley, Joseph F., and James D. Wright. "Gun Acquisition and Possession in Selected Juvenile Samples" (government report). Washington, DC: National Institute of Justice, 1993.

———. *In the Line of Fire: Youth, Guns, and Violence in Urban America.* Hawthorne, NY: Aldine de Gruyter, 1995.

Sherrill, Robert. *The Saturday Night Special and Other Guns with which Americans Won the West, Protected Bootleg Franchises, Slew Wildlife, Robbed Countless Banks, Shot Husbands Purposely and by Mistake and Killed Presidents—Together with the Debate Over Continuing Same.* New York: Charterhouse, 1973.

Sloan, John, et al. "Handgun Regulations, Crime Assaults and Homicide: A Tale of Two Cities," *New England Journal of Medicine* 319, no. 19 (November 10, 1988): 1256–63.

Smith, Dan. "Davis Oks Assault-Weapons Limits, Handgun Bill," *Sacramento Bee* (July 29, 1999): A2.

Smith, Tom W. "A Call for a Truce in the DGU War," *Journal of Criminal Law and Criminology* 87, no. 4 (1997): 1462–69.

Smolowe, Jill. "The NRA: Go Ahead, Make Our Day," *Time* (May 20, 1995): 18–21.

Snyder, Jeffrey R. "A Nations of Cowards," *Public Interest* 113 (fall 1993): 40–55.

———. "Fighting Back: Crime, Self–Defense, and the Right to Carry a Handgun." Washington, DC: Cato Institute, 1997.

Spitzer, Robert J. *The Politics of Gun Control.* Chatham, NY: Chatham House, 1995.

Stern, Marcus. "A Semi-Tough Policy on Illegal Workers," *Washington Post National Weekly Edition* (July 13, 1998): 22.

Stillman, Richard. "The Peculiar 'Stateless' Origins of American Public Administration and Consequences for Government Today," *Public Administration Review* 50, no. 2 (March/April 1990): 156–67.

Stone, Deborah. *Policy Paradox.* New York: W.W. Norton, 1997.

Sugarmann, Josh. *The National Rifle Association: Money, Firepower, and Fear.* Washington, DC: National Press Books, 1992.

Suro, Roberto. "Targeting Gun Makers with a Cigarette Strategy," *Washington Post National Weekly Edition* (January 4, 1999): 30.

Suro, Roberto, and Philip P. Pan. "Laws Omission Disarms Some Police," *Washington Post* (December 27, 1996): A16.

Tonso, William R. *Gun and Society: The Social and Existential Roots of the American Attachment to Firearms.* Washington, DC: The University Press, 1982.

———. "Social Problems and Sagecraft: Gun Control as a Case in Point," in ed. Don B. Kates, Jr., *Firearms and Violence.* San Francisco: Pacific Institute for Public Policy Research, 1984.

———. *The Gun Culture and Its Enemies.* Bellevue, WA: Second Amendment Foundation, 1990.

————. "Guns and the Ruling Elite," *Liberty* 10, no. 1 (September 1996): 40–44.

Toobin, Jeffrey, "The Plot Thins: The Oklahoma City Conspiracy That Wasn't," *New Yorker*, January 12, 1998.

Tribe, Lawrence H., and Akhill Reed Amar. "Well-Regulated Militias, and More," *New York Times* (October 28, 1999): A31.

U.S. Congress, House of Representatives. Subcommittee of the Committee on Interstate and Foreign Commerce. *Hearings on the National Firearms Act.* 73rd Congress, 2nd Session, April and May 1934.

————. Subcommittee of the Committee on Interstate and Foreign Commerce. *To Regulate Commerce in Firearms, Hearings.* 75th Congress, 1st Session, 1937.

————. Subcommittee on Crime, Committee on the Judiciary. *Handguns and Crime.* 94th Congress, 1st Session, March 20, 1975.

————. Committee on the Judiciary. *Events Surrounding the Branch Davidian Cult Standoff in Waco, Texas, Hearing.* 103rd Congress, 1st Session, April 28, 1993.

U.S. Congress, Senate. Committee on Commerce. Subcommittee on S.885, S.2258, and S.3680. *To Regulate Commerce in Firearms, Hearings.* 73rd Congress, 2nd Session, 1934.

————. Committee on the Judiciary, Subcommittee to Investigate Juvenile Delinquency. *Federal Firearms Act, Hearings.* 89th Congress, 1st Session, 1965.

————. Committee on the Judiciary, Subcommittee to Investigate Juvenile Delinquency. *Federal Firearms Act, Hearings.* 90th Congress, 1st Session, 1967.

————. Committee on the Judiciary, Subcommittee to Investigate Juvenile Delinquency. *Federal Firearms Legislation.* 90th Congress, 2nd Session, 1968.

————. Committee on the Judiciary, Subcommittee to Investigate Juvenile Delinquency. *Handgun Crime Control—1975–1976.* 94th Congress, 1st Session, Vols. I and II, 1976.

————. Committee on Appropriations. *Oversight Hearings on Bureau of Alcohol, Tobacco, and Firearms.* 96th Congress, 1st Session, July 11, 1979.

————. Committee on the Judiciary, Subcommittee on the Constitution. *Gun Control and Constitutional Rights, Hearings.* 96th Congress, 2nd Session, September 15, 1980.

————. Committee on Appropriations. *Proposed Dissolution of the Bureau of Alcohol, Tobacco, and Firearms, Hearings.* 97th Congress, 2nd Session, 1982.

————. Committee on the Judiciary, Subcommittee on the Constitution. *The Right to Keep and Bear Arms, Hearings.* 97th Congress, 2d Session (1982).

U.S. Sentencing Commission, *Federal Sentencing Guidelines Manual* (Washington, DC: 1998).

VandeHei, Jim. "On the Hill: Guns 'n' Poses," *New Republic* (June 28, 1999): 15–18.

Violence Policy Center. "Gun Shows in America: Tupperware Parties for Criminals." Washington, DC: Violence Policy Center, 1996.

Vizzard, William J. "The Evolution of Gun Control Policy in the United States: Accessing the Public Agent." DPA dissertation, University of Southern California, School of Public Administration, 1993.

————. "Crafting for Compromise." Paper presented at the Academy of Criminal Justice Sciences, Boston, March 1995.

————. "The Impact of Agenda Conflict on Policy Formulation and Implementation: The Case of Gun Control," *Public Administration Review* 55, no. 4 (July/August 1995): 341–47.

————. *In the Crossfire: A Political History of the Bureau of Alcohol, Tobacco, and Firearms.* Boulder, CO: Lynne Rienner, 1997.

————. "No More Wacos" (book review), *Police Quarterly* 1, no. 2 (1998): 111–19.

————. "Reexamining the Importance of Firearms Investigations," *FBI Law Enforcement Bulletin* 68, no. 5 (May 1999): 1–9.

————. "A Systematic Approach to Controlling Firearm Markets," *Journal of Firearms and Public Policy* 11 (fall 1999): 177–220.

Wachtel, Julius. "Sources of Crime Guns in Los Angeles, California," *Policing: An International Journal of Police Strategies and Management* 21, no. 2 (1998): 220–39.

Walsh, Sharon. "The NRA Fires Back," *Washington Post National Weekly Edition* (March 8, 1999): 30.

Walter, Jess. *Every Knee Shall Bow*. New York: HarperCollins, 1995.

Washington Post. "Fire at Will," June 26, 1968.

Webster, Daniel, et al. "Reducing Firearms Injuries," *Issues in Science and Technology* 7, no. 3 (spring 1991): 73–80.

Weil, Douglas. "Gun Control Laws Can Reduce Crime," *The World and I* (February 1997): 301–10.

Weiss, Carolyn. "Ideology, Interest, and Information: The Basis of Policy Positions," in ed. Daniel Callahan and Bruce Jennings, *Ethics, the Social Sciences, and Policy Analysis*. New York: Plenum, 1983.

Weiss, Laura B. "House Blocks Proposed Gun Regulations," *Congressional Quarterly* 36, no. 24 (June 17, 1978): 1557–58.

White, Jack E. "First the Flame and Then the Blame," *Time*, June 17, 1996.

Wildavsky, Aaron B. *Speaking Truth to Power: The Art and Craft of Policy Analysis*. New York: Little, Brown, 1979.

Williams, David C. "Civic Republicanism and the Citizen Militia: The Terrifying Second Amendment," *Yale Law Review* 101, no. 3 (1991): 551–615.

Wills, Garry. "To Keep and Bear Arms," *New York Review of Books* (September 21, 1995): 62.

Wilson, George C., and Peter Carison. "The Ultimate Stealth Plane," *Washington Post National Weekly Edition*, January 6, 1996.

Wintemute, Garen, Stephen Teret, and Jess Kraus. "The Epidemiology of Firearms Deaths Among Residents of California," *Western Journal of Medicine* 146, no. 3 (March 1987): 374–77.

Wolfgang, Marvin E. "A Tribute to a View I Have Opposed," *Journal of Criminal Law and Criminology* 86, no. 1 (fall 1995): 188–92.

Wright, James D. "Second Thoughts About Gun Control," *Public Interest* 91 (spring, 1988): 23–39.

Wright, James D., and Peter H. Rossi. "Weapons, Crime, and Violence in America: Executive Summary" (government report). Washington, DC: National Institute of Justice, 1981.

————. *Armed and Considered Dangerous: A Survey of Felons and Their Firearms*. Hawthorne, NY: Aldine de Gruyter, 1986.

Wright, James D., Peter H. Rossi, and Kathleen Daly. *Under the Gun: Weapons, Crime, and Violence in America*. Hawthorne, NY: Aldine de Gruyter, 1983.

————. "The Great American Gun War," in ed. Lee Nisbet, *The Gun Control Debate*. Buffalo, NY: Prometheus Books, 1990.

Wright, Kevin N. *The Great American Crime Myth*. Westport, CT: Greenwood Press, 1985.

Wright, Richard T., and Scott H. Decker. *Armed Robbers in Action*. Boston: Northeastern University Press, 1997.

Yang, Bijou, and David Lester. "The Effects of Gun Availability on Suicide Rates," *Atlantic Economic Journal* 19, no. 2 (June 1991): 74.

Young, John T., David Hemenway, Robert J. Blendon, and John M. Benson. "The Polls—Trends: Guns," *Public Opinion Quarterly* 60, no. 4 (winter, 1996): 634–50.

Zahn, Margaret A., and Patricia L. McCall. "Homicide in the Twentieth-Century United States: Trends and Patterns," in ed. M. Dwayne Smith and Margaret A. Zahn, *Studying and Preventing Homicide*. Thousand Oaks, CA: Sage Publications, 1999.

Zawitz, Marianne W. "Guns Used in Crimes" (government report). Washington, DC: Bureau of Justice Statistics, 1995.

Zimring, Franklin E. "Is Gun Control Likely to Reduce Violent Killings?" *University of Chicago Law Review* 35 (1968): 721–37.

———. "Firearms and Federal Law: The Gun Control Act of 1968," *Journal of Legal Studies* 4, no. 1 (1975): 133–98.

Zimring, Franklin E., and Gordon Hawkins. *A Citizens Guide to Gun Control*. New York: Macmillan, 1987.

———. *Crime Is Not the Problem*. New York: Oxford University Press, 1997.

INDEX

ABOUT THE AUTHOR

WILLIAM J. VIZZARD is a professor of criminal justice at California State University–Sacramento. Prior to beginning his teaching career at the University of Wisconsin–Oshkosh in 1994, Dr. Vizzard was a deputy sheriff with the Fresno County (California) Sheriff's Department and served 27 years as a special agent, supervisor, and manager with the Bureau of Alcohol, Tobacco, and Firearms (ATF), serving in seven offices, including six years at ATF Headquarters. He is the author of *In the Crossfire: A Political History of the Bureau of Alcohol, Tobacco, and Firearms* (1997) and numerous articles on gun control and policing.